Manipur-Myanmar Historical Connections

About the Editors

Aheibam Koireng Singh (M.A., Ph.D.) is Assistant Professor, Centre for Manipur Studies, Manipur University, Canchipur, Imphal West District, Manipur. He is formerly the General Secretary of Manipur University Research Club. He is also the life member of Indian Tourism Congress, Manipur Historical Society, and North East India History Association. He specializes in India's North East regional studies of election, ethnicity, inter-group and inter-community relations, conflict, peace building, and issues of governance. His authored and edited books, "Ethnicity and Intercommunity Conflicts: A Case of Kuki-Naga in Manipur", "Miniature India in Motion: Movements in Recent Past and Present Manipur" are well received for its rich material content and critical insights. He can be contacted at <akoireng@gmail.com>

Shukhdeba Sharma Hanjabam (M.S.W., Ph.D.) is Head, Department of Social Work, Indira Gandhi National Tribal University, Regional Campus, Manipur, Makhan Kangpokpi District, Manipur. He completed his Ph.D. from the School of Social Work, Tata Institute of Social Sciences, Mumbai and post-doctoral from University of Florida, Florida, USA (2014-15) as Fogarty International Centre Fellow. He is also the life member of North East India History Association; Manipur Historical Society; and Indian National Trust for Art and Cultural Heritage (INTACH), New Delhi. He also had successfully completed research projects under the sponsorship from ICSSR, New Delhi and Manipur Commission for Protection of Child Rights, Manipur. He can be contacted at <hanjabam@gmail.com>

Manipur-Myanmar Historical Connections

Edited by
Aheibam Koireng Singh
Shukhdeba Sharma Hanjabam

CONCEPT PUBLISHING COMPANY PVT. LTD.
NEW DELHI-110059

ISBN: 978-93-5439-078-4 (HB)
ISBN: 978-93-5439-079-1 (PB)

First Published 2022

Published and Printed by

Concept
Since 1974

Concept Publishing Company Pvt. Ltd.
A/15-16, Commercial Block, Mohan Garden,
New Delhi-110059 (INDIA)
T: 91 11 41101460
E: publishing@conceptpub.com, *W*: www.conceptpub.com

Cataloging in Publication Data--Courtesy: D.K. Agencies (P) Ltd. <docinfo@dkagencies.com>

Manipur-Myanmar historical connections / edited by Aheibam Koireng Singh, Shukhdeba Sharma Hanjabam.
pages cm
Contributed articles.
Includes bibliographical references and index.
ISBN 9789354390784 (HB)
ISBN 9789354390791 (PB)

1. Manipur (India)--Relations--Burma. 2. Burma--Relations--India--Manipur. I. Singh, Aheibam Koireng, editor. II. Hanjabam, Shukhdeba Sharma, 1983- editor.

LCC DS450.B93M36 2022 | DDC 327.540591 23

ꯗꯥ. ꯔꯥꯖꯀꯨꯃꯥꯔ ꯔꯟꯖꯟ ꯁꯤꯡꯍ
डॉ॰ राजकुमार रंजन सिंह
Dr. Rajkumar Ranjan Singh

सत्यमेव जयते

विदेश और शिक्षा राज्य मंत्री
भारत सरकार, नई दिल्ली
Minister of State for External Affairs & Education
Government of India, New Delhi

Foreword

It is a matter of great delight and personal satisfaction that the book titled "Manipur – Myanmar Historical Connections," which is an outcome of a collaborative effort by eminent academicians, military experts, freelance researchers, well known cultural exponents, and others, is coming out very soon.

Manipur and Myanmar have had rich and shared cultural heritage and linkages since the very early times. Manipur, too had political and treaty relations with Myanmar as early as 1470 AD. The erstwhile Kingdom of Manipur had affinities with the erstwhile Kingdoms of present South Asia such as Ahom (Assam), Cachar, Tripura, and South East Asia such as Pegu, Awa, Shan, and Siam. Manipur had trade relations with the countries like Burma, China, British India, Arab and Greek world. One of the Indian trade route to China and South East Asia also lay through Manipur.

The book traces the interwoven history and shared past of these two erstwhile nations, i.e., Manipur – Myanmar, that could redefine the Manipur-Myanmar Relations and consequently, India-Myanmar Relations. These areas remain less explored despite the importance of Northeast India, particularly Manipur, and its connection with Myanmar and South East Asia.

Of late, with India's Act, East Policy gaining prominence, the Indo-Myanmar region and its land and people have started generating increased attention and the eagerness to know of it. I hope and look forward that this book which throws light on the shared cultural heritage of Myanmar and India, particularly Manipur, which otherwise is also known as India's gateway to South East Asia, will be well received by the professional and general amateur readers alike.

I also strongly feel that such academic ventures, which are of great significance but otherwise continued to remain a less ventured territory receiving the least attention from the academic community, should be deservingly encouraged by giving institutional support.

I wish the book a grand success and happy reading.

Jai Hind

(Dr. Rajkumar Ranjan Singh)

Office : Ministry of External Affairs, Jawaharlal Nehru Bhawan, New Delhi- 110 001
Tel : 011-4901 6636 **Fax :** 011-4901 6740

Acknowledgements

At the outset, we would like to start by appreciating and acknowledging our contributors for making valuable contributions in the form of book chapters.

We thank the Editorial team of Kangla Lanpung (Volume XII Issue I: Summer 2018, pp. 113-138), for their permission to reproduce the chapter "The Meitei (Kathè) Crown Service Groups in Myanmar From The Earliest Times to the End of Monarchical Rule" by Nwe Ni Hlaing.

We also acknowledged the intellectual and moral support from the following:

- Prof. Naorem Lokendra Singh, Hon'ble Vice-Chancellor, Manipur University; and Prof S Mangi Singh, Dean, School of Social Sciences, Manipur University.
- Prof. Shri Prakash Mani Tripathi, Hon'ble Vice-Chancellor; Prof. Alok Shrotriya, Director (Academic); Prof. Rakesh Singh, Dean, School of Social Sciences; Dr. Ng Ngalengnam, Director; Indira Gandhi National Tribal University, Amarkantak and Regional Campus, Manipur.
- Prof. G.P. Parsain, Hon'ble Vice-Chancellor, Tripura University and former Dean, School of Social Sciences, Manipur University; and
- Prof. Kuldip Chand Agnihotri, Vice Chancellor, Central University of Himachal Pradesh.

We also would like to thank Shri Chanam Hemchandra Khaba Manucriptologist and Shri Thokchom Thoiba, Cultural Activist for their guidance in locating and accessing some of the important ancient literatures relating with Manipur-Myanmar Connections.

We also would like to put on record our sincere appreciation to Shri A. Dhanachandra Sharma, Manipur; Shri Swapnil Shermale, Convener, Intellectual Forum of North East for giving us the required moral support to complete this book in a time bound manner.

Last but not the least, we expressly owe our indebtedness to one and all who are associated in one way or the other in bringing out this book.

Contents

THEME-III

Manipur-Burma Relations

THEME-IV

Political Engagement

Abbreviations

AC	:	Assembly Constituency
ACWF	:	All Community Welfare Forum
AD	:	Anno Domini
AEP	:	Act East Policy
AMESCO	:	All Manipur Ethnic Social and Cultural Organisation
AMSU	:	All Manipur Students Union
AMUCO	:	All Manipur United Clubs Organisation
ASEAN	:	Association of South East Asian Nations
BCIM	:	Bangladesh-China-India and Myanmar
CLK	:	Chanura Lamjinglen Kangleipak
CNPO	:	Chandel Naga Peoples Organisation
CII	:	Confederation of Indian Industries
CONSOCOM-RGM	:	Consolidation Committee Manipur Revolutionary Government of Manipur
CRPF	:	Central Reserve Police Force
CSDS	:	Centre for Study of Developing Societies
IGP	:	Inspector General of Police
DGP	:	Director General of Police
FDI	:	Foreign Direct Investment
GATT	:	General Agreement on Tariffs and Trade
HERICOUN	:	Ethno Heritage Council
HTC	:	Hill Tribal Council
INCB	:	International Narcotics Control Board
IPSA	:	International Peace and Social Advancement
KCSI	:	Knight Commander Star of India

KCP/MFL	: Kangleipak Communist Party/Miyamgi Fingang Lanmee
MYC	: Moreh Youth Centre
KDF	: Kuki Defence Force
KIC	: Kuki Inpi Churachandpur
KIM	: Kuki Inpi Manipur
KSO	: Kuki Students Organisation
KWUHR	: Kuki Women Union and Human Rights
KYKL/MYL	: Kanglei Yawol Kanna Lup/Meeyamgi Yawol Lanmi
LEP	: Look East Policy
MCM	: Meitei Council Moreh
MDC	: Moreh Development Council
MMCM	: Meitei Muslim Council Moreh
MPCC	: Manipur Pradesh Congress Committee
MSC	: Meitei Society Churachandpur
NKCLL	: Nupi Khunnai Chaokhat Lamjing Lup
NLG	: Naga Lim Guard
NSUC	: Naga Students Union Chandel
NWUC	: Naga Women Union Chandel
OCI	: Overseas Citizen of India
OEG	: Opening of the Eastern Gate
PBD	: Pravasi Bharatiya Diwas
PIO	: Person of Indian Origin
POM	: People of Manipur
POMO	: People of Manipur Origin
PREPAK	: Peoples Revolutionary Party of Kangleipak
PSA	: Pravasi Samman Awards
SDPO	: Sub Divisional Police Officer
SPDC	: State Peace and Development Council
TIPS	: Threatened Indigenous Peoples Society
TS	: Tamil Sangam
UCM	: United Committee Manipur
UPF	: United Peoples Front
USDP	: Union Solidarity and Development Party
UNDCP	: United Nations Drug Control Programme
UNLF	: United National Liberation Front

Contributors Profile

Dr. Chirom Rajketan Singh is Associate Professor, Department of Manipuri, Manipur University, Canchipur. He can be contacted at < crketan@yahoo.in>

Dr. Heisnam Nilkant Singh is Associate Professor, Department of History, Y.K College, Wangjing, Manipur. He can be contacted at <heisnamnilkant@gmail.com>

Dr. Kakchingtabam Ruhinikumar Sharma is Assistant Professor, Department of History, Ideal Girls College (Government of Manipur), Akampat, Imphal-East-795001, Manipur, India. He can be contacted at <kruhinikumar@gmail.com>

Dr. Kamei Budha Kabui is Assistant Professor, Department of Tribal Studies, Manipur University of Culture, Palace Compound, Imphal-795001, Manipur. He can be contacted at <budhakamei@gmail.com>

Dr. Konsam Himalay Singh (PVSM, UYSM, AVSM, YSM) retired as a Lt. General of Indian Army. He is presently the Member, Consultative Group of Government of Manipur, Naga Peace Talks; and Visiting Scholar, Department of National Security Studies, Manipur University. He was also the former Chairperson, Manipur Public Service Commission. He can be contacted at <himalay27@yahoo.com>

Laiphrakpam Nishikanta Singh, VSM & BAR, is Chairperson, Manipur Public Service Commission. He retired as Lt. General, Indian Army. He served as a professor in Army War College and also in Indian Military Training Team in Bhutan. He can be contacted at <nishiby555@gmail.com>

Dr. Laishram Suresh is medical practitioner by profession. He is also a Director of Himalayan Cultural Research Centre. He has presented papers in various seminars, conferences and other academic platforms. He also has some respectable publications to his credit.
He can be contacted at <sureshlaishram2019@gmail.com>

Dr. Leisangthem Chandramani Singh (b. May 1934 – d. April 2020) was two times Deputy Chief Minister of Manipur and Speaker of Manipur Legislative Assembly. Some of the well-known books he authored are — "History of Manipur", "The Boundaries of Manipur", and "Athoubasingee Ningshing Numit".

Dr. Mangangcha Thoudam Achou is Assistant Professor, Oriental College (Autonomous). He can be contacted at <mtmanipuri@gmail.com>

Manglemjao Singh Sorokhaibam, IPS (Retd.) is Ex-Inspector General of Police, Government of Manipur. He also was formerly a Lecturer in Geography, Thoubal College, Manipur. He can be contacted at <soromanglem2010@gmail.com>

Prof. Naorem Lokendra Singh Hon'ble Vice-Chancellor, Manipur University. He can be contacted at <lokendranaorem2015@gmail.com>

Dr. Ngangom Jayshree Devi is Research Associate, Centre for South East Asian Studies, Manipur University. She can be contacted at <jayshreeng@gmail.com>

Dr. Nongthombam Jiten is Research Associate, Centre for Myanmar Studies, Manipur University, Canchipur, Imphal-795003, Manipur, India. He can be contacted at <jiten_nongthombam@yahoo.co>

Dr. Nwe Ni Hlaing (Late) was Lecturer, Department of History, University of Mandalay. She was one of the Manipuri Diaspora who actively worked to documents the historical connections of Manipur and Myanmar in order to strengthen the relationship. Among the Manipur Diaspora, she is also known as Takhelambam Nandeshwori and resided at 19th Street 102 Quarter, Mindee Eekin, Mandalay Division. She died in an unfortunate incident of car accident on 01/11/ 2016 at Mandalay.

Dr. Puyam Rakesh Singh is Research Fellow, Indian Council of World Affairs, New Delhi. He can be contacted at <khuman_mei@yahoo.com>

Dr. Rajkumar Ranjan Singh is Hon'ble Minister of State (External Affairs & Education), Government of India. He was elected as the Member of Parliament (Lok Sabha) from the Inner Manipur Parliamentary Constituency.

Sanamani Singh Yambem at the time of preparing the chapter incorporated here in this volume (which actually was first published as an article in the Bulletin of the Division of History, Centre of Post Graduate Studies, JNU, Imphal, 1974) was a member of the faculty of the Jawaharlal Nehru University in 1974. Subsequently, he joined the Reserve Bank of India as a Direct Recruit Officer in 1978. He demitted office as a General Manager. He also served as Pro Vice Chancellor of ICFAI University of Mizoram. He can be contacted at <yambem.ss@ gmail.com>

Dr. Sanasam Amal Singh is Research Associate, Centre for Manipur Studies, Manipur University. He can be contacted at <amalsanasam@ rediffmail.com>

Dr. Th. Suresh Singh, besides an MD in Community Health Administration from DU, he is Ex-Health Director, Manipur, with experience of combating dreaded bird flu endemic in Manipur in 2007. With 2 WHO Fellowships from Holland and UK, has 2 letters of Appreciation from the Goverment of Manipur for his outstanding works in the field of Health and FW. Besides conferring Bharat Excellency Award in 1997, his name was also included in the *Rising Personalities of India* published by the International Penguin Publishing House in 1998. As a columnist, published about 100 leading articles in 2 leading local newspapers, including 3 recent ones in New Delhi based prestigious *Financial Express* about present Corona pandemic. He is also a human right propagandist to the core. He is also well-known for his authored book, "The Endless Kabaw Valley (British Created Vicious Cycle of Manipur, Burma and India)", Quills Ink Publishing, 2014. He can be contacted at <drsuresh2059@gmail.com>

Dr. Sylvia Yambem is Guest Faculty, Department of History, Manipur University. She can be contacted at <sylvia.yambem@gmail.com>

Prof. Yumnam Mohendra Singh is formerly Principal of Oriental College, GoM, Imphal; and Director, College Development Council, Manipur University. He is also the author of the well-known book, "Status of Manipur".

Introduction

Manipur had enjoyed the fortune and glory in the past and experienced sorrow and vicissitudes of her long history. Manipur and the present country of Myanmar, erstwhile Burma, were two ancient kingdoms in Asia having its own history, interwoven in such a way that it is corresponding to each other. Eminent Archaeologist Okram Kumar Singh in his studies conducted during the last many years has established beyond doubt that Manipur passed through various phases of prehistoric culture, *viz.* Palaeolithic Culture, Hoabinhian Culture and Neolithic Culture. As Hoabinhian Culture spread far and wide in the region, there is a strong possibility of the land and its people having connection with the Southeast Asian countries particularly with Myanmar (Burma). It is because of the interwoven history and shared past of these two erstwhile nations that India could easily access to this part of the country and establish cordial relationship with Myanmar so swiftly. Manipuris and Myanmar shares joys and sorrow for over two thousand years as good neighbours and people of Manipur should be instrumental in strengthening the bilateral ties of India and Myanmar which together are trying to find out a great economic growth in the Asiatic map.

Of late, the various activities of exchanging of ideas and sharing experiences in different spheres of life have taken place which brings the people from both sides of the border closer to each other thereby playing a key role not only in Manipur-Myanmar Relations but also consequently India-Myanmar Relations. The traditional relation of friendship and cooperation between the two countries could be deepened and intensified further to each other's mutual benefit. No doubt, at some stages of history, before the advent of the British, there had been a story of struggle for supremacy between the people of Manipur and Burma known to the Manipuris as Awa after the Ava dynasty that ruled Burma from Mandalay in upper Myanmar. In the fluctuating fortune between the two sides, the Burmese had shown the might and thrusting power of the famed Manipuri Cavalry who, armed with the deadly Arambais, forced the Burmese to retreat.

When the Burmese took their revenge and occupied Manipur, they returned home with members of these famed horsemen and they formed the advance thrust when king Alungpaya attacked Thailand in Chiangmai. The British, eager to save their interest from growing French influence in the Bay of Bengal, saw an ally in Manipur. Thus was born the Manipur Levy under charge of Maharaja Gambhir Singh, which drove the Burmese away. But the Manipuris, who were taken as war captives to meet the Burmese requirements of skilled artisans, soldiers and scholars settled down in and around Mandalay and became part of the mosaic of Burmese people, treated as one and equal. Even then there are still considerable number of people who still harbour the perceived past wounds of seven years devastation (1819-1826) and it comes dominant to their minds whenever any discourse on Manipur-Myanmar comes up. Such mindset needs to be done away within the light of emerging realities and finding ways of benefiting together.

Keeping this in consideration, this book which altogether consists of 24 chapters is organised into six themes. The first chapter, **'The Tribes of Nong and Nung Race: Common Ancestry of the Early Population of Northeast India, Myanmar and Southwest China'** by **Laishram Suresh** by referring to various authentic sources concludes that the people of the Northeast India and Myanmar are the tribes whose ancestral roots were the Lai and Tien tribes of Kating (Katien), Kamai and Katik of the Nong Race from Koubrau or Kabrau highland Plateau of Manipur, the gorgeous Koubrau Kham Prefecture and it extends up to Myanmar and the highland of southwest China forming Nonglon (Leithak) and Leirol (Leikha). The Nung Race who migrated from the Neolithic sites of Karau of Qinghai, Himalaya and adjoining region in 5000 to 1500 BC and migrated along great rivers of China and Brahmaputra reached Sichuan and Yunnan Kham Prefecture, Northeast region then to the Present Myanmar. So, the early population of Northeast India, Myanmar and Southwest China were mainly the tribes of Nong and Nung Race.

The second chapter, **'Manipur-A Bridge between Indian Subcontinent and Burma, South East Asia, China and Far East in Ancient Times'** by **L. Nishikanta Singh** while highlighting that since ancient times, Manipur was connected well with the rest of the world and also internally arrives at a conclusion that the early land routes between India and Burma passed through Manipur. In the own words of the author, "it can be safely concluded that Manipur was well connected since the beginning of the civilization. In fact, Manipur served as a bridge between Indian Subcontinent and Burma, South East Asia, China and Far East. Hence, it is most befitting to term Manipur as the gateway to East for our beloved country India."

The third chapter, **'Soraren Macha Khunkumba: Ancient Manipuri Manuscript relating to the Shans'** by **Naorem Lokendra Singh** and **Yumnam Mohendra Singh** analyses the ancient Manipuri manuscript 'Soraren Macha Khunkumba' which deals with 'the settlement by the son of God of Heaven' available in the custody of the local Manipur Pandits. The manuscript written in archaic Manipuri script contains a number of sentences relating to the history of the Pongs (Mao-Shan). The first half of the manuscript deals with a mystified story of the God of Heaven 'Soraren' asking his sons — 'Khullee' and 'Khullai' and other kinsmen to go down and enstablish settlements on the earth. The second half, which constitutes historically the most interesting and useful portion, deals with the military adventure of Samlongpha, the younger brother of the Mao-Shan king Su-kan-pha in Manipur and the neighbouring areas. The last portion of the manuscript also deals with the relationship between the Pong King Kheekhomba and Meitei king Keeyamba. The analysis leads one to believe that the Meities are in some way or other ethnically and culturally closely related to some of the branches of the great Tai People.

The fourth chapter, **'Evaluating Meitei-Pong (Shan) Relations and the Conquest of Khampat from Sorarel Machana Khunkhumba'** by **Manglemjao Singh Sorokhaibam** thoroughly studies and highlights the Manipuri ancient text 'Sorarel Machana Khunkumba', which could literally be translated as 'The Sons of Heaven Descending on the Earth' which is supposedly a Shan Chronicle found in Manipur towards establishing the Meitei-Pong (Shan) relations.

The fifth chapter, **'A Brief Note on Shan Polity'** by **Heisnam**

Nilkant Singh highlights that the Shans are the largest and most widespread population in South East Asia who are known as Laos in Laos, Yunnan Tai in the South China, Tribal Tai in northern Vietnam, Tais in Thailand, Ahom in Brahmaputra valley and Kabos in Manipur. The geographical extend of the Shan States is 1,60,000 square kilometers almost a quarter of the present Myanmar. During the olden days, the Shans settled an area covering what is now in Assam state of India, the southern part of Yunnan, the Shan states of Burma and the northern part of Vietnam. This chapter attempts to focus mainly on the Shan polity that evolved since the early time by using archival materials.

The sixth chapter, **'Outlining Manipur-Shan Relation'** by **Kakchingtabam Ruhinikumar Sharma** attempts to reconstruct the relationship between Manipuri-Shan in its historical perspective and show how their interaction had influenced the course of Manipur history in her evolution from a chiefdom based political system to a mature feudal polity in the eighteenth century, the period which witnessed the zenith of power and glory and beginning of the process of decline and downfall of Manipur kingdom as well. It concludes that Ahom-Shan relationship had a great bearing on the future course of the history of Manipur.

The seventh chapter, '**Manipur-Burma Relations from the Beginning of the Eighteenth Century to the Treaty of Yandaboo, 1826**' by **Sanamani Singh Yambem** surveys the relationship between Manipur and Burma based on available materials, some primary, and others secondary. Giving detailed historical accounts, the chapter concludes with convincing authentication that by the end of 1826, Manipur, which had become a subordinate of Burma, regained her independence and despite the British Agency, she enjoyed greater elbow room in deciding her policies than she has done in the late eighteenth and early nineteenth centuries.

The eighth chapter, **'Burma and Manipur Relations (1714-1826)'** by **Yumnam Mohendra Singh** relies on various material sources such as archival, colonial British accounts, scholarly historical writings etc. to highlight, among others, in chronological sequence the Burma and Manipur relations starting with the marriage of King Charairongba's daughter to the Toungoo King of Burma (1698-1714),Toungoo king's ill treatment of Chakpa Makhao Ngambi's, the defeat of Burma by Garibaniwaz to fulfil his father, Charairongba's wishes to revenge the ill treatment of

Chakao Makhao Ngambi and the other exploits of Garibaniwaz, and later the crushing defeat inflicted by Alaugpaya on the Manipuris. It concludes with the 1st Anglo-Burmese War coming to an end by the Treaty of Yandaboo, 1826. As its consequent outcome, Gambhir Singh was recognized as the Raja of Manipur by the king of Ava as per the Article Second of the Treaty. Accordingly, the Burmese renounced its claim on Manipur.

The ninth chapter, **'Manipur's Political Relations with her Neighbour Burma: From the Middle of 15th Century to the Treaty of 1826'** by **Kamei Budha Kabui** attempt to delve into the political relations of Manipur with her neighbour Burma from the middle of 15th century to the treaty of Yandaboo, 1826. Manipur was in frequent contact with the Burmese and Shans since the occupation of Kabaw valley. There were also trade contact and social relationship between the two countries. It is truth that Kabaw valley was under the political control of Manipur till 1826 except for some periodical occupation by Burmese now and then, which the Manipuri king destroyed by war and established the genuine right and at the same time right by conquest. Kabaw valley, a fertile land is rich in natural resources and, also strategically important so Manipur and Burma tried to establish control over the valley. There were conflicts and wars between the two countries. The Kings of Manipur invaded Kabaw valley and conquered it. In 1738, Garibaniwaz invaded Burma and this was his most successful invasion of Burma. The Burmese forces were ready to face the invasion but in the battle, they were defeated and Manipuri forces sacked Sagaing; and planted the standard of Manipur. But, with the emergence of Konbaung dynasty, the Burmese invaded Manipur time and again. In 1819, the Burmese invaded Manipur and devastated the country, which is known as seven years devastation in the history of Manipur. The first Anglo-Burmese war came to an end with treaty of Yandaboo, 1826 which recognized the Gambhir Singh as the Raja of Manipur. Gambhir Singh re-conquered the Kabaw valley, but failed to incorporate any provision relating to it in the treaty. This led to the loss of the Kabaw valley.

The tenth chapter, **'The Meitei (Kathè) Crown Service Groups in Myanmar from the Earliest Times to the End of Monarchical Rule'** by **Nwe Ni Hlaing** highlights that The Meitei (Kathè) had settled along the Yangtze River in China from about the 2nd century BC and then they moved in Sichuan region. Later they migrated from the south-eastern Tibet to Hukong Valley, Chindwin region and Kachin region. From that earliest time onwards they lived Chindwin valley and scattered into the Manipur plain [*sic*]. Some Meitei (Kathè) groups arrived and stayed in those areas: in Somra tract, along the Ayeyarwady valley, Thaung Thut, Yaw, Monywa, Sagaing. Meitei (Kathè) are Tibet-Myanmar family. Their sub-family members are Chin, Kachin, Myanmar, Naga, Thet and Lo Lo. Therefore, some of their languages are found closely related to Chin, Kachin and Myanmar. During the time of Myanmar King, the Manipur State was under the rule of Myanmar Kings and also became as one of their tributary States. Due to the military conquest of Myanmar Kings, the Meitei (Kathè) group arrived in Myanmar royal cities including from Meitei royal families to commoners and bondsmen [*sic*]. They had settled so long in Myanmar kingdom. The reason to this long lasting settlement safely and securely, might be attributable, to their services rendered to the Myanmar people and the King, which can be seen in the renowned services of court Brahmins (Kathè Ponna) in the palace, Myin Su in the famous name of Kathè cavalry, Lamaing Su (royal cultivators), Thwei-Thauk Su (Blood-bond Brotherhood), Boatmen and other crown service groups. They were widely utilized by Myanmar Kings. This show that Kathè people had served Myanmar Kings with might and main, intellectually and physically, without sparing their lives for the interest of the King and the people. They are still living together with Myanmar people particularly around the former royal capitals and throughout Myanmar.

The eleventh chapter, **'Manipur-Burma Relationship and the British Empire'** by **Sylvia Yambem** highlights that The Treaty of Yandaboo, which concluded the first Anglo-Burmese War of 1824-26 stipulated the King of Ava to recognize Gambhir Singh, as Raja of Manipur. Neither Gambhir Singh, nor the princely kingdom of Manipur was party or ally to the war or negotiations, however, this was the beginning of a series of colonial stipulations, rules and orders, which regulated and controlled the relationship between the independent kingdoms of Manipur and Burma. For the British Empire in India, this need to regulate the Manipur-Burma relationship was determined by the political necessity of the North Eastern Frontier, which was imperative to the political-economic-defensive strategic security of the Empire in India. Geo-strategically located Manipur was the entry-point for the Burmese troops into

Bengal, the Eastern Frontier. Manipur was also the entry point to Burma. The dynamics of colonialism transformed the Manipur-Burma relationship from a relationship marked by internecine warfare, raids, punitive raids and also diplomatic friendly relationship and cultural assimilation to a regulated, moderated and controlled alliance to meet the capitalist imperialistic needs of the British Empire.

The twelfth chapter, **'Garibaniwaz (Pamheiba)-The Master of Manipur and Upper Burma (West of Irrawaddy) (1709-1748)'** by **Manglemjao Singh Sorokhaibam** describes Garibaniwaz, more popular locally as Pamheiba was the greatest king Manipur has ever produced in its historical existence since more than 2000 years. The chapter ends by citing the remarks of eminent historian, Prof. N. Joykumar that "The year AD 1738 was the most significant period so far the military campaign of Garibaniwaz was concerned against Burma. As recorded in Ningthourol Lambuba king Garibaniwaz attacked and occupied several places like Metu (Mydeu), Makang, Taprang and from these places the Manipuri forces collected a large number of war booty and the entire villages were completely devastated. In this way, the repeated attacks by Manipur king Garibaniwaz from 1719 up to 1749 has weakened the Burma king considerably."

The thirteenth chapter, ***'Samsok Ngamba*-An Old Manuscript showing Manipur-Burmese Relation'** by **Chirom Rajketan Singh** chronicles the Manipur-Burmese linkages from *Samsok Ngamba,* a manuscript that gives a vivid account of Manipur-Awa relations. Pamheiba ascended the throne on Wednesday 20th of Thawan (July-August.) 1709 AD. He vowed that he would attack Awa as his father Charairongba had said before his death. In 1717 when the Awas asked again for his daughter's hand he took it as an opportunity to attack upon them. With this intention he agreed to send his daughter and attacked them. In *Samsok Ngamba,* the description of the war is written in such a way that it look like the war took only one or two months. But from the concluding part of the book it can be known that King Pamheiba conquered and ruled certain areas in Awa for about seven years. The time corresponds to that given in *Chitharol Kumbaba*. Pamheiba first attacked Samsok in 1717 AD. He attacked Chanta in the month of Poinu (November-December) 1722 A.D. Samsaok which was conquered by King Pamheiba lies in Sagaing Division of today. It is said that Kaunghmudaw Pagoda that lies in this division was marked on its door with 7 sword marks by King Pamheiba to show that it was under his control. From such manuscripts like *Samsok Ngamba,* it could be known that Manipur was a well-known nation state in the South East Asia before it finally merged with India.

The fourteenth chapter, ***'Awa Ngamba*-The Last War of Manipur and Burma'** by **Chirom Rajketan Singh** deals with *Awa Ngamba* which is one of the manuscripts of Manipur written in Meitei script. It was written in 1871 during King Chandrakirti's rule. This manuscript mainly depicted the courageous feat and religious practices of King Gambhir Singh. During the time of king Garibaniwaz, Manipur expanded its territory by annexing many parts of Burma. There were constant feuds amongst his sons so the Burmese took advantage of the situation and often invaded Manipur and terrorized the Meiteis. In 1819, the Awas completely defeated the Meiteis during the time of King Marjit and Manipur came under the rule of the Awas. The Meitei princes fled Manipur and took shelter in other lands. Till the middle of 1825 Manipur remain under the rule of the Awas. Many Meiteis were taken as prisoners of war. The Awas chose kings of their choice and ruled Manipur through them. The people of Manipur fled to Assam, Tripura and Bangladesh and settled there. They were unable to face the atrocities of the Awas. This period was called the Seven Years Devastation in the history of Manipur. At this time, the brave Meitei Prince Gambhir Singh gathered all the patriotic Meiteis and organized a Meitei army at Cacchar in order to drive out the Awas from the soil of Manipur. The Awas also invaded and conquered many parts which were under the British rule. Even Cacchar was not spared. The British together with Gambhir Singh succeeded in driving out the Awas from Cacchar. Impressed by Gambhir Singh's valour, the British helped him in the war against the Awas. Gambhir Singh again occupied Manipur from the hands of the Awas and ruled again. His territory expanded till Ningthi river (Chindwin river). Regions in Kabow Valley which were a part of Manipur were given to Burma with the consent of the king of Manipur by the British under the context of improving trade relations. Another part of the book reflected the religious stories told by King Bheigyachandra to his son Gambhir Singh when he was a child and the discussion on the practices of rule of law. In many instances during his rule, King Gambhir Singh often took the help of his father's teachings while taking decisions. King Bheigyachandra introduced Vaishnavism religion in Manipur and made the people follow this religion. King Gambhir Singh also patronized this religion. The goodness of this religion is also discussed in some part of the book. Gambhir Singh's belief in the ancestorship of Manipuris in the *Mahabharata's* hero Arjuna is also written in this book. But the British told Gambhir Singh that there were no such records in the old manuscripts of Manipur. So there was even a discourse on this in the Royal court of Manipur. All these events are written in the manuscript. After Kabow Valley was given to Burma King Gambhir Singh became heartbroken and he died soon after. This article focuses mainly on the war between Manipuris and Burmese and the courage shown by King Gambhir Singh as depicted in the manuscript called Awa Ngamba.

The fifteenth chapter, **'The Problem of the Kabaw Valley'** by **Leishangthem Chandramani Singh** highlights that possessing the Kabaw Valley which is a narrow strip of level land between the mountains which form the eastern boundary of the Manipur Valley and the Ninghthee River was considered indispensable by the Rajas of Manipur and Burma not only for its economic importance arising from rich teak woods, but also for the border security of their respective countries and naturally they endeavoured to extend their sovereignty over that valley. The chapter describes successive border disputes arose in that valley during the years following the First Anglo-Burmese War (1824-26) which the Government of Bengal came forward as the arbitrator over this intricate problem and its outcome.

The sixteenth chapter, **'How Manipur Lost Kabaw Valley to Burma during Negotiation'** by **Th. Suresh Singh** while describing about lost Kabaw Valley which is about four times the size of present Manipur and is at present under the Burmese control stated that the valley had been a bone of contention between Manipur and Pong/Burma (present Myanmar) which for a maximum period was under the control of Manipur kings. Kabaw Valley was a part of Manipur during period from 1467-1709 AD where 12 kings reigned, i.e. from Kyamba to Charairongba. The same continued till the beautiful valley was handed over to Burma in exchange for his Manipuri throne in 1813 by incompetent King Mangle Marjit after Garibaniwaz's death. Kabaw Valley was, however, regained by Maharaja Ghambhir Singh in December 1825 with British help.

Thus, the Valley was under Burma for a brief period of 12 years only. However, Ghambhir Singh's hard earned victory and re-conquest of Kabaw Valley was made negative by the British due to bad negotiation strategy. The Burmese Government was paying 500 Sicca Rupees (i.e. more than Indian Rs. 6,270 at that time) per month. That means Manipur was getting the same rent since 25 January, 1834 till Nehru's second visit to Manipur. The British at least kept a scope to revert the Valley back to Manipur (Compensation Agreement). At least they have a partial favour to Manipur. Nehru in his second visit went to Kohima together with the Burmese Prime Minister U Nu, and there Nehru handed over Kabaw Valley to Burma on a platter even without the compensation clause and the consent of the Manipur people and without the approval of India's Parliament. This has created an apple of discord between Manipur, Burma and India. And Manipur has lost Kabaw Valley for ever. The author concludes by looking forward to the present generation of researchers to fill in the gap of presenting important facts in true Manipur historical perspective. It also expressly wish that present lot politicians would take up Kabaw Valley in appropriate forum in order to regain the Valley back as strong historical and legal background favour Manipur.

The seventeenth chapter, **'Matrimonial and Social Relationship between Manipur and Myanmar: Before the Reign of Nongda Lairen Pakhangba (33 AD-158 AD)'** by **Mangangcha Thoudam Achou** highlights the relation between Myanmar and Manipur in different subjects, particularly the matrimonial and social relationship from the pre-historic period. The transport and communication was done through the hills passes of Manipur valley. It also analyses the matrimonial and social relationship between Manipur and Myanmar in two contexts, one from the reign of Nongda Lairen Pakhangba, 33 AD to 158 AD in the beginning of Konnachak (era) and another before the reign of King Nongda Lairen Pakhangba. The social relationship between Myanmar and Manipur are also analysed according to the contents in the old manuscripts by dividing into two ways – i.e. view from creation of Universe and another view from religious matter.

The eighteenth chapter **'Satyamala Devi-The Most Fortunate Manipuri Princess in the 18th Century Southeast Asian History'** by **Manglemjao Singh Sorokhaibam** highlights that Satyamala Devi was the daughter of Maharaja Garibaniwaz @ Pamheiba's brother Khamlang Pamsaba who had been brought up by Garibaniwaz as his own daughter. Manipur during the time of Garibaniwaz (1709-1748) was at its peak in its military expeditions in the neighbouring kingdoms. During this time Burmese King Mahadhammaraja Dipati's repeated request to the Manipuri King seeking the hand of a Manipuri princess ultimately led to the sending of princess Satyamala Devi as Awa Leima in 1749 and she became one of the queen of Mahadhammaraja Dipati, the last king of Toungoo Dynasty and titled as "Maha Devi". In the meantime, Ava was sacked and destroyed in 1752 and hundreds of royal families including the king were deported to Pegu including Maha Devi and there were mass massacre. However, fortunately "Maha Devi" was not killed but made the queen of Pegu by King Binnya Dala. A few years later in 1757, Alaungphaya forces attacked Pegu and Maha Devi was captured yet again and made the wife of the Alaungphaya. Thus, Satyamala Devi, the daughter of Khamlang Pamsaba, one of the brother of Maharaja Garibaniwaz, who was Wangkheirakpa becoming the queen of two kings in successive events of Burma and lastly a wife of the great King Alaungpaya in 1756 can be described as one of the most fortunate Manipuri princess in the history of Southeast Asia and South Asia.

The nineteenth chapter, **'Cross-Border Ethnic and Historical Connect: Manipur and Myanmar'** by **Konsam Himalay Singh** highlights the geographical and the historical setting of the sub-Himalayan region which is bounded by the mighty Irrawaddy River to the East, the river Brahmaputra to the West, Himalayan range to the North and the Bay of Bengal to the South is marked by mountainous and hilly landscape interspersed by the beautiful valleys and riverine terrain. The most powerful and historically documented kingdoms that existed in the areas; The kingdom of present day Manipur, which was established around the 1st century AD; the competitive expansion of their influence resulted in frequent wars between the kingdom of Manipur and the ruling powers in Burma (Ava) since the beginning of 15th century despite having limited social and cultural exchanges; wars and forced migrations; contribution of the Kathes (Manipuris) in the making of Burmese Empire; Manipur's trade relations with countries like Burma, China, and British India; the broad culture and traditions among the hundreds of ethnic groups in the region which had broad common ancestry and could not be separated from each other; the royal historical link; places settled by Manipuris in Myanmar; and the present status and reality of the historical and ethnic connect. It concludes by looking forward that the much talked about ancient wisdom in the old Manipuri Puyas that "Nongpok Thong Hangba" (Opening of the Eastern Gate) of Manipur would bring greater peace and progress in the Manipur-Myanmar relationship within the larger framework of Indo-Myanmar friendship in the future.

The twentieth chapter, **'Cross-Border Migration and Cultural Dynamics of Ethnic Groups between Myanmar and Manipur'** by **Sanasam Amal Singh** enunciates that migration of people is as old as human mankind. And migration across borders and oceans is as old as nation-states. This process brought forth a very good positive impact in the political and social life of the existing surrounding environment. In the long history of coexistence between Myanmar and Manipur the activities of cross border migration or movements played important roles. The cross border movements were mostly associated with trade and commerce, war captives and matrimonial alliances. From these aspects the chapter attempts to highlight the early ethnic Shan migration in Manipur and the Meitei settlement in Myanmar. It also looks into the cultural influence brought by the ethnic migrant groups in the regions of Myanmar and Manipur.

The twenty-first chapter, **'Manipur and Kabaw Mangsa (Min Thar): Revisiting the Linkages'** by **Ngangom Jayshree Devi** while drawing for a revisit of the linkages Manipur had with the people of Kabaw valley highlights that the Southeast Asian country Myanmar and the Manipur which share borders also have a long shared history. Historically political developments at different points in time led to redrawing of the erstwhile kingdom of Ava now Myanmar and the then Princely state of Manipur in the Nineteenth century. At that era, the happenings in this part of the world were largely shaped by the British Colonial power and as per their accord Kabaw valley was ceded to Ava in 1834 AD, a move still viewed by many Manipuris as not wholly justifiable. Boundary divides the land but people can still maintain the linkages for mutual growth and development with due loyalty to their respective countries, a theory now accepted by countries including India thus influencing in shaping its foreign policies. Thus, India's 'Act East Policy' (1992) transformed to 'Act East Policy' (2014) provides provisions for interface between Manipur and Myanmar with opportunities to develop and strengthen connectivity through trade, culture, people-to-people contacts and physical infrastructure. The new policy has consequently removed the political wedges blocking the connection between Manipur and Myanmar thereby offering the right time and opportunity to revive the past linkages. Against such backdrop, this chapter attempts to study linkages between a place call Mangsa/ Mungsa/Min Thar just near the Manipur-Myanmar border in Sagaing region with Manipur from a historical perspective.

The twenty-second chapter, **'Comparative Studies on Manipur and Myanmar (Burma) within the South East Asian Paradigm: An Overview'** by **Nongthombam Jiten** at the very outset reiterates that Manipur in North East India and Myanmar are immediate neighbours in terms of physical and human geography, as well as culture, and interlocked historical development. Northeast India, including Manipur had remained as an 'obscure' spot in the minds of the scholars on Southeast Asia. Academic information about the very ancient structures of polities, the social and cultural developments through time, their adaptations to the environments, their response to external stimuli as well as relationships in war and peace, and the organization of authority relations between their own rulers and the ruled etc. have not been comparatively studied by contemporary scholars. The challenges before modern scholars interested in comparative studies of the two pre-colonial polities are enormous as Manipur-Myanmar comparison in terms of polity construction, organisation and impact on social and political histories are still to be undertaken by the native scholars. There is a need for an autonomous treatment on the studies of Manipur and Myanmar of pre-colonial times till the present. The chapter concludes that research works on the comparative studies particularly on Manipur and Myanmar within the South East Asian paradigm will be a holistic approach for understanding Myanmar in particular, and South East Asia in general could be an asset for the policy-makers and planners too.

The twenty-third chapter, **'India-Myanmar Connectivity: Prospects for a Land-Linked Manipur under the 'Act East' Policy'** by **Puyam Rakesh Singh** highlights that India's 'Act East' policy has added momentum to India's connectivity with the Eastern neighbours in the last few decades. Since the launching of the 'Look East' policy in the early 1990s, India's engagement with Myanmar has seen major changes in various sectors including connectivity between the two countries. At present, India-Myanmar relations also constitute an important pillar of the Indo-Pacific region particularly in the Bay of Bengal region. The two neighbouring countries have stepped up maritime security cooperation and naval exchanges recently. Given the geo-strategic environment where competition between the US and China is gaining momentum, China's growing influence in Myanmar and India's role as a counterpoise to China will shape the regional dynamics in the 21st century. Amidst such a fast changing strategic environment, India's Northeast Region (NER) in general and Manipur in particular will see major development of connectivity with the neighbouring ASEAN (Association for South East Asian Nations) nations. Apart from bilateral cooperation, India-Myanmar connectivity is driven by emerging global supply chain disruptions, the China factor, India-ASEAN Connectivity Initiative, development of NER and security of the Bay of Bengal. Strategically located between the Brahmaputra and Ayeyawady rivers with the Trilateral Highway passing through the state, Manipur is an important stakeholder towards building connectivity with the ASEAN nations. To understand the emerging trends in connectivity, this study also looks into the implications of Myanmar's political and economic reforms especially in the field of infrastructure development in Chin State and Sagaing Region under the Myanmar Sustainable Development Plan (2018-2030). This chapter is an attempt to analyse the major facets of India-Myanmar connectivity projects and prospects for transformation of landlocked Manipur into a land-linked state under the 'Act East' policy.

The twenty-fourth chapter, **'Indo-Myanmar Region: A Geo-Strategic Study'** by **Rajkumar Ranjan Singh** while emphasising the need for a detailed analysis of the tactical relations in between the tri-nations, namely India-China-Myanmar intends to study the vibrant geopolitical pulses throbbing along Myanmar's border which shares with five countries, namely Bangladesh 193 km, China 2,185 km, Laos 235 km, Thailand 1,800 km and India 1,463 km. India dominates Myanmar's western side just as China dominates its northern borders. Thailand borders the entire east of Myanmar except for a narrow strip that borders Laos. The location of Myanmar is one of the strategic and bridges of India, linking South and Southeast Asia. But at the same time, the geostrategic location of Myanmar at the tri-junction of East Asia, Southeast Asia and South Asia is of critical significance to India. The transformation of 'Look East Policy' into the much coveted 'Act East Policy' has also added to the significance of Myanmar in India's considerations of foreign policy. India is a neighbour which Myanmar cannot afford to ignore. Reciprocity on the Indian side is visible in supporting Myanmar to promote democratic values and re-build its institutions along with socio-economic reforms. The two countries have also signed several bilateral investment promotion agreements facilitating their venture in each other's country. There is also demand that Indian Government should introduce International bus service linking Moreh with Mandalay. The bus service linking Moreh with Mandalay would not only just help the traders, but also bring in tourists from Myanmar to India. Both India and Myanmar have agreed to start a Cultural Exchange Programme (CEP) with wide range of activities including dance, music, yoga, Thang-Ta, Martial Arts etc. to deepen the close bonds between the peoples of India and Myanmar. Education is a crucial area where India exercises competitive advantage in Myanmar for building a sustainable academic partnership between the two countries. For boosting its engagement with Myanmar, India has kept its focus on 'Development Assistance', supported through grants-in-aid, lines of credit, training programmes, and provisions for expert knowledge and capacity building initiatives. Regime transformation and political developments in Myanmar since the last few years have opened a new chapter in India-Myanmar relation. Given the political transformation taking place in Myanmar, the country offers immense opportunities for re-engagement which India may use to its strategic advantage. The traditional relation of friendship and cooperation between the two countries could be deepened and intensified further to each other's mutual benefit.

THEME-I

Common Ancestry and Connecting Routes

1
The Tribes of Nong and Nung Race

Common Ancestry of the Early Population of Northeast India, Myanmar and Southwest China

Laishram Suresh

The recent discovery of new archaeological sites revises the human habitation timeline on Tibetan Plateau. Human ancestors first set foot on the interior of the Qinghai-Tibetan Plateau around 30,000 to 40,000 years ago, according to new research by Scientists from the Chinese Academy of Science (CAS).[1] These finding moves back to the earliest data of habitation in the interior by 20,000 years or more. The research team was led by Dr. Zhang Xiao Ding and Prof. GAO-Xing from the Institute of Vertebrate (IVPP) of CAS. The prehistoric cultural artifacts from Nwya Devu provide important archaeological evidence of the survival strategies of early anatomically and behaviourally modern people to what is arguably the most rigorous terrestrial environment on earth. It also allows analysis of Palaeolithic exchange and interaction between East and West possible migration.[2]

The Himalayan mountain range encompasses an unparalleled landscape featuring some of the planet's highest peaks providing a formidable barrier separating the Tibetan plateau from the Indian subcontinent.[3] The region also constitutes an ethnic and linguistic contact zone as it marks a crossroad of three different religions (Islam, Hinduism and Buddhism) and two language families, that is, Indo-European and Sino-Tibetan, with Sino-Tibetan partitioning into the Chinese and Tibeto-Burman (TB) sub-families. Speakers of the latter represent the majority of the Himalayan inhabitants whereas the Indo-Europeans are restricted to the south by the extensive chain of Himalayan mountains ranges. The geo-political partitioning of TB-speaking groups include Tibet, Nepal, Northeast India, Bhutan, Burma, Southwest China and parts of Southeast Asia.[4] Two opposing views on the origin of TB populations have been proposed. Both models invoke demi diffusion for the dispersal of the language subfamily. Su *et al.*[5] postulate the upper and middle Yellow River basin as the ancestral source of TB people. In contrast, Van Driem[6] argues for the Yangtse River in Sichuan province as the homeland of TB-speakers, with subsequent northward migrations to the fertile plains of the Yellow River valley where Neolithic civilizations flourished.[7]

Regarding the genetic affinities present among Tibeto-Burman (TB) groups from Northeast India have been ascribed to geographic contiguity rather than linguistic affiliation.[8] The same group suggested that, given its geographical proximity, Burma most likely provided the source population for the Manipur and Tripura territories, whereas those from the northern region (Arunachal Pradesh, Mizoram and Sikkim) have been populated primarily by Tibetans.[9] Unfortunately, the study did not incorporate both probable parental source populations to assess their phylogenetic relationships to the Northeast Indian groups. Other studies based on Bhutanese and Nepalese 'Y-STR'[10] profiles revealed isolation and drift among these Himalayan collections, with a pronounced effect of drift observed in Bhutan. Nevertheless, haplo type sharing indicates possible gene flow between them or from a common source population.[11] To evaluate the genetic relationships between the Himalayan collections and the neighbouring TB-speaking populations at the regional level, six Northeast Indian TB groups were included in the phylogenetic and statistical analyses performed using the 13 core Combined DNA Index System-Statimax Trip Release (CODIS-STR) loci. These Northeast Indian TB groups map distantly from both the Himalayan and East Asian populations in the studies, inconsistent with previous Y-chromosome and mitochondrial DNA (mtDNA) studies which report a high degree of genetic homogeneity between Himalayan and Northeast Indian TB groups.[12]

The discrepancy observed between Y-chromosome and microsatellite polymorphisms in the Northeast Indian TB groups may be explained by a male founder effect from Northeast Asia and their subsequent genetic isolation for an extended period of time following their arrival.[13] The studies suggest that the Northeast

Asian ancestry for the Himalayan populations with subsequent genetic admixture in Kathmandu and Newar populations from South Asia. South Asian influences in Tibet and Tamang are negligible most likely due to the natural barrier presented by the Himalayas. Tamang, Tibet and Bhutan display close genetic affiliations in all analyses possibly indicating a shared common ancestry. The biparental markers examined in this study reveal unique genetic profiles for the Northeast Indian TB groups, which are distinct from their Himalayan counterparts implying limited gene flow, geographic isolation and/or founder effects.

The tribes of the Karau (Kharup) and the adjoining Neolithic sites of Tibet, Chamdo Kham, of Qinghai region, Himalaya mountain range and its extension of minor gorgeous Koubrau Kham[14] prefecture of the Northeast India has played an important role in shaping the population landscape of the region by demarcating east-west migration and restricting human dispersals, especially from Indian subcontinent into the Tibetan plateau and northeast India.The geo-political partitioning of TB (Tibeto-Burman) speaking groups include Tibet, Nepal, Northeast India, Bhutan and Burma (Myanmar).

The North Eastern tip of India, flanked in the north by the Himalaya and in the south by the Bay of Bengal, constitutes a unique narrow passageway that connects the Indian subcontinent to East Asia and South East Asia. This flank is thought to have been a crucial corridor for human migrations between these two sub-continental areas of East Asia and Southeast Asia. It is pertinent in this context that the Indian subcontinent has been considered as a major corridor for the migration of human population to the East Asia. With the unique geographical position, North East India is the only region which currently forms a land bridge between the Indian subcontinent and South East Asia, hence hypothesized as an important passage for the initial peopling of Southeast Asia.[15]

A team led by B. Mohan Reddy studied the Austro-Asiatic Tribes of Northeast India provide Hitherto Missing Genetic Link between South and Southeast two major routes have been proposed from the initial peopling of East Asia; one *via* Central Asia to Northeast Asia, which subsequently expanded towards Southeast Asia and beyond, and the other through India to Southeast Asia and further to different regions of East Asia. It is pertinent in this context that the Indian subcontinent has been considered as a major corridor for the migration of human populations to East Asia. With the concept of its unique geographic position, Northeast India is the only region which currently forms a land bridge between the Indian subcontinent and Southeast Asia, hence hypothesized as an important passage for the initial peopling of East Asia. However, Austro-Asiatic speakers, hypothesized as probably the earliest settlers in the Indian subcontinent and references they are in, are also found in other parts of India as well as in East/Southeast Asia. Therefore, if Northeast India had served as an initial corridor, then the Austro-Asiatic tribes of this region should provide hitherto missing genetic link, which may reflect genetic continuity between Indian and East/Southeast Asian populations. Based on genetic studies of mtDNA and Y-chromosome markers, observed genetic discontinuity between the Indian and Southeast Asian populations and inferred that Northeast India might have acted as a barrier rather than the facilitator of the movement of populations both into and out of India.

In the study of "Antiquity, geographic contiguity and genetic affinity among Tibeto-Burman populations of India"—Bimonthly Academy Journal—Published by Tayler & Francis—Society for the Study of Human Society documented the genetic affinities present among TB groups from Northeast India have been ascribed to geographic contiguity rather than linguistic affiliation. The same group also suggested that, given its geographical proximity, Burma most likely provided the source population for the Manipur and Tripura territories, whereas those from the northern region (Arunachal Pradesh, Mizoram and Sikkim) have been populated primarily by Tibetans.[16]

Before coming to the discussion of Manipur Religious cosmology we need to understand the two terms of Nong and Nung ethnic people in the Chinese and southeast Asian context. Nong people are believed to be the branch of Zhuang nationality, settling in Yunnan and Guangxi of Southern China. Like the Vietnam's Nung, they live in border areas. The autonyms and exonyms referred to various branches of Nong around these areas at present. The historical and anthropological perspectives, proto-Tai linguistic classification of Nong/Nung as a subgroup of Central Tai. But Nung are Nungish languages family of uncertain affiliation within the Sino-Tibetan Language spoken in Yunnan, China and Burma. They include: Derung, Rawang, Nung (Anong,

Along, Anung). The Thai Nung are a Diac people who speak one of the central Tai languages, in China, they belong to the Zhuang minority people group. The central Nung group living primarily in the northern Vietnam and southern Guangxi are Tai ethnic group. According to the Vietnam census, the population number is about 10,83,298 by 2019. Nung has traditionally been classified as central Tai language within Kra-dai or Diac family. The Kra-Dai speaking people living across a substantial region of East and Southeast Asia are commonly considered to originate in South China. On the other hand, Laurent Sagart (2008) proposes that Kra-Dia is a later form of FATK, a branch of Austronesian belonging to subgroup Puluqis, developed in Taiwan, whose speaker migrated back to the mainland, both to Guangdong, Hainan and north Vietnam around the second half of the 3rd millennium BCE.[17] There is puzzle why some Nung ethnic groups speak Tai-Kadai Language and some Nung speak Sino-Tibetan-Nungiest language.

Nong people are a branch of Zhuang nationality, settling in Yunnan and Guangxi of Southern China. Like Vietnam's Nùng, they live in border areas. The autonyms and exonyms referring to them show that there are various branches of Nong around these areas. The linguistic classification of Nong/Nung language first, then, some historical evidences and anthropological perspectives, gathered from surveys and documents about Nong ethnic groups in Southern China, are additionally proposed. According to some phonological criteria, Proto-Tai linguistic classification grouped Nung/Nong as a subgroup of Central Tai. There are arguments amongst scholars whether some Nong dialects in Southern China can also be identified as a subgroup of Northern Tai dialects or not. According to the historical records and ethnohistory, a rebel leader of Nong in 11th century named Nong Zhigao became interesting information for further researches.

Now-a-days, even though Nong people are culturally influenced by Han Chinese, they still maintain their ancestral culture and tradition. In southwest China and Southeast Asia there are numbers of Nung and Nong tribes, but puzzle remained in the study of Nong and Nung. Some Nung speak Tai-Kadai language and some other Nung speak Tibeto-Burman Languages, similarly, some Nong tribes speak Tai-Kadai and some other speak Tibeto-Burman.

The Rawang people are an ethnic group who inhabit far

northern Kachin state of Myanmar (Burma). According to cultural research and their own oral traditions, the Nung-Rawang are most likely Mongolian descendants who moved south from the Mongolian steppes to the 3 river region—Mekong, Yangtze, Salween of China.

During the second millennium, the Nung-Rawang migrated south-west into the Himalayas at the top of Burma, seeking fertile farm lands. They settled in some of the most remote valleys and mountains in all of Burma. The Nung-Rawang are a proud, peaceful, industrious, agriculturally based mountain people known for their stability, hospitality, and colourful traditions. Living in the beautiful and isolated regions of northern Burma, they have also become prosperous through the plentiful supplies of jade and gold in their region. During the British colonial period, their very existence was thought to be a myth, as incoherent reports of "Pygmy tribes" in the mountains of north Burma surfaced from time to time. The Drung, a sub-tribe of the Nung-Rawang are short in stature, and are known for their crossbow hunting skills, and an extensive anthropological study has been initiated on this remote ethnic group by Dr. P. Christiaan Klieger of the California Academy of Sciences, since 2001.

Considering all the above relevant documents of research works let us now see what religious cosmology and other old legendary textual records of Manipur documented in the peopling of the Northeast India and Myanmar. The geo-political partitioning of TB (Tibeto-Burman) speaking groups include Tibet, Nepal, Northeast India, Bhutan, Burma, Southwest China and parts of Southeast Asia.[18]

The Religious Cosmology 'Leithak Leikharol'[19] and 'Pudin (Putien)'[20], the old legendary textual records of Manipur believed to be compiled by 'Leinung Tharuk Asheiba', the royal Pena singer of Prince Nongda (Nongdalai Pakhangba)[21] of 1st century AD.

The mythological and historical timelines of the ancient 'Taibangpal', the world of 'Taipang'[22] and World of Proto-Tai had great Hangko eras and great Chak eras. The Hangko era was a great Era of Lai and Tien having four divisions each namely;'Koi' or 'Ko' or 'Ka Hangko', 'Thoi-Hangko', 'Tai-yo Hangko' and 'Poi-yo Hangko'. Similarly, the four Chak eras are 'Hayi Chak', 'Haya Chak', 'Khunung Langba Chak' and' Konna Chak' eras. The names of the Hangkos and Chaks are the names of the dominant tribes of the eras. According to 'Meihoubarol'[23] text of late Moirangthem Narendra, the tribes of *Kating, Kamai* and *Katik* are given as the names of the tribes in the Hangko eras.[24] Again, the same text says the Hangko era was an era of Lai people. Before the Hangko era, the world of Taipang race was in darkness and when A-tien-kok emerges as a leading chief, the darkness ended. The Hangko era was founded by Lai people and Tien the ruling clan of Lai. The Name Taiyo and Poiyo Hangko indicates that the two Hangko era were dominated by proto-Tai of Tai-yo tribes descendant of Tien of Koubrau Kham prefecture and Poi of TB tribe of Tibetan Plateau.

The Gorgeous 'Kham Koubrau' or 'Kabrau'[25] plateau was the first settlement site of Lai people in the Koi or Ko or Ka Hangko period and still today the sacred sites of the Koubrau mountain of ancestral Lai primogenitors are worshipped by the valley people during New Year's weeks. Old records in the ritual songs of Laiharaoba and textual records says: "*Awang Koubrau (or Kabrau) Asuppa, Laiyam khunda Ahanba......*", literary meaning is—Lai was the foremost settler of the Koubrau Mountain. The Lai from Manipur Koubrau Kham Plateau expanded to the surrounding highland of Thangjing, Wangpurel, Chingkhei and Marjing. In the later period of Hangko eras, the Lai people settled down at the basin of the lakes. There is another mountain of same name Kabrau located at the border of India and Nepal, which can be clearly seen from Dzongri in Sikkim. This Kabrau and Koubrau much be of similar tribes of Lai named the two mountains with slight variation in sound. It appears that in the late Palaeolithic and early Neolithic period, the Lai people from Koubru of Manipur might have moved Northward and reached Kabru of Northeast at Nepal border and might have moved eastward to reach Shanthong Mountain of eastern China in late Palaeolithic and early Neolithic periods.

Hayi Chak era was an era of Lai and Mi tribes, King Kangba was the first king of the Muang city state of Manipur in 1500 BC. The Maung city state of King Kangba was known as Kang-Muang, at the present Kang-muang village of Imphal west district. King Kangba had nine sons, namely Koikoi, Teima, Yangma, Tasharot, Wurel Khuba, Wurelhanba, Yerem, Khapi and Langba. Koikoi remained at Kangmaung and ascended the throne of Muang under his coronation name Moriya Phampalcha, Teima became Meitei-man-pi, Yangma migrated southward and established Mayang city state, Tasharot went out south-westward and established

Takhel (Tripura) city state, wurel Khuba went towards Koubrau and established Moirang princedom, Yerem went southward and established Pasha city state, Khapi migrated eastward and established Khakhe at southwest China, Langba went southward and established Erangka (Erakan).[26]

According to Kangbaron text, during the time of King Muriya or Moriya (Muang-Laiya, the land of Lai people)[27] different waves of Chakpa tribes migrated from Karau highland to Manipur crossing the Northwest hill ranges[28] in 1450-1400 BC, as the present Manipuri calendar 'Moriya Phampalcha Kumshinglon' is 3418-3419 in 2020 AD that means 1400 BC and this is calculated from the Divine Lai year. The Karau tribe abandoned their home land in 1750 to 1500 BC and Chakpa reached Manipur around 1400 BC. The Chakpa tribes reached Manipur in different waves and time period, and settled down in different sites of the lake and river basins of Manipur. The Chakpa from the valley of Manipur migrated to Chakpa Ango-Ye Basin (Khyiang River) or Kabaw valley and established number of villages. In the textual records of 'Ningthourol Lambuba', 'Khuman Ningthourol Lambuba', 'Cheitharol Kumbaba' mentioned of Chakpa Village in the Chakpa Ango-Ye Basin from early period. The hill range along the river side recorded is still known as Chakpa Ango Ching to the people of Manipur and the river of Chakpa Ango-Ye River. The Chieng (Qiang) of Himalayan tribe is recorded as earliest tribe in Chak era in 'Moirang Ningthourol Lambuba', the Chieng established their polity and came to be known as Chienglei. Chienglei means the land of Chieng or Qiang.

The text of Kangbarol also recorded the migration of the son of King Kangba and Prince Pong son of King Moriya or Muanglai reached Khyiang River Basin and moved north-eastward and said to have established Pong or Muang Pong or Muang Pang (Mupang) city state at the highland region of Khage, Kha-Khe the southwest highland of Yunnan and Shan state region. In the Yunnan legend, Yunnan was ruled by an Indian prince of Maurya Ashoka and his children ruled Yunnan for many centuries. This Muariya is not the Mauriya of Ashoka but the Muanglaiya of King Kangba and Moriya of Haye Chak era. The present Kabaw Valley is recorded in Burmese history as Muariya tract, as the descendants of King Muanglaiya migrated along this river basin to reach Highland region of southwest China in Haye Haya Chak eras. The principality of Sumjok (Tuanghtut) and Kari (Kali-myo) are believed to be established by the descendants of King Muariya Phampalcha. Moirangtem Narendra in his book 'Meihoubarol' recorded that Manipur prince captured the ancient city state of Yunnan and the prince name is recorded as Mengshi Khomba, the conqueror of Mengshi kingdom southwest China. Again, Yunnan people believed that a prince from India ruled Yunnan and his descendants ruled for many centuries.[29]

The word Karau is a day-to-day uses to address highland, sky and when people died, people believed that the souls ascended to Karau highland, heaven or the ancestral homeland. In the text of 'Pakhangba Karau Nongkawa'[30], recorded the honorific names of the kings, princes, princesses and noblemen whose souls ascended to the ancestral heavenly highland of Karau. In the text, 365 entities were divinized for their great contribution for the mankind and worshipped as ancestral deities still today.

The Tibeto-Burman people currently living in the Yi-corridor clearly retain the historical memory that their ancestors came from "the North" in their epics, legends, and cultural customs. For example, the Qiang people living by the upper reaches of the Minjiang River say in their legends that their ancestors came from the Gansu-Qinghai region[31], (Changshou Ma, 1984) while the legends of the Yi people and the ancient records written in Yi language claim that their ancestors were originally from "outside the land of the yaks" (*maoniujiaowai,* today's plateau region in Sichuan), and according to Nakhi legends, their ancestors came from the upper reaches of the Jinsha River (Upper stretches of the Yangtze River, it flows through the provinces of Qinghai, Sichuan, and Yunnan in West China); the Lisu people say that their ancestors came from the upper reaches of the Lancang River (Upper half of Mekong River), and the Jingpo (Kachin) people say their ancestors came from an unspecified area of the Qinghai-Tibetan plateau.[32] Today the tradition of "escorting the soul" is still very common in the funerary customs of the Yi sub-group living in the southern part of the Tibetan-Yi Corridor: this practice consists of inviting a priest after somebody dies (each ethnic group has different names for priests: the Yi people call them *bimo,* the Nakhi people[33] call them *dongba,* and so on), to read the sacred book for escorting the soul of the deceased, in order to help their soul find the land of their ancestors, one station after another.[34] Even though the paths and the toponyms along the routes of the "escorting the souls" of each nationality are completely different, all of them are directed "northward". The "escorting the souls" traditions of the Yi, Nakhi, Hani, Lisu, Lahu, Jinuo, Pumi, and Jingpo (Kachin) people are the most representative and prominent.[35] This is a real reflection of the history of the migration from north to south of the ancestors of the Tibeto-Burman group. Just as ethnologist Li Shaoming said: "Each group of the Tibeto-Burman people living in the valleys of the six rivers of the Tibetan-Yi Corridor share a history of migration from north to south."

The text of 'Pakhangba Nongkawa'[36] and 'Kangbarol' proves that the Tibeto-Burman speaking people was also the ancestor of the valley and hill people migrated from Neolithic site of Karau and surrounding region of Kharup (horde of Kha people).[37] 'Kangbarol' mentioned of the migration of Chakpa tribes from Karau to the valley of Manipur, indicating that they migrated from Karau and Kharup[38], Neolithic site of Chamdo, Qinghai region of Himalaya. Most of the Chak or Chakpa population moved eastward from Manipur valley to Chakpa Ango-Ye (Khyiang Ye or Chindwin River) basin and came to be known as Sak, Thet tribes to the Myanmar. In Kabaw valley Magazine, published at Tamu, Muang Nwe Than, the editor after studying the manuscripts of the Shumsok (Thaunghtut) or Pong principality of Kabaw valley, he wrote that the earliest known tribe of Kabaw valley was Sak or Thet, they later shifted to Yerang Yeya Chao River Basin (Ayeyarwady Basin). This Sak and Thet are corrupted word for Chak, Myanmar pronounce *Cha* and *Sa* as *Ta*, for Assam as *Atan*, *khy* or *ky* as *ch* and *iang* as in, *khyiang* is pronounced as Chin. Mentioned may be made, the new Chin-Kuki tribes pronounce *'L'* as *'G'* and for old group as *'R'*, Old Kuki Chin group called Imphal River as Run River and new Kuki Chin called Gun River, Meitei called land as Lam, old Kuki called land as *'Ram'*, and new Kuki Chin called *'Gam'*. Meitei called dead as Shiba or *siba* and Kuki Chin called *Athi* or *Thita*, here *'s'* is *'t'*.

The Karau culture (3300 to 2000 BC) was a Neolithic culture in Tibet. The culture cultivated foxtail millet. The Karuo Neolithic site was discovered in 1977 at Chambo Country, Chamdo Prefecture, Tibet, Qinghai, Himalaya and excavated from 1978 to 1979. Karau is located at about 3,100 m (10,171 ft.) above sea level[39], the site covers an area of 10,000 m^2. Over 7,000 artifacts have been discovered at Karuo, including 1,060 stone artifacts, 1,284 pottery shards and

4,755 bone objects. It is one of only a few archaeological sites on the Tibetan Plateau dating back so far, and it is in good enough condition for the foundations of houses to still be found, along with roads, walls, and stone altars in addition to the individual artifacts.[40] Appearance-wise, the pottery at Karuo shows many similarities with pottery found at Majiayao sites, primarily the later phases, Machang and Banshan; however, the Karuo pottery was made using different methods and appears to be merely imitative. The tool assemblage at Karuo also shows similarities with those found at sites in western Sichuan.[41]

The remains of 34 houses were found at the site. During the earlier stages, the houses at Karuo were round and semi-subterranean. During the later stages, the houses at Karuo were rectangular and subterranean. The later houses were more solidly built and represent a shift to more permanent habitation at Karuo.

Karuo is the site of the oldest permanent settlement in Tibet and represents the earliest evidence for agriculture on the Tibetan Plateau. Agriculturally, the people at Karuo relied primarily on Foxtail Millet, while some evidence for broomcorn was also discovered. The oldest evidence for foxtail millet at Karuo dates to around 5000 to 3000 BC. The people of Karuo also supplemented their diet with hunting.[42]

The residents of Karuo suddenly abandoned the settlement around 1750 BC. This is likely due to a change in climate, as Karuo likely required optimal conditions (higher temperatures) for foxtail millet to be grown successfully; Karuo coincided with a period of warmer temperatures in the region, and a return to cooler temperatures likely made foxtail millet cultivation at the site untenable. Broomcorn millet requires even higher temperatures for cultivation, so the broomcorn millet found at Karuo must have been obtained from trade with lower elevation sites.

The Neolithic cultural features of the Tibetan-Yi Corridor also displayed two clear-cut traits: firstly, the ruins in the areas closer to the upper reaches of the Yellow River are the oldest ones, while the ones farther away from the upper reaches of Yellow River are more recent; secondly, the closer the ruins are to the Gansu-Qinghai area, the more distinct are their cultural features, while the farther they are, the weaker these traits get. This explains why Historical linguistics studies suggest the origins of the Tibeto-Burman ethnic group and its separation with the Chinese language certainly happened in the upper reaches of the Yellow River. These Neolithic inhabitants who migrated southward to the Tibetan-Yi Corridor about 6000 years ago were the main pioneers of the Tibetan-Yi Corridor, as well as the earliest ancestors of the Tibeto-Burman ethnic group.[43]

In the Manipur religious cosmology *Leithak Leikharol, Pudin* and many other old texts recorded of Pinaidaba (unknown parents); of five tribes who called out from Nonglon (Yunnan Fu or Nong Fu) and Leikha (low land of Indo-China region) were recorded, namely Tien-liren, Lai-liren, Khayirel, Taoyirel, Lentaorel. Among these five tribes two tribes of Lai and Tien belong to Nong ethnic group and the Kha-Yirel, Taoyirel and Lentaorel belong to Nung ethnic groups. Nung tribes are Tibeto-Burman linguistic tribes and probable Nong of proto-Tai tribes. The Karau Nung people who migrated along the great rivers of China reached Sichuan and Yunnan Kham Prefectures from Karau and surrounding areas came to be known as Chak-Kha tribes and Nung Karau or Kharup who descended along the Brahmaputra River reaching Northeast to Manipur were of different tribes of Chakpa or Chak ethnic group. The Chakpa or Chak when they reach Kabaw Valley came to be known as Sak or Thet and later reached Ayeyarwady Basin. The tribes of Nung Ethnic of South-west China and that of Manipur when they reached Myanmar they came to be known as Thet, Sak or Sek, Kadu, Kantu and Gunnan, Thambanti etc. The river of Chindwin or Khyiang River was known as Chakpa Ango, the river of the Chakpa tribes of Chakpa Angoching, the hill range along the Chindwin River. The present river of Chindwin is recorded in different names according to the tribes that settled along the basin of the river in the course of history. The river was known as Nam-Kham River (Nam for water and Kham for Gold) by the Shenwi or Shenbi Kabo Ye, or Shenwi Kabo Ye, Chakpa Ango Ye River, Khyiang Ye River etc. The generic names indicate that the River basin was passed down by different tribes when stronger tribes dominated the basin one after another. *The Royal Chronicle of Manipur, Ningthourol Lambuba, Ava Ngamba, Sumjok Ngamka* and many other old records give the tribes who once occupied this basin from early period. *Poireiton Khunthokpa* mentioned of Shenwi Kabo, Chakpa, and Chakha Tangkhul and Chakha Maring tribes in the valley and adjoining hill sites. The earliest name of the Kabaw Basin of Chindwin was known as Kualkham. The Thongnang Man-taoriba was the earliest tribe of the present Chin hills at the basins of the Thongnang Yachu Ye of Kualdyn River. The Thongnang later shifted to Mizoram and Chittagong region and lastly established Thongnang city state in the Chittagong and Takhel (greater Tripura region). In old text, the Tripura and lower Assam region was known as Thongnang Takhel or Thongnang Mayang. The Tripura tribes or Thongnang Man tao yi shows that Man Tao and Yi belong to the tribes of ancient Southwest China. Thongnang was a tribe of Kual of Kualkham, the earliest name of Kabaw Valley who migrated to Chin Hill, Mizoram and Chittagong region and the name Kualdyn or Kuladyan also indicates that the river was named with reference to Thongnang Mantaoriba tribe. Tureirol Lambuba and Tutenglon recorded that from early era to 2nd century AD, the Thongnang tribes occupied the region of Chingnung Hut River gorge of Manipur River or Imphal River southward hill ranges.[44]

Poireiton Khunthokpa text clearly mentions the names of the different tribes of valley and hill region of Manipur. The text mentions Chak-Kha Tangkhul, Chak-Kha Maring and cognates of Pagan tribes of Mayol Molshang, Anan and Tarao Chak-Kha tribes, Chakha Maram and Chak-Kha Kapoi (Kaboi of Rongmei, Laingmei and Ziangmei), Kharam, Moirang and Meitei, Chak-Kha Kharam (Chothe). So, the above tribes were aboriginal tribes of Manipur from many centuries before the arrival of prince Poireiton and Prince Nongdalai through Yunnan Kham region.[45]

From the records of Manipur religious cosmology, the earliest known tribe of Myanmar was Chakpa known as Thet or Sak tribes and Austro-Asiatic tribes. The Thet and Sak tribes reached Myanmar in 1500 to 1400 BC but the exact time of the arrival of Austro-Asiatic tribes is not known but during the migration of the Tien princes from Tien Kingdom of Nong-Fu or Yunnan-Fu and his people of southwest China in 2nd BC to 1st AD, population of two to three cubic feet were found in the upper Ayeyarwady Basin and Kachin-Yunnan-India adjoining region.[46]

Before the arrival of Nongdalai Pakhangba, the northeastern part of the valley was dominated by three Sorarel (Heavenly) tribes of Kha Nganba, Luwang and Chienglei. The Chakpa Nung princedoms of Tubu developed at the lake basin were Luwang (Luang), Khuman, Chienglei, Mangang, Khaba, Nganaba and Nong princedom was Moirang, Koubrau and Shelloi tribes and later Nongthoucha and Poi tribes of Chak-Kha Poireiton.[47]

The Nung tribes of Chak-Kha from Yunnan Kham Southwest China and Chakpa from Manipur valley developed numbers of city states in the two great rivers of Khyiang and Ayeyarwady River basin known as Tagaung Dyansty, Pyu Dynasty, Kanren and Thet Dyansty. These tribes are now put under Pyu city states of Tigua, Beiktenu, Simon, Halin, Pagan, Maingmaw, Binnak, Sri Kstra who flourished from 3rd or 2nd century BC to mid-9th century AD to 11th century AD when another wave of TB tribe known as Mrama reached upper Ayeyarwady River Basin in the middle part of the nineth century established Pagan Dynasty and dominated Tibeto-Burman speaking Pyu city states one after another.

Considering the above statement, the people of the Northeast India and Myanmar are the tribes whose ancestral roots were the Lai and Tien tribes of Kating (Katien), Kamai and Katik of the Nong Race from Koubrau or Kabrau highland Plateau of Manipur, the gorgeous Koubrau Kham Prefecture and it extends up to Myanmar and the highland of Southwest China forming Nonglon (Leithak) and Leirol (Leikha). The Nung Race who migrated from the Neolithic sites of Karau of Qinghai, Himalaya and adjoining region in 5000 to 1500 BC and migrated along great rivers of China and Brahmaputra reached Sichuan and Yunnan Kham Prefecture, Northeast region then to the Present Myanmar. So, the early population of Northeast India, Myanmar and Southwest China were mainly the tribes of Nong and Nung Race.

NOTES

1. Mihai Andrei (29 November, 2018). "New archaeological site revises human habitation timeline on Tibetan plateau", in *Science Daily*. Chinese Academy of Science Headquarters.
2. X.L. Zhang, B.B. Ha, S.J. Wang, Z.J. Chen, J.Y. Ge, H. Long, W. He. W. Da, X.M. Nian, M.J. Yi, X.Y. Zhou, O.Q. Zhang, Y.S. Jin, O. Bar-Yosef, J.W. Olsen, X. Gao (2018). "The earliest human occupation of the high-Altitude Tibetan Plateau 40 thousand to 30 thousand years ago", in *Science Daily*.
3. Gayden, T., Cadenas, A.M., Regueiro, M., Singh, N.B., Zhivotovsky, L.A., Underhill, P.A. *et al.* (2007). "The Himalayas as a directional barrier to gene flow", in *Am. J. Hum. Genet.* 80,. pp. 884-894.
4. Cordon, R.J. Ethnologue (15th Edn., 2005). *Languages of the World.* (SIL) International, Dallas.

5. Su, B., Xiao, J., Underhill, P.M., Deka, R., Zhang, W., Akey, J. al. Y. (1999). "Chromosome evidence for a Northward migration of modern humans into East Asia during the late Ice Age", in *Am. J. Hum. Genet.* 65, pp. 1718-1724.
6. Van Driem, G.L. (2002). "Tibeto-Burman Phylogency and Prehistory: Languages, Material Culture, and Genes", in Bellwood, P. & Renfrew (eds). *Examining the Farming Language/Language Dispersal Hypothesis,* pp. 233-249.
7. Van Driem, G.L. (2005). "Tibeto-Burman vs. Indo-Chinese Implications for Population Geneticists, Archaeologists and Prehistorians", in Sagart. L., Roger Blench and Alicia Sanchez-Maza (eds.). *The Peopling of East Asia: Putting together Archaeology, Linguistic and Genetics.* Routledge. Curzon, Taylor and Frances Group, London.
8. Krithika, S., Trivedi, R., Kashyap, V.K. & Vasulu, T.S. (2005). "Genetic diversity at 15 microsatellite loci among the Adi Pasi population of Adi tribal cluster in Arunachal Pradesh, India", in *Leg. Med. (Tokyo)* 7, pp. 306-310.
9. Krithika, S., Trivedi, R., Kashyap, V. K., Bharati, P. & Vasulu, T. S. (2006). "Antiquity, geographic contiguity and genetic affinity among Tibeto-Burman populations of India: A microsatellite study", in *Ann. Hum. Biol.* 33, pp. 26-42.
10. A Y-STR is a short tandem repeat (STR) on the Y-chromosome. Y-STRs are often used in forensics, paternity, and genealogical DNA testing. Y-STRs are taken specifically from the male Y chromosome. These Y-STRs provide a weaker analysis than autosomal STRs because the Y chromosome is only found in males, which are only passed down by the father, making the Y chromosome in any paternal line practically identical.
11. Parkin, E.J., Kraaj Enbrink, T., Van Drien, G.L., Tshering of Gaselo, K., de Kniftt, P. & Jobling. M.A. (2006). "26 locus Y-STR Typing in a Bhutanese Population Sample", *Forensic, Sc. Int.* 161, pp. 1-7.
12. Su, B., Xiao, J., Underhill, P., Deka, R., Zhang, W., Akey, *et al.* (1990). "Y-Chromosome evidence for a northward migration of modern humans into Eastern Asia during the last Ice Age", in *Am. J. Hum. Genet,* 65, pp. 1718-1724.
13. Corduax, R.G., Saha, N. & Stone King, M. "The northeast Indian passageway: A barrier or corridor for human migration?", in *Mol. Boil, Evol.* 21.
14. In Moirang Ningthourol Lambuba, the Koubrau Mountain is recorded as Kham Yoi and the prince who came down to Moirang princedom is recorded as gorgeous Koubrau Kham prince.
15. Su, B., Xiao, J., Underhill, P., Deka, R., Zhang, W., Akey, J. *et al.* (1999). "Y-Chromosome evidence for a northward migration of modern humans into Eastern Asia during the last Ice Age", *Am. J. Hum.*

Genet. 65, pp. 1718-1724.
16. Krithika, S., Trivedi, R., Kashyap, V.K., Bharati, P. & Vasulu, T.S. (2006). "Antiquity, geographic contiguity and genetic affinity among Tibeto-Burman Populations of India: A Microsatellite Study", *Ann. Hum. Biol.* 33, pp. 26-42.
17. Wilson & Vy (1976). p. 11.
18. Su, B., Xiao, J., Underhill, P., Deka, R., Zhang, W., Akey, J. *et al.* (1999)."Y-Chromosome evidence for a northward migration of modern humans into Eastern Asia during the last Ice Age", in *Am. J. Hum. Genet.* 65, pp. 1718-1724.
19. 'Leithak Leikharol' deals with the Meitei mythology of the creation and describes how the Almighty Atiya Guru Sidaba got his two sons—Asiba and Khonjin Tinthokpa.
20. 'Pudin' is early Manipuri manuscript dealing with the subject matter of Cosmogony which gives an account of the genesis of the universe, birth of human beings and also the origin of the clans.
21. Nongda is Nong-Tai, and his coronation title as Nongda-lairen-pakhangba (Nong-Tai-Lai-ren Pakhangba).
22. Taibangpal: is Taipangpal, the region where Tai Pang people live or inhabited. Taipangpal is the world of Taipang Race, the proto-Tai people of Taipang world.
23. 'Meihoubarol' deals with genealogies of the Meitei clans, subclans or families wholly or singly.
24. *Meihoubarol* written and edited by Narendra Moirangthem, published by Dr. Moirangthem Rangjana, 2005, p. 10.
25. Kourau is address as "Kham-Yoirel" in Moirang Ningthourol Lambuba, which means gorgeous Kham.
26. Nongthonban Angou Luwang (ed. & trans., 1976). *Kangbarol.* Tamar Publication, Imphal, p. 3.
27. Mu is the shortened form of Muang, for city state. In *Ningthourol Lambuba,* "Leipak Khunda aphababu Mu kauye". Ri is Li and Li is Lai.
28. *Op.cit.* Nongthonban Angou Luwang (ed. & trans., 1976). *Kangbarol.* pp. 5-6.
29. The. Rev. Geo, W. Clarke (2nd Edn. 1974), "On the Aboriginal Tribes of Western Unnan", in *Ptolemys Geography of Eastern Asia.* Oriental Books Reprint Corporation, N. Delhi.
30. Chanam Hemchandra (ed. & trans., 2000). *Pakhangba Nongkawa.* Chingtam Press, Imphal.
31. Ma Changshou, DI and Qiang, Shanghai People's Publishing House, 1984, pp.166-181.
32. Meng Mo (1980). *Chronicles of Puliof the Anshun Government records, Guizhou, cites the ancient record in Yi language, Yi book of Luogui.* Vol. 22.
33. Nakhi or the Nashi people are an ethnic group found at the foothill

of the Himalayas in the Yunnan Province and the Sichuan Province in China. The Nashi are believed to be descendants of Proto-Qinghai, an ethnic group living in the Tibetan plateau. The proto-Nakhi moved to the basins of Nujiang River then to the Along River in the present Sichuan Province.

34. Shi Shuo (2001). *Ethno Origin of the Tibetan People and the Ancient Civilization of Eastern Tibet*. Sichuan People's Publishing House, pp. 54-65.
35. Yunnan Bureau for the Plan of the Publication of Nation, 1989; Ling Fuxiang, 1993.
36. *Op. cit.* Chanam Hemchandra (ed. & trans., 2000). *Pakhangba Nongkawa.*
37. Lairup and Tienlup-horde of Lai and Tien people, so Kha rup means horde of Kha tribe.
38. Karau is also known as Kharup.
39. Qiu, Jane (2015). "Who are the Tibetans?", in *Science*. 347 (6223).dol: 10.1126/science. 347.6223.708.
40. ChinaCulture.org Archieved 2009-01-08 at the Wayback Machine.
41. Guedes, Jade d'Alpoim (2015). "Rethinking the spread of agriculture to the Tibetan Plateau", in *The Holocene*. Doi: 10,1177/09596836155858352
42. Gruschke, Andreas (2004)."The Karo culture in: The Cultural Monuments of Tibet's Outer Provinces", in *Kham—Vol. 1. The TAR part of Kham*, White Lotus Press, Bangkok 2004, S. pp. 166-170.
43. Shi Shuo (2006). *"The Regional classification of Neolithic cultures in the Tibetan Yi corridor and their relation to the Gansu-Qinghai Region"*, in Bashu (Part-III) *Cultural Studies*. Bashu Books.
44. Tureirol Lambuba and Tutenglon. Ms.
45. Chanam Hemchandra (ed. & trans.). *Poireiton Khunthokpa*. Chingtam Press, Imphal.
46. Chanam Hemchandra (ed. & trans. 2010). *Leithak Leikharol*. Chingtam Press, Imphal.
47. *Ibid.*

2
Manipur-A Bridge between Indian Subcontinent and Burma, South East Asia, China and Far East in Ancient Times

Laiphrakpam Nishikanta Singh

Since ancient times, Manipur was connected well with the rest of the world and also internally. Trade between Manipur and Yunnan province of China since ancient times is recorded in the Royal Chronicle of Manipur. In fact, the people of Manipur possibly learnt brick making from the Chinese. The Chinese knew how to make bricks, called it as 'chek' in their language. The same word was introduced in Meitei-lon as 'brick'. According to the chronicle, a Meitei king attacked the principal Chinese village (or town) along with many brave Meitei warriors and defeated their chief Chouopha Hongdei. The Royal Chronicle records that in 1632 A.D., King Khagemba constructed a brick wall at the western gate of Kangla Fort. It appears that the art of brick making was acquired from the Chinese prisoners who were captured during the Chinese invasion of the eastern frontier of Manipur. Meidingu Khagemba (1597–1652) was known as the "Conqueror of the Chinese" (Khagi: Chinese and Ngamba: conqueror). He consolidated and expanded his father's kingdom of Meitrabak, later successfully defending it from foreign invaders such as the Muslims, the Kachari and the Shans of the Kabaw Valley. Muslim settlement became more prominent after 1606 A.D. with the establishment of a Muslim Personal Law Board headed by a Qazi appointed by the king. Khagemba introduced bell metal currency in the kingdom and a number of coins from his reign have been found.

The above clearly brings out Manipur was in contact with Indian, Burmese and Chinese people and traders, further indirectly with Thai and Roman people/traders in the early centuries of the Christian era. Some writings also indicate that Manipur was known to the Arab, Persia, Greece, Rome, China, Burma, Shan and other countries. Asian international trade route passed through the state.

Determining the exact details on the age of communication linking the civilisation and settlement in Manipuri with the rest of the world is difficult. However, there are certain direct or indirect evidences which help us to conclude that there were settlements and population in Manipur as early as 8th century B.C. There are also evidences that people migrating into Burma passed through Manipur. It is mentioned that even prior to the beginning of the Christian era, these routes have been used by traders, common people and invaders. D.G.E. Hall, in his book *"History of South East Asia"*, mentions of a road connecting lower Burma with India *via* the bank of the Irrawaddy, the bank of Chindwin and Manipur.

In the 2nd century B.C., there was a regular trade route from Chinato Afghanistan and Europe passing through Manipur, Assam and Northern India. A historian wrote that accessibility through Upper Burma was difficult but from 2nd century B.C., the Chinese used a trade route passing through the Irrawaddy and Salween River corridor and also along Chindwin through Manipur. The caravans from China to Europe, passing through Manipur took more than three months to reach Afghanistan. By about 900 B.C., prince Abhiraj of Sakya dynasty travelled through Manipur valley and settled at Ava (Burma). Colonel Gerini in his researches on Ptolemy's Geography writes, "According to Burmese Royal Chronicles (Maharjavamsa), Dhajaraja, a king of Sakya race, settled at Manipur about 550 B.C." In about 548 B.C., a group of Teleng People from Kalinga had also passed through the hill routes of Manipur and settled in Burma.

Of the many routes through the valley and hills of Manipur connecting the Surma valley, the Brahmaputra valley and the Kabaw valley, the following are worth mentioning:

(a) Heirok Route *via* Machee Kabaw, to Ava (Burma).
(b) Aimol Route to China and South-Eastern Asia.
(c) Ngar Chingjen Route (Ngariyan Route) to Eastern countries of Asia.
(d) Tongjei Maril Route (Old Cachar Road) to Cachar, Tripura, Sylhet.

(e) Ngaprum Chingjin Route (New Cachar road) to West including Assam.
(f) Acqui Route (Northern Route) also known as Tekhao Route to Assam, Nagaland and other Northern areas including Jorhat.

By the 6th century B.C. people from different parts of India could easily enter the Manipur and Imphal valley through one of the above routes and further they could easily travel to Burma. These routes were used by traders, common people and invaders. Hence, it can be easily said that in the ancient times, Manipur was one of the gates through which there was cultural flow between India on one hand and Burma and South-East Asia on the other. The hill routes of Manipur were also used by people of India forgoing to Burma and the Far East. These routes in general had west-east orientation in spite of the high hill ranges which are generally running parallel north to south with deep river valleys and gorges in between the ranges. These routes, in spite of the difficult terrain, were used throughout the ancient and medieval periods. The hill routes mostly converged at Imphal and again diverged in different directions to connect different places in Burma in the east and south, and Cachar and Assam in the west.

Surface transportation was the only means of transport for movement of people and goods in Manipur and also with the neighbouring countries those days. Though there was limited river transportation using various types of small country boats. These were mostly used in the valley for movement of goods as well as people. But being small, these boats had very limited carrying capacity to carry only about 20 maunds (8 quintals).

The main goods passing through Manipur consisted of silk textile and silk goods, bamboo and cane products, gold and horses. These goods were sent to the Western countries as well as to Burma and China, traders, armed forces, pilgrims, especially the Buddhists, were the main source of passenger traffic.

In spite of all-out effort, nothing much has been found as historical evidences or records of the roads both in the valley and the hills, before the Christian era. King Pakhangba, the first Manipuri king, ascended the throne in 33 A.D. At the same time, a horde of immigrants also arrived in or about 33 A.D. They entered Manipur through the hill routes. They also proceeded towards the Kabaw valley and further into Burma. Pakhangba developed trade and commercial contacts with neighbouring kingdoms. The succeeding kings had also constructed a few more roads in the valley. King Ayangba had constructed a road in the eastern part of Imphal. It served the people of Manipur for many centuries and still exists and was named Ayangpalli. It forms the eastern boundary of Imphal Municipality.

On the other hand, during the medieval period, Manipur was divided into seven principalities. There was continuous conflict amongst them for supremacy. As a result of this, a little progress was there on the construction of roads due to fights among the principalities. The principalities were connected with each other by roads and also water route.

When King Loiyamba (1074-1122) ascended the throne, there was a marked improvement in the economic condition of Manipur. Even though there were political disturbances and fights and invasions from outside, roads were constructed by the successive rulers. In 1536-37, king Kabomba (1523-42) opened a new route to Assam. It facilitated the cultural contacts between people of Manipur and Brahmaputra valley. During the reign of king Khagemba (1597-1652) in about 1630, there was a marked improvement of roads resulting in better transportation of goods and other stores. However, there was great difficulty in the road construction work due to the terrain; and also the forest environment which was infested with wild animals. King Paikhomba (1666-1690) improved the road from Chinga to Mongsangei in 1675. He maintained trade with Burma, Cachar and Tripura.

The above activities resulted in existence three different routes which connected Cachar and Sylhet with Manipur. They were the main artery for trade and commerce movement of people and military personnel between Manipur and British India located in Assam and Bengal during the later medieval period. These three routes as are given below:

(a) *The Kabow route (also known as Aquee route)*: Earlier the route was used frequently but after the 1st Burmese War it was less frequently used. The total distance from Imphal valley was about 140 km.
(b) *The Kala Naga Route*: This route connected Assam with

Lumlangdong (Bishnupur) in Manipur *via* Khoupum, with distance of about 133 km.

(c) *The Khongjai or Kuki Route*: This route passed through Khongjai (Kuki) area on the western bend of river Barak entering in the Manipur valley at its south-western corner.

On the other hand, another three routes connecting Manipur with the Kabaw valley in Burma existed as given below:

(a) *The Muchee (Machi) Route*: This started from Thoubal in Manipur *via* Heirok and Muchee to Tamu in Burma. Through this route, the distance from Thoubal to Tamu was about 75 km.

(b) *The Imole (Aimole) Route*: This also started from Thoubal and Tamu was about 80 km long. This route had a few steep and precipitous passes.

(c) There was another route north of the above two routes, which started at Sekmai (Nongpok Sekmai) in Manipur, passing through the villages of Tangkhul tribes, entered the valley of Kabaw a few miles west of Sumjok.

Besides the abovementioned lines of communications, there were several other minor routes to reach southern areas of Kabaw valley through the hills. There were eight different routes from Tamu to reach Ningthi (Chindwin).

But with the arrival of the British, during the reign of Maharaja Gambhir Singh (1825-1834) things changed. There was a reorientation of economic and commercial life. Construction of roads was given importance, especially in the hill areas, for easier movement of laden animals, camels, carts, military troops etc. The construction of Cachar Road was taken up in 1837 and completed in 1844. Though this road became excellent for foot passengers and pack animals, it remained quite narrow and steep for large-scale wheeled traffic. Besides this road, Maharaja Chandrakirti Singh (1834-1886) agreed to the construction of a road in the northern section through Naga Hills to link up Manipur with the Brahmaputra valley. This became the present day the Imphal-Dimapur Road and was completed in 1881, and became much more important than the Cachar Road.

The above resulted in the undermentioned four roads to the west from Manipur:

(a) The Naga Hills and Assam Road towards the north of Imphal *via* Mao and Kohima which is the present day Imphal-Dimapur road.
(b) The Rezepemah and Kenoma Road. It was basically a bridle path and passes over an extremely broken country and which crossed over by very steep ranges.
(c) The Cachar Road *via* Khoupum valley and Bishnupur.
(d) The Acqui Road or the Upper Cachar Road.

Towards the East, Manipur was linked with Burma through several roads. But the better ones are as given below:

(a) The Mache Route.
(b) The Aimol Route.
(c) The road from Imphal valley to Yangoupokpi *via* Haitukpokpi and onwards to Kabaw valley.
(d) The road from Manipur to Moreh *via* Pallel led direct to Kabaw valley.

All these roads were generally well planned. In the valley it avoided multiple crossing of water body instead followed one convenient side of the water body as far as possible. Further, the roads in the valley were like those of Assam, Burma and other rice-growing countries. They were raised a few feet above the rice fields wide enough for one cart, about 20 yards in some places, fairly levelled. The bridges were fit for laden mules, but not for carts and were frail and bamboo/wooden structures. In the hills, a convenient spur was selected and followed up to one of the suitable passes on the range, and down to any convenient spur on the other side. The roads were unpaved both in the valley and also in the hill. The hill routes were very narrow and steep, at some places suitable only for foot passengers and laden mules.

Thus prior to the Anglo-Manipur war of 1891, there were about ten main roads radiating from Imphal, as given below:

(a) The Naga Hills and Assam Road on the north,
(b) The Tangkhul country road on the north east,

(c) The Eastern road,
(d) Three roads starting from Thoubal to Burma,
(e) Two Langthabal or Central valley roads on the south,
(f) The Western Road, and
(g) The Kangchupkhul, Acqui or Upper Cachar Road.

Another road connecting Imphal valley with Burma is the Tedim Road. This was developed during the Second World War and fierce battles took place along this road between the Allies on one side and the combined INA and Japanese forces on the other, as this road was chosen as a major axis of advance by the Japanese and the INA forces.

Starting from Imphal, the road runs South *via* Bishnupur and Moirang to connect with Lamka, the district headquarters of Chudachandpur, which is 62 km from Imphal. From here it goes further south and touches the India-Burma international boundary at Behang village on the Indian side. The distance from Lamka to Behang is 59 km. A narrower and unmetalled portion of the Tedim Road crosses the international boundary and moves into the mountainous Chin State (formerly known as Chin Hills) in Burma. From the border it stretches another 144 km, cutting across the Manipur River at Nakzang village and finally ending at Tedim which is a major administrative town in the north of Chin State. Beyond Tedim it is well connected by a 92 km road with Kalemyo in Burma. The total length from Imphal to Tedim is 265 km.

The origin of this road can be traced back to January 1857, when Maharaja Chandrakirti Singh led a 1,500-strong punitive expedition against the Kamhau-Suktes in the Chin Hills. Another account states, in the late 19th century, British civil servants Bertram S. Carey and Henry N. Tuck discovered the existence of a route from Imphal to Tedim *via* Kakching, Sugnu, Lenglakot and Tonzang.

But it was only during the Second World War that the road actually developed. Despite heavy casualties, the retreating British soldiers put up stiff resistance against the Japanese and INA Forces to give some breathing space to the India Command to get ready, not only to defend the Indian frontier, but also to prepare for the launch of a counter-offensive operation in Burma. But the question was how to avoid the Kabaw valley, which was known as the 'valley of death' because of Japanese ambushes and the 'killer' malaria. The answer to this came in the form of a proposal to construct an alternative road from Imphal to Kalewa not through the Tamu but *via* a mountainous road in Chin Hills. In June 1942, therefore, it was decided also to develop a second road. The alignment chosen was along the bridle-path from Imphal to Tedim and further to the final great Letha Range to the Chindwin valley. According to Lieutenant-Colonel Towers, in September 1942, the idea was further reinforced when General William Slim decided to defend the lone defensive position at Tedim. The task for construction was given to the Sappers of the 17 Indian Division. The original plan was to complete the road in time for the winter campaign of 1942-43, but the limited numbers of engineers and labourers caused delays. Sappers started the work in late 1942. First, the Imphal to Torbung road, a distance of 53 km, was converted into an all-weather road. Construction continued towards the southern frontier to make a jeepable road from Torbung to Tedim. Meanwhile, construction work was also underway from Tedim. In May 1943, a jeep finally reached Tedim from Imphal. The length of the Tiddim Road between Imphal and Tedim was 265 km. Apart from a stretch in the plains of Manipur, almost 200 km of the road passed through the mountainous region. This road later witnessed some of the fiercest battles of the war.

It can be conclusively said that the early land routes between India and Burma passed through Manipur. Thus, it can be safely concluded that Manipur was well connected since the beginning of the civilization. In fact, Manipur served as a bridge between Indian Subcontinent and Burma, South East Asia, China and Far East. Hence, it is most befitting to term Manipur as the gateway to East for our beloved country India.

THEME-II

Manipur-Shan Relations

3
Soraren Macha Khunkumba

Ancient Manipuri Manuscript Relating to the Shans

Naorem Lokendra Singh and *Yumnam Mohendra Singh*

Soraren Macha Khunkumba (the settlement by the son of God of Heaven) is an undated and unpublished manuscript available in the custody of the local Manipur Pandits. The manuscript written in archaic Manipuri script contains a number of sentences relating to the history of the Pongs (Mao-Shan). The first half of the manuscript deals with a mystified story of the God of Heaven 'Soraren' asking his sons—'Khullee' and 'Khullai' and other kinsmen to go down and establish settlements on the earth. The second half, which constitutes historically the most interesting and useful portion, deals with the military adventure of Samlongpha, the younger brother of the Mao-Shan king Su-kan-pha in Manipur and the neighbouring areas. The last portion of the manuscript also deals with the relationship between the Pong King Kheekhomba and Meitei king Keeyamba.

Soraren Macha Khunkumba very categorically states that Samlongpha visited Manipur during the reign of King Khongtekcha of Manipur. The specific year and period of Samlongpha's arrival at Manipur is still very controversial and therefore, it is necessary to take a look at the history of the neighbouring country where Mao-Shan people migrated from their homeland and settled finally. It is universally accepted that the Ahoms settled in A.D. 1228 in Assam. Based on this fact of history, it may be safely said that Samlongpha visited Manipur in the first half of 13th century and not in last part of 8th century.

Soraren Macha Khunkumba described Samlong's forays to Manipur and the neighbouring kingdoms for collection of tributes on the instruction of his elder brother king Sukampha. The manuscript not only refers to a number of elephants and horses that accompanied Samlong and his army but also categorically stated that the Shan Prince brought along with him six sophisticated weapons, i.e. a big sabre, a multi-pronged spear, a powerful bow with arrows, a big shield, a rope and a powerful hammer. After a successful trip to the eastern kingdoms, Samlong came towards the western kingdoms. First, he went to the 'Basa' kingdom which according to Pemberton was the capital of Cachar. The king of 'Basa' requested him to detonate the hill ranges surrounding his country. The Shan prince complied with the request and levelled the hills which blocked the sight of the sun. It seems that the Shan troops made some positive changes in the difficult hilly terrain of the region and the Basa kingdom had thus improved its environment. The king of Basa became awe-stricken and offered a lot of gold, silver, horses, elephants etc. as tributes. Samlong too was satisfied with the treatment meted out to him. Subsequently, Samlong asked the Basa king to pay tribute to his brother king Sukampha.

Samlong then came towards 'Takhel' (Tripura) where he was received by the local raja. From there he crossed 'Khepu mountain' and reached 'Ngaprum ranges' of Manipur. When he saw the land of the Meiteis, he was very unimpressed by the presence of vast masses of swamps. He thought that the land was not prosperous enough to feed his horses, elephants and other retainers. He, therefore, turned towards Moirang where he was received by the local chief and his officers. After assessing the resources of the place, Samlong directed the local rulers to pay regular tributes consisting of seasonal products of the place like 'Heikak' (an edible aquatic plant) and 'Hentak' (an edible preparation made from small dried fish) to Magaung.

Samlong left Moirang after staying for some time. He skipped the land of the Meiteis as it seemed to be poverty-stricken and turned towards 'Thoubal Maru' on the north. The Manipuri king, Khongtekcha hurriedly went to meet him and impressed upon him to stay at the valley for some time. The Shan prince ultimately agreed and he stayed at 'Apong Ingkhol' at Imphal for ten years. During his stay at Manipur, Samlong probed deeply about the traditional ritual places like 'Kanglamen', 'Kuchu' and the big stone slab at the capital. In the course of his interactions with the local ruler he once pointed out that some time in future, scholars of Pong, Khaki, Meitei, Bengal and Burma will take interest in matters related to the place. The manuscript also stated that the Shan prince identified spots within the Kangla as future sites for 'Kanglasha' (Dragon), 'Shangai Yumpham' (royal house) and also instructed that 'Goddess Lairemma' (the family goddess) should be worshipped at a particular room inside the royal house known as 'Lapyen Ka'. The Manipuri ruler was not only given a three layered umbrella for occasional use but also helped in preparing a royal dress mostly made of gold. The Manipuri king was told that he was his real grandson. Samlong left Manipur for Tekhao (Assam). On the way he sent his servant Choumaong, to go in advance to Mogaung and inform king Sukampha and their mother of his successful venture. For reasons unknown, the messenger turned treacherous and the manuscript stated that Choumaong incited Sukampha against Samlong. King Sukampha was impressed upon to kill his brother Samlong through poisonous food. The conspiracy to kill Samlong came to the knowledge of their mother, who reported in advance to Samlong about the possible attempt at his life. Such a reality had hurt Samlong and he decided to relinquish any sort of relationship with Mogaung. He, therefore, went towards Assam from where he requested his elder brother Sukampha to send him his wife, children and also expressed his desire to settle at Assam. King Sukampha was very happy to know this and he readily gave away 50 villages to Samlong, who ruled in Assam for some time. During his reign Samlongpha instructed his son 'Chounakham' and other officers to pay annual tributes of gold and silver to Sukampha, his elder brother. He, however, died after taking the 'dried poison food' which Samlongpha preserved as sent by his elder brother. The manuscript contains the instruction given to his son before his death about the construction of burial place of his dead body. He also gave advice to his son about the administration of his kingdom. After Samlongpha, his son Chounakham became king of Assam.

The manuscript again discuss in detail the relationship between Meitie king Kyamba and Shan king Khikhomba. The two kings decided to attack and destroy the Khambat principality as the king of Khambat had once abducted a Manipuri princess meant for the Shan king. The manuscript narrates the circumstances leading to their rendezvous at an appointed place for joint attack against the chief of Khambat. The appointed day was to be known only when the 'Khongumelei' (an orchid plant) which were planted by the two kings in their different countries blossomed. The plants were separated from the original one. Because of differences in the nature of topography in the two kingdoms, the flowers blossomed on different days. Nevertheless, the two kings met after some time and defeated the king of Khambat. After their successful venture, the relationship between the two kings became closer. The two kings sat together on the same seat and had meals from the same plate. They also divided the kingdom of the chief of Khambat and fixed the boundaries respectively. The division of the Khambat kingdom between the two kings may be taken as the genesis of the claim of Manipuri king on the portion of the Kaba valley. The Pong king gave 22 (twenty-two) items of various articles as his gifts to the Meitei king. The title of 'Chouphahem' was conferred on the Meitei king by the Pong king. The Meitei king gave 3 (three) items, of articles as gifts to the Pong king. There was exchange of cultural items between the two kings according to the manuscript.

Although the manuscript does not deal with the social and economic aspect of the Shan-Meitei relationship, it seems that a lot of cultural, social and ethnic criss-crossing had taken place. This is clearly reflected in the Manipuri manuscript 'Nongpok Haram' (migrants from the east). European writers like E.W. Dun, R. Brown, Col. Mcculloch and R.B. Pemberton stated that the Shan invader had brought some fundamental changes in the dress as well as food habit of the local indigenous people. It appears that Samlongpha replaced the traditional practices of the people chewing dried fish with that of betel nut.

As one go through the Tai rituals, there are striking similarities between many of the ritual practices of the Tais and those of the Meiteis. The Tai concept of 'Khwen' has its Meitei counterpart in the 'Thawai Mi Koukhatpa'. The Tai practices of cutting the umbilical chord of a new born baby and burying the placenta in a part of the family house, the exposure of the mother after child birth to fire (Meining Kumba in the case of Meiteis), the third day birth ritual of the new born child on a bamboo tray (sixth day ritual in the case of a Meitei child), the traditional hair style of the Tai women as well as head gear of the Tai men all drew striking similarities with those of the Meiteis, worthy of an in-depth analysis.

In this connection, it may not be out of place to mention the following few references to throw light on the origin of the 'Meitei'. The 'Krathong Lamlen' an unpublished chronicle in Archaic Meitei script says 'Pakhangba' you stay here, your name is Meitei. Brian Houghton Hodson says that Meitei is one of the branches of the great Tai (JASB 1853, pp. 14-15). A.R. Col Quhown in his 'Amongst the Shans' (p. 207, Foot Note) says Manipuris call themselves as Meitei. P. Gogoi in his 'Asamat Prachalit Pouranik Akyan Samuhar Mui Bichar' (In Assamese, p. 4) says that the Meiteis are called 'Mung Kasse' by the Burmese. The 'Mung' belongs to the Ai-Lao race of the Tai according to Dodd (as mentioned by P. Gogoi in 'Tai and Tai Kingdom', p. 21). In the Manipuri chronicles 'Man (Mee)' is called 'Pong'. To cite as an example, Poireiton Kunthokpa says 'Hayee Ngeida Meepu Pong Koye'—(in olden days Man was called Pong). In 'Chakparon Lol', the reason for calling man as Pong is given. It says in second creation, the man was created. But the man so created was big in the middle. So man was called Pong. In common parlance of the Meiteis, the question "Mee-Pong Lapra" (meaning whether any man comes) is used. Thus 'Mee' (Man) is equivalent to Pong. The Kabuis, one of the important hill people of Manipur called the Meiteis as 'Tai Mei'. Hill people of Manipur usually call Man as 'Mei or Me'. The above analysis thus leads one to believe that the Meities are in some way or other ethnically and culturally closely related to some of the branches of the great Tai People.

[This paper was originally published at the *Journal of Historical Research*, Vol. IX, 1999, Dibrugarh University, pp. 71-76.]

4
Evaluating Meitei-Pong (Shan) Relations and the Conquest of Khampat from Sorarel Machana Khunkumba

Manglemjao Singh Sorokhaibam

According to a Manipuri ancient text 'Sorarel Machana Khunkumba'[1], which could literally be translated as 'The Sons of Sorarel (Heaven) Descending on the Earth', supposedly a Shan Chronicle found in Manipur has mentioned that, after the devastation of the Pong capital at Mungmaorung by the Chinese forces under the leadership of General Yachangshu, the King Sugnpha with his eldest son Sukeepha @ Samahpa escaped to Pokka (Pagan) or Awa. The king sent his first son in search of his queen mother and other sons, ultimately Samahpa met with the mother and other brothers, and narrated about his father sheltering at Awa. In the meantime, Khakis (Chinese) came to know about the sheltering of Pong king at Awa, and demanded to handover the Pong king. The Chinese General in the meantime threatened the Awa to devastate their kingdom if not hand over the king. The Awa ministers hurriedly discussed the matter and hand over the king secretly in the night. But in the meantime, the queen without knowing these facts about the arrest of the Pong king she sent a messenger to inform about her hide in that region but arrested the messenger by Chinese forces and his whereabouts was not known. Later the queen gave birth to another son and lived at a place called 'Heitup-pokpi' as a temporary capital with all five together. Then Chinese came to know about all these and devastated the place and arrested the eldest son Sumihpa (Samahpa) or Sukeehpa and again they fled to Hkampti (Khampti) and stayed there for two years. Thereafter in the year Kapsi they established their capital near the river Namkong (Namkwang), they called the place Mungkong (Mogaung). After three years Suhumhpa died in the Haisinga (Lakli) II O II.

After this his brother Suponghpa @ Sakhanhpa became king and borne one son namely Suhunghpa. During this time in the year 'hunghou' got one 'yai pung' of ching-yaishin an extraordinarily big drum, its sound reach up to two days journey. He reigned for 28 years happily and died in the year (Lakli) Kaimet. After this younger brother Suhup-pha became king in 1368 A.D.[2] After his three years reign he with a large force attacked with a vow to avenge the treachery of the Awa (Pagan King) who had surrendered his father Sugnam and brother to the Chinese (Khagi, Yunnan) General Yachangshu (Yachangshi). His forces destroyed Awa, conquered and seized Sagaing. After reigning 29 years he died in the year Kakao.[3]

Suhung-Pha

Suhungpha (Soo-hoo-pha) was succeeded by his nephew (son of his brother Sukhanghpa) Suhunghpa (Soohoonghpa). He had four sons, namely:

1. Suhenhpa @ Suhungkham,
2. Hungshe (Satapansang),
3. Chao-Swee-Nok,
4. Souramkham, both of the 2nd and 3rd sons belong to Papham clan. Suhenpha @ Suhungkham scattered Awa country, 2nd son Hungshe @ Chaw Hoongsang scattered Mung Yang; the 3rd son Chao-Swee-nok scattered Kaksa; the youngest Showramkham attacked Khampat. Suhungpha reigned for 50 years and died in the year Kasou Lakli.

Suhungkham @ Suhonghpa

Then Suhungkham, the eldest son of Suhungpha succeeded his father and became the King of Pong at Mungkong (Mogaung). He had one son Aipengpha-nakham and later issued two daughters, namely—Anangyi-Kankham-Phong and Nangei-Choikham-Khu. These two princesses when they became beautiful damsels of marriageable age, the king of Pong informed to all the chiefs of his tributary principalities expressing his willingness to marry to any of these chiefs. The Mung Yang chief proposed for the elder, and the second was proposed by the Hkampat chief. Both of the proposals were accepted. In the next year in 'Kapnyi Lakli' on a very auspicious day the first daughter was sent off to the chief of Mung Yang and the second daughter to the Chief of Khampat in the year 'Haisi Lakli'. But when the younger princess and her party was passing through Mung Yang, the elder sister intercepted and pleaded to the younger that her sister if proceeded to Khampat there won't be any communication when something happen to them and there shall be much distress and requested by the elder to dissolve the engagement and requested their father and got accepted the request, and both became the queens of Mung Yang chief. On hearing the news Khampat chief was very angry and 'Souramkham' the Khampat chief, tributary to Mungkung (Mogaung) send a message that if the Mungkong king's daughter has been given to Mung Yang, the necessary dowry he was to have receipt still be paid; and also requested a remission of three years tribute reporting that the tribes around were disturbing and he was to fight with them. The remission of the tribute for three years was accepted. Khampat chief, indignant at the treatment he had received, built a strong fort and dig thanga-pat (moats) under a pretended apprehension of the tribes around and prepared to fight against the Pong King.

The Pong King Suhonghpa send an Embassy called Chao-Lang Hai to the Meitei King Kyamba (1470) (Seeking a hand of a Meitei princess).

After few years, the Pong King Suhonghpa @ Suhungkham sent one embassy (manai angamba) named Chao-Lang Hai to the court of Meitei king requesting a hand of a princess. The Meitei king accepted the request but informed Chao-Lang Hai to wait for one year. After a deep thought as there were no princess, the Meitei King send one Sekta girl (Sekta chanu) after naming her as 'Sekmu Urabi' escorted by Chao-Lang Hai and party. On way near the Sekmu foothill (Sekmu Ching khong) the princess was carried off by the Khampat chief and his party, who were lying in wait, but the Pong nobleman effected his escape and reached Pong capital and narrated the whole incident. The Pong King was furious on learning the news and decided to fight Khampat with the combined forces of Meitei King.

The Pong King send an emissary to the Court of Meitei King for a joint invasion against Khampat (Khambat).

Pong King send one emissary again to the court of Meitei King and the emissary on arrival narrated the whole incidents and requested of joint invasion against Khampat as requested by the Pong King; and further one bunch of 'Khongkan Melei Urei', Khongkan Melei orchid which was brought from Pong was divided into two and one part was given to the Meitei king; another part taken by the emissary; and further appointed each other to meet for the war when the orchid starts to grow its new stems.

The Pong King, when the orchid starts growing new stems marched towards the Kabow Valley for invasion against Khampat, but the Meitei King was not reaching and waited there, and send his man to inform Meitei King, but met with Meitei King on the way. He was late because the Meitei land was colder climatically than that of the Mungkong (Mogaung or Mungmao). They met there and then they happily proceeded towards Khampat jointly, and reached there.

On reaching Khampat the Pong King suggested the Meitei King to enter Khampat Fort from the western side and he was to enter from the east. They also constructed two forts as the battle may take some days. There were great fighter but they could not enter Khampat easily as Khampat was well fortified. There were sound of paddy pounding inside the fort and singing songs sending a message that the Khampats were well settled inside the fort; and later the Pong King with the Meitei King discussed about leaving the place as Khampat was so well fortified that it shall be impossible for them to devastate it, but in the meantime one old woman, who had been starved for days escaped from inside the fort and requested them to provide some food, also narrated that the Khampat also suffered due to lack of food inside, and what they were pounding inside were not paddy but pounding pebbles and husked paddy bran to produce sound only; and they are about to surrender soon. Then the old woman was provided with food. Thereafter, the Pong King suggested the Meitei King to enter the fort by digging tunnel from the western side by night; and himself and his men from the east, and to see the next morning who first entered inside the fort. The Meitei King with his men entered in the night itself and devastated the camps; whereas the Pong King entered in the next morning. The Khampat King fled away by a white elephant, while his queen with his two sons—Kaikhang and Kaimang—fled on a vehicle (gari) in front of the King and reached Mung-O-Mangtra and the whole fort was completely devastated and turned into ashes. A big hall was constructed inside the fort and a big throne was installed and the two kings sat together and ate together on the same royal plate in the victory ceremony.

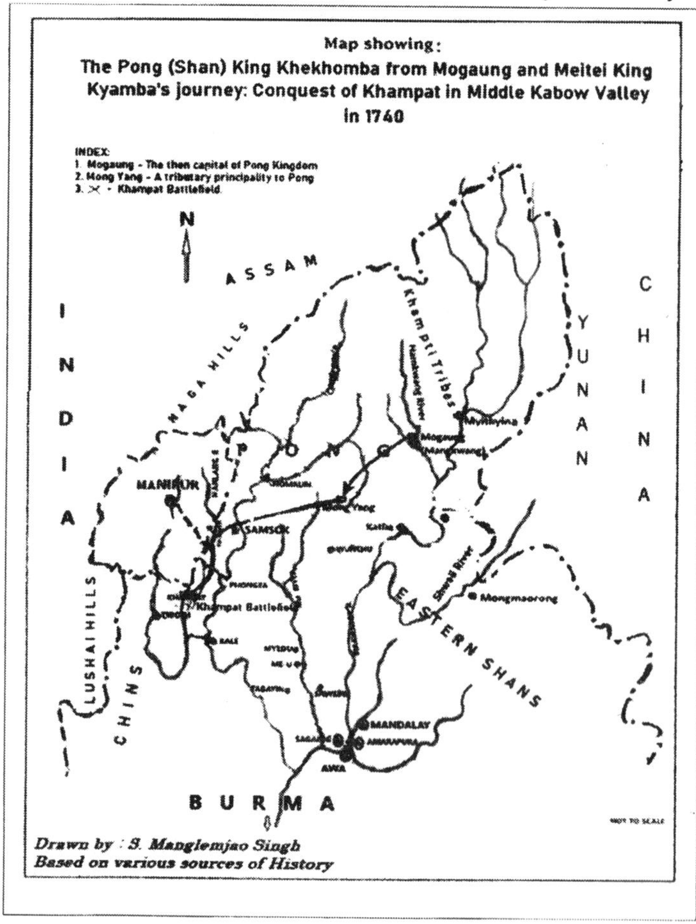

Naming of the Two Kings after the Victorious Battle of Khampat (1470 A.D.) and presentation Ceremonies

Thereafter, the king of Pong declared the new victory names for himself and for the Meitei King. The Pong king Suhongpha was named as "Chaopha-hum Kekhomba" and the Meitei King as "Chaopha-hom Kingyamba."[4] On the great satisfaction of the Meitei King's performance during the war against Khampat, the Pong king arranged to offer the following presents to the Meitei King and handed over:

(a) One gold senpot sprinkle with thousand diamonds (Tampha lising ama thinba),
(b) One betel box made of gold (kwagok),
(c) One silver kwagok,
(d) One kwagok for keeping the matured fruits,
(e) One gold kong-khao,
(f) One plate for keeping the gold kong-khao,
(g) One gold pad for keeping the gold plate,
(h) One brass plate,
(i) One silver plate,
(j) One gold khujai,
(k) One silver khujai,
(l) One gold khuteisen,
(m) One silver khuteisen,
(n) One three pointed gold sword,
(o) One gold dragon engraved armpit (tal in original Manipuri),
(p) One gold four footed throne,
(q) One three storied umbrella (Sekpil mathol ahum longba),
(r) Two Kanghei White colour (Humai, Chamor etc. used as hand fan), and
(s) Complete set of King's costume (Ningthougi Potloi Suna).

Then the Meitei king Kyamba was perturbed on what should be presented to his beloved Epu (respected grandfather King) king in return. Then, he has presented the following:

(a) One Sangkai,
(b) One Cock, and
(c) Two Sandang (Mithun) to the Pong King.

But the Meitei King was not satisfied with these gifts and then he had taken out his own shirt and presented to the Pong King;

and Pong King was very much satisfied with the manner and acts of the Meitei King.

Then the Pong King Chaopha-Hum Kekhomba declared the Meitei King's the newly given name—Chaopha-hom Kingyamba again in front of all audiences and ended the victory celebration of the day. Thereafter, the Pong King again declared the next day's programme of boundary demarcation between the Shan Kingdom of Pong and The Meitei Kingdom (Also known as the Boundary Treaty of Meitei-Pong of 1470 in the history of Manipur).

Next day morning, the Pong King Chaophahum Kekhomba and the Meitei King Chaophahom Kingyamba @ Kyamba met together and conducted the procedure as such: Both traverse to some demarcation points and identified the boundary of the Meitei King as follows:

1. On the South as far as Mratong demarcated by the celebrated Dwarf Mango tree area;
2. On the East—five days journey from beyond Chindwin (Ningthee) river all lands bounded by Loichari Hills;
3. On the North the Dwarf Mango Areas of Munghkam-Mungwang; and
4. On the West up to the land where Sun sets. (The place where this demarcation negotiated was in the east, and the Kingdom of Manipur which was at that time only known as Meitei King's dominion is very much in the west so as the Pong King had demarcated as such). Thereafter, they came back to 'Song Hsuk'[5] and halted the night. During the night Meitei King Kyamba intercepted a conversation between one Samjok (Shan) common man and one Meitei; the Samjok arguing that even the Pong King had given Songhsup (Samjok) to the Meiteis they won't be the servants of the Meiteis. King Kyamba was not happy with that kind of conversation of Samjok and Meitei. Next day morning King Kyamba hurriedly met the Pong King Chaophahum Kekhomba, and inquired that the land 'Epu' has given to your 'Esu', the Meitei King comprised Songhsuk (Samjok) or not. The Pong King Chaopha-hum Kekhomba told the Meitei King Chaopha-hom Kyamba (Kingyamba) that he had given land bounded by Loichari Hills on the east which is lying far east and Samjok is very

> close and very much within the territory he has given, and with a slight smile murmured that his Esu King was so silly.

Then Pong King told Meitei King that if he is not willing about Samjok let that place be their meeting place during their visits, but the tributes shall be received by the Meitei King only. Then both of the Kings went towards the Dwarf Mango tree area and sat below the big two branched Mango tree and ate together; and discussed about their departure to their own capitals. Hearing about the programme of returned journey of the two kings, the Pong King's maid cook and the Meitei King's cook Koiremba who had been husband and wife since their meeting during this itinerary committed suicide by tightening them together by a cloth packed with a big stone and immersed and drowned inside the water as they pre-decided that both of them were faithful servants and they won't be allowed to live together as husband and wife by the two kings.

Thereafter, Kyamba requested the Pong King addressing as 'Epu' to give Epu's Trumpet blower (Pere Khongba) that was accepted readily; and the Pong King requested for Langte Drummer (Langte Pung Yeiba), and that was also accepted. The drummer was a Sekta (a man from Sekta Village) and generally called him (the drummer) as Pungyeib-O. Thereafter, Pong King wished Meitei King to return him safely to his capital and reign there with long life and to live with sweet memories of their friendship. He (Pong King) also narrated that in the year Kapchao he was 37 years, but three times coronation together he had been on the throne for 30 years, whereas Kyamba told him he (Kyamba) was 27 years and his coronation was since 3 years only. The Pong King wished him to reign long with pomp and grandeur, and their good days together may be remembered in the days to come with the grace of heavenly gods. He (Pong King) also told Kyamba that their meeting was in the year Kapchou (Lakli Kapchou), i.e. in the year 1470.[6] Thereafter, both the kings departed for their respective capitals. Later, Pong King died after reigning 70 years in the year Kamou Lakli.[7] According to Manipur History, Kyamba also died in year 1508, at the age of 64 after reigning 40 years of glorious history of conquest and administrative reforms. During his time many Shans from Kabaw Valley were also absorbed within the Meitei Society.

NOTES

1. *Sorarel Machana Khunkumba* (a Pong Shan Chronicle found in Ma: ipur in Unpublished Manuscript), Author is the custodian.
2. As mentioned in B.R. Pemberton, *The Eastern Frontier of India 1835*, New Delhi, rp. 1998.
3. B.R. Pemberton, *The Eastern Frontier of India*, New Delhi, 1835, rp. 1998, p. 112. In addition, a very unexpected confirmation of the event is found in Appendix of Crawford's Embassy to Awa.....the destruction of Zakaing (Sagaing) and Penya is mentioned as having been effected in the year 1364 A.D. Major Burney also discovered the same circumstances recorded in the 6th Vol. of the Maha Yazawanor the Great History of Ava, where the destruction of both cities is said to have been effected by the Shan king Thokyenbwa.
4. 'Khambat' which the author has written as 'Khampat' was the capital town of Khambat section or principality of Kabow Valley, which is located on the bank of Khambat River. This region is also known as Kiang-Khambat. Hence both of the Pong King and Meitei King had been named in relation to Kiang-Khambat.
5. Samjok to the Meiteis, Thuangdoot to the Burmese.
6. Pemberton mentioned as 1474 after comparing Burmese, Myanmar records.
7. Pemberton has given Pong King's year of demise as 1512-1513 A.D.

OTHER WORKS CONSULTED

Brown, R., *Statistical Account of Manipur 1873*, New Delhi, rp. 2001.

Dun, E.W., *Gazetteer of Manipur 1886*, rp. 1992, Delhi.

Gangumei Kamei, *History of Manipur*, Vol. One, New Delhi, 1991.

Hemchandra, Chanam, *Ningthourol Lampupa*, Imphal, 2018.

Sharma, B. Kulachandra, Mayamba Garibaniwaz (Manipur) 2000, Imphal, Manipur.

Singh, Konsam Manikchand, *Descent of the Scion of Sorarel on the Earth* (Sorarel Machana Khulkumpa), Imphal, 2014.

Singh, L. Ibungohal and N. Khelchandra Singh, *Cheitharol Kumbaba* (tr., Royal Chronicle of Manipur), Imphal, 1967, 2nd ed. 1989.

Singh, L. Joychandra, *The Lost Kingdom: Royal Chronicle of Manipur*, Imphal, 1995.

Singh, N. Joykumar, *Emergence of Manipur as a Nation State*, New Delhi, 2015.

Singh, N. Khelchandra, *Ariba Manipuri Sahitya gi Itihas* (tr., History of Ancient Manipuri Literature), Imphal, 1969.

Singh, Oinam Bhogeshwar, *Ningthourol Lambuba,* Imphal, 1967.
Singh, R.K. Jhalajit, *A Short History of Manipur,* Imphal, 1965.
Singh, R.K. Snahal, *A Short History of Manipur,* Imphal, 1989.

5
A Brief Note on Shan Polity

Heisnam Nilkant Singh

Introduction

The Tais are the largest and most widespread population in South East Asia. The extent of the distribution of the Tai race stretches from Brahmaputra valley in the west to Kwang-Tung province in China and from southern Yunnan in the north to Kara in Malay in South. It lies between the latitude 7° N to 26° N and longitude 94° E to 110° E. The Tai settlement is divided into western groups, Eastern groups, Southern groups, Central Mekong river groups and Central upland groups. The Tais are named differently according to their various inhabited areas. Thus, the Tais are known as Laos in Laos, as Shan in Upper Burma, Yunnan Tai in the South China, Tribal Tai in northern Vietnam, Tais in Thailand, Ahom in Brahmaputra Valley[1] and Kabos in Manipur.

The geographical extent of the Shan States is 1,60,000 square kilometres almost a quarter of the present Myanmar. The states are bordered by China and Tibet in the north, Laos and Thailand to the east and Myanmar to the south and west.[2] It extends approximately between latitude 20-24° N and 9-10° E longitude.[3] During the olden days, the Shans settled an area covering what is now in Assam state of India, the southern part of Yunnan, the Shan states of Burma and the northern part of Vietnam, in the area stretching for more than seven to eight thousand 'li' (mile) in length.[4]

"Not only does the tradition assert that these Shans of Upper Burma are the oldest branch of the Tai family, but they are always spoken of by other branches as the Tai Long or Great Shans, while the other branches called themselves Tai Noi and Little Shan. From the Nam Mao, the Shans spread south-east over the present Shan

States, North into the present Hkamti region, and west of the Irrawaddy River in all the country lying between it, the Chindwin and Assam." In this region, many big and small of the Shan people settled and formed tribal union.[5] From the Han Dynasties to the Tang and Song dynasties onward, the Shan-Tai ethnic group make close relation. They also waged war for supremacy against the neighbouring Funan and Zhenla of the Mon-Khmer language group, Annam of the Vietnamese language group. Their struggle continued up to the middle of the 18th Century A.D.[6]

D.K. Wyatt in his book '*Thailand: A Short History*', analyzes about the polity of Tai in general but does not mention a particular Tai group like the Shans of Upper Burma. Similarly, E.R. Leach in his book '*Political System of Highland Burma*' discusses about social institutions and domain but not highlight about the development of polity. Therefore, the present chapter attempts to focus mainly on the Shan polity that evolved since the early time by using archival materials.

Migration and Settlement

According to E.R. Leach, the Shans are territorially scattered, but fairly uniform in culture. All Shan settlement area are associated with rice cultivation. The Shan are scattered about in hill area at random and settlement are always found associated with irrigated wet paddy land.[7] It is presumed that the Shans migrated from their original homeland to different directions of mainland South East Asia and North East region of present India. They migrated owing to defeat in the war of supremacy amongst the different ethnic groups or defeat in the hands of superior powers, and in some cases search for new fertile areas where livelihood materials are abundantly available and thus enable them to expand their political frontier.

From time to time, the upland Taimuang (domain) defended itself either militarily or diplomatically against neighbouring Muang powers such as the hill people and China. They mainly fought to maintain law and order and to settle inter-village conflict over the question of land or water right or cattle thefts.[8] Soon after their advent in Shwali valley, the two brothers Hkun Lu and Hkun Lai quarreled over the subject of precedence. Therefore, Hkun Lu left the country and he arrived after moving some miles at a place near the Uyu River, a tributary of the Chindwin where he founded the city of Mong Kong Mong-Yawng. "Tradition and the statement of all the hitherto discovered chronicle assert that the Nam Mao or Shweli valley and its neighbourhood, Bhamo Mong Mit, Hsenwi were the first home of the Shans in Upper Burma. In order to search virgin land, the Shans from the Nam Mao spread south-east over the present Shan states, north into all the country between the Chindwin and Assam."[9]

There is a legendary account of the establishment of Western Shan States. That, the four brothers, namely Tho-Kaw-bwa, Thongan-bwa, Tho-kyan-bwa and Tho-hon-bwa founded their respective Bien or Ban (village). (Their mother was Chinese princess named Saw Hla and father was a white tiger found in the Shan region). The first son established Bein-Kawng and later this was changed to Mong Kawng-Mogaung. The second son founded Bein-Mit or Mongmit country. The third set-up their respective countries like Bein-Yang and the fourth established Bein-Hso or Wyinghso or Wunho.[10] Besides, different hordes of Shans also entered the valley of Manipur in pre, proto and historical periods.

It is clearly mentioned in the Tai chronicles that the Tai send expeditions to colonize different far-flung and neighbouring regions. However, in order to make fulfil his aim, he organized the men of his *Muang* and sent a military expedition under the leadership of one of his sons or brothers. The conquered areas were brought under the control of the princes. Characteristically, sons might thus be sent out in order of their seniority, leaving the youngest son to succeed the kingdom of his father.[11]

During the kingship of Sao Hso Hkan Hpa, Mao Shan Empire expanded widely. The King sent his brother Sao Hsam Long Hpa to conquer more territory. He was able to set-up number of the tributary states, probably more Shan migration took place during his time. King Hkun Lai sent forth his descendants to administer the neighbouring Kingdoms. Those of the countries ruled by his descendants are given below:

(1) Ai Hkun Luwang was the king of Lung Kung or Tuguang.
(2) Hkun Hpa was the king of Mong Yang (Mohnyin). He paid a tribute of ten lakh horses.
(3) Hkun Ngu or Khunju was the king of Lamung-Tai, i.e. La Bong was Cheingmei. He paid a yearly tribute of three hundred.

(4) Hkun Kawt Hpa was the king of Yon Long or Mong Yang. He paid yearly tribute a quantity of gold.
(5) Hkun La was the king of Mong Kala or Kale. He paid water of the Chindwin River as tribute.
(6) Hkun Hsa was the king of Ava and paid tribute yearly 2 (two) viss rubies.
(7) Hkun Su was the king of Mong Yawn.[12]

Shukapha with some of followers including 8 (eight) nobles and 9000 men, women and children left his mother country. He migrated westward and entered the present Assam where he defeated aboriginal tribes like Morans and Boharins. Thus, Shukapha established Ahom kingdom in 1228 A.D.[13], usually, a large number of upland low-lying Tai agriculturist in northern fringe of the Khmer Empire during the 11th and 12th centuries. Of course, they were successful in setting up smaller principalities, namely Lannatai, Cheingsaen, Ngoengang, Puyao, Rad, Bangyang and Luwang Prabang.[14] Later on in 13th century A.D., the combined forces of prince Khun Bang Klang Tao of Bang Yang and Khun Pa Mung of Rad defeated Khmer commander at Sukhathai. Thus, the first Tai kingdom of Sukhothai was founded under the kingship of Sri Indradit.[15]

Socio-Economic and Political Life

In a nutshell, the pattern of Shan political development was primarily concerned on the following line. One is pristine development through a different stages of human civilization and another is secondary way development made by conquest or confederation. Since time immemorial, the Shans mostly dwelt in the sub-tropical river basins and plains of the Shan Plateau, which is drained by the Salween River. With the passage of time, the big and small Shan community or tribe came into exist.[16] "According to the Shan chronicle, the heaven sent rulers and their descendants to organize the construction of towns and village, established boundaries between principalities and appointed honorable men as ministers and officials."[17] Since the Shan society was more patrilineal than matrilineal; father was regarded as the sole head of the family (pu or paw Kruna). Usually, in a Shan society life involved around the family. The number of scatter Shan families were bound together and formed village (ban or been or waan). The establishment of the village led to existence of the head of the village (Paw Ban or PuGe or Pu Gang). On the other hand, different Shan rulers were responsible to establish Shan villages. According to D.K. Wyatt, "family was the base line of both socio- and political unit of the Thai."[18]

Generally, most of the Shan settled in small endogamous villages and thus had a long tradition of community works. In Southern China and Indo-China peninsula, some groups of the Thai people still practiced their traditional custom of communal ownership of land. In the primitive stage of settlement, a single family enjoy a free holdership of land in which the group it belonged to occupy a certain common territorial and a number (a single family) was permitted to cultivate it freely within the occupied territory, depending upon his labour ability. In due course, such system had developed into a commune ownership of the property (the land) and cooperative labour among the entire member.[19]

In the olden days, on the Shan plateau areas, small groups of Shan families settled together forming a tiny community. However, the community expanded into either hamlet or bigger villages due to mainly increase of population. It was from the pre-Buddhist period that it was mandated for villagers to attend meetings compulsorily by every household, which was held at the premises of an elder to select village head (Paw Bean or Pu Gang). Such meeting came to be held at either monastery or the house of the elders after adopting the Buddhism as state religion.

The Shans practice wet-rice cultivation in their permanent fields as their major occupation accompanied by animal husbandry as secondary to agriculture. Besides the Shan villagers were engaged in various types of occupations such as weaving, carpentry, pottery, tool making, mining, paper making, silversmith, fishing etc. Normally, the average rice villages consisted 200-500 individual. Villages were located in river valleys or in pockets of level lands in the hills, always near water and frequently in the midst of a bamboo grove.

Probably, every villager was rightly counted as the subject of prince. The cultivators were liable to pay tribute to the *Muang* or domain according to the number of rice fields and buffalo they possessed. It is possible that some villages were subject to provide labour for the cultivable fields of the ruler while the other villages were ready to supply household member consisting *mahouts* to look after the elephants, gardeners for the palace gardens and women to weave, embroider and maintain royal clothes. On the other hand, some privileged families were given hereditary rights to contribute their sons as palace guards.[20]

Muang or Mong (Domain)

With the passage of time several big and small villages collectively emerged as *muang* or *mong*. A *mong* was governed by a hereditary chief named *Sawbwa* or *Sao-hpa*. It is recorded that as many as fifty *muang* were established in different parts of Shan state region. The rise of these *muang* varied from one state to another state. The smallest *muang* was *Namtok* measuring 14 square miles while the largest *muang* was *Kentung* which was 12,000 square miles. According to Susan Conway, "in a geographical sense *muong* means a territorial unit centred in a river valley. A *muang* ruler came primarily from a prominent local family whose claim to sovereignty was accepted. In general a *muang* had one main city where the ruler lived possibly in some smaller towns, if it was a large *muang* then many great and small village society based on mutually beneficial relationships with people coming together for water management, agricultural labour and trade, for defence and social interaction."[21] In such a way, primary or pristine Shan state emerged to the Upper Burma or Southern Yunnan in many years back.

"There were many grades of native officials appointed by the princes of more powerful *muang* to collect tribute. These officials were liable to report to the princes at least once a year. Some are locally styled *Sao-hpa* by the people although they have no right to the title. When this is the case, their ancestors were probably ruling chiefs, who in former times were conquered, remaining subjects to more powerful princes, but permitted to govern their districts on payments of yearly tribute."[22] Official representative was appointed to watch over spirit guardians to protect and care important spirit shrines and get ready for seasonal festivals.[23]

The Shan princes strongly believed that their ancestors were linked with heavenly gods. Their concept of divine origin was strengthened by the Buddhist idea of kingship. Probably, a Shan prince was customary to perform monkhood for a certain period before ascending to the throne. Since the adoption of Buddhist, the Shan princes paid more attention to the pious deeds relating to Buddhism in order to earn more prestige or loyalty from the subjects. The word *Chaofa* or *Saohpa* (lord of the sky or heavenly lord of the sunset) was addressed to senior Shan prince. Usually, a prince who governed a small principality was frequently referred to as *Chao* or *Saohpa* was the final over his subject; but in a specific case, his clemency from senior Buddhist monks. Though, the law of primogeniture was maintained in Shan society, the succession was often disputed as polygamy was practiced by the princes.[24] With the occupation of Shan region by the Burmese, *myosa* (eaten of the town) who looked after the town area was appointed and they were authorized to collect taxes in local affairs.[25]

NOTES

1. Leber, *Ethnic Group of Mainland South Asia*, New Haven, 1964, p. 190.
2. Suan Conway, *The Shan Culture, Art and Crafts*. River Book Company Ltd., Bangkok, 2006, p. 11.
3. Chen Lufan, *Whence Came the Thai Race? An Enquiry*, Kunning, 1989, p. 133.
4. J. George Scott assisted by I.P. Hardman I.C.S. *Gazetteer of Upper Burma and Shan States* in Five Volumes, Part 1, Vol. 1, Rangoon, 1990, p. 194.
5. *Ibid*., pp. 195-196.
6. Chen Lufan, *op. cit*. pp. 127-128.
7. E.R. Leach, *Political System of Highland Burma*, 1954, pp. 29-30.
8. D.K. Wyatt, *Thailand, A Short History*, New Haven, 1984, pp. 8-9.
9. J. George Scott (compiled) and J.P. Hardiman I.C.S. (assisted), *op. cit*. p. 194.
10. *Op. cit*., pp. 202-203.
11. D.K. Wyatt, *op. cit*., p. 9.
12. J. George Scott and J.P. Hardiman, *op. cit*., p. 220.
13. R. Sh. Gulap Chandra Barua, *Ahom Buranji from the Earliest Time to the end of Ahom Rule* (translated, ed.), Guwahati, 1985, pp. 24-25.
14. Rong Syamanda, *History of Thailand*, Bangkok, 1981, pp. 18-19.
15. W.A.R. Wood, *History of Siam*, revised ed., Bangkok, 1933, pp. 51-53.
16. Chen Lufan, *op. cit*., p. 126.
17. Suan Conway, *op. cit*., p. 33.
18. D.K. Wyatt, *op. cit*., p. 7.
19. Sakurai Yumio, *Formation of Vietnam Village*, Tokaya, 1987, pp. 42-43.
20. Maurice Collies, *Lords of the Sunset, A Tour in the Shan States*, Faber and Faber, London, 1938, rp., Bangkok, 1996, p. 131.

21. Suan Conway, *The Shan Culture, Art and Crafts*, River Book Co. Ltd., Bangkok, 2006, p. 16.
22. Mrs. Leslie Milne and Wilber Cochrane, *Shans at Home,* London, John Murray, 1910, p. 186.
23. Suan Conway, *op. cit.*, p. 18.
24. Harry L. Tilly, *Wood Carving of Burma*, Superintendent of Government, Printing & Stationery, Rangoon, 1903.
25. Maurice Collies, *op. cit.*, p. 130.

6
Outlining Manipur-Shan Relation

Kakchingtabam Ruhinikumar Sharma

Introduction

In this chapter, a humble attempt is made to reconstruct the relationship between Manipuri-Shan in its historical perspective and show how their interaction had influenced the course of Manipur history in her evolution from a chiefdom based political system to a mature feudal polity in the eighteenth century, the period which witnessed the zenith of power and glory and beginning of the process of decline and downfall of Manipur kingdom as well. Some of the source materials though of primary nature are already published and this discussion is more in the nature of an analytical study. Apart from *Cheitharol Kumbaba*, the royal chronicle of Manipur and other historical and semi-historical texts, reports and accounts written in the nineteenth century by the British officials and reporters having posted or connected with Manipur are also used as additional source of information.

Manipur, an ancient kingdom in South-east Asia, now a constituent state of India lies between 23°51′N to 25°41′ latitude and from 93°2′ 'E' longitude to 94°47′ 'E' longitude.[1] Strategically located in the extreme north-eastern corner of India bounded on the north by the state of Nagaland, on the north-east, east and south by Myanmar (Burma), on the south-west by Mizoram, on the west and north-west by the state of Assam.

Archaeologist Okram Kumar Singh in his studies conducted during the last many years has established beyond doubt that Manipur passed through various phases of prehistoric culture, *viz.* Palaeolithic Culture, Hoabinhian Culture and Neolithic Culture.[2]

As Hoabinhian Culture spread far and wide in the region, there is a strong possibility of the land and its people having connection with the Southeast Asian countries particularly with Myanmar (Burma).

Manipur, hemmed in all sides by mountain ranges is an isolated hilly tract on the eastern frontier of India. Geologically, the state of Manipur belongs to the Alpine system of young folded mountains which came into existence as a result of the Tertiary folding of the sedimentary strata formed in the shallow Tethys Sea, some 40 to 90 million years ago. The present-day landscape of the state bears an indelible impression of the organic movements which took place at the time of first and second Himalayan upheavals.[3]

The state of Manipur is almost rectangular in shape with a fertile alluvial plain in the centre surrounded by hill ranges on all sides. It is bounded by Naga Hills (present-day state of Nagaland) on the north, Assam on the west, Lushai Hills (present state of Mizoram) on the south-west, Myanmar (Burma) on the east and south-east. Physically, Manipur can be divided into three regions, *viz.* (i) the Manipur Hills, (ii) the Manipur Valley, and (iii) the Barak Basin. The Manipur hills consist of a series of parallel ranges extending between the Naga Hills in the north and Mizo and Chin hills in the south. These hills trending north-east to south-west, slanted towards south and dominate the regional landscape. The hills of Manipur broadly fall into two groups—the Manipur eastern hills and the Manipur western hills. The eastern hills form a compact and continuous chain along the present Indo-Myanmar border for about 200 kms. The Manipur western hills spread over the entire western part comprising parallel ridges and valleys running north to south for about 180 kms.[4] On the other hand, the valley extends right up to the foot of these hill ranges with an inclination from north to south.

Manipur being one of India's gateways to South-East Asia had throughout the centuries attracted immigrants from the east and the west. The Mongoloid elements predominated in the valley as well as in the hills with some non-Mongoloid elements who speak Tibeto-Burman languages. Manipur's population consists of three major ethnic groups, the Meiteis of the valley, the Nagas and Kukis of the surrounding hills.

Manipur-Shan Relation

One of the early references to Manipur-Shan connection could be found in the Khuman-Meitei conflict during the reign of Puranthaba (1247-1263 A.D.). The Khumans who were completely subdued and had already accepted Meitei suzerainty made a vain attempt to re-establish their political authority during the reign of Puranthaba (1247-1263 A.D.). In an attempt to regain their supremacy, the Khumans invaded the territory of the Shelloi Langmai in the eastern hills. The Shelloi Langmais in turn sought the help of Meitei King to drive away Khumans. The Meitei King completely defeated the Khuman forces at Poirei. This was the last battle marking the Meitei conquest of Khuman principality.[5] Since then the Khumans were completely absorbed into Meitei kingdom. However, taking advantage of the weakened position of the Khuman principality, the Shan dwellers of Kabaw valley in Chindwin basin of Upper Burma invaded the erstwhile Khuman territory during the reign of Meitei king Khumomba (1263-1278 A.D.). In this face-off, the king himself leading from the front defeated the Shans on the bank of Ikop lake and several Shan soldiers were captured as war prisoners.[6]

Thus, with the beginning of fourteenth century, history of Manipur witnessed the increasing power of the Meitei kingdom in terms of expansion of her military power and authority. Thangbi Lanthaba was succeeded by Kongyamba (1324-1335 A.D.) whose reign was marked by invasion of the kingdom by a group of people from the west referred to as Thongnang Mayang in the chronicles who were a group of Bengalee refugees driven out of Bengal by the Muslims and who came to Manipur for settlement.[7] Some leaders of the invading force along with 200 soldiers were taken as prisoners.

With the beginning of fifteenth century, history of Manipur witnessed the increasing power of the Meitei kingdom in terms of expansion of territory and consolidation of Ningthouja political authority. The reign of Punshiba (1404-1432 A.D.) not only saw the conquest of a number of tribal villages but also witnessed the extension of the kingdom into interior tribal areas of the surrounding hills. The military expeditions carried out by the king in the interior hilly and tribal areas were aimed at the consolidation of the Ningthouja rule in the Kingdom of Manipur. Ningthoukhomba, son of Punshiba ascended the throne in 1432 A.D. who was known as the conqueror of Tamu. Except for the Moirang territory, his father had already accomplished consolidation of the Kingdom covering most part of Manipur valley, north-western, north and north-eastern hills. To facilitate the expansion of territorial limits of the kingdom Ningthoukhomba by following an aggressive policy made attempts to conquer the neighbouring areas. He followed a policy to provoke both the Shan principality of Tamu and Moirang principality into a quarrel both of whom had been into conflict with the successive Meitei kings for quite some time. Having succeeded in creating distrust and enmity between them, Ningthoukhomba carried out a series of raids to Tamu between A.D. 1432 and 1443. The king next drew his attention towards the Moirang territory. Ningthoukhomba along with his nobles invaded and overran the whole territory of Moirang principality. In the form of tribute, the Moirangs presented "Leishang" to the Meitei king. Here it may be mentioned that it was the first significant defeat of Moirang, though not totally crushed in the hands of the Meiteis. Control over the territory of Moirang strengthened economy of the Meitei state. The growing feudal structure of the kingdom during the reign of Ningthoukhomba was evident as indicated by the ranks of nobles who accompanied the king and participated in several military expeditions including the invasion of Moirang. In 1443 A.D., Ningthoukhomba led another military expedition to the village of Akla inhabited by the Kabaw Shans in the eastern frontier. In this expedition, the elephant of the Akla chief and many warriors were captured as war booties. Afterwards the king turned towards the south-east and invaded the Tarao village of Louchingphei. One of the most memorable events of the reign of Ningthoukhomba was the raid of the kingdom by the Tangkhul tribes of Tuisem village while the king was far away from the capital leading military expeditions at Akla and Tarao Louchingphei. The Meitei queen Linthoingambi dressed in the guise of man not only ward off the invaders but also arrested Henpuringba, chief of the Tuisem Tangkhul. It is no wonder that since the time of Yabirok, Nongda Lairen Pakhangba's mother, Meitei women had played a decisive role in socio-economic and political affairs of the land and whenever a serious crisis/threat befall the kingdom. Since the time of Laisna, (wife of Nongda Lairen Pakhangba) successive Meitei queens have been presiding over the Pacha Shanglen, a court dealing with cases relating to women like adultery and bigamous affairs, meted out punishments thereby assisting the affairs of the state in enforcing accepted norms of behaviour and morality. Ningthoukhomba's rule attracted immigrants from the east and west. Some Kabaw Shans (perhaps war captives) were allowed to marry Manipuri women and were ultimately absorbed in Meitei society. Without exaggeration it may be observed that during Ningthoukhomba's rule, despite the autonomy of Moirang, the Meitei state was completely formed and the Ningthouja Kingdom had more or less become a feudal state.

With the accession of Kyamba (Thangbwai Ningthouba) at the throne in 1467 A.D., history of Manipur opens a new chapter. Accounts given by *Cheitharol Kumbaba* and supplemented by other chronicles give far more reliable information in reconstructing history of the kingdom. The growing power and strength of the Meitei state was reflected in the military aggrandisement and policy of territorial expansionism adopted by this great king. Having already accomplished the consolidation of the kingdom by his able predecessors, Kyamba shouldered upon himself the responsibility of expanding the territorial limits of his kingdom far beyond the mountainous regions. Having acknowledged the increasing power of Kyamba and his country, in 1470 A.D., the king of the Shan kingdom of Pong proposed to the Meitei ruler to participate in a joint military expedition in the trans-Chindwin basin which was the home of several Shan principalities. As Kyamba was already looking for opportunities to expand his kingdom, he readily agreed to the proposal of joint military expedition. *Cheitharol Kumbaba* records that the joint forces of Manipur and Pong invaded and conquered Kyang, a Shan principality in the Kabaw valley. The chronicle further mentions that the victory over Kyang was celebrated by renaming Thangwai Ningthouba as Kyamba, the conqueror of Kyang. The most notable outcome of the joint military expedition was the conclusion of a treaty of friendship between the two countries which fixed the boundary between Manipur and Pong. The major portion of fertile Kabaw valley which was known for its agricultural and forest products was annexed to Manipur. Here it may be mentioned that the bilateral treaty concluded between Manipur and Pong was the first of its knd entered into between Manipur and another foreign country which was well recorded in the royal chronicle of Manipur and Pong Meitei Lamyen Lairik. About the treaty G. Kabui observes thus, "This was the first international recognition of the kingdom of the Meiteis by a power in upper Burma. The kingdom of Manipur was a full-fledged sovereign country with internal and external independence in the true sense of the term."[8] Another notable development during the reign of Kyamba was the invasion of Manipur in 1504 by the Mayangs (Thongnang) from the west. The identity of the invaders is still not clearly established; however, the invaders were defeated and repulsed by the Manipuri forces. Not only known for military exploits Kyamba was also an efficient ruler. He added two new revenue districts or circles, *viz.* Naharup and Ahallup Pana in addition to the existing six Panas already established by Loiyumba in 1110 A.D. The introduction of the keeping of the royal chronicle known as *Cheitharol Kumbaba* from the year 1467 A.D. was perhaps the greatest contribution of Kyamba to the cultural heritage of Manipur. Cheiraoba, the festival marking the end of the year was also introduced by the king.

The successful rule of Kyamba attracted hordes of immigrants from the east and west to Manipur who in course of time adopted Manipur as their homeland and the liberal policy of the king allowed the foreign elements to be absorbed in Meitei society. The Shans or Pongs or Kabaws came here and became the subjects of the rulers of Manipur in Kabaw valley. The Muslim expansion in eastern India forced many Brahmins to flee their homeland. Many of these displaced Brahmins migrated to Manipur and settled here permanently. Many of them were employed by the king to look after the Hindu temples and to act as astrologers. The Lairikyengbams were other non-Brahmin migrants who were employed as royal scribes. The Brahmins and Lairikyengbams married Manipuri women. They adopted Manipuri (Meiteilon) as their mother tongue. In the later periods, there are evidences of Manipuri Brahmins accompanying the Meitei kings and taking part in military expeditions. The arrival of Brahmins and other groups of people into Manipur and their subsequent absorption into Manipuri society may be regarded as an indication of the beginning of a pluralistic pattern of society in Manipur.

Another notable feature of Kyamba's reign was the beginning of Vishnu worship in Manipur thereby laying the foundation of Hinduism in Manipur which saw its zenith during the eighteenth and nineteenth centuries. Kyamba is reported to have constructed a Vishnu temple at Lamangdong where an image of Lord Vishnu was installed and worshipped by the Brahmins. The place where

Vishnu temple was constructed came to be known as Bishnupur. Though worshipping of Vishnu was started, perhaps under royal patronage, evidences available so far do not suggest the king being converted into Hinduism. Kyamba remained a follower of the traditional Meitei religion. After a reign of forty years he died in 1508 A.D. at the age of sixty-four. Kyamba was one of the greatest rulers of Manipur. Except for Moirang principality which enjoyed a fair amount of autonomy within Manipur kingdom, the territorial limits of Kyamba's kingdom extended up to Kabui country in the west, to the eastern part of the Chindwin River in the east, covering the whole of Manipur valley had made Manipur a power to be reckoned with by the Shan states in upper Burma. Doubtless to say, Kyamba was a great conqueror, a wise statesman, an able administrator who made significant contribution to culture and civilisation of Manipur. Thus Ahom-Shan relationship had a great bearing on the future course of the history of Manipur.

NOTES

1. W.W. Hunter, *Imperial Gazetteer of India*, Vol. XVII, 1908 (New edition), p. 184.
2. O.K. Singh, *Stone Age Archaeology of Manipur*, Imphal, 1997, pp. 1-155.
3. R.P. Singh, *Geography of Manipur*, NBT, Delhi, 1982, p. 1 5.
4. Vedaja Sanjenbam, *Manipur: Geography and Regional Development*, New Delhi, 1998, pp. 18-19.
5. O. Bhogeshwore, *op. cit.*, 1967, pp. 121-147.
6. Gangmumei Kabui, *History of Manipur*, New Delhi, 1991, p. 170.
7. *Ibid.*, p. 137.
8. *Ibid.*, p. 196.

THEME-III

Manipur-Burma Relations

7
Manipur-Burma Relations from the beginning of the Eighteenth Century to the Treaty of Yandaboo, 1826[1]

Sanamani Singh Yambem

Manipur shares a long border with Burma and almost two-thirds of Manipur's frontier is with Burma. These two areas, due to their long common frontier and the warlike nature of their people, were involved in a number of clashes and the quest for the political domination by one over the other may be traced back to the fifteenth and sixteenth centuries. However, due to the scarcity of reliable sources and till such time when old records shall be dug up, the knowledge of the relationship between these two areas, if not obscure, will remained blurred. The object of this chapter, will be to survey the relationship between Manipur and Burma based on available materials, some primary, and others secondary.[2]

Manipur-Burmese relationship, or for that matter, the very history of Manipur, though obscure in the sixteenth and seventeenth centuries, enters into some degree of certainty with the opening of the eighteenth century. It was Garib Niwaz who was able to consolidate the whole of Manipur territory and not only was he successful in his internal consolidation, but was able to drive away the successive waves of Burmese attacks on Manipur. Burma raided Manipur in 1712, 1724, and 1725. Garib Niwaz not only repelled the Burmese raids but was able to establish his sway over the trans-Chindwin area.[3]

Thus, the opening decade of the eighteenth century saw the Manipuris able to conduct an independent foreign policy, and her relations with Burma was one based on an equal footing. This was, however, not to continue for long, as, with the death of Garib

Niwaz at the hands of his eldest son, Ajit Shah, a period of anarchy and confusion entered Manipur. Garib Niwaz was murdered by his son Ajit Shah in December 1748.[4]

The death of Garib Niwaz brought chaos and confusion into the internal policies of Manipur, and brought the relations with Burma on even more favourable conditions with Burma. But though enmity between Burma and Manipur continued during the period from 1748 to 1760, when Jai Singh agreed to rule along with his brother may be considered as one of comparative peace for no major armed clash or outbreak of hostility took place.

This however did not mean that the necessity of preparing the Manipuri forces and strengthening their capacity was overlooked by Manipur. The threat of the Burmese and their apprehension of Burmese overtures prompted Jai Singh to enter into diplomatic relations with the English Government.

Jai Singh was convinced that with his limited resources both in men and material, it would not be possible for him alone to repel the Burmese.[5] Meanwhile, it came to the knowledge of Jai Singh that Ajit Shah was presenting his case to the British Government through the Raja of Tripura. Ajit pleaded that he has been unfairly disposed from the throne. Aware of the moves taken by Ajit Shah, Jai Singh deputed in July 1762 his agent Haridas Gossain with a letter to Mr. Herry Verstatt, chief of Chittagong Factory, explaining the reasons for Ajit Shah's dethronement. Haridas Gossain consulted the British authorities and advocated the basis on which Jai Singh was on the throne of Manipur.[6]

The arrival of Haridas Gossain at Chittagong was highly opportune. The rapid growth of Burmese under Alungpaya (1752-1760) was viewed with concern from Bengal. The Burmese King at the instigation of the French who were then at war with the British (Seven Years War, 1756-1763) destroyed the English settlements at Negris, an island at the mouth of the Irravaddy. It was at this juncture that Haridas Gossain arrived at Chittagong and made his preparations for an alliance between the Manipuris and the British.

After a series of negotiations an agreement was reached between the British and the Manipuris. In their eagerness to secure British support Manipur not only agreed to pay their expenses but also to compensate for the loss suffered by the British at their defeat at Negris. In return, the British agreed to send a contingent of

6 companies of sepoys to Jai Singh in order to enable him to secure back the areas captured by the Burmese from him.

Any close scrutiny of the treaty which was also the first formal agreement signed between the English and the Manipuris would make it amply clear that it was at the first instance the threat of any such agreement being made between Ajit Shah and the English which prompted Jai Singh to conclude the treaty with the English. Equally important was the challenge of the Burmese both to the English as well as to the Manipuris which further compelled an agreement between the two powers.

The first three clauses of the treaty were directly related to the Burmese problem. The English agreed to assist Jai Singh to recover the areas which had been lost to the Burmese. Jai Singh, by the second clause agreed to pay for the maintenance of the British troops, a price he had to pay for the British protection. It may be recalled here that this agreement falls under the general category of treaties signed between the English and the other Indian states particularly towards the end of the eighteenth century and the first quarter of the nineteenth century. But, what would be of more importance here is the fourth clause in which the question of the Burmese threat was taken up to be a major problem, not merely for the Manipuris identified as common the injuries done to the British and Manipuris by the Burmese. On the other hand, the Burmese threat was recognised as of equal importance to both the Manipuris and the British, on the other hand, and, more significantly, Manipuri's Burma policy was henceforth to be tied up with the interests of the British.

However, even before the treaty could be ratified by the East India Company, Shah Alam's urgent appeal for help against Ahmad Shah Abdali made it difficult for the Company to dispatch any European troops to the assistance of Manipur. But considering the advantage it would bring to the English, although the troops were not dispatched, the agreement was duly approved on 4 October, 1762.[7]

Meanwhile, political conditions in North-East India improved considerably during the following years and the urgency of sending British troops also declined. During this period the Manipur-Burma relations stood on almost same level as it was when Jai Singh has ascended the throne. This period again is marked by scarcity of information and from 1792 onwards till about 1809, information is unreliable. From this period until 1809, we have no trace of any further intercourse with this petty state.[8]

On the death of Gour Shah in 1763, Jai Singh again ruled Manipur uninterrupted for a period of 36 years. But on his death in 1799, another war of succession occurred. Labana Chandra succeeded his father but was murdered by his brother Madhu Chandra, but the latter was not able to rule for any length of time.

While this internal strife among the Manipuri princes was going on, the Burmese from across the border were making plans for new attacks. The Burmese had by this time made further advances in the direction of North-East India. The Manipuri princes even at this moment of imminent danger did not offer any combined resistance against the Burmese. On the contrary, they further divided themselves into various opposing groups. Chourjit, the brother of Madhu Chandra, joined hands with Marjit, and the combined forces, defeated the other group, occupied the throne. At this stage, although Marjit was made the Jubaraj and the Senapati, he was not satisfied with it and after an attempt to oust his brother, Marjit, went to Burma and requested the help of the Burmese King, Badawpaya (1779-1819). The Burmese readily complied and a large Burmese force invaded Manipur and placed Marjit on the throne.

Marjit, though he secured the throne of Manipur became a mere vassal of Burma and wanted to get rid of Burmese tutelage. However, having failed in his attempt, he fled to Cachar. While at Cachar, the three brothers parcelled out to Cachar and remained as divided as before. Thus, Manipur lost her independence, the reasons for which being primarily the consequences of the internal disputes which came out in Manipur and which resulted in a number of factional fights, among the successors of Raja Jai Singh.[9]

With her loss of independence, Manipur entered what was perhaps one of the darkest periods of her history. While the brothers remained unreconciled among themselves, the Burmese attacked again, and in 1819, completely devastated the country. The same year, Marjit fled to Cachar, and remained there until 1826. This period of seven years, referred to locally as 'Charu Taret Khuntakpa' may be considered as the high water mark of Burmese domination over Manipur. At the same time, it may be considered the end of one phase of the relationship between the Burmese and the Manipuris for thereafter the latter was no longer on equal terms with the Burmese.

Before 1819, the two countries pursued independent foreign policies, the Burmese, however, enjoyed greater freedom of manoeuvre. The threat of invasion came mainly from the Burmese and this was all the more potent for the internal strife among the Manipuri princes. Manipur on her part was able to pursue an independent foreign policy only in the early eighteenth century when internal dissension had not yet set in.

By the middle of the eighteenth century, however, there was a noticeable change for the problem of the Burmese threat was not merely a problem for Manipur alone but was equally grave for the British also. It was the realization of this problem, common to both the British and the Manipuris, that led to the Treaty of 4 October, 1762. With the British involvement, Manipur was no longer able to conduct a purely independent foreign policy with respect to Burma. The British connection thereafter could not be ignored although its importance varied from time to time.

With the opening of the second decade of the nineteenth century, Manipuri's relations with Burma assumed a different character. The British involvement with Manipur has been on a low key owing to the former's preoccupation in other parts of India. However, the ambitious design of the king of Burma entering Cachar and with the assigning of the throne of Chachar to Govind Chandra, the British attitude changed from one of indifference to alarm. They felt the necessity of re-establishing the Manipur dynasty as a bulwark against the Burmese invaders. Thus, negotiations between the British and Gambhir Singh were resumed so that a strong government could be created in Manipur as a buffer between the British and the Burmese.[10]

Thus assured British help, Gambhir Singh planned his entry into Manipur. He was allowed to raise a contingent called the Manipur Levy formed of 500 Manipuris and Cacharis. David Scott, the then British Agent in the North East frontier of India, was appointed by the Governor-General to make an on-the-spot report on the situation in Manipur. He recommended that the policy of non-intervention be abandoned in favour of encouraging the Manipuris to resist and shake off the Burmese domination. Convinced by Scott's report, the Governor informed Gambhir Singh that his only chance of regaining the throne lay in the active support and co-operation that the British could extend to him.[11]

Gambhir Singh decided to march on Manipur with his

Manipuri Levy armed by the British. They set out for Manipur on 25 May, 1825, and, despite bad weather and inadequate supplies, managed to reach Manipur by 10 June, 1825. Gambhir Singh then left for Sylhet leaving only 300 men and local armed volunteer to garrison Manipur.

Gambhir Singh started his second campaign on 4 December, 1825 and on arrival at Manipur found that most of the Burmese forces have stockaded themselves at Tamu in the south-east corner of the Valley. The Sumgok Raja of Kabaw valley offered some resistance to the Manipur advances, so Gambhir sent a detachment against him. But the enemy proved too strong, so Gambhir Singh and Captain Grant had to march to the assistance for these forces and joined them on 18 January, 1826.[12]

On 19 July, 1826, the combined forces assaulted the Burmese positions; and though the Burmese made several spirited sorties to drive out the Manipuris, they were resisted with even greater spirit. By the night of 22 January, the Burmese began their retreat and completely cleared the stockade.[13]

The Anglo-Burmese war came to an end with the signing of the Treaty of Yandaboo on 24 February, 1826, and under Article 2 of this treaty, "His majesty the King of Ava renounced all claims upon and will abstain from all interference with the principality of Assam and its dependence and also with the contagious petty States of Cachar and Jyntea. With regard to Munnipore, it is stipulated that should Gambhir Singh desire to return to that country, he shall be recognised by the King of Ava as Raja thereof."[14]

As for treating Gambhir Singh as an independent sovereign ruler of Manipur or as a vassal king, the treaty was not explicit. This question attracted the anxious attention of the Government of Bengal for it was the desire of the British that Manipur should be treated as an independent kingdom. An independent kingdom, inhabited by a people with a deep-rooted antipathy to the Burmese between the Burmese and British territories was then regarded as desirable from British point of view. At the same time, it was considered insecure to leave Manipur as a dependency of Burma. The Supreme Council, therefore, resolved that if the Burmese regarded Manipur as their dependency, the matter should be settled by negotiation.[15]

Crawford, the Resident-designate for Ava, reported that Burma considered Manipur an independent country and wanted the

British also to treat her as such. They even desired that Gambhir Singh should not maintain European Officers at his Court. Though the problem of the presence of foreign officers at Manipur was not resolved, the independent status of Manipur was recognised by Burma. On the conclusion of the Burmese War, Manipur was declared independent.[16]

Thus, by the end of 1826, Manipur, which had become a subordinate of Burma, now regained her independence and despite the British Agency, she enjoyed greater elbow room in deciding her policies than she has done in the late eighteenth and early nineteenth centuries.

NOTES

1. Reproduced from the Bulletin of the Division of History, Centre of Post Graduate Studies, JNU, Imphal, 1974.
2. I must express my deep sense of gratitude for the assistance provided to me by Dr. Chandramani who made some of the materials in his collection available to me.
3. Hall, D.G.E, *A History of South-East Asia*, London 1955, p. 324.
4. Jhaljit Raj Kumar, *A Short History of Manipur*, p. 142.
5. Chandramani, L., *British relations with Manipur, 1824-1891*, unpubl. Ph.D. Diss., Gauhati University, p. 10.
6. Quoted in Chandramani, p. 10, n. 5.
7. Chandramani, *op. cit.*, p. 11.
8. Pemberton, R.B., Capt., *Report on the Eastern Frontier of British India*, 1835, p. 188.
9. Phayre, Sir Arthur, *History of Burma from the earliest times to the First War with British India*, p. 220.
10. Bannerjee, A.C., *The Eastern Frontier of British India*, p. 244.
11. Secret consultations, 20 April, 1824, nos. 2 & 4, quoted in Chandramani, *op cit.*, p. 28.
12. Wilson, Horance Haymen, *The Narrative of Burmese War 1824-1826*, pp. 252-253.
13. *Ibid.*, pp. 253-254.
14. Aitchison, *Treaties* etc. Vol. II, pp. 149-150.
15. Lahiri, R.M., *The Annexation of Assam*, p. 58.
16. Brown, R., *Statistical Account of Manipur*, 1873.

8
Burma and Manipur Relations (1714-1826)

Yumnam Mohendra Singh

The Toungoo dynasty of Burma started to decline during the last part of the 17th century A.D. Minrekawdin or Shri Pawar Mahadhamma Raja, king of the Toungoo dynasty of Burma was very weak. He was as a mere figure. He reigned for nearly twenty six years from 1673-1698. During his reign the real power was in the hands of a small coterie of ministers. Minrekawdin died in 1698. He was followed by three kings. They were: (i) Sane (1698-1714), (ii) Taninganwe (1714-33), and (iii) Mahadammayaza (1733-52). They were all non-entities like Minrekawdin.[1] Two forces took advantage of the weakness of the Toungoo dynasty. One was from inside Burma. The Mons of Burma were dreaming of the restoration of their old kingdom of Pegu. They took full advantage of the weakness of the Toungoo kings of Burma. The other force was from outside Burma. Manipur was a little trans-Chindwin mountain State. It also started to take full advantage of the weakness of the Toungoo dynasty of Burma.[2]

Sane, the Toungoo king of Burma (1698-1714) sought for the hand of Manipuri princess.[3] He sent his envoy to Manipur for contracting the matrimonial alliance. The Ava envoy arrived at the Court of Manipur in 1702.[4] During those days, Charairongba (1697-1709) was the king of Manipur. He expressed his willingness for the matrimonial alliance with the Burmese king on certain conditions. Certain villages in the Burmese territory were once tributary to Manipur. The Manipuri king wanted the return of the villages to Manipur before the matrimonial alliance.[5] The Burmese king readily accepted the condition imposed by the Manipur king. Chakpa Makhao Ngambi, the daughter of Charairongba, accordingly left for Burma on Friday, the 23rd day of the month of Manipuri Poinu of Sakabda 1626.[6]

Charairongba had become old. During the last part of his reign, he received the news from Burma that the Burmese king had degraded his daughter Chakpa Makhao Ngambi from the status of the chief queen. On the death bed, he instructed his son Garibniwaz to teach a lesson to the Burmese king for the ill treatment meted out to Chakpa Makhao Ngambi. Charairongba died in 1709.[7] In Manipur, Charairongba was succeeded by his son Garibniwaz. In Burma, Sane was succeeded by his son Taninganwe (1714-33). In 1717 January, the new Burmese king sent another envoy for the hand of another Manipuri princess.[8] Garibniwaz took this as an opportunity for weaking vengeance on the Burmese king for the wrong done to his sister, Chakpa Makhao Ngambi. At the same time, the Burmese king had not yet also returned the villages as agreed upon as the condition for the marriage of the Manipuri princess. Garibniwaz accepted the proposal from the Burmese king for a new Manipuri princess on the Chindwin river. This was the place where the first Manipuri princess was received by the Burmese king. Garibniwaz determined to devastate the whole of Upper Burma. He left Manipur for Samjok in 1717 under the garb of a marriage party. The Burmese were waiting at the appointed place for the reception of the Manipuri princess. The Manipuri soldiers swooped on the waiting Burmese. A fight between the Burmese and the Manipuris ensued. The fight ended in the discomfiture of the Burmese; 90 Burmese men and 110 Burmese women were captured by the Manipuris.[9]

The Burmese received the news of the Trickish attack of the Manipuris on the Burmese. The King of Burma retaliated by sending a large force to Manipur. However, the Burmese were defeated by the Manipuris in the Kavaw Valley. The booty captured by the Manipuris including 157 Burmese.[10] In 1723, the Burmese decided to feed at their ancient grudge against Manipur. The Burmese, therefore, invaded Manipur. They entered Manipur valley from two directions. The Burmese encamped at a place near Wangjing, 17 miles south of Imphal. Garibniwaz, king of Manipur personally led the Manipuris. The Burmese were defeated. Two thousand Burmese were captured by the Manipuris.[11] Again in 1724 and 1725 king Garibniwaz invaded Burma. He defeated the Burmese force at the mouth of the Naglung river. In retaliation, the Burmese penetrated into the valley of Manipur in 1726. The Burmese attack was repulsed by the Manipuris. On this occasion, the entire three divisions of Burmese army were captured by the Manipuris.[12]

Mahadmmayaza Dipali was the last king of Toungoo dynasty of Burma. He reigned from 1733 to 1752. He succeeded his father Taninganwe in 1733. Garibniwaz of Manipur crossed the Chindwin river in 1735. He attacked and destroyed the town of Myedo of Burma on the banks of the Mao river. Garibniwaz carried off numerous Burmese captives in this attack.[13] In 1737, the Burmese king sent a large army to Manipur. The Burmese army consisted of 7000 foot, 700 horses and 20 elephants. The Manipuris defeated the Burmese in a pitched battle and killed the Burmese Commander. Garibniwaz of Manipur entered Shewbo district of Burma. He destroyed the district with fire and sword and carried away large booty.[14]

In 1738, Garibniwaz of Manipur led an expedition to Burma. He crossed the Chindwin river of Burma. He attacked and dispersed a Burmese army of 15,000 foot, 3,000 horses and 30 elephants. In the same year after the rainy season was over, Garibniwaz at the head of a force of 20,000 men invaded Burma. He defeated a Burmese army out of three divisions. He captured Sagiang, the ancient capital of Burma after overwhelming the stockades put up round it by the Burmese. The famous Kaungmudaw Pagoda of Burma was stormed by the Manipuris. While entering the Pagoda, Garibniwaz slashed at a door with his sword and the gash may still be seen.[15] They massacred its garrison and burnt every house and the monastry up to the wall of Ava. The Manipuris had been recently converted to Hinduism. Their Brahmin priests advised them that they would obtain blessedness by bathing in the Irrawaddy at Sagaing. The religious fanaticism stimulated the Manipuris to the acts of successful daring. The Manipuris performed the religious ceremony of their forefathers on the Chindwin.[16]

In 1739, Garibniwaz of Manipur invaded Burma with a force of 20,000 men. But this time he failed to make an attack on the Burmese position at Myedoo. Garibniwaz was deserted by his allies, the Cacharis. After suffering much losses he was compelled to retire to his country.[17] In 1749, Garibniwaz with an army of 20,000 foot, 3,000 horses crossed the Chindwin. When he was ready to cross the Irrawaddy for an attack on Ava, the capital of Burma, his standard was blown down during the night. Garibniwaz took the blowing down of his standard as a bad omen. He, therefore, returned without fight by presenting a daughter to the king of Ava.[18] Garibniwaz, the enterprising and successful ruler had as many as ten wives. King Garibniwaz had a fascination for the third wife. Chitsai was the second son by his third wife. Garibniwaz abdicated the throne of Manipur in favour of Chitsai. The king rejected the rightful claim of his eldest son Shamshai by his first wife. Chitsai immediately after his ascending the throne of Manipur exiled his father to Burma.[19] When Garibniwaz was in Burma, the fall of Ava was imminent on slaught of the Mons. He returned towards Manipur. Chitsai received the news of the return of his father to Manipur. He sent a party with the avowed object murdering his father. The old king along with Shamsai and other nobles was killed on the bank of the Chindwin.[20] Chitsai was unpopular and weak. In 1752, the treacherous Chitsai was expelled by his own younger brother Bharatsai with the approval of the people. Chitsai took shelter in Cachar.[21]

In 1753, Bharatsai was again expelled from Manipur by Gourasham who was also known as Maramba. Gourasham was the eldest son of Shamshai, the eldest son of Garibniwaz.[22] The accession of Gourasham marked the restoration of the direct line of succession which was violated by Garibniwaz.[23] Immediately after the dethronement of Bharatsai, Gourasham became king of Manipur in 1752. He made his younger brother Jay Singh heir-apparent. Gourasham was a cripple.[24] He evolved a device so that his brother Jay Singh and himself should become king alternatively for a term of five years.[25] He also wanted to fortify his position. He, therefore, made his maternal uncle Wahengbam Khelemba, as the chief of Moirang. However, Khelemba had a spirit of independence. Khelemba was waiting for an opportunity to strike at his nephews.[26]

In Burma, the Toungoo dynasty was a new power. It rose to power in the early 16th century. It conquered Lower Burma. It made Pegu their Capital. The Toungoo kings launched the policy of fusion of the Mons with the Burmese successfully. Bayinnaung (1551-1581) started conscription of the Mons for his numerous wars. The conscription increased the hatred of the Mons for the Burmese. This had resulted in the outbreak of rebellions of the Mons. The Toungoo rules took up repressive measures against the Mons. These measures intensified their hatred for the Burmese. The policy adopted by Thalun (1629-1647) to pacify the Mons did not work well. The Mons continued to migrate out of the country. Mahadham mayaza Dipali (1783-1852) of the Toungoo dynasty wanted to guard the northern frontiers of Burma from the erruptions of the Manipuris. In order to achieve the objective, he transferred the capital from Pegu to Ava in Upper Burma. The Mons took the transfer as a sign of weakness of the Toungoo dynasty. The Governor of Pegu in 1740 revolted against the Burmese king. He declared Pegu independent of Ava. This was the last cause for the rise of the Mons. The Burmese Governor did not try to win over the local population. On the other hand, his hand fell heavily upon the local Mons. They rose against the Governor and killed him. They drove out the Burmese Governors of Martaban and Tavoy. The Mons then set up their independent kingdom at Pegu under Lord Htaw Bhudaketi. They decided to attack Ava with the object of destroying the Burmese kingdom. They took Prome and Toungoo and subjugated all the countries towards the south. In 1747, Htaw Budhaketi retired and his Chief Minister was chosen as the king. The Mons Commander Talaban made full scale invasion of Upper Burma. Ava was captured in 1752 and the last Toungoo king Mahadammayaza (1733-1752) was deposed. Finally, he was killed.[27]

Alaungpaya of Moksobomyo resisted the Mon detachment sent to receive the allegiance of his town. He defeated the Mon attack made on his stronghold led by Talaban in person. By 1754 all Upper Burma passed into the hands of Alaungpaya. He captured Prome in 1755. The chiefs of Toungoo, Henzarda, Myaungmya, Bassein and the Arakanese district of Sandoway submitted to Alaungpaya. In 1755, he took Dagon which he named Rangoo.[28] Since Burma was weak it was unable to take retaliatory actions effectively against the Manipuri raids under Garibniwaz. Manipur, however, was only a small State with a very small population as compared to Burma. Under a strong Burmese king, it was but natural for Manipur to pay more than the full price for her depredations against Burma. A new Burmese dynasty under the leadership of Alaungpaya was ready to strike at Manipur.[29] On the other hand in Manipur after Garibniwaz, there began a series of sordid internal wars. The character of the wars was the most savage and revolting. In the wars sons murdered brothers. There was not a single trait of heroism to relieve the dark scene of blood and treachery.[30]

When Gourasham of Manipur started his rule after expulsion of his uncle Bharatsai, Alaungpaya of Burma received an invitation from one of the Manipuri princes to instal him on the throne of Manipur. Alaungpaya, therefore, invaded Manipur in 1755.[31] Alaungpaya also did not satisfy himself with the consolidation of his authority in Upper and Lower Burma. He invaded Manipur and Siam.[32] The Burmese army was led by a relative of Alaungpaya. The Manipuris under the command of Heir-Apparent Jai Singh met the Burmese army at Tummu. The Manipuris retreated and fought at Kakching. Gourasham, king of Manipur also joined the fight in person. The Manipuris were defeated by the Burmese. Manipur was devastated by the Burmese. The Burmese left Manipur after nine days. The Manipuri king and the inhabitants were taking shelter in the surrounding hills during the Burmese stay at their country. After the Burmese left, the king and the population came down to the plains from the hills.[33] The Burmese devastation of the plain of Manipur is known as the "Khoolthak Halba" or Primary devastation.[34]

In 1759, the term of Gourasham was over. Jai Singh assumed the regal power.[35] As soon as Jai Singh resumed the administrative reigns of the country, he had to meet the biggest Burmese invasion of Manipur. The Burmese invasion of Manipur in 1759 was led by Alaungpaya. Bharatsai on his expulsion by Gourasham went to Burma. He requested Alaungpaya to place him on the throne of Manipur. Alaungpaya personally led the invasion against Manipur.[36] He proceeded up to the Chindwin with a fleet of boats, subdued the western bank of the Chindwin inhabited by the Kathe Shans or Shans tributary to Manipur. There he disembarked, crossed the Ungoching hills by the Khambat route, marched through the Kabo valley and entered the valley of Manipur by the Imole pass at Pulel. At Pulel, Alaungpaya was met by the Manipur army. Alter a sanguinary fight, the Burmese defeated the Manipuris. Alaungpaya left Imphal after thirteen days. He set-up a stone inscription. He left garrisons at Tummu and Thangsut and returned home with his booty. Manipur was ruled for a period of three years by the Moirang Chief as the Burmese nominee.[37]

The crushing defeat inflicted by Alaungpaya on the Manipuris was disastrous for the Manipuris. Manipur was devastated. Thousands of people of men, women and children were seized by the Burmese and carried as captives to Burma. The Manipuri captives were settled in Mong Nai, Ava, Amarapura in the southern pans of the Kyaukse district and at Mogok. The Brahmin captives from Manipur were made astrologers at the Court of Ava. The Manipuris also formed a cavalry regiment in the Burmese army.[38] The main cause for the success of the Burmese invasion led by Alaungpaya was due to the use of fire-arms by the Burmese. The Manipuris did not have the taste of fire-arms before. They had the experience for the first time of the use of fire-arms in the invasion led by Alaungpaya.[39] During the Mon-Burmese fight, Alaungpaya got 35 cannons each throwing a 24 lb. ball seized from the two ships sent from Pondicherry as the help to the Mons. The crew numbering over 200 of the two ships were also enlisted in the Burmese army as gunners. The Anglo-Burmese Agreement of 1757 also gave Burma every year a cannon throwing a 12 lb. with 200 viss powder. The Burmese used large quantities of fire-arms which they procured from both the French and the English[40], against the Manipuris. On the other hand, the Manipuris entirely depended on the dao, spear and bow and arrow against the Burmese.[41] The Burmese invasion of Alaungpaya compelled the Manipuris to look for their new weapons to match their adversary.

The English people heard about Burma before they founded the East India Company in 1600. The Company did not take interest in Burma during their early adventures in this subcontinent. The reason was that Burma did not produce species which were demanded by the Europeans. The company also wanted to avoid clash with other powers which were her enemies in Europe. In those days, Burma was treated as being under the influence of the Portuguese. However, in 1747, the Company obtained permission from the Burmese king for construction of a house and a dock at Syriam. The East India Company received opposition from the Dutch and competition from the interlopers. They later on had withdrawn their factory at Syriam.[42]

The French recognised the Mon king and the English inclined to recognise Alaungpaya during the fight between the Mons and the Burmese (1740-1757). In 1757, an agreement was signed between Burma and the British, by virtue of which the Burmese obtained every year a cannon throwing 12 lb. with 200 viss powder which Burma was in dire need. In return, the Burmese exempted customs duty for the British. The Burmese also ceded Negrals in perpetuity to the British with right to fortify it.[43]The British allowed the refugees from Mons and Burmese sides during their fight to visit and stay at Negrais. The Mons traders who were among the refugees exchanged their wares for four or five musket in payment, from the British. Armenian merchants who were hit by the East India Company's monopoly reported to Alaungpaya. The British also as traders supplied the Mons with weapons. Alaungpaya sent his brother to inquire into the allegation made by the Armenian merchants against the British. Alaungpaya's brother did not report anything wrong against the East India Company. Alaungpaya imprisoned his brother and he sent 2,000 men against the British at Negrais. The Burmese commanders and the Governor of Bassein went inside the fort saying that to be delivered to the English manager of the fort. At the same time, the Burmese army were hiding in the nearby bushes. When the Burmese commanders and the English manager were sitting down for break-fast, the Governor of Bassein gave a secret sign to the hiding Burmese soldiers. On receipt of the signal 2000 men rushed out from their hiding place and attacked the English.

As a result, the Englishmen of the fort including one hundred Indians were killed. This is called Massacre of Negrais which took place on 6th October, 1759. The Burmese burnt the fort and carried away the cannon.[44] In 1761 Capt. Alves was sent to demand for the compensation of the massacre. Naungdawgyi who succeeded Alaungpaya refused the payment of compensation. However, he granted the Company permission to reopen trade with a specific condition that the English should not go to Negrais. Capt. Alves reported that the king looked on all that were killed at Negrais, whether guilty or innocent as born to die there.[45] When the British were confronted with the question of reparation of their Negrais ill-treatment. The case of Manipur came up before the English officials at Chittagong. At the same time, Jai Singh of Manipur was trying to save his country from the devastation of the Burmese army. Chitsai who was expelled from Manipur took advantage of the precarious condition. Chitsai Singh presented his case before the English at Chittagong through the help of Tripperah king. He pleaded for the English help for his installation on the throne of Manipur. He contended that he had been unjustly ousted by his brother from Manipur.[46] Jai Singh came to know of Chitsai's movement. He sent his Vakil Haridas Gossai with a letter to Mr. Vereist at Chittagong. Jai Singh apprised the English official at Chittagong of the reasons for the ouster of Chitsai from the throne of Manipur. The English Officials examined the case of Manipur. They rejected the case of

Chitsai. The English Officials at Chittagong had not only decided to support the claim of Jai Singh of Manipur to the throne of Manipur but also expressed their willingness to help Jai Singh in the war against the Burmese.[47]

Haridas Gossai also convinced the English Officials at Chittagong about the existence of the possibility of an extensive British trade from India to China. He pointed out that the Chinese merchants used to bring their merchandise as far as Manipur when Burma and Manipur were in good relations. He further pointed out the great commercial interest that to be accrued to the East India Company from Manipur after the expulsion of the Burmese from Manipur. He further emphasised that East India Company would be able to secure favourable terms from the Manipuris. Haridas Gossai placed a proposal containing terms of articles to Capt. Verelst which was the basis of an alliance to be negotiated between them on behalf of their respective masters. After some discussion, the terms of the alliance were finally settled on the 14th September, 1762. The alliance was signed at Chittagong by Haridas Gossai on behalf of Jai Singh, king of Manipur. Mr. Verelst forwarded a copy of the alliance to Mr. H. Vansittart, President of Board for approval to the Board and also requested him for a force for the expedition against Burma. The expedition on arrival at Manipur immediately was fruitful to demand satisfaction from the Burmese for all the injuries the British received from the former at Negrais and Pegu.

The case of Manipur came up before the Board for consideration on the 4th October, 1762. The Board found the articles very favourable. The proposed expedition against Burma was also to give advantages to the Company if it was proved successful. The Board decided to call for the opinions of Colonel Coote and Major Carna on the proposed expedition before it was finally approved. On the 11th October, 1762, the proposed alliance with Manipur against Burma came up for consideration before the Board. At the same time, the President of the Board Mr. Vansittart placed the case of Shah Alam, king of Delhi and his Vazir Shuja-ud-daulah who were earnestly applying for British help to gain possession of Delhi. The Board decided not to sanction any expedition against Burma. It thought that it was unwise to detach anybody of European troops to distant Meckley in view of the grave situation prevalent in northern India. However, the Board also held at the same time that they would not miss the opportunity of contracting an alliance with the Meckley Rajah. The opportunity was very favourable to the East India Company as it might open a road to them for obtaining reparation from the Burmese for the repeated ill-treatment of the Factory at Negrais.[48]

The Board finally decided to fix a post at Manipur. The objects of the post were to gain exact intelligence on the strength and character of the Burmese and the situation of the country and also to cultivate further friendship with the Manipur Rajah. The post should consist of six companies of sepoys—four from Calcutta and two to be drafted from Capt. Grants Battalion at Chittagong under the command of Lt. Archibald Winston, with two other officers, Lt. John Stables and Esnign Scotland. The Board informed the officers at the Chittagong factory of their decision with the condition that Mr. Verelst might either accompany the troops himself or send Mr. Marriot or Mr. Rambold and that the troops should be under the order of the officer accompanying them. The Chittagong officers were further instructed that case should be taken not to proceed any further or commence hostilities against the Burmese, until further instructions in this behalf were received from the Board.[49] The Manipur expedition reached Chittagong about December 1763 from where it proceeded towards its final destination under Verelst in January 1763. In April 1763, it reached Khaspur near Badarpur. However, it was not to reach its destination. The main reason was that the expedition suffered from rain and disease in the midst of pestilential marshy lands. This had resulted in the reduction of the number of soldiers. The remaining few retreated to Jainnagar on the left bank of the Barak river. The expedition returned to Bengal later on.[50]

The bodyguards of Jai Singh, king of Manipur committed the murder of a certain Brahmin missionary. As a mark of mortification for the murder, Jai Singh handed over the legal power to his brother Gourasham. This was in 1761 before the expiry of his term of power for five years.[51] Gourasham on assuming the real power confirmed all the articles of the alliance entered into by his younger brother Jai Singh with the English. This was effected through the accredited agents of Gourasham Singh at Chittagong. The agents were Anantasai and Jaganath Das.[52] According to the terms of agreement, English troops were to be employed in Manipur. The expenses for the maintenance of the troops were to be borne by Manipur. Gourasham pleaded his inability to pay in cash. The reason given by Gourasham was that the country had been badly damaged by the Burmese invasion. He agreed to meet the expenses by the "products of Meckley". The products were to be measured in the scale and conditions approved by the East India Company. The products of Manipur were valued at Rs. 56,850 annually. Articles worth Rs. 26,050 were to be paid by the Manipuri king within one month after the arrival of the English troops at Raung Roong.[53] The treaty between Manipur and British was the first diplomatic relation between the two parties. This was the direct product of the political relations between Manipur and Burma.

While Alaungpaya was in Manipur, he received the news of the revolt of the Peguers. He was forced to beat a retreat from his stay at Manipur.[54] On reaching Burma, Alaungpaya laid the siege of Ayutia in 1700 and during the seige he was hopelessly wounded. Later on he succumbed to the injury on his way to his capital.[55] Alaungpaya was succeeded by his son and successor Naungdawgyi (1760-63). During this short reign nothing was done towards Manipur. Naungdawgyi was succeeded by his brother Hsinbyushin in 1763. He transferred his capital from Shwebo to Ava. Hsinbyushin revived the career of conquest and aggrandizement of his great father Alaungpaya.[56] In Manipur, Jai Singh ascended the throne of Manipur on the death of his brother Gourasham in 1763, the same year in which Hsinbyushin ascended the Burmese throne. Khelemba, Chief of Moirang of Manipur wanted some additional lands from Manipur. He requested the Manipuri king Jai Singh for cession of the lands. Jai Singh, the Manipuri king refused to comply with the request of his maternal uncle Khelemba of Moirang. Khelemba decided to strike at Manipur with the Burmese help. In order to get help from the Burmese, Khelemba of Moirang gave his daughter in marriage to the Burmese king.[57] In 1764, Hsinbyushin of Burma invaded Manipur. He defeated the Manipuris first at Tummu and secondly at Kakching. Manipur was devastated by the Burmese. Jai Singh of Manipur fled to Cachar. The inhabitants of Manipur took shelter in Moirang. The Burmese placed Khelemba on the throne of Manipur. The Burmese then left Manipur with large captives.[58]

During the stay of Jai Singh of Manipur in Cachar, he made contact with the officials of the Ahom king Rajeswar Simha (1752-1768). The king of Cachar Ramchandra was related to Jai Singh of Manipur. The Cachari king also made communication to the

Ahom king on behalf of the Manipuri king. The Ahom king gave permission for interview to the Manipuri king. The Cachari king and the Manipuri king were accompanied by Barbura to the Court of Ahom king. The request of Manipuri for help from the Ahom king to drive out the Burmese from Manipur was complied with by the Ahom king. An army consisting of 40,000 men including the Gargaon and the Gauhati recruit was sent under the command of Majindar Phukan. The Ahom army in the accompaniment of Jai Singh, Manipur did not find out the correct way for Manipur. Therefore, they entered into the dense forest in the middle of Charaideu Hill where the army suffered a great loss. They finally returned with a loss of two-thirds of the men and provisions. This is the Latakati-Ran in the history of Assam.[59] After the failure of the first expedition, the Ahom king Rajeswar Simha sent another expedition in 1767 under the command of Khangia Phukan. Jai Singh, king of Manipur accompanied the expedition. This time the army took a different route to avoid the mistake committed in the previous expedition. The army proceeded to Raha, then to Cachar from where it proceeded towards the frontiers of Manipur. The Ahom army halted on the bank of the Merap river. When Jai Singh reached the hill villages of Manipur, where the inhabitants welcomed him. Jai Singh proceeded towards Manipur with the inhabitants.[60]

The Ahom army numbered 80,000 men. The bigger part of the army encamped at Raha. Jai Singh accompanied 10,000 men up to the Merap river where the Ahom army halted.[61] After the arrival of Jai Singh, the Moirangs were destroyed. The inhabitants of Manipur who took shelter in Moirang during the devastation of the valley came down to it from Moirang. In 1768, the Moirang king on his way from Ava to Manipur was killed.[62] The Khangia Phukan sent Mamath Naga Bara with two hundred men to see the condition of Jai Singh. King of Manipur conveyed his gratitude to the Ahom king for his assistance. Jai Singh also expressed his readiness to send tributes as well as princess Kuranganayani to the Ahom king Rajeswar Simha. Kuranganayani was daughter of Gourasham, brother of Jai Singh. She was also known as Phonda Lokpi. She was escorted to the Ahom king in the accompaniment of Manmath Bara along with dowry.[63] The Ahom king constructed houses for the Manipuri princess at Sonarinagar near the river Talao. Rajeswar Simha made Kuranganayani his Barkuari, chief queen.[64]

After the death of Rajeswar Simha in 1769, the Moamarias, a religious sect professing Vaishnavism rose in revolt against Lakshmi Singh, brother and successor of Rajeswar Simha. The rebels ousted the Ahoms and occupied Rangpur, the capital city. Ragha Moran, one of the principal leaders of the rebels took Kuranganayani as his wife. A conspiracy was hatched between Ram-Krishnai and Kuranganayani to kill Ragha. The plan was successfully executed when Kuranganayani struck Ragha with a sword just below the calf. When Ragha fell down, Ram-Krishnai severed the head. Lakshmi Singh regained his throne.[65] In 1788, Moamarias under Tati forced Ahom king Gourinath Singh flee from Rangpur towards Gauhati. Gourinath solicited help from Jai Singh who sent a small force of 700 to help the Ahom king under the command of his priest Thakur Ram.[66] The Manipuri army failed to report to Buragohains camp as directed by Gourinath Singh and the force returned suddenly to their own country after plundering Assamese village on the Assam-Cachar frontier.[67] Gourinath Singh of Assam made a fresh request to Jai Singh of Manipur for help. In compliance with the request, Jai Singh himself commanded the Manipuri force at the head of 800 effectives and 84,000 irregulars in 1790.[68] Jai Singh met Gourinath at Khutarmur in December 1790. Jai Singh proceeded with his army to the Boragohains camp.

Jai Singh in the company of his son Modhuchandra Singh arrived with his army at Jorhat. Jai Singh was conducted by the Baragohain Teaok from where he was sent to attack the Moamarias at Rangpur. The Manipuri force halted at Gauri Sagar. Modhuchandra Singh went in advance with the detachment towards the Ahom capital. He was able to force his way into Rangpur fortress by avoiding the route where the Moamarias kept their batteries concealed in the softy gross and impenetrable reeds. He massacred the Moamarias of every age and sex. However, Modhuchandra had to abandon his offensive as he got the news that the Moamarias killed a great number of Manipuris by opening guns on his father's army. Modhuchandra on reaching his father's place experienced the same fate as that of his father. Modhuchandra Singh was forced to beat a retreat on the first of the well-directed fire of the Moamaris cannon.[69] Jai Singh of Manipur left Assam after leaving 700 men for the service under the Boragohain.[70] The 700 Manipuris also left Assam without further fight. On their arrival at Manipur, they were punished in public for running away from the battle-field.[71]

The Chinese invaded Burma in 1769. But they failed to take Kaungton. The Chinese proposed for peace. The proposal was accepted by the Burmese Commander. Accordingly an agreement was reached between the two parties. The terms of agreement included the retreat of the Chinese peacefully, the restoration of trade between the two countries, exchange of decennial missions between the two monarchs to remove misunderstanding between them. The two countries were never to fight each other again. The Burmese king Hsinbyushin heard the return of the Chinese army without annihilation. He was very angry. He ill-treated the families of his victorious generals who saved him and his kingdom. The Burmese armies heard the news of the ill-treatment of their king to their families. They were afraid of their king and of their return as they knew they would meet the same fate as that of their families. By this time, Manipur had shown signs of marked prosperity after the last devastation by the Burmese. The news of this rapid restoration of progress reached the generals of the Burmese army. They decided to appease their king with the booty to be taken from Manipur. They were sure that sufficient booty would be collected from Manipur in case of a raid. In January 1770, the Burmese army instead of their return to home, invaded Manipur.[72]

In this Burmese raid of Manipur, the Burmese army accompanied two Manipuri officials Ghanasham and Moirangjam Togindra from Burma. The Burmese army devastated the country.[73] Jai Singh of Manipur fled to Cachar. During the flight of Jai Singh to Cachar, Keibiram was placed on the throne of Manipur. Bhavanand, brother of Jai Singh, who was carried away by the Burmese army came to Manipur with the Burmese army to contest for the throne of Manipur. The Burmese party was met by the Manipuri Party led by Keibiram at Tusarok. In the fight that ensued Keibiram was killed. Bhavanand placed his brother Kukecla on the throne of Manipur and left for Burma.[74] When Jai Singh returned from Cachar in 1772 he was received by Kokeelanand. The regal powers were thus assumed by Jai Singh.[75] In 1773, the Burmese again invaded Manipur. The defeated Manipuri king Jai Singh fled to Cachar. The Manipuris lost five cannons in the fight at Tamu and the Burmese remained in possession of the country for a period of five months. Jai Singh of Manipur returned from Cachar next year.[76] Jai Singh fled four times from Manipur to Cachar between 1775 to 1782 when he made four successful attempts to regain his throne. From 1782 to 1798, Jai Singh ruled the country without any disturbance from his enemies as he made a compromise with the Burmese in 1782.[77] Jai Singh of Manipur became tired and exhausted by his constant lights with the Burmese. In January 1798, he abdicated the throne in favour of his eldest son Labanya Chandra and proceeded to Nadiya on a pilgrimage where he died one year after in 1799 near Bhagovangola on the banks of the Ganges.[78]

In Manipur, after the death of Jai Singh, Labanya Chandra came to the throne of Manipur in 1799. In Burma Heinoyushin died in 1776. He was succeeded by his inefficient son Singu (1776-1782). Singu, the Burmese king had a short reign as he was ousted through a palace intrigue which placed Bowdapaya, a son of Alaungpaya on the Burmese throne. Bowdopaya had a long reign of 37 years (1782-1819).[79] There was a Burmese raid on Manipur in 1800. The Manipuris repulsed the raid at Tummu.[80] In 1801, Labanya Chandra was assassinated as a result of a conspiracy hatched by his own brother Modhuchandra.[81] Alter the death of Labanya Chandra, Modhuchandra ascended the throne of Manipur. On ascending the throne, Modhuchandra made his brothers Chourjit Singh and Marjit Singh as Jubraj and Senapati respectively.[82] In 1803, Chourjit fled to Cachar from where he invaded Manipur. Marjit Singh was to resist the advance of Chourjit Singh. However, Marjit Singh instead of fighting made a common cause with Chourjit Singh against their brother Modhuchandra. The combined force of Chourjit and Marjit Singh forced Modhuchandra to take refuge in Cachar. Chourjit became king of Manipur while Marjit was made heir-apparent. Modhuchandra Singh, the fugitive king of Manipur married a daughter of the Cachar king. Modhuchandra invaded Manipur. However, he was killed in action in 1804.[83] Marjit Singh conspired to usurp the throne of Manipur in the year 1806.[84] But he failed in his attempt to capture the throne of Manipur. He fled to Burma. The Burmese effected a compromise between Chourjit and Marjit. There was a temporary reconciliation between Chourjit and Marjit. However, the compromise did not last long. Marjit Singh in 1808 again revolted against his brother Chourjit Singh. Marjit Singh suffered defeat on two occasions in the hands of Chourjit Singh. Marjit finally fled to Cachar from where he reached Ava through Arakan.[85] Marjit Singh stayed for seven years in the Court of Burma. During his stay, Marjit presented his case before the Burmese king. At the beginning, the Burmese were unwilling to render their help for Marjit against his brother Chourjit Singh. Finally Marjit succeeded in inducing the Burmese to take up his case for which he agreed to renounce all claims on the Kubo Valley and to become dependent king of Burma.[86] The Burmese king in order to settle the case through negotiations summoned Chourjit Singh to the Court of Ava. Chourjit on his part did not comply with the Burmese summon.[87] In 1812, a Burmese army of one lakh invaded Manipur to place Marjit Singh on the throne of Manipur.[88] Two Burmese divisions were formed at Tummu in the Kubo valley. One was led by Marjit Singh and the other was led by the Somjok Chief. The division led by the Sumjok Chief encamped at Heirok. This was routed by the Manipuris under Petumber Singh, nephew of Chourjit Singh. The other led by Marjit Singh gave battle to Chourjit Singh at Kakching. After a fight which lasted for five days, Chourjit was defeated. He fled to Cachar. The Burmese army left Manipur after a stay of ten days by placing Marjit Singh on the throne of Manipur. Marjit became king of Manipur in 1813.[89]

In Burma on the death of Crown Prince in 1808, Bodowpaya immediately proclaimed Bagidaw, son of the deceased Crown Prince as the heir-apparent. Bodawpaya died in 1819 and Bagidaw became king of Burma.[90] The new Burmese king decided to commemorate the coronation on 2nd November, 1819 with extraordinary pomp and grandeur. All the tributary kings were summoned to pay homage personally to the new king. Marjit Singh of Manipur was also summoned. Marjit Singh was entirely indebted to Bagidaw as it was due to the friendly exertions of Bagidaw that Marjit Singh was able to become king of Manipur. Much waters had flowed down the Imphal river since the becoming of Marjit Singh as the Manipuri king. As soon as he was placed on the throne of Manipur, Marjit Singh dismissed his allies. He forcibly cut teak timbers from the Kubo Valley which was ceded to Burma. Marjit finally constructed a gilded house which should not have done by a dependent king of Burma. These arbitrary actions of Marjit Singh of Manipur, made the relations between Manipur and Burma strained. Marjit incurred the displeasure of the Burmese king. Though Marjit received the summon from the Burmese king, he tactfully tried to avoid his presence in the coronation ceremony of Bagidaw. Marjit Singh expressed his inability to attend the ceremony on account of the hostile attitude of his brothers Chourjit Singh and Gambhir Singh who were staying in Cachar. The Burmese took an opportunity of dethroning Marjit from the throne of Manipur on account of his failure to attend the coronation of the Burmese king. In 1819, the Burmese king sent immediately an army to punish the recalcitrant Marjit Singh of Manipur. The two parties met at Kakching, the venue for previous fights between the Burmese and the Manipuris. The fight ended in the complete defeat of Marjit Singh of Manipur. He fled to Cachar as usual. Manipur was occupied by the Burmese. Subol Singh was placed on the throne of Manipur as the Burmese nominee. He was supported by a large Burmese army. Manipuris numbering three lakhs were taken as captives of Burma. This is known as the Seven Year Devastation (Chahi Taret Kjioontakpa) in the History of Manipur.[91]

Garibniwaz and Jai Singh, the two Manipuri kings maintained cordial relations with Cachar through matrimonial alliances. Garibniwaz and Jai Singh gave their daughters in marriage to the kings of Cachar. Garibniwaz received assistance from the king of Cachar during his Burmese invasion in 1739. Jai Singh of Manipur also took refuge at least three times in Cachar when he was driven out by the Burmese. Sons of Jai Singh also took refuge in Cachar whenever they were defeated and expelled by their rivals in Manipur. Cachar was converted into a base for the Manipuri princes for their depredatory activities against their rivals in Manipur. The conversion of Cachar into a base for the Manipuri princes produced results which were disastrous for the existence of Cachar itself. In 1812, Chourjit Singh was expelled by Marjit Singh from Manipur. Chourjit Singh came along with his brother Gambhir Singh to Cachar. Chourjit Singh of Manipur applied for assistance to Govind Chandra of Cachar for invasion of Manipur. Govind Chandra rejected the application of Chourjit Singh to invade Manipur. The ground of rejection of the application of Chourajit Singh by Govind Chandra was that Govind Chandra had the same degree of relationship with the Manipuri brothers. Chourjit left Cachar for Calcutta, for securing help from the British. Chourjit also failed to get help from them. Chourjit Singh then came to Jaintia. Where he made an alliance with Ram Singh of Jaintia and began to create trouble for the king of Cachar.[92] Gambhir Singh who stayed at Cachar was taken in the service of the king of Cachar as Commander-in-charge of the army at a monthly payment of Rs. 35.[93]

Marjit Singh fled to Cachar in 1808. During his stay in Cachar he picked a serious quarrel with Govind Chandra, brother of Cachar king. The cause of the quarrel was over a "hockey pony of quite exceptional excellence." Govind Chandra developed a fascination for the pony belonging to Marjit Singh. He made an offer for the pony to Marjit Singh who rejected the offer. Overwhelmed by the desire for the pony, Govind Chandra took possession of the pony forcibly.[94] Marjit Singh could not forget this episode and to feed fat for his ancient grudge on Govind Chandra, Marjit Singh invaded Cachar in December, 1817.[95] In the fight at Rangpur on the bank of the Barak river, Govind Chandra was forced to retreat. Following the initial success, Marjit Singh made an advance up to Badarpur which was on the fringe of the English territory. This attracted the attention of the Magistrate of Sylhet who sent troops to guard the frontier of the company. Marjit Singh of Manipur had made himself the master of Cachar. He sent a communication to the Magistrate of Svlhet requesting him to appoint a European Officer to keep Govind Chandra and Gambhir Singh in check so that they might not wage any war against Marjit Singh. The Magistrate of Sylhet rejected the request of Marjit Singh. However, the Magistrate of Sylhet assured Marjit Singh of Manipur that there was no occasion for fight with him provided Marjit Singh did not cause any disturbance on the frontier of the Company.[96]

Chourjit Singh from Jaintia responded to the appeal made by Govind Chandra for assistance against Marjit Singh of Manipur. Chourjit Singh came to the rescue of the Cachar king Govind Chandra. Marjit Singh apprehended the influence of Chourjit Singh on his army. On hearing the advance of Chourjit Singh, Marjit Singh of Manipur made a retreat hastily to Manipur.[97] Marjit Singh of Manipur was evicted from the occupation of Cachar immediately after the eviction of Marjit from Cachar, Govind Chandra had to face a serious threat. This threat led the ouster of Govind Chandra from the throne of Cachar. Chourjit Singh persuaded Gambhir Singh to leave the services of Govind Chandra. Gambhir Singh left the Cachari service. Chourjit and Gambhir Singh in conjunction with Tularam began to commit atrocities in Cachar. Govind Chandra of Cachar was unable to secure assistance from the English against his enemies. He ultimately escaped to Sylhet.[98] The plains of Cachar felled in the hands of Chourjit Singh and Gambhir Singh. The northern hilly region of Cachar went in the hands of Tularam.[99]

At about the same time in 1819, Marjit was expelled from Manipur by the Burmese. He was received kindly by Chourjit Singh. Marjit Singh handed over the royal insingnia along with the sacred images of Govind and Binamchandra to Chourjit Singh.[100] The Manipuri princes from Cachar began to launch their offensive against the Burmese with a view to regain their hereditary throne. In 1821, the first attack on the Burmese in Manipur was led by Hirachandra, son of Labyana Chandra. He was able to make a surprise attack on a Burmese detachment of 500. The Burmese were defeated and 200 were captured.[101] In 1822, Pitambar *alias* Yumjaotaba, son of Madhuchandra was sent to assist Hirachandra. The two brothers made a joint effort to dislodge the Burmese, through guerrilla warfare for about 8 months. Unable to achieve their objective they retired to Cachar.[102] In another attempt Hirachandra Singh defeated Subol, the Burmese nominee on the throne of Manipur. Hirachandra and Subol received Pitambar who was sent by Chourjit Singh in 1823. Pitambar himself assumed the royal authority.[103] Gambhir Singh immediately entered Manipur with a small force and deposed Pitambar Singh who took his flight to Burma.[104] For want of adequate supplies, Gambhir Singh was forced to retire to Cachar.[105] The vacuum on the throne of Manipur was immediately filled by the Burmese with Jai Singh as their nominee. Jai Singh reigned for 2 years only. The next Burmese nominee was Jadu Singh.[106] He ruled for 2 years. Jadu Singh was followed by the Burmese nominee Radhob Singh who had also 2 years rule to his credit.[107] The last Burmese nominee on the throne of Manipur was Bhadra Singh with a rule of only one month.[108]

In Cachar, a fresh quarrel broke out between the three Manipuri princes. Marjit Singh who had the dream of becoming king of Manipur made a conspiracy with Gambhir Singh to drive out Chourjit Singh from Cachar. Chourjit Singh, eldest of the three had a legitimate claim on the throne of Manipur.[109] Chourjit Singh who received Hilakandi from Govind Chandra for his assistance, fled to Sylhet following the conflict between the brothers.[110] Hilakandi passed in the hands of Marjit Singh and the rest of south Cachar was in possession of Gambhir Singh.[111] In Sylhet, Chourjit Singh applied to the British Magistrate to make charge of his territory in Cachar.[112] In 1823, the situation in the eastern frontiers of the British had become critical. Manipur and Assam had been virtually under the hands of the Burmese since 1819. Cachar was under the Manipuri princes. The possibility of falling these

Manipuri usurpers of Cachar prey to or reconciling themselves with the Burmese was present. The situation on the Chittagong frontier also assumed alarming proportion.

The news of the movements of the Burmese forces leading towards Cachar made the local British Officers to take cognizance of the strategic importance of Cachar. Negotiations at once, with the Manipuri princes were opened. Govind Chandra of Cachar was excluded from the purview of the negotiations.[113] Gambhir Singh alone claimed full sovereignty of Cachar. He lodged strong objection to the negotiations being opened with Chourjit Singh and Marjit Singh. Gambhir Singh at the same time sought for the British protection.[114] The British Officers received evasive and unsatisfactory replies from Gambhir Singh. Gambhir Singh's dubious connections with the Burmese authority in Manipur were also detected by the British Officers at this stage of negotiations. The case of Gambhir Singh was dropped by the British Officers. The British finally decided to reinstate Govind Chandra to the throne of Cachar and the Manipuri princes were to be provided pensions from the revenue of Cachar for their stay in the British territory.[115] On January 17, 1824, the fight between the advancing Burmese army and the British took place at Vikrampur. The intimation by the Burmese Commander of their objective to place Govind Chandra on the throne of Cachar and to effect arrest of the Manipuri princes was negatived by David Scot. The British refused to hand over the Manipuri princes to the Burmese. They also informed the Burmese that they were to place Govind Chandra on the throne of Cachar. On February 13, 1824, a fight ensued between the British and the Burmese at Badarpur. The British were able to score their victory in the engagement. But they suffered a defeat in their attack on a Burmese stockade near Dudpatli.[116] The Burmese retired to Manipur.[117] A breathing space was created by the retreat of the Burmese from Cachar. This was followed by the declaration of the British protection of Cachar by a Treaty entered into between the British and Govind Chandra on March 6, 1824.[118]

The British declared war against the Burmese on 5th March, 1824. The outbreak of the 1st Anglo-Burmese War (1824-1826) made Manipur a part of the theatre of the War. Manipur was the gate for the Burmese to Assam and Cachar. It was in the hands of the Burmese on the eve of the outbreak of the war. The necessity for the utilising services of the Manipuri princes in order to put pressure on the Burmese in Manipur was urgently felt. Gambhir Singh was a bold and aspiring soldier. The British choice fell on Gambhir Singh. The British Officers gave an assurance to Gambhir Singh that he should be made king of Manipur after the liberation of the country from the yoke of the Burmese. The share of Chourjit Singh in the governance of the country should be excluded. The British assurance induced Gambhir Singh to lead an expedition against the Burmese in Manipur. Accordingly Gambhir Singh joined the services of the Company at Badarour in April 1824. The British arrangement with Gambhir Singh angered Chourjit Singh. He made an attempt to excite a revolt amongst the Manipuri recruits of a British Battalion. The obnoxious role of Chourjit Singh was detected by the British. He was accordingly deported to Nadia where he was paid a monthly pension of Rupees one hundred.[119]

The hostilities between the British and the Burmese in Cachar were renewed. Gambhir Singh joined the abortive attack of Colonel William Innes made on the Burmese stockade at Talain for three days on July 6-8, 1824. By the close of October 1824, the Burmese army in Cachar retired to Manipur.[120] After the evaluation of Cachar by the Burmese, the British prepared the plan for occupation of Manipur. The British thought that the active engagements of the Burmese in the operations in Arakan and the Delta would minimise the chance of strong opposition from the Burmese in the Manipur operation. Brigadier-General Shuldham, Commanding Eastern Frontier determined to march to Manipur. Arrangements were made for the construction of a road from Dudpatli towards Manipur.[121]

On February 24, 1825, General Shuldham arrived at Banakandi. The geographical conditions of the country and the incessant rains made it not possible for him to complete the road through which he was to advance towards Manipur.[122] In December 1825, Gambhir Singh decided to fulfil the unfinished task left by General Shuldham. Gambhir Singh with the permission of the British marched with his "Manipur Levy of 500 who were paid and supplied with arms by the British Government to conciliate Gambhir Singh, it was further proposed that even if he would fail to retain the possession of Manipur, he would receive a provision of land either in Cachar or in Assam for himself and his followers. (Secret proceeding 1826, February 17, No. 20). He was accompanied by Lieutenant Pemberton. Gambhir Singh left Sylhet on May 17,

1825 and finally reached the western limit of the valley of Manipur on June 10, 1825. On the approach of Gambhir Singh, the Burmese retreated from the capital of Manipur and later from the Andro village, 10 miles away from the capital.[123] Gambhir Singh returned to Sylhet by the end of June by leaving 300 men at Manipur.[124]

Gambhir Singh for the second time returned to Manipur on December 18, 1825. He was accompanied by Captain Grant. When Gambhir Singh came to know the withdrawal of the Burmese troops from the Kabaw Valley, he sent his troops early in January 1826.[125] The advance of Gambhir Singh's army was resisted by the Chief of Shamjok of Kabo Valley. Gambhir Singh and Captain Grant led the troops in person and dispersed the Burmese army.[126] On February 1, 1826, Gambhir Singh arrived on the western bank of the Chindwin river of Burma to find the desertion of the entire district by the Burmese army. Even the district on the opposite of the river was found deserted.[127] The 1st Anglo-Burmese War came to an end by the Treaty of Yandaboo, 1826. By the Article Second of the Treaty, Gambhir Singh was recognized as the Raja of Manipur by the king of Ava.[128] The Burmese renounced its claim on Manipur.

NOTES

1. Hall, D.G.E., *History of South East Asia*, London, 1955.
2. Hall, *History of Burma*, p. 73.
3. N. Khelchandra and L. Ibungohal, *Cheitharol Kumbaba*, Manipur Sahitya Parishand, Imphal, p. 55.
4. *Samjok Ngamba*, ms., p. 2.
5. *Ibid.*, p. 5.
6. W. Yumjao Singh, *An Early History of Manipur*, Imphal, 1966, p. 40.
7. R.K. Sanahal Singh, *Manipur Itihas*, p. 50.
8. *Manipur Itihas*, p. 54. Also see, W. Yumjao Singh.
9. W. Yumjao Singh, *An Early History of Manipur*, p. 41. Also see *Cheitharol Kumbaba*, p. 66.
10. *Ibid.*, p. 67.
11. *Cheitharol Kumbaba*, p. 67. W. Yumjao Singh, *op. cit.*, p. 42.
12. *Cheitharol Kumbaba*, p. 73.
13. Pemberton, *Report on the Eastern Frontier*, p. 39.
14. *Ibid.*, p. 38. Also see R.K. Sanahal Singh, *Manipur Itihas*, p. 54. Also see, W. Yumjao Singh, *An Early History of Manipur*, p. 47. and *Cheitharol Kumbaba*, p. 73.
15. Pemberton, *op.cit*, p. 38.

16. *Ibid.*, p. 38.
17. *Ibid.*, p. 39.
18. *Ibid.*, p. 17.
19. W. Yumjao Singh, *op. cit.*, p. 52.
20. R.K. Jhalajit Singh, *A Short History of Manipur*, p. 142.
21. W. Yumjao Singh, *op. cit.*, p. 52.
22. *Ibid.*
23. *Ibid.*
24. Capt. E.W. Dun, *Gazetteer of Manipur*, p. 38.
25. R. Brown, *Statistical Account of Manipur*, p. 60.
26. W. Yumjao Singh, *op. cit.*, p. 53.
27. Hall, *op. cit.*, p. 389. Desai, *Pageant of Burmese History*, pp. 84-86.
28. Hall, *op. cit.*, pp. 401-404. Desai, *op. cit.*, pp. 87-88.
29. Desai, *op. cit.*, p. 110.
30. W. Yumjao Singh, *op. cit.*, p. 53.
31. *Ibid.*, p. 53.
32. A.C. Banerji, *Eastern Frontier of British India*, p. 27.
33. W. Yumjao Singh, *op. cit.*, p. 53.
34. Pemberton, *op. cit.*, p. 41.
35. W. Yumjao Singh, *op. cit.*, p. 53.
36. R.M. Natha, *Background of Assamese Culture*, p. 93.
37. Pemberton, *op. cit.*, p. 41. Also see Desai, *op. cit.*, p. iv. Also see Brown, *op. cit.*, p. 61.
38. Hall, *op. cit.*
39. Desai, *op. cit.*, p. iii. Pemberton, *op. cit.*, p. 41.
40. Harvey, *Outline of Burmese History*, pp. 128-129.
41. R.K. Jhalajit Singh, *op. cit.*, p. 151. Pemberton, *op. cit.*, p. 41.
42. Abdul Ali, *Notes on the Early History of Manipur*, 1923, pp. 3-4.
43. Desai, *op. cit.*, p. 117. Also see Harvey, *op. cit.*, p. 128.
44. *Ibid.*
45. Harvey, *op. cit.*, p. 136. Also see Desai, *op. cit.*, p. 118.
46. Abdul Ali, *op. cit.*, p. 6.
47. *Public Proceedings*, Vol., 1762, pp. 232-240.
48. Abdul Ali, *op. cit.*, p. 6.
49. *Public Proceedings* (Vol. 1862, pp. 239-40, September 1762 to November, 1764), p. 85.
50. Abdul Ali, *op. cit.*, p. 6.
51. W. Yumjao Singh, *op. cit.*, p. 54.
52. *Cheitharol Kumbaba*, *op. cit.*, p. iii.
53. Abdul Ali, *op. cit.*, p. 7.
54. Pemberton, *op. cit.*, p. 41.
55. *Ibid.*, p. 41.
56. Hall, *op. cit.*, p. 411.
57. R.K. Sanahal Singh, *op. cit.*, p. 74.

58. *Cheitharol Kumbaba,* p. 111. Yumjao Singh, *op. cit.,* p. 56. R.K. Sanahal Singh, *op. cit.,* p. 74. Pemberton, *op. cit.,* p. 44. Desai, *op. cit.,* p. 111.
59. S.K. Bhuyan, *Tungkhungia Buranji,* pp. 50-59. G.C. Barua, *Ahom Buranji,* pp. 286-288.
60. *Ibid.,* pp. 288-289.
61. W. Yumjao Singh, *op. cit.,* p. 57.
62. *Cheitharol Kumbaba,* p. 112. W. Yumjao Singh, *op. cit.,* p. 57.
63. *Cheitharol Kumbaba,* p. 112. Ahom Buranji, p. 290.
64. *Cheitharol Kumbaba,* p. 112.
65. S.K. Bhuyan, *Tungkhungia Buranji,* p. 73.
66. *Cheitharol Kumbaba,* p. 141.
67. S.K. Bhuyan, *Anglo-Assamese Relations,* p. 232.
68. *Ibid.,* p. 233.
69. W. Yumjao, *op. cit.,* p. 60. *Cheitharol Kumbaba,* pp. 145-46.
70. *Ibid.,* p. 146, S.K. Bhuyan, *op. cit.,* p. 236. W. Yumjao, *op. cit.* p. 60.
71. *Cheitharol Kumbaba,* p. 147.
72. Desai, *op. cit.,* p. 99. Harvey, *Outline of Burmese History,* p. 142.
73. *Cheitharol Kumbaba,* p. 122.
74. *Ibid.,* p. 113. Also see W. Yumjao Singh, *Manipur Itihas,* p. 57.
75. *Cheitharol Kumbaba,* p. 113.
76. *Ibid.,* pp. 114-115. Also see W. Yumjao Singh, *op. cit.,* p. 57.
77. Pemberton, *op. cit.,* p. 45.
78. Brown: *Statistical Account of Manipur,* p. 62. Pemberton, *op. cit.,* p. 45.
79. Hall, *op. cit.,* p. 414.
80. *Cheitharol Kumbaba,* p. 167.
81. N. Gourachandra Singh, *Kartagee Macha Ibungoo Mari,* pp. 30-31.
82. *Cheitharol Kumbaba,* p. 169.
83. Pemberton, *op. cit.,* p. 46.
84. *Cheitharol Kumbaba,* p. 199.
85. W. Yumjao Singh, *op. cit.,* p. 62.
86. *Cheitharol Kumbaba,* p. 204. Pemberton, *op. cit.,* p. 46.
87. W. Yumjao Singh, *op. cit.,* p. 63.
88. *Ibid.*
89. Pemberton, *op. cit.,* p. 65.
90. D.G.E. Hall, *op. cit.,* p. 596.
91. *Cheitharol Kumbaba,* pp. 207, 211. W. Gourachandra, *Kartagee Macha Ibungo Mari,* pp. 117-118. Pemberton, *op. cit.,* pp. 47, 48. A.C. Banerjee: *Eastern Frontier of British India,* p. 31: Han *op. cit.,* p. 596. Desai: *op. cit.,* p. iii.
92. S.N. Sen, *Records in Oriental Languages,* Vol. I, Bengali letters, letters No. 162, 163.
93. *Foreign Political Proceedings,* 14 November, 1828, No. 19.
94. B.C. Allen, *Assam District Gazetteer,* Vol. I, Cachar, pp. 25-26.
95. S.N. Sen, *op. cit.,* Nos. 162 & 163.

96. S.N. Sen, Letter No. 163.
97. Pemberton, *Report on Frontier*, p. 48.
98. S.N. Sen. *op. cit.*, Letter No. 166.
99. *Ibid.*, No. 162-3, 166.
100. *Ibid.*
101. Pemberton, *op. cit.*, p. 48.
102. Pemberton, *Report on Eastern Frontier*, p. 48. *Cheitharol Kumbaba*, p. 213.
103. *Ibid.*, p. 214. Also See Pemberton, *op. cit.*, p. 48.
104. Pemberton, *op. cit.*, p. 49. *Cheitharol Kumbaba*, pp. 213-214.
105. Pemberton, *op. cit.*, p. 49. Also see R.K. Sanahal: *Manipur Itihas*, p. 90.
106. *Cheitharol Kumbaba*, p. 216.
107. *Ibid.*, p. 216.
108. *Ibid.*, p. 218.
109. Pemberton, *op. cit.*, p. 49. W. Gourachandra Singh, *Kartagee macha mari*, p. 121.
110. R.M. Nath, *Background of Assamese Culture*, p. 93.
111. Pemberton, *op. cit.*, p. 49.
112. *Foreign Secret Proceedings* 1823, November, No. 19.
113. *Foreign Political Proceedings*, 17 January, 1823, No. 6. *Secret Proceeding*, November 14, 1823, No. 19.
114. *Foreign Secret Proceeding*, November 14, 1823, No. 19.
115. *Foreign Political Proceeding*, 28 November, 1823, No. 6.
116. *Foreign Secret Consultation*, March 5, 1824, No. 18.
117. *Secret Consultation*, March 12, 1824, No. 19.
118. Aitchinson, No. XII.
119. *Foreign Political Proceedings*, April 20, 1824, No. 6.
120. Wilson, *Documents Illustrative of the Burmese War*, Calcutta, No. 96.
121. *Ibid.*, No. 98. Appendix No. 14.
122. *Ibid.*, No. 171.
123. *Ibid.*, No. 104.
124. *Ibid.*, No. 105.
125. *Ibid.*, No. 165(B).
126. *Ibid.*, No. 166(C).
127. *Ibid.*, No. 167(B).
128. Treaty of Peace concluded at Yandaboo.

9
Manipur's Political Relations with her Neighbour Burma

From the Middle of 15th Century to the Treaty of 1826

Kamei Budha Kabui

Introduction

Manipur literally means the land of gems. It was during the reign of Garibniwaz that the term was formally introduced is one of the northeastern states of India.[1] In the distant past, Manipur was called by different names like Kangleipak, Poireipak, Meitrabak etc. These indigenous names appeared to have indicated certain areas of the present state during various phases in the early period. A charming hilly state which had once divided into Assam and Burma (Myanmar) before the creation of present states such as Nagaland, Arunachal Pradesh, Meghalaya and Mizoram out of Assam. Manipur had enjoyed the fortune and glory in the past and experienced sorrow and vicissitudes of her long history. It had witnessed the transformation from a primitive tribal state to an independent kingdom and later on from native state of British India to a state of the Indian union. Multiple ethnic groups in the valley and at the surrounding hills occupy the state. These ethnic groups belong to Mongoloid racial stock and speak Tibeto-Burman languages.

Method and Materials

The study is purely historical approach based on available primary and secondary sources. Secondary sources include published books, articles, souvenirs etc.

Manipur had regular contact with the Burmese and Shans since the occupation of Kabaw valley in the 15th century as the Kathe Shans (Kabaws) were the subjects of Manipur Kingdom. In addition, there were constant trade contact and social relationship between Manipur and Burma. The 15th century was an important era because Manipur kingdom was in the military enhancement and expansion of its territory. The indigenous sources tell about the Manipuri military expeditions to Kabaw valley and conquered the valley in the first half of the 15th century. However, in the opinion of colonial officer R. Brown, about 300 years ago, Pakungba raja after consolidation of Manipuri power invaded and occupied the Kabaw Valley.[2] It was during the reign of Khumomba (1263-1278), the Kabaws invaded the Khuman; Khumans with the help of Khumomba drove out the Kabaws and some Kabaws were captured. In the year 1443, Ningthoukhomba (1432-1467) raided Alka inhabited by Shans in Chindwin basin of upper Burma and conquered it.[3]

Then, King Thangwai Ningthouba along with Choupha Khekhomba, the king of Pong invaded Kyang (a Shan principality of Kabaw Valley) and conquered it. Since Thangwai Ningthouba conquered Kyang, the Manipuri king was known as Kyamba (the conqueror of Kyang). The two kings celebrated their victory with great pomp, and did demarcate their boundaries under the friendly treaty concluded between the two rulers. This was the first ever treaty Manipur had entered into with a foreign country. Manipur boundary extended up to Mungkhang Muwai and the land of the dwarf mango groves was for Pong; in the east, it was up to Loijiri Hills, in the south up to Miyatong Hill. Regarding Samjok, the western portion was for Manipur and the eastern portion was for Pong.[4] Thus, a key portion of Kabaw was ceded to Manipur. According to Pemberton, Manipur and Pong sent a joint military force in the Kabaw valley and defeated the raja of Khumbat in 1475 and divided the conquered country between the two kingdoms and Kubo was annexed into Manipur in 1475.[5] This treaty and demarcation clearly indicates recognition of Manipur Kingdom by a power in upper Burma as the former exercised full-fledged sovereign power having internal and external independence in the true sense of the term.

After the conquest of Kabaw valley, Manipur gave free hand to the Shan princes to rule their respective territories but with the payment of annual tribute which they paid in the form of silks and paddy. The only responsibility of Manipur was to give protection to the Kabaw Valley from Burmese invasions and to avert armed conflicts among the princes. So, Manipur maintained a network of intelligence in the Kabaw Valley perhaps which is not known to the Shan princes. According to Late Prof. Kabui, the officials of Manipur were regularly placed on duty in strategic positions in Kabaw valley such as Tammu and Angoching Hills located on the west bank of Chindwin River.[6] In strategic points of Kabaw valley and the route connecting the valley, Meitei villages were established. The most important village was Kwatha, a betel nut planting village; it was established by Kyamba. Since the political relation between Manipur and Shan principalities in Kabaw valley was important, the vassal states were to be clearly watched and controlled. This was done mainly to integrate Kabaw valley with mainland Manipur.

The Kings of Manipur sent numerous military campaigns to Kabaw valley and Chindwin basin. But in the beginning of 16th century, the heirs of Kyamba were incompetent to sustain maintaining strong political grip over Kabaw valley. Due to physical distance from Kangla, the capital of the kingdom and the absence of direct administration over them, these tributary principalities tried to be free from political control of Manipur. There were bigger Shan states in upper Burma. And the central political power of Ava also gave encouragement to them. However, it was Mungyamba (1562-1597) who regained his control over them. Mungyamba invaded Mungkhong Mungyang in the eastern border of the Kabaw valley and defeated Shan ruler. He captured guns, a golden statue of a cock and five chiefs like Chaopha Mangtra, Chaopha Womsing etc. Mangsha was also defeated and its Chief Khangcheng was taken prisoner. In the year 1571, he invaded and conquered Samjok; in the next year 1572, the Kabaw Shans were defeated. In 1578, the Khamram was fixed as the boundary between Manipur and Shan states. Again in 1582, Mungyamba sacked Samjok and in 1597, he conquered Kyang and Shan Yathek in Kabaw valley.[7]

Khagemba (1597-1652) was the great ruler of Manipur. He acquired proper training of warfare, and diplomatic skills from his father. He conquered more territories and expanded the territory of

Manipur further besides consolidating his control over the whole Angoching and Kabaw valley. In 1602, Khagemba invaded Kyang and captured 177 as prisoners. In 1607, Samjok was invaded by him and 60 men were taken as prisoners. In 1614, he raided in Kyang in which he captured Maramba (a white horse) and invaded Samjok again. In 1649, he conducted last raid to Samjok and devastated. He also invaded Angoching Hills on the bank of Chindwin River.[8] Thus, Khagemba consolidated his position in the Kabaw valley.

The Shan principalities were subdued by frequent military attacks of Manipur. But in the last year of Khagemba's reign, the Burmese under Toongoo dynasty tried to establish their control over the Shan states in upper Burma. So Khagemba came into conflict with the Burmese. The Burmese (Ava) invasions in 1648 and 1651 in the eastern frontier in the Kabaw valley were repulsed. Prince Mungyamba defeated Burmese in the first invasion and captured two prisoners. Some years later, the Avas invaded again but were defeated but some nobles were killed. It occurred in the year 1651.[9]

Khunjaoba (1652-1666), son of Khagemba attacked Samjok twice. In the attack, he recovered cattle, buffaloes and elephants as spoils. He raided over the Chakpa Angoching village near the Chindwin River. He also defeated the Avas and captured their Chief Choupha Mangtra. In 1657, he completely destroyed Mangsataba (a tiny principality in the Kabaw valley).[10] Like his predecessors, Paikhomba (1666-1697) also invaded Samjok in 1692 and captured fifteen prisoners; and seized a number of shields, swords, guns and houses. In 1693, an expedition was sent to gather paddy from Samjok, which was kept at the royal granary. The Burmese attempted to invade Manipur across the Chindwin River in 1692. The invading Burmese were driven out.[11]

The reason of frequent invasion of Kabaw valley by the kings of Manipur is despite military control over them, there was no administrative integration of Kabaw valley with mainland of Manipur. And the Shan people could not be completely won over because of severe administration of Manipur on the conquered Shans. The social relationship between the Kabaws and Manipuris was not strong because the Shans followed Buddhism. Simultaneously, the Shan connection with Shan bigger states was very strong because of socio-economic and cultural contacts. As a result, the Manipuri kings established a very strict political control over Kabaw valley. It is in the light of this not so friendly situation that Kabaw valley was controlled for the access to and control of the natural resources in that. And it also provided a safety to the kingdom of Manipur from the Burmese invasion.

In the year 1702, envoys were sent by the king of Toongoo dynasty of Ava for asking hand of a Manipuri princess. Charairongba, the king of Manipur gave his daughter Chakpa Makhao Ngambi in marriage to the king of Ava. But this marriage ran sour and created military and diplomatic problems between the two countries.[12] The princess was ill-treated at the court of Ava. One death wish of Charairongba was to invade Burma and take revenge of the ill-treatment of his sister. This instruction was given to Garibniwaz. Garibniwaz was waiting for the opportunity to defeat the Burmese. So he strengthened his position in the eastern hills and in the Kabaw valley.[13]

A new era began with the succession of Garibniwaz (1709-1748) at the throne of Kangla in 1709. Garibniwaz was one of the greatest kings of Manipur had ever produced. He played an important role in shaping the future of Manipur. He led a number of military expeditions to Burma and devastated the country and gave a death blow to the Toongoo dynasty of Burma, Kabaw valley was in possession of Manipur. Garibniwaz fought wars with Burma over three decades (1717-1748). In 1718, the Burmese crossed the Chindwin River and penetrated into Manipur. Garibniwaz along with his forces fought against the Burmese at Wangjing village. The Manipuri forces had cavalry which equipped with *arambai* (a deadly sling). The Burmese were defeated at the battle of Wangjing. In the battle, 157 Burmese soldiers were captured as prisoners.[14] The Burmese invasion of Manipur after crossing Chindwin was possible because of weak control over Kabaw valley. In 1723, the Burmese invaded Manipur. A ferocious battle between the Burmese and Manipur was fought on the bank of Lokchaoyi stream at Wangjing. The Manipuri forces had 4000 tribal soldiers, 5000 Meitei soldiers and 300 well trained cavalry. The Burmese war elephants proved to be alarming for the Manipuri cavalry. At one phase, the Burmese had the upper hand. Finally, Manipuri cavalry and infantry broke through the northern side of the Burmese forces. The cavalry brought chaos on the Burmese foot soldiers and this resulted flee of the Burmese soldiers from the battlefield. This retreat put the Burmese forces in complete disorder and they were defeated.[15] In 1724, Garibniwaz made an invasion of Burma, while repulsing a

Burmese force which made incursion in the eastern frontier across the Chindwin River. And in the year 1725, the Burmese invaded Manipur again with 30,000 strong army but they were defeated. In 1735, Garibniwaz made successful invasion in Burma. He crossed the Chindwin River and attacked Mayedoo on the bank of the Moo River within Shwebo province of the Kingdom. The Manipuri soldiers destroyed the whole town or village of Mayedoo. The king captured 6 war elephants, 100 horses and 1000 muskets. He also occupied the Soipret pagoda. These raids were conducted in 1736. There was a counter invasion of Manipur by the Burmese in 1737. But the Manipuri forces killed two-third of the Burmese including their drunken general.[16]

In 1738, Garibniwaz along with his strong force of 20,000 including cavalry invaded Burma and this was the most successful invasion of Burma by Garibniwaz. King Mahadhamma Yaza Dipati of Burma and his strong force consisting of 85,000 infantry, 3000 horses and 30 elephants were ready to check the invasion. In the battle, the Burmese forces were defeated and Manipuri forces sacked Sagaing, set ablaze houses and monasteries; and planted the standard of Manipur. Samjok was the biggest, most powerful and a great source of revenue in Kabaw valley so Garibniwaz invaded Samjok seven times.[17] During his reign, the boundary of Manipur extended far beyond Ningthe on three directions of north, east and south as well.[18] "Manipur in olden days possessed a famous breed of ponies, larger and better bred that come from the Shan states. On these ponies were mounted the formidable cavalry that in the last century made Manipur feared throughout upper Burma, and enable her rulers on more than one occasion, to carry their victories arms within sight of Ava, where their Raja Pamheiba erected a stone pillar to commemorate the event."[19] In the words of G.E. Harvey, "In 1738 when the king garrisoned these two places (Myedu and Tabayi) and Mingin in the upper Chindwin district against them, they (Manipuris) simply cantred past, camped at Thalunbyu west of Sagaing, burnt every house and monastery up to the walls of Ava, and stormed the stockade built to protect the Kaunghmudaw pagoda slaughtering the garrison like cattle in a pen and killing the commandant, a minister of the Hluttaw council; the old door leaves of the pagoda's eastern gateway show a gash made by the sword of Garibniwaz when he was forcing an entrance."[20]

The third Burmese empire at Ava was set-up by Alaungpaya of

Konbaung Dynasty (1752-1886) after driving away the rebellious Mons. Alaungpaya brought a change in the political situation in Burma and in its neighbouring countries like Manipur. After the death of Garibniwaz, Manipur also witnessed a series of chaos. The sons of the great king intrigued for power and this resulted in bloodshed and series of fratricidal killings. On the other hand, Alaungpaya, decided to drive away the English traders from Burma and defeat Manipur as revenge for earlier aggressions.[21] In this situation, the Burmese forces invaded Manipur time and again and devastated the country. In the invasion, the Burmese used advance weapons and firearms.

Bhagyachandra (1762-99) made a marathon fight to liberate his motherland, Manipur from the Burmese yoke. In 1813, Marjit Singh became king of Manipur with the help of Burmese and as a price Kabaw Valley was ceded to Burma. He also promised to renounce all the claims over the Kabaw valley.[22] Thus, Kabaw valley was in the possession of Burma from 1813 to 1825, for twelve years. But before 1813, except for some time during Bhagyachandra's flight to Assam, Kabaw valley was always in the possession of Manipur. Pemberton has stated that "The territories of Munepoor have fluctuated at various times with the fortunes of their princes, frequently extending for three or four days' journey east beyond the Ningthee or Khyendwen River, and west to the plains of Cachar."[23]

In 1819, Bagyidaw ascended the throne of Ava. Soon quarrel started between the Burmese king (1819-1838) and Marjit Singh (1814-1819) over the latter's negative response to attend the coronation of the former and the cutting of timber by Manipur in the Kabaw Valley. Marjit Singh thought that the request to extend help was mainly due to friendship relationship. So, there was no question of subordination. Under this notion, Marjit Singh did not go to attend the coronation ceremony. As a result, the Burmese forces invaded and devastated Manipur. This is commonly known as Seven Years Devastation (1819-1826), a dark period in the history of Manipur. Not only Manipur, the Burmese forces also occupied Assam. The aggressive action of the Burmese led to the outbreak of the First Anglo-Burmese War (1824-26). Gambhir Singh with the help of British raised a group of patriotic soldiers called Manipur Levy which was put under the command of Captain Grant and Lt. Pemberton. Gambhir Singh with his Levy drove out the Burmese from Manipur, up to the western bank of Ningthe[24] and re-conquered the Kabaw valley in 1826.[25] James Johnstone wrote, Ghambir Singh along with his Levy under Grant and Pemberton in a short time not only was Manipur cleared, but the enemy driven out of the Kabaw valley. Later on he was recognized as Raja of Manipur and the Kabaw valley was included within his territory.[26] It is also stated that during the war Manipur forces captured Khambat, Wokhong, Tummu, Mungsa, Samjok comprising the whole extent of the Kabaw valley from Khambat and Kale. The first Anglo-Burmese war came to an end with the treaty of Yandaboo in 1826 and Ghambir Singh became the Raja of Manipur. However, the treaty of 1826 did not mention anything about the Kabaw valley which became a bone of contention between the two countries. This led to the loss of the Kabaw valley.

Conclusion

After observing the above facts, we can conclude that there was frequent political contact of Manipur and Burma from the middle of the 15th century on the subject of Kabaw valley. Another factor of contact is the matrimonial alliance which also affected their relationship. It is a fact that Kabaw valley was under the political control of Manipur till 1826 except for some periodical occupation by Burmese now and then, which the Manipuri King devastated by war and established the legitimate right and at the same time right by conquest. In the opinion of a colonial official, Manipur held a considerable territory east of the Chindwin River in subjection, at other times only the Kabaw valley, a strip of land, inhabited by Shans, and lying between Manipur proper and the Chindwin. For the greater part of 18th century, the Kabaw valley unquestionably belonged to Manipur, and it was never in any sense a Burmese province, a feudatory of great Shan kingdom of Pong.[27]

NOTES

1. Gangmumei Kabui, *History of Manipur*, Vol. 1, New Delhi, 1991, p. 1.
2. R. Brown, *Statistical Account of Manipur*, Mittal Publications, New Delhi, 2001, p. 59.
3. Ibungohal Singh & N. Khelchandra Singh (Ed.) (1989). *Cheitharol Kumbaba*, Imphal, 1989, p. 19. Also see Oinam Bhogeswar Singh (Ed.), *Ningthourol Lambuba* (up to Pamheiba), Imphal, 1966, p. 219.

4. Ibungohal Singh & N. Khelchandra Singh, *op. cit.*, pp. 19-20. Also see B.C Allen, *Gazetteer of Naga Hills and Manipur*, Mittal Publications, New Delhi, 2002, p. 13.
5. R.B. Pemberton, *Report on the Eastern Frontier of British India*, Calcutta, 1935, pp. 117-118.
6. Gangmumei Kabui, *History of Manipur*, Vol. 1, New Delhi, 1991, pp. 210-211.
7. Ibungohal Singh & N. Khelchandra Singh, *op. cit.*, pp. 29-31. Also see Kabui, *op. cit.*, 1991, p. 205.
8. Ibungohal Singh & N. Khelchandra Singh, *op. cit.*, pp. 37-41. Kabui, *op. cit.*, 1991, pp. 211-13. & R.K. Jhalajit Singh, *A Short History of Manipur*, Imphal, 1965, p. 102.
9. Kabui, *op. cit.*, 1991, p. 213.
10. Jhalajit, *op. cit.*, 1965, pp. 108-109.
11. *Ibid.*, 112.
12. Kabui, *op. cit.*, 1991, p. 236.
13. *Ibid.*, p. 244.
14. *Ibid.*, p. 245.
15. *Ibid.*, pp. 245-246.
16. *Ibid.*, p. 247.
17. *Ibid.*, pp. 243-248; J. Roy, *History of Manipur*, Imphal, 1958, p. 36.
18. Dr. Suresh, 'Endless Kabaw Valley', in *Huiyen Lanpao*, Vernacular Manipuri daily, 2011.
19. Major-general Sir James Johnstone, *Manipur and Naga Hills*, Cultural Publishing House, Delhi, 1983, p. 81.
20. G.E. Harvey, *A History of Burma*, London, 1926, p. 208.
21. Kabui, *op. cit.*, 1991, p. 266.
22. *Ibid.*, p. 25; Naorem Sanajaoba (Ed.), *Manipur Treaties and Documents 1110-1971*, Vol. 1, New Delhi, 1993, p. 43.
23. R.B. Pemberton, *op. cit.*, 1935, p. 22.
24. Sanajaoba, *op. cit.*, 1993, p. 46.
25. R.K. Sanahal Singh, 'Kabaw Valley: A Retrospect', in *The Backbone*, Vol. 1.
26. Major-general Sir James Johnstone, *Manipur and Naga Hills*, Cultural Publishing House, Delhi, 1983, pp. 85-86.
27. Johnstone, *op. cit.*, 1983, p. 81.

OTHER WORKS CONSULTED

Acharyya, N.N., *Manipur in the Eyes of Foreign Historians*, N. Sanajaoba (Ed.) *Manipur: Past and Present*, Vol.1, Mittal Publications, New Delhi, 1988.

Kabui, Gangmumei, *The Lost Territory of Manipur: Cession of Kabaw Valley*, N. Sanajaoba (Ed.) *Manipur: Past and Present*, Vol. 1, Mittal Publications, New Delhi, 1988.

10
The Meitei (Kathe`) Crown Service Groups in Myanmar from the Earliest Times to the End of Monarchical Rule

Nwe Ni Hlaing

Introduction

According to the studied guess of scholar, Myanmar ethnic races who belonged to the Tibeto-Myanmar family had settled at their native place of the upper reaches of Yellow River and T'aung valley in China since 3,000 years ago.[1] When S'hang Dynasty was established in 16th century B.C., Tibeto-Myanmar lived side-by-side with the S'hang Chinese. In 14th century B.C., Tibet Myanmar moved to Kansu and the north-west of Sichuan provinces. The Tibeto-Myanamr [*sic*] races were known by the Chinese as Chi'en. Between 15th and 12th centuries B.C. Chi'en settled in Yangtse valley and Sichuan, the western provinces of China and some lived in the Yunnan province.[2] At the beginning of the Christian Era, the people belonged to Tibeto-Myanmar family were attributed to move into present day Myanmar.[3] They were divided into three groups, namely those who entered into the Eastern Tibet, those who penetrated into Bramaputtra valley and Assam and those who entered into Myanmar. One group after another moved into Myanmar in different times. The earliest groups entered into Myanmar were Bama and ethnic races related with early Bama, Thet, Chin, Kachin and Naga.[4]

Bama and early Bama arrived Myanmar *via* Mekhong, Thanlwin and Mekha River routes and some entered Myanmar *via* Yon-chiang in Yunnan Province.[5] Meanwhile, Lo Lo entered Myanmar *via* Mekha River route. Thet, Chin, Kachin and Naga tribes entered from the north-west region of Myanmar. Actually, the advent of Thets was earlier than Chins and Kachins and they spread to upper reaches of Chindwin River and Manipur.[6]

Chin, Kachin and Naga firstly moved to Eastern Tibet *via* China from there entered into Myanmar through the Malikha and Chindwin Valleys via north-western passes of Myanmar.[7] They settled in Hukong Vally[8] [*sic*]. During the fourth century A.D., Chins were supposed to enter Hukong valley to settle along with Kachin and Naga.[9] Later, they were enforced to move to the upper reaches of Chindwin River by Kachins. Some scholars attributed that Meitei (Kathe`) races who belong to the same family of Chins, once they lived with Chin and Kachin in Hukong valley and along the Chindwin valley.[10] The myths and oral history of Meitei reveal that they descended from the same ancestors and lived in the same region.[11] At the beginning, Meitei (Kathe`) lived along side with Chins in Chindwin valley and some Meiteis (Kathe`) who settled in Somara Hill and Ireel Valley of Manipur enabled to establish a dynasty, however some Meiteis (Kathe`) continued to live with Chin races in Myanmar. Between 4th and 15 centuries A.D, Chin races settled in a wide area stretching from Chindwin valley to Manipur valley.[12] Later they spread to Sagaing, Mague, Pokokku, Monywa and Ayeyawaddy valley.[13]

Races

Chins belong to the Tibeto-Myanmar speaking family and sub-family is the Assam-Bama group—one of the major races of Assam-Bama. Chins belong to the same family of Bama, Naga, Kachin, Thet, and Lo Lo.[14] Kuki Chin race was sub-divided into 53 Chin tribes and Meitei (Kathe`) was comprised as one of the Kuki Chin Tribes.[15] Linguistically, some words of Meitei are closely related with those of Chin, Kachin and Myanmar.[16] Therefore, they lived in the same place, descended from a same family and shared common culture.

Myanmar called Meitei as Kathe` which was derived from Shan word "Cassay"[17] and the land where Kathe` settled was known as Myinde`.[18] It is attributed that the name Myin-te` was called after the name of its inhabitants Meitei.

List of Photos

Kathè Inscription in Sein kone quarter at Sagaing

Kathè Temple in Mindè Ekin quarter at Mandalay

King Nongpok Nningthou and Ema PanThoibi in Dawnabwa quarter at Mandalay

Kathè Temple in Moza at Sagaing

Meitei Kathè Temple at Letthama Village

Nat Shrine in Yekyi Pauk Village

Kathè House at Datarle Village

Kathe` Horseman in 1855 (Dr. Tin Maung Kyi Collection)

Kathe` Boatment (Dr. Tin Maung Kyi Collection)

Meitei (Kathe`) State under Myanmar King's Rule

During pre-colonial period, Manipur had been one of the vassal state of Myanmar kings, Myanmar chronicles mention that Myin-te` khayaing—district is comprised in the territories of Myanmar during first Tagaung Kingdom. Following evidence reads:

> As Kathe` also being Chin since the reign of King Kan Yaza Gyi who resided at Kalay Yazagyo and Myin-te` khayaing had been put under his rule, Mawyingyi Bon Za Noe shall rule Kathe`.....[19]

Above mentioned statement indicate that Kathe` races were termed as Chin races and the state they inhabited was called Myin-te` Pyi. The territorial boundary of Kathe` state was Po-khaung mountain range and the land located to the west of Po-khaung range was knoun [*sic*] as Myin-te` khayaing. Jambudipa Oksaung Kyan mention the four boundaries of Kathe` state thus:

> In the east there is Chindwin River,
> In the south is the land of Thaung-thut and the land on the other side,
> In the west is the North Pin-le` (Thein) North village and Tha-kho (Nga) ywa, and
> In the north-east Hmaing wei-myei region and the land on the other side. [20]

The territorial boundaries[21] during Bagan period mention the western boundary of Myanmar is as far west as Padeik Khaya-kala (region) and accordingly indicate that Assam and Manipur had comprised in the territories of Myanmar. During the Hanthawaddy Hsinbyushin of Taungoo period, the north-western boundary of the empire of Myanmar covered the whole state of Kathe`. According to the Shwezigon Pagoda Inscription of Shwethahlaung Hill, it is known that Kathe` state comprised in Thunaparanta Taing—the north-west region of Myanmar to the west of Ayeyarwaddy River in King Minye` Kyawhtin of Inwa. Similarly, Bonsan Tulut Monastery Inscription of Shwebo, dated 1765 A.D., mentions that Manipur comprised one of the 16 taings—divisions of Myanmar in Konbaung period. These evidences indicate that Meitei (Kathe`) had been one of the vassal states of Myanmar throughout monarchical rule. However, in the negotiation of Yandaboo Treaty after the first Anglo-Myanmar war (1824-26), the kingdom of Myanmar had to relinquish Taninthayi, Rakhine and Manipur. From that time onwards, Manipur became a state of British-India. In addition, the Article 11 of Yandaboo Treaty prescribed that all Assamese and Manipuris under Myanmar king shall be surrendered to the British Government to deport to the Manipur [*sic*]. However Myanmar government did not comply the British demand and informed that the Assamese and Manipuris who became the subjects of Myanmar government voluntarily settled in Myanmar and accordingly it is impossible to surrender them to the British Government.[22] By this way, Manipuris and Assamese and their descendants settled in Myanmar up to present day.

Relations between Meitei (Kathe`) and Myanmar under Monarchical Rule

Throughout history Kathe`-Myanmar relations took the form of both hostile and friendly relations. The frequent outbreak of war prevailed between Myanmar and Manipur from Taungoo to the first half of Konbaung dynasties. King Bayinnaung (1551-1581) of Taungoo Dynasty, King Thalun (1628-1648), King Minye` Kyawhtin (1673-1698), King Taninganwe (1714-1733), King Maha Dhammar-rajadipati (1733-1752) of Nyaung-yan Dynasty, King Alaungmintaya (1752-60), Myeidu Min (1763-1776), Badon Min (1782-1819) and Sagaing Min (1819-1826) of Konbaung Dynasty waged the war against Manipur. As the Myanmar kings launched expeditions and occupied Manipur, Kathe` rajas occasionally over-ran Myanmar territories. It is interesting to note that some weak Manipuri rajahs established friendly relations with the kingdom of Myanmar through the matrimonial alliance, i.e they submitted their daughters to the kings of Myanmar to establish amicable relations. Anyway, the Kathe` communities had emerged in Myanmar through the conscription of war captives by the successive kings. Kathe` people and their descendants were organized into miscellaneous crown service groups and were allotted lands for residence and subsistence.

After the occupation of Manipur by King Alaungmintaya, over 2000 Kathe` horsemen were organized into king's cavalry groups.

They were offered gold, silver, clothings and other provisions and lands for residence and subsistence.[23] During Myeidu Min's reign, Kathe` royalties were allowed to settle in the south-east corner of Innwa.[24] The Kathe` people, totalled over 40,000, had continue to arrive in the reigns of King Badon and Sagain Min. They were populated in Sein-don, Hsin-tat, Bye`-ta-yaw, Mo-za and Linzin in Sagaing, Nwa-no-daw-su, Leik-hsan-khun, Shwe-kyet-yet, Shwe-khe`, Nge-toe, Hsin-daing (East), Hsin-daing (West), Da-da-le, Le-thama-su, Pagyi-su, Ponna-su, Myit-tu, Yei-gyi-pauk, in Amarapura and Ma-de`E-kin in Mandalay.[25] Now-a-days, Meitei (Kathe`) and their descendants settled in Mo-za-su in Sagaing Township, Ponna-zu, Pa-gyi-zu, Kokko-zu, Ta-da-le, Yei-kyi-pauk, let-tha-ma-su in Amarapura Township and Ma-de`Ekin, Thamidaw-zay Quarter, Pe-hlaw-gyaung, Hnin-si-gyan, Ku-gyi-kon and Po-pe-kon Quarters in Mandalay[26] (See photo). It is interesting to note that their ancestores were not war captives [*sic*]. They voluntarily came to Myanmar to serve the Myanmar kings. It is attributed that some of them entered Myanmar in pursuit of good opportunities for their living. Of the Kathe` who settled in Myanmar as non-war captives, Kathe` Brahmans (Ponnas) were the most outstanding class and they served the king as the court astrologers, advisers and royal prohita supervisor who arranged the royal coronations[27] etc. Any way, it is suggested that Kathe` mingled each other in accordance with their races, culture and social norms.

Crown Service Groups in Myanmar

As mentioned above, varieties of Kathe` comprising royalties, Kathe` Ponnas, crown servicemen, commoners and bondsmen settled in Myanmar. The advent of Kathe` royalties was partly created by the diplomatic relations. When king Bayinnaung defeated Manipur in A.D. 1558, Kathe` Rajah submitted his daughter to the king for peace.[28] From that time onward, Kathe` royalties settled in Taungoo. During the reign of King Sa-ne in 1732, Maripuri Rajah submitted his daughter Hnin Long Khang. She was allowed to enjoy the taxes from Popa Town as Popa Myoza. She had two sons Maung Phyu and Maung Min. During the reign of Maha Dhamarajadipati in 1749 Kathe` Rajah again submitted his daughter to the king. King Dhamarajadipati conferred her the title of Maha Devi and her son Khura Letpa, the title of Min ye`

Sithu. When Inwa was shocked by the Mons, Princess Popa and Maha Devi were deported to Hanthawaddy (Bago) along with the deposed king. Suprisingly, Maha Devi was installed as a queen by the Mon King and was conferred the title of Thirizeya Mingala devi. After the conquest of Hanthawaddy by Alaungmintaya, she was submitted to the King Alaungmintaya.[29]

During Myeidu Min's reign, Moriang Rajah submitted his daughter Ton-taw wadi as bride. She was allotted Za-Yun Town in Badon reign. Other sons and daughters of Manipuri Raja were also allotted towns as fiefs as follows:

Son	Maung Shwe Pyei	...:..	Kalay Town
Daughter	Shin Nan Yit	......	Za-yun Tow
Younger son	Maung Shwe Ko	......	Kalay Town
Daughter	Min Shwe Gon	......	Htan-da-bin[30] Town

All of the sons and daughters of Manipuri Rajah settled in Amarapura. In 1807 Kathe` Rajah and his brother submitted their daughter and sister to king Badon respectively.[31] They were allowed to enjoy equal privileges of other queens and royal siblings and to live in the palace. ven. Shan-ga-lay-kyun Sayadaw and Nun Me Kin were renowned descendant of Kathe` royalty.

In addition to the Kathe` royalties and servicemen, Kathe` Ponna served the successive kings in accordance with their qualification. Here it is need to explain the meaning of Ponna. The word Ponna derived from Hindu word "varna" which means a person who observed the noble precept. In other words, it means saintly person, or priest. Ponna is a derivative word of Bonna which was used by the Mons in Bagan period and it did not refer to a certain race.[32] For instance, the word Kathe` Ponna means a Kathe` who followed the noble precept. Likewise, Rakhine Ponna, Myanmar Ponna, Bayanathi Ponna, Thai Ponna mention that the races who practised the noble precept.

Ponnas were categorized in accordance with the duties such as Kathe` Shippa Ponnas because each eight Ponnas had to attend the royal ceremonies at the left and right places of the King. The king allowed this status only to Kathe` Brahmin. An order of Badon Min, dated 21 January, 1818, read thus:

Shitpa Ponna (Eight member Brahmin) shall not do Shit Hko-obeisance, to members of Royalty and Ministry.[33]

Shitpa Ponna who arranged royal coronation ceremonies

were allowed to use insignia of rank such as decorated head dress, golden shoulder sash etc. Like shippa Ponna, Ko-pa ponna were important for their duties of propition of nine planets in Brahmanical concept. The king selected some Shippa and Ko-pa Ponna to appoint royal purohita or scholar. On 17 October, 1839, Thiri Thattama Maha Yazaguru was appointed as scholar.[34] On 5 May, 1842, Ponna Scholars were assigned the duty of compiling calendar.[35] It is attributed that as the calendar was essential for any religious, economic and social performances, the duty of Ponna scholar was more important than that of other officials. In some cases, the king assigned ponna scholars to other duties on the ground of their physical and mental prowess. When Rakhine frontier problem broke out between Myanmar and British-India, Ponna scholars accompanied Zeya Kyawhtin, official in-change of Myanmar delegation, to discuss with the British.[36] They also served the duty of diplomacy when the Rajah of Vesali submitted his daughter.[37] During the First Anglo-Myanmar war, some Ponna scholars were attached to the army of Maha Bundula to investigate the position of British forces in Nepan (Saingpa), Pyinsala, Sheindra and Laknow.[38] When the Second Anglo-Myanmar war broke out, Ponnas were attached to the armies to arrange occult science to uplift the morale of the servicemen.[39] In addition the king appointed Pyin-nya-shi na-yi-dawhmu Ponna scholar who supervised the watch tower to calculate the Myanmar stand and time. In order to deal with the affairs of Ponnas, the king usually appointed Ponna-wun-official in-charge of Ponnas and Ponna Sa-Yei-Clerk of Ponnas in addition, the evidence mention the appointment of Ponna Thatha-na-paing supreme head of Ponna ecclesia order. In 1805, king Badon appointed Ponna Atitra U Hla as Ponna Thatha-na-paing.[40] During king Mindon's reign, Ponna wun and Ponna scholars were offered insignia of rank including golden shoulder sash of twelve strings jewelled ear-plug, head dress etc. like the Myanmar court officials they were conferred the titles.[41]

During king Mindon's reign, Nga Ba Gyi, grandson of Ponna Wun, was despatched as state scholar with 15 other candidates. In 1820 Kathe` a-mat Nga Phyu was conferred the title of Zeya Wattana Kyawhtin to administer Manipur as town govermor[42] [*sic*]. Some Kathe`scholars were installed as ywa-za—fief holder of certain village in Sagaing Min's reign. For instance kathe` scholar Zaya Brahma was allotted Nga Le Ngauk Village, Yaza Parohita Brahma was allotted Hladawgyi Five villages and Wuntha Brahma was allotted Kyei Hsin Inn village respectively.[43] An order, dated 20 July, 1787, mentions the name Kyatpyin Kathe` Myothugyi Nga Shun and it is suggested that Nga Shun was installed to the office of myothugyi— town officer.[44] During King Mindon's reign Maha Thiri Pandita Dhammarajaguru was allotted Son-myo as fief,[45] by this way the king installed Kathe` to the rank of Myothugyi, Myowun, Myoza and Ywaza [*sic*].

The king also provided lands and paddy for their subsistence. Shippa Ponnas and Koe-pa Ponnas were allotted 1201 pes of paddy lands located in Thinpankon below Aungpinle lake by King Mindon.[46] In 1841, a royal order was passed to provide paddy for some Shippa and Koe-pa Ponnas.[47] They were also exempted from paying taxes whenever they sold their houses or lands in Ponna village.[48] In 1861, there were about 850 Ponans serving in the place and total population of Ponnas was about 2,000.[49] All of them were allotted lands and paddy as the monthly provision. In addition they enjoyed the privilege of the insignia of ranks and titles which were not lesser than that of Myanmar court officials. It is interesting to note that most of the Ponnas came to Myanmar to serve the kings and some came for missionary works and a few came to learn astronomy and fortune telling.

Through monarchical period, the crown servicemen played a vital role in the administration and warfare. Some were renowned for their economic performances. The able kings in warfare employed war captives from neighboring countries to extend their influence. The captive servicemen made their utmost efforts in the formation of army and administration.

Meiteis (Kathe`) were also organized into miscellaneous groups. They were mostly seem in the su-gyi—the group important for military and non-military servicemen such as daing—shield-bearers, lamaings—crown cultivators and win-koyan—palace guards and royal bodyguard. Some were recruited into the group of Hsin-daw-thi elephanteers. An order of king Badon, 1784 A.D., mentions as follows:

> Nga San Hmat, son of Kathe` Rajah altogether nineteen men were organized Nga San Hmat Thwei-thauk groups. The status of this group shall equal to the Banya Kyandaw Thwei-thauk of Chiengmai.[50]

Above metioned elephant group led by thwei-thauk Nga San Hmat was recruited by the King Hsinbyushin when he conquered Manipur. Nga San Hmat and his followers were believed to be the Kinsmen of Kathe` Rajah. He and his family members were recorded in the list of golden treasury. In 1164 M.E (1802 A.D.), Thwei-thank Ngapi Nganpa, age 39 and Thursday born, was examined and answered thus:

> He was brought to Myanmar since King Hsinbyushin's reign and was organized in Hsin-taw-ti Thwe-thauk group by Myin-wun and Myin sayei in 1151 ME (1784 A.D.)..... Hsin-si Thiri Kaw Pi Nga-pa shall enjoy insignia of ranks comprising grown, head dress etc.[51]

In 1808, the Kathe` horsemen were transferred to the group of elephanteers. The thwei-thauks of newly recruited honsemen were the natives of Shwe Kyu Pauk and Da-Ze Kon villages.[52] The list submitted by Hsin Sachi (cleark of elephanteers) Gazan Ye` Thu in 1170 ME (1808 A.D.) mentions the population of elephanteers as follows:

List of Elephanteers, 1170 ME (1808 A.D.)

Elephanteers	*1145 ME (1783 A.D.)*	*1167 ME (1805 A.D.)*	*Location of Groups*
Hti-paung-kha	31	12	Royal Capital
Mad`e	73	12	Royal Capital
Taung-Kyi	42	8	Royal Capital
Suka (Yodaya)	128	9	Royal Capital
Shwe Lun Zu Quarter	68	96	Royal Capital
Narakan (groups)	14	3	Royal Capital
Hisngyon (Yayi Group)	32	11	Royal Capital
Hsingyon (Awa)	18	17	Royal Capital
Yayi (Yodaya)	31	18	Royal Capital
Hsin-daing Kathe`	162	100	Royal Capital
Hsin-daing Akkabat	42	24	Royal Capital
Hsin-daing Shan pike (Added)	18	10	Royal Capital
Hsin gon (Added to collect Yodaya elephant fodder)	×		
Total	671	341	
Sagaing	39	1	Sagaing
Purchased Kathe` (Mingun)	-	15	Sagaing
Total	39	16	

Source: Parabaik MS, No.pu-0004, Ludu Library, Mandalay Collection.

All of the above mentioned elephanteers, comprising Kathe` servicemen, settled in Inwa and Sagaing. In 1182 ME (1825

A.D.), Mani Yaza and thwei-thauks from Shwe Kyu Pauk, Hsin-swe-put village, Mauk-kaing, Hsi-nan, Htan Thon Gwa, Yin-pon, Taungthaman, Tein-pya, Bon-Oe, Hsat-kon, Lin-sin-kon, Hlwa-su and Yadanagu were added to the Manipuri Elephant groups. In 1182 ME (1820 A.D.), Manipuri Raja and his kinsmen taken from Maknipur [*sic*] were organized into elephant groups. Following list reads:

Family of Kathe` Raja who were organized into Elephant group

Title conferred in 1182 M.E. (1820 A.D.)	*Title conferred in 1199 M.E. (1837 A.D.)*	*Male*	*Female*	*Town*	*Remark*
Yaza Thinkhaya	U-dein Teza Nawrahta	3	3		
Kammathein Sitha	U-dein Zeya Nawrahta	3	4	Bon-Oe	
	Nawarth U-dein Kyaw	2	1		
Nga Han Tha	La Pon Kaw	2	2		Two monk
Saka-tata	Paw la-te	3	1	Bon-Oe	
Kasan Nawta	Nga Lo-paw	1	1	Mi-pa-chei	
Thuye` Kamatha	Thiha U-dein Nawahta	1	2	Bon-Oe	
Zeya Yawtha	Sandayaw	4	2	Bon-Oe	One Novice
Nga san Hla`s son	Nga la Ba	3	2		
Nga shwe pwint's son	Thuya Udein Nawrahta	1	2	Bon-Oe	
Nga San Taw's son	Tonpa	1	1	Lebo	
Nga Kya's son	Su Rupa	4	2	Bon-Oe	
Maung Tha Yaza Thiha's son	Hton Kanaung Mani Udein Nawrahta	3 4	3 3	Shwe Kya Pauk/ Sa daw Quarter Bon-Oe	
Nga Han Pon's son	Udein Teza Nawrahta	4	2	Bon-Oe	
Nga shwe Min's son	Nga Kya Yoe	1	2	Shwe Kyu Pauk	

Source: Sayin, 2003 (c), pp. 102-112.

Similarly in 1199 ME (1837 A.D.), Nemyo Mani Yazashein and his family were organized into Mani Yaza Shein thwei-thauk group. Some servicemen of above mentioned elephanteers were conferred titles. Wundauk—assistant commandant of elephant group was conferred the title of Nemyo, hsin-sa-chi—clerk of elephant group and hsin-san-thugyi were conferred the title of Nawrahta. Those who obtained the title of Nemyo were offered two red umbrella and one red velvet trouser as insignia of rank.[53] Those who obtained the title of Nawrahta were offered one red umbrella, one gold sword and one velvet trouser in 1879. They were also allotted lands for subsistence. Following figures read as:

List of cultivated lands Allotted to the 25 Manipure Thwei-thauks in Elephant Group

Village	*Pe*	*Seik*
Chan Thamagyi-ywa	85	
Pyipa	15	
Chin-ywa	35	
Non-Nge	10	
Mekkhaya	10	
Sabathein	7	2
Taing Malan	44	
Myinthi	6	2
Ma The`	47	
Pan Sun	5	
Thin Ti (Two Villages)	91	
Thi khaung	31	2
Naung Saing	20	3
Khan Ti	69	2
Ti Taw	27	2
Nga Pyet	38	
Chan Thama-nge	27	
Total	**572**	**13**

Source: Sayin 2003 (c), 114.

In 1837 during King Thiyawaddy's reign, the king allotted 20 pes each for thwei-thauk gyi, 10 pes for mounted servicemen and 25 pes for servicemen of Manipuri elephanteers. In his reign, the list of irrigated lands allotted to Kathe` servicemen can be seen as follows:

List of Irrigated lands Allotted to the Kathe` Servicemen

	Additionally Allotted Lands	*The Land already allotted*	*Weir*
1	95 pes	83 pes	Nwa-det
2	15 pes	15 pes	Nwa-det
3	6 pes 2 seiks	6 pes 2 seiks	Nwa-det
4	15 pes	15 pes	Nwa-det
5.	35 pes	35 pes	Pyaung-pya
6.	15 pes	15 pes	Pyaung-pya
Total	**181 pes**	**169 pes 2 seiks**	

Source: Sayin 2003 (c), 115.

In addition, the lands allotted to other villages were extracted to grant Meitei (kathe`). Following list reads:

List of lands extracted from other villages to grant Kathe` Servicemen

Village (Extracted)	*Transferred to (Kathe`)*	*Total*	*Added*	*Drop-off*
Thinti-ywa	95 pes	95 pes		
Saing ma-lan-ywa	15 pes	18 pes	3	
Myinthi-ywa	6 pes 2 seiks	6 pes 2 seiks	-	
Extracted from mi Hla Taik	10 pes	15 pes	-	
Chin-ywa	35 pes	42 pes	7	
Naung-saing	20 pes 3 seiks	15 pes		5 pes 2 seiks
Total	**182 pes 1 seiks**	**191 pes 2 seiks**	**10**	**5 pes 2 seiks**

Source: Sayin 2003 (c), p. 114.

Elephant played a vital role in the army formation and battle fields. They were used to mount guns and weapons as well as to use as pack animal. As Kathe` elephanteers had the privilege to enjoy the land, they became the cultivators during the peace time.

In addition to the elephant groups, Kathe` horsemen played an important role in the army formation of Myanmar and they comprised in su-gyi group. The crown servicemen were divided into sugyi, su-nu, su-gyan and su-thei. Su-gyi groups were comprised military servicemen such as thwei-tauk, cavalry, muskets, and elephanteers. After the conquest of Manipur by king Alaungmintaya, about 2000 households of Kathe`s and Akkabat were brought into Myanmar. They were organized into cavalry groups by granting lands for residence and subsistence. Horse figure was tattooed on the abdomen of the Kathe`cavalryman. During king Thibaw reign, there were 833 Kathe`s cavalrymen.[54] Actually, the advent of Kathe` horsemen prevailed since the conquest of Manipur by king Bayinnaung. The classical poems of that period known as ya-du and maw-gun record of achievements of the king written in poetic form reveal that the people during Taungoo period were familiar with "goolie game" or present day polo. It is known that the goolie game was the Manipur origins and is assumed that Kathe` horsemen had served king Bayinnaung in Taungoo period. When Sino-Myanamr [*sic*] war broke out in 1769 in Myeidumin's reign, 500 Kathe` horsemen accompanied with Myanmar armies to fight against the Chinese.[55] During the First-Anglo Myanmar War in 1824, the British defeated in the Rakhine front by the attach Kathe` horsemen.[56] In 1852, the Second Anglo Myanmar war, the Kathe` cavalry troops marched to the battle field of Han tha-waddy and Mottamma columns under the chief of Kathe` cavalry Maha-Thi-ha dhamma Yat.[57] Similarly in the Third Anglo Myanmar War, the Kathe` Akkabut cavalry troops fought against the British in Sagaing front under the leadership of Akkabut Myin-wun Min-gyi maha min Htin Ya-za.[58] The Kathe` cavalry could make considerable achievement in the battle-fields. During Konbaung period, Kathe` horsemen were populated in Kyaukse district.[59] Leik san khun village in Amarapura township had been a cantonment area of Kathe` cavalry. An order of King Badon, dated 18 October, 1808, reads thus:

> Kathe` who have now been collected together, may or may not tally with the list of Kathe` made in 1805, just register which kathe` belongs to which group and let them all the marching troops.[60]

The order mentions that Kathe` people and their descendants were organized into crown service groups and able men were recruited in the infantry groups. An order, dated 10 October 1808, mentions that:

> Kathe` Akkabut Hpwe` Yin Sayin-Original list of Kathe` Akkabut (armed men), shall be orgnized into one Myin Zu-group of Horsemen, and one Lay Zu-group of Archers;

> send Lu Daw Su—Group of Better Men, here under the charge of leaders chosen from people who hare had the Ayeik Ma Htwet.[61]

The able Kathe` and Akkabats who were not comprised in the crown service groups were selected to recruit in cavalry group and archers. Similarly, the order dated 19 October, 1808 mentions that:

> Kathe` who are originally in the services of Prince Pyay, Prince Pagan, Prince Makkhaya and Prince Mindon shall remain so but any extra men shall be added to any one of the Horse Groups, these horse men under eight leaders shall join the marching 5,000 Kathe` men under Nay Myo Gamani Thin Gyan.[62]

The role of Kathe`cavalry in Myanmar armed forces was still important in the battle-field. Customarily, the king offered pa-so—neither garments and turbans to the horsemen totaled over 700.[63] They were headed by myin-gaung-chief of horsemen and myin-zis—mounted cavalry officer. In May 1885, when Nga Lin, officer of Kathe` cavalry regiment passed away, Nga San Ya was appointed as cavalry officer and Nga Shwe Hla of Taug-tha-man cavalry group passed away, his son Nga lela Shein was selected by their followers as the Kathe` chief of Taung-tha-man cavalry group.[64] During king Thibaw's reign, a Kathe` prince was appointed as the Kathe` Myin-wun—Commandant of Kathe` horse and appointed as let-thon-daw-kaing—the trusted officials who had to keep the royal regalias such as sword, lance, musket ect. [*sic*]. He was offered the title of Minhla Minhtin Yazashein to take charge the house-hold cavalry. This evidence mention that Kathe` faithfully served in the royal palace. Minhla Minhtin Thurein was appointed as Akkabat Myin-wun.[65] The duties of myin-win were to take charge of the defence of kingdom, to systemize the conscription of security servicemen, to convey the instructions and order of the king, Hlut-taw and byei-daik to the subordinate cavalry officials. The battles participated by the cavalry groups reveal the important role and valour of horsemen.

Customarily, various Kathe` cavalrymen were marked with tattoo. On 10 October, 1808, horsemen were tattooed the emblem of brahmani duck, archers were marked with diamond shape and servicemen of su-yin—original groups were tattooed with fighting peacock.[66] During king Thiaw's reign, 825 Kathe` horsemen were allotted 13,090 kyats as salary.[67] In addition to the granting of salary, Kathe`and Akkabat horsemen were allotted cultivated lands. Following table mentions thus:

List of wet-rice and Dry Cultivated Lands Allotted to Kathe` Horsemen

Horsemen	*Original Pes*	*Flooded Area*	*Dry Cultivated Land*	*Wet-rice Land*	*Location*
Kathe` Akkabat	1545 pes 2 seiks 400 pes	50 pes 2 Seiks	200 pes	1495 pes 200 pes	Inside and Below Aungpinle Lake
Kathe`s Horse-men (to cultivate kaukyi paddy)	450 pes		330 pes	120 pes	Outside Mingala canal

Source: Sayin, 2003b, pp. 280, 283.

The cavalry regiments played an important role in the king's army due to the quick mobilization in the field.

Kathe` servicemen can be seen as the royal boatmen who settled along the Ayeyarwaddy River. Royal boatmen groups were divided into boat or war-canoe groups, barge groups and hlaw-ga—boat with high and ornamented prow and stern. A list of brick kiln servicemen, dated 22 October, 1782, reveals that the Kathe` boatmen were employed in the establishment of Amarapura new capital. The list also describes the names of the officers and fleets such as Htwet-taing-ya kathe` fleet and pyaing-daing-ya kathe` fleet under Nga Pi and Nga Naung, Baung-thein kathe` fleet under U-dein Zayathu, Bon-daw-Nainggan kathe` fleet[68] under she-win sa-chi let-ya Thikha kyaw htin, In-pyauk fleet, Tha-byu fleet and Ye`-lun-kyaw fleet. They were assigned as the brick kiln servicemen. In time of war, they had to alert for the military duty. An order of king Badon, dated 2 November, 1808, reads:

> Boatmen shall serve as fighting men under Let Yway Gyi Hmu—Chief of Big Selected Groups.[69]

In some cases, Kathe` boatmen had to serve under the princes King Badon put Kathe` boatmen under the charge of Crown Prince and Prince Kalay [*sic*]. An order dated 15 May, 1810, mentions thus:

> Kathe`, belong to Pyine Daing Ya Boat Group, are transferred to San Ywei Boat Group and they shall serve Crown Prince. Kathe`, belonging to Marabin Boat Group are transferred to Prince Kale service.[70]

The royal fleets were assigned not only military duty but transportation and fishery. They were offered lands for their subsistence. Many cultivated lands were allotted to San-Ywei Kathe` boatmen.[71] The successive kings paid great attention to the performance of boatmen. They arranged occasional regatta festival to up fifth the qualification of boatmen. The boatmen faith fully served the kings to the best of their ability.

Another important group which was comprised Kathe` servicemen was lamaing-crown cultivators. Since the reign of King Alaungmintaya in A.D. 1758, Kathe` were populated in letwe`-taw and let-ya-taw lamaings.[72] They continued to serve as lamaing under king Myedu and Badon. An order, dated 8 August, 1787, mentions thus:

> Either Manipuri or Burmese Royal Land cultivators shall never be conscripted into the fighting forces; they shall work only in the economic interest of the king.[73]

Lamaing groups were primarily categorized into Shwe-nan-yo lamaing and Aungpinle lamaing. Kathe` also served in the other small groups such as black smith, carpenter, weaver, tailoring, white-lime washers, escorts, servicemen of western court etc.[74] Some Kathe` were employed in the ruby mines in Mogok District. They were also employed in silver and lead mines.[75] An order was passed for the other chiefs not to molest the Kathe` servicemen because they being the tax-payers of palace.[76] Anyway Kathe` not only had to engage the occupations they acquainted but also follow the king's instructions to serve at the necessary groups. They even served the princes and princesses as the household servants. An order, dated 21 October, 1808, reads:

> Prince Kale, Prince Ranaung, Princess Zayun and Princess Htan Da Bin have many kathe` who had never been enlisted in any work group.[77]

As the princes and princesses belonged to the Kathe` royalty, the Kathe` household slaves came together with them as the inheritance from their parents. The other Kathe` household slaves served other princes and princesses.

Conclusion

The advent of Kathe` in Myanmar society prevailed since the Taungoo period. They served Myanmar kings in various capacities [*sic*]. They arrived into Myanmar not only as the captives but some of them moved into Myanmar since the time immemorial. Variety of Kathe` strata including royalty, servicemen, commoners, Kathe` Ponnas, and slaves came to Myanmar through ages. Successive Myanmar kings employed them in accordance with their expertise and offered titles and insignia of ranks to the Kathe` servicemen and officials. Ordinary servicemen were granted lands for their subsistence and residence. Over time, Kathe` ywa-zas, myo-zas, Kathe` Ponna-wuns, Kathe` Cavalry commandant, Kathe` scholars and royal advisers prevailed in Myanmar officialdom. Kathe` scholars served the kings with their mental prowess and Kathe` horsemen, elephanteers, boatmen faithfully served the king with their skilfulness in respective service groups including su-gyi—major armed groups and su-thei—small groups of craftsmen.

The advent of Kathe` in Myanmar society brought about the changes in Myanmar culture and way of life to some extent.

Acknowledgment—Firstly, I want to express deeply indebted to Dr. Ba Maung, Minister for Social Affairs, Hakha Town, Chin State for his valuable advice in writing this chapter. My sincere thank goes to Professor Dr. Yee Yee Win, Head of History Department, University of Mandalay for her guidance to prepare this chapter. I also gratitude to my parents, my brother and his colleagues for their encouragement.

BIBLIOGRAPHY

Primary Sources

i. *Amarapura Shwe Myo Taw ti Sartan, Pe,* Ms. No. 1791, Mandalay Library Collection.
ii. *Konbaung-khit Sayin Pa-de-tha,* (A.D. 1752-1885) (collection of Sayin) edited by Htun Yee, vol. 3, Japan.
iii. *Parabaik,* Ms. No. 0020, Lu-du Library Collection.

iv. *Parabaik,* Ms. No. 0004, Lu-du Library Collection.

v. *The Military Expedition to Panwa (Ramu), Parabaik,* MS. No. 756, National Library Collection, Yangon.

vi. *The Royal Orders of Burma (A.D. 1598-1885),* Part VI, edited and translated by Dr. Than Tun, Centre for Southeast Asia Studies Kyoto, 1987.

vii. *The Royal Orders of Burma (A.D. 1598-1885),* Part VII, edited and translated by Dr. Than Tun, Centre for Southeast Asia Studies Kyoto, 1988.

viii. *The Royal Orders of Burma (A.D. 1598-1885),* Part VIII, edited and translated by Dr. Than Tun, Centre for Southeast Asia Studies Kyoto, 1988.

ix. *The Royal Orders of Burma (A.D. 1598-1885),* Part IX, edited and translated by Dr. Than Tun, Centre for Southeast Asia Studies Kyoto, 1989.

Secondary Sources

1. Chit Thein, (1965) *Shae-haung Mon Kyauk-sa Poung Chok,* Archaeology Department.
2. Charney Michael W. (2004) *Southeast Asian Warfare,* Leiden.
3. Crawford, (1829) *Journal of an Embassy from the Governor General of India to the Court of Ava in the year 1827,* London Henry Colbun.
4. Enriquiz, C.M., (1932) *Races of Burma,* Yangon, Government Printing.
5. Grant Brown, (1960) *Burma Gazetteer, Upper Chindwin District,* Rangoon, Superintendent, Government Printing.
6. *Han tha-waddy Aye-taw Pon Maw Kun U Dan,* (2006) edited by Dr. Toe Hla, Historical Research Centre, Lowis, C.C., (1910) *The Tribes of Burma,* Rangoon, Government Printing.
7. Luce G.H., (1959) *Chin Hills-linguistic Tour, Journal of Burma Research Society,* Vol. XLII, June.
8. Luce G.H., (1968) Burma Languages, *the Journal of Burma Research Society,* Vol LI, i, June.
9. Lehman F.K., (1963) *The Structure of Chin Society,* University of JUinois Press.
10. Maung Maung Tin, (2005) *Shwe–nan–thone War-ha-ra Abi-dan* (Dictionary of Royal Terms), Yangon, Yarpyae Yarpyae Book House.
11. Maung Maung Tin U, (2004) *Konbaung-zet Maha-Yazawin Taw-gyi* (The Great Chronicle of Konbaung Dynasty), Vol. II, Yangon, Yarpyae Press.
12. Maung Maung Tin U, (2004) *Konbaung-zet Maha-Yazawin Taw-gyi* (The Great Chronicle of Konbaung Dynasty), Vol. III, Yangon, Yarpyae Press.
13. Naga Bo Theik Tin Twe, Yadana Ti-Ka Maha Yaza-win, Yangon, Ponya

Press, 1967.
14. Rosan, (1958) *Migration Route of Chin-Kuki-Mizo,* Yangon, Ywet.
15. Sein Sarpe, 2014.
16. Roy J., *History of Manipur,* Calcutta.
17. Sai Aung Tun, (1999) *A Multi-ethnic Myanmar and the Challenge,* Part I, Yangon.
18. Scott J.G. and J.P. Hardiman, (1900) *Gazetteer of Upper Burma and the Shan State,* Part I, Vol. I, She-haung Sar-pe Tu-te thi Ta-U, *Nan Hmu Nan-yar A-sin thazar,* Vol. I, Part I.
19. Shwe Kaing Tha, (1959) *A-Hnit Ta-yar Pyae Mandalay,* (Mandalay centenary) Kyi Pwa Ye Press, Than Tun Dr., (1988) *Essay on the History and Buddhism of Bruma,* Scotland: Kiscadale Publication.
20. Than Tun Dr, (2002) *Khit haung Myanmar Yazawin* (History of Ancient Myanmar), Yangon, Innwa Press, Than Tun Dr, (1968) *Ne-Hlei ya-zawin,* Yangon, Nant-thar taik press.
21. Than Tun Dr, *A-maint taw-hte-ka Thamaing, 3.*
22. Tin U, (2012) *Myanmar Min Ok-chok-pon sa-dan hnit Bodaw.*
23. *Paya-gyi ei Ya-za-that Khaw-thaw A-meint-daw tan-gyi* (Royal Edicts by King Bodawpaya), V. volume, Yangon, Seik ku-Cho Cho Press.
24. Thiri U Zana, (2001) *Loka Byu-har Kyan,* Yangon, Ministery of Culture.
25. Toe Hla Dr, (1990) *Ponna Lu-hmu A-phwe' A-Si toe-tet Pyaung Le lar Pon Thamaing,* Project Paper, History Department, Mandalay.
26. Toe Hla Dr, (1995) *Chin Twin Myit-thar Mu-Ayear,* Yangon.
27. Toe Hla Dr, (2004) *Kong baung-khit Kye-let Lu-hmu Si-pwa ba-wa,* (Socio Economic History of Rural Society) Yangon, Historical Research Centre.
28. Vumson, (1986) *Zo History,* Aizawl India published by the author Yi Sein U, (2011) *Selected Writing of U Yi Sein,* comiled by U Taw Kaung, Yangon.
29. *Zambudipa U-shaung-kyan,* (2005) edited by Dr. Than Tun, Yangon Universities Press.

NOTES AND REFERENCES

1. U Yi Sein, *Selected Writing of U Yi Sein,* compiled by U Taw Kaung, Yangon, 2011. p. 27 (Henceforth: Yi Sein, 2011).
2. Vumson, *Zo History,* Aizawl India published by the author. 1986, p. 27 (Henceforth: Vumson, 1986).
3. C.C. Lowis, *The Tribes of Burma,* Rangoon, Government Printing, 1910, p. 5.
4. C.M. Enriquiz, *Races of Burma,* Yangon, Government Printing, 1932, p. 24 (Henceforth: Enriquiz, 1932).

5. (a) Dr. Than Tun, *Essay on the History and Buddhism of Bruma,* Scotland: Kiscadale Publication, 1988, p. 3. (b) Yi Sein, 2011, p. 442.
6. G.H. Luce, *Burma Languages, the Journal of Burma Research Society,* Vol. LI, I, June 1968, pp. 33-34.
7. F.K. Lehman, *The structure of chin society,* University of JUinois Press, 1963, p. 12.
8. Rosan, *Migration Route of Chin-Kuki-Mizo,* Yangon, Ywet Sein Sarpe, 2014, p. 180. (Henceforth: Rosan, 2014).
9. G.H. Luce, *Chin Hills—Linguistic Tour, Journal of Burma Research Society,* Vol. XLII, June 1959, pp. 19-22.
10. (a) LIAN. H. Sakhong, *In Search Chin Identity,* Thailand, NIAS Press, 2003, p. 15. (b) Vomsum, 1986, p. 29.
11. Vomsum, 1986, p. 30.
12. Grant Brown, *Burma Gazetteer, Upper Chindwin District,* Rangoon, Superintendent, Government Printing, 1960, pp. 25, 28.
13. Enriquiz, 1932, p. 8.
14. Dr. Than Tun, *Khit haung Myanmar Yazawin* (History of Ancient Myanmar), Yangon, Innwa Press, 2002, p. 43.
15. (a) Vumson, 1986. (b) Sai Aung Tun, *A Multi-ethnic Myanmar and the Challenge,* Part I, Yangon, 1999, p. 31.
16. J.G. Scott and J.P. Hardiman, *Gazetteer of Upper Burma and the Shan State,* Part I, Vol. I, 1900, p. 684.
17. J. Roy, *History of Manipur,* Calcutta, 1958, p. 2.
18. *The Military Expedition to Panwa (Ramu), Parabaik,* MS. No. 756, National Library Collection, Yangon (Henceforth: *Parabaik* MS. No. 756).
19. U. Tin, *Myanmar Min Ok-chok-pon sa-dan hnit Bodaw Paya-gyi ei Ya-za-that Khaw-thaw A-meint-daw tan-gyi* (Royal Edicts by King Bodawpaya), V. volume, Yangon, Seik ku-Cho Cho Press, 2012, p. 196 (Henceforth: Tin, 2012).
20. *Zambudipa U-shaung-kyan,* edited by Dr. Than Tun, Yangon Universities Press, 2005, p. 94.
21. Tin, 2012, pp. 192, 193, 194.
22. Crawford, *Journal of an Embassy from the Governor General of India to the Court of Ava in the year 1827,* London Henry Colbun, 1829, pp. 490, 493.
23. Maung Maung Tin, *Shwe-nan-thone War-ha-ra Abi-dan* (Dictionary of Royal Terms), Yangon, Yarpyae Bookhouse, 2005, p. 267 (Henceforth: Maung Maung Tin, 2005).
24. *Parabaik* Ms. No. 756.
25. Dr. Toe Hla, *Ponna Lu-hmu A-phwe' A-Si toe-tet Pyaung Le lar Pon Thamaing,* Project Paper, History Department, Mandalay 1990, p. 5.
26. Dr. Nwe Ni Hlaing, *Myanmar Naing-ngan-tho Kathe' Lu-myo Mya Win-yauk La-chin Hnint Kathe' Luhmu A-Phwe' A-si* (The advent of

Kathe' Tribes into Myanmar), Project Paper, Department of History Mandalay, 2010, p. 18.

27. *The Royal Orders of Burma (A.D. 1598. 1885)*, Part VII, edited and translated by Dr. Than Tun, Centre for Southeast Asia Studies Kyoto, 1988, p. 438. (Henceforth: ROB, VII).
28. *Han tha-waddy Aye-taw Pon Maw Kun U Dan*, edited by Dr. Toe Hla, Historical Research Centre, 2006, pp. 62, 65.
29. (a) Thiri U Zana, *Loka Byu-har Kyan*, Yangon, Ministry of Culture, 2001, pp. 189-193. (b) Naga Bo Theik Tin Twe, Yadana Ti-Ka Maha Yaza-win, Yangon, Ponya Press, 1967, p. 182.
30. *Parabaik*, MS. No. 756.
31. *The Royal Orders of Burma (A.D. 1598-1885)*, Part VI, edited and translated by Dr. Than Tun, the Centre for Southeast Asia Studies Kyoto, 1987, p. 423. (Henceforth: ROB, VI).
32. Chit Thein, *Shae-haung Mon Kyauk-sa Poung Chok*, Archaeology Department, 1965, p. 53.
33. ROB VI, p. 633.
34. *The Royal Orders of Burma (A.D. 1598-1885)*, Part VIII, edited and translated by Dr. Than Tun, Centre for Southeast Asia Studies Kyoto, 1988, p. 423. (Henceforth: ROB, VIII).
35. ROB, VIII, p. 744.
36. Zeya Kaw Htin, *Majjama Desa A-ye taw-pon.*
37. ROB, VII, p. 424.
38. ROB, VIII, p. 424.
39. *The Royal Orders of Burma (A.D. 1598-1885)*, Part IX, edited and translated by Dr. Than Tun, Centre for Southeast Asia Studies Kyoto, 1989, p. 646. (Henceforth: ROB, IX).
40. Tin, 1963, Vol. IV, p. 253.
41. She-haung Sar-pe Tu-te thi Ta-U, *Nan Hmu Nan-yar A-sin thazar*, Vol. I, Part I.
42. U Maung Maung Tin, *Konbaung-zet Maha-Yazawin Taw-gyi* (the Great Chronicle of Konbaung Dynasty), Vol. II, Yangon, Yarpyae Press, 2004, p. 203 (Henceforth: Maung Maung Tin, 2004 b).
43. ROB, VIII, p. 321.
44. ROB, IV, p. 541.
45. ROB, IX, p. 456.
46. ROB, IX, p. 358.
47. ROB, VIII, p. 735.
48. ROB, IX, p. 648.
49. Shwe Kaing Tha, *A-Hnit Ta-yar Pyae Mandalay*, (Mandalay Centenary) Kyi Pwa ye Press, 1959, p. 166.
50. *Konbaung-khit Sayin Pa-de-tha*, (A.D. 1752-1885) (collection of Sayin) edited by Htun Yee, Vol. 3, Japan, p. 93 (Henceforth *Sayin*, 2003*c*).
51. Sayin, 2003*c*, p. 96.

52. Sayin, 2003*c*, p. 97.
53. Dr. Toe Hla, *Chin Twin Myit-thar Mu-Ayear*, Yangon, 1995, pp. 146-147.
54. Sayin, 2003*c*, p. 364.
55. Maung Maung Tin, 2004*c*, p. 332.
56. Michael W. Charney, *Southeast Asian Warfare*, Leiden, 2004, p. 164.
57. Maung Maung Tin, 2004*c*, p. 85.
58. Maung Maung Tin, 2004*c*, p. 470.
59. Dr. Than Tun, *Ne'-Hlei ya-zawin*, Yangon, Nant-thar Taik Press 1968, p. 178.
60. ROB, VI, p. 142.
61. ROB, VI, p. 136.
62. ROB, VI, p. 607.
63. Maung Maung Tin, 2004*c*, p. 126.
64. *Parabaik*, Ms. No. 0020, Lu-du Library Collection.
65. Maung Maung Tin, 2004*c*, p. 490.
66. ROB, VI, p. 607.
67. Maung Maung Tin, 2005, p. 267.
68. *Amarapura Shwe Myo Taw ti Sartan*, Pe Ms. No. 1791, Mandalay Library Collection.
69. ROB, VI, p. 160.
70. ROB, VI, p. 246.
71. Sayin, 2003*b*, pp. 269, 273.
72. Dr. Toe Hla, *Kong baung-khit Kye-let Lu-hmu Si-pwa ba-wa*, (Socio-Economic History of Rural Society), Yangon, Historical Research Centre, 2004, p. 3.
73. ROB, IV, p. 562.
74. ROB, VI, p. 627.
75. ROB, IV, p. 541.
76. Dr. Than Tun, *A-maint taw-hte-ka Thamaing*, p. 33.
77. ROB, VI, p. 146.

11
Manipur-Burma Relationship and the British Empire

Sylvia Yambem

The Treaty of Yandaboo, which was concluded after the first Anglo-Burmese War of 1824-26, stipulated the King of Ava to recognize Gambhir Singh, as Raja of Manipur. Neither Gambhir Singh, nor the princely kingdom of Manipur was party or ally to the war or negotiations, however, this was the beginning of a series of colonial stipulations, rules and orders, which regulated and controlled the relationship between the independent kingdoms of Manipur and Burma. For the British Empire in India this need to regulate the Manipur-Burma relationship was determined by the political necessity of the North Eastern Frontier, which was imperative to the political-economic-defensive strategic security of the Empire in India. Geo-strategically located Manipur was the entry-point for the Burmese troops into Bengal, the Eastern Frontier. Manipur was also the entry point to Burma. The dynamics of colonialism transformed the Manipur-Burma relationship from a relationship marked by internecine warfare, raids, punitive raids and also diplomatic friendly relationship and cultural assimilation to a regulated, moderated and controlled alliance to meet the capitalist imperialistic needs of the British Empire.

The First Anglo-Burma War

The first Anglo-Burmese war of 1824-26 was a turning point in the history of Manipur-Burma relationship. The war between the East India Company and Burma was fought over territorial-political-economic control over the states located on the North Eastern

Frontier of India or the North-East Frontier of Bengal (henceforth NEF).[1] The eastern frontier states constituted a boundary line or sometimes referred to as a tract embracing the hill ranges north, east and south of the Assam Valley, as well as the western slopes lying between Bengal and independent Burma, with its outlying spurs and ridges (Mackenzie, 1884, p. 1). The area occupied by the numerous savage races, demarcated a mountainous boundary between the English dominion of Bengal extending up to Sylhet in East Bengal, and an independent Burma, who were constantly engaged in raids and warfare against each other and with Burma. This eastern frontier beyond the administrative-market centre of Sylhet had been demarcated by the Company as a buffer zone, not only against the raiding hill tribes but also against the Chinese and the Burmese (Cederlöf, 2014, p. 3).

The NEF was of strategic importance to the Company's interest in India, as well as to Burma who by the 18th century emerged as an important political power in South-east Asia. Burmese territorial aggrandizement in the eastern frontier escalated under the Konabung dynasty and the aggressive political ambition of its king Alaungpaya (Alompra) began to radically alter the political situation in Burma *vis-à-vis* not only the eastern frontier states of Manipur, Assam, Cachar and Jaintia but also towards Bengal, which was the Company's frontier dominion (Kamei, 2019, p. 312).[2] Sylhet came under the Permanent Settlement Revenue Administrative system, and by the end of the 18th Century, commerce and security in Sylhet became important to the Company's eastern frontier. The Company's interests and dominance over east Bengal was, therefore, closely interlinked to the developments in this eastern frontier, and most importantly to its ability to control the frontier.

Certain factors, however, compounded the Company's eastern frontier problems. The eastern frontier was unknown to the English and Captain R. Pemberton in the Report on the Eastern Frontier of British India published in 1835 (after the First Anglo-Burma War) had emphasized on the need to gather knowledge of the eastern frontier for:

> when at the commencement of the Burmah war, our ignorance of the whole frontier became manifest, and it was found that the records of Government furnished no information that could in the slightest degree direct or

> facilitate the advance of those armies, which it became evident were necessary to preserve the integrity of our dominions (1835, p. 2).[3]

The Company's knowledge on the eastern frontier at the time of the outbreak of the war was moreover economically and commercially driven. The records of the Departments of Revenue and the Political and Secret Department showed varying information on the developments in the eastern frontier. While the Revenue Department files of the 1820s did not mention any escalating conflicts while the Political and Secret Department reported on Burmese fortifications in Assam and the best routes *via* which the Company's troops would reach Assam (Cederlöf, 2014, pp. 44-45).

Despite this information limitation on the frontier, defence and security of its territories was integral to the Company. Hence when in 1823 the Burmese encroached westwards into India *via* the northwestern frontier and primarily into the territories in Chittagong increased, the Calcutta government stationed a police contingent or thana at Shahpuri island.[4] Their were, however, conflicting claims over the Shahpuri island—both the British and the Burmese believed Shahpuri island to be theirs, hence in their defense while the Burmese believed that they were not encroaching on the territory of the English, the English believed that they were defending their territory against Burmese aggression.[5] This was another factor in the eastern frontier, the problems of conflicting territorial claims and the fluidity of the terrain, worsened by the fact that the frontier had never been delimited and the forested mountainous riverine natural barriers made it difficult to accurately assess the border, exposed the vulnerability of the frontier to Burmese attack—especially since the Burmese occupied Assam and Manipur. Hence, the Burmese's continued advance from Manipur to Cachar, a bordering dependency of the British province of Bengal made the British Government declare war on Burma on 5th March, 1824.

The treaty of Yandaboo (signed on 24 February) 1826 which concluded the first Anglo-Burma war, reiterated the significance of the security of the eastern frontier against Burmese threat and other external aggressions. The Treaty made the king of Burma not only renounce all claims upon Assam and the states of Cachar and

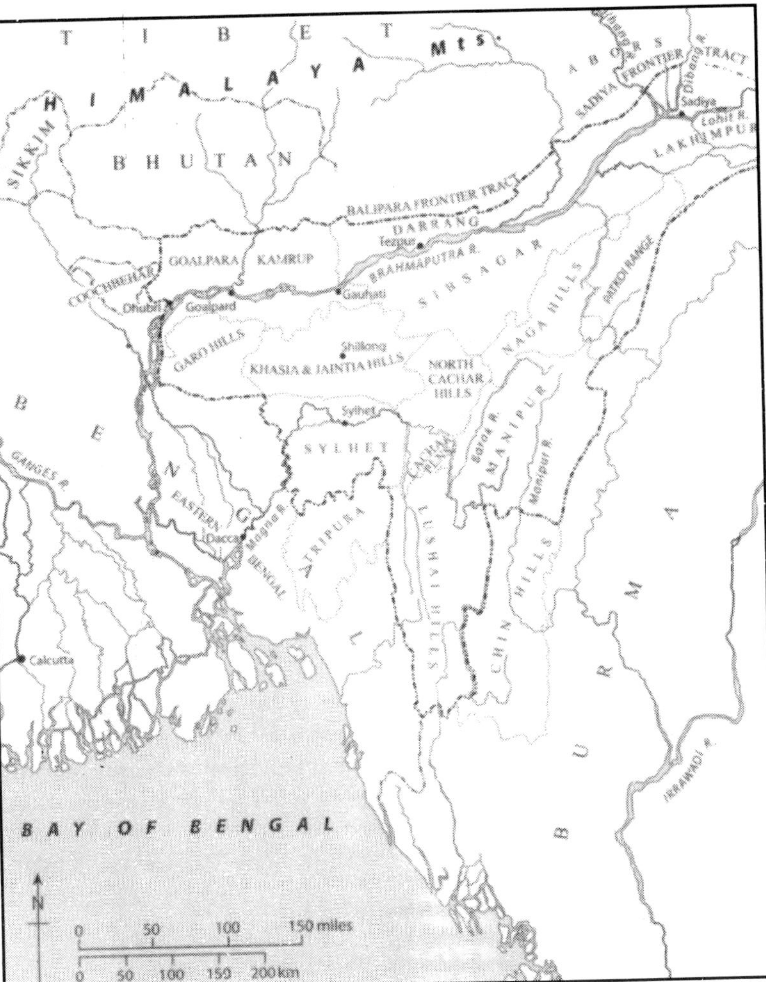

Map: Map of British Assam in 1931 (C.S. Mullan, Census of India 1931, Vol. III, Part I, Report, Shillong, 1932 cited in Zou and Kumar, 2011)[6]

Jaintia but to also abstain from any future interference. The treaty also resulted in the annexation of Ye, Tavoy, Mergui, Arakan and Tennasserim. Thus not only did the treaty end the Burmese domination in the Brahmaputra and the Barak valley but as seen in the case of Manipur whose independence and King was to be appointed by the

English and acknowledged by the Burmese, the treaty succeeded in establishing a friendly barrier state against all future Burmese invasions. The treaty, transformed the Manipur-Burma relationship from a relationship marked by internecine warfare, raids, punitive raids and also diplomatic friendly relationship and cultural assimilation to a regulated, moderated and controlled alliance to meet the capitalist imperialistic needs of the British Empire.

Manipur, Burma and the English in the Eastern Frontier

The history between Burma and Manipur is replete with incessant warfare, raids, and punitive raids for control over land and economic resources, as well as diplomatic alliances and shared cultural traits. For instance, the Manipuri king Kyamba's (Thangwai Ningthouba) conquest of the Kabow valley from the Shan kingdom of Pong in upper Burma in 1470 resulted in constant contestation between Manipur and Burma over the control of the Kabow valley. The *Cheitharol Kumbaba* (the court chronicles of the kings of Manipur) also mentions two such Burmese invasions of 1648 and 1651 over the Kabaw valley that was successfully repulsed by Manipur. *Cheitharol Kumbaba* also lists 7 military expeditions against Samjok during the reign of the Manipuri King Garib Niwaz or Pamheiba. It was during the reign of Garib Niwaz that the Manipuris organized numerous raids against Burma—historical records mention that in 1725, the Burmese forces were defeated at Maglung river, in 1726 the King successfully repulsed a Burmese force comprising 30,000 men, in 1735 Garib Niwaz crossed over the Ningthee river and destroyed the Burmese town of Myedoo, defeated two Burmese armies and ravaged the territory from the banks of the Khodoung Khyoung to Deebayen in 1737 and in 1738 Garib Niwaz even occupied the ancient capital of Zakaing (Sagaing).

The Burmese also organized numerous invasive campaigns including counter-raids against Manipur. The most devastating attacks targeted at territorial expansion in the northeastern frontier occurred after the reign of Garib Niwaz. The tragic death of Garib Niwaz at the hands of his younger son Chit Shai (also known as Ajit Shai was the first patricide in the royal history of Manipur) and the contest for the throne among his sons reduced the status of Manipur from a strong power and the centre of political gravity (Kamei 2019). King Alaungpaya raided Manipur in 1755, an event known as koolthakahalba or the primary devastation and in 1758 Alaungpaya armed with modern weaponry acquired from the French and the Portuguese entered Manipur through Pallel, marched to the capital defeated King Gourshyam and even stayed for 13 days.[7] In 1764, Hsin-byn-Shin, the new Burmese king again invaded Manipur's Kabow valley, and defeated King Bhagyachandra at Tamu.

In 1765, the Burmese under Shembegwen once again invaded Manipur forcing king Jai Singh to flee to Cachar, and in place the Burmese reinstated Eringba on the throne of Manipur. Though Jai Singh was successful in dethroning the Burmese anointed king, the period between 1765-1782 witnessed numerous clashes between Manipur and Burma, each time ending with Jai Singh fleeing to Cachar and the Burmese appointing their puppets as king of Manipur, as seen in the case of the appointment of Moirang raja as the king of Manipur. It is reported that between 1775-1782, Jai Singh made no less than four attempts to regain the throne of Manipur, and was successful each time. The death of Jai Singh was followed by a period of intense struggle for the throne amongst his sons. This period saw succession of kings beginning from Robinchandra who ruled till 1801, then Modhuchandra until 1806 and then Chourjit Singh. Chourjit Singh's reign also did not last long as Marjit Singh, his brother made numerous unsuccessful attempts to capture the throne. Marjit Singh attacked Manipur in 1812 with the help of the Burmese and captured the throne. In return for Burmese military support, Marjit agreed to renounce Manipur's claim on the Kabow valley and was to acknowledge dependency on the king of Burma. Chourjit Singh meanwhile fled to Jaintia.

The Manipur-Burmese relationship, however, soon soured when Marjit Singh refused to attend the accession ceremony of Bagyidaw in 1819, though other factors such as the cutting of timber in the Kabow valley and the erection of the gilded palace also contributed. As retaliation, king Bagyidaw in 1819 raided and occupied Manipur. This event popularly known as the *chahi taret khunthakpa* that lasted for a period of 7 years (*chahi taret*), is one of the most devastating attacks by the Burmese on Manipur. The resulting Burmese invasion once again forced Marjit to flee to Cachar, where he reconciled with Chourjit Singh.

These developments in Manipur and the *chahi taret khunthakpa*, however had wider implications in the eastern frontier. The constant feuding between Manipur and Burma exposed the territorial vulnerability of the NEF to constant Burmese threat and the region's political instability, which if un-checked would also facilitate future Burmese aggression in the frontier. Burmese influence in the eastern frontier was also not limited to Manipur; between 1817 and 1826, the Burmese invaded Assam on three occasions, Assam became a Burmese protectorate state and in 1822 a Burmese province.[8] Cachar was also impacted by the Manipur-Burma feud. Physically Manipur was located between Cachar and Burma; forming one highway connecting Assam, Cachar on one side and with Burma on the other side. Like Manipur, Cachar was equally vulnerable to the Burmese as the Manipuri kings in the event of a Burmese invasion always sought refuge in Cachar. The event of *chahi taret khuntakpa* which forced the Manipuri king to flee to Cachar created political instability in Cachar leading to the overthrow of its king Govind Chandra by the three Manipuri brothers—Chaurjit, Marjit and Gambhir Singh. The Burmese as mentioned earlier also staked claim over some parts of eastern Bengal on the ground that Burmese conquest of Arakan naturally transferred the territorial rights over these areas of eastern Bengal to Burma.

By 1823-24, the constant Burmese invasions into the eastern frontier along with incidents such as the Shahpuri island or the elephant-hunters case had convinced the British under Lord Amherst that the Burmese had encroached into the British side of the river Naf. To deal with the eastern frontier, the British government under Lord Amherst adopted measures for strengthening the northeastern frontier *via* a two-pronged approach:

- Firstly in terms of military strategic defence 15 companies of regular native infantry were to be kept as reserved at the borders of Assam and Cachar in case of any Burmese aggression.
- Secondly to "develop a barrier of friendly states" by encouraging and supporting the original inhabitants of those countries (i.e. the eastern frontier states), to expel the Burmese from the British frontier of Assam, Manipur and Arakan.[9]

This need to develop barrier states was important. Burma's relationship with this eastern frontier was not exclusive to conflict and hostility, but also shared deeper cultural-social traits. The frontier tribes including the Burmese shared similar Mongoloid physical features with the Burmese, food habits and even were in nature tribal and warrior like. The repeated attacks, invasion and capture also facilitated the exchange of socio-cultural traits. Marriage relationships, for instance to conciliate with the Burmese was practiced by the Manipuri kings who would offer their daughters to the Burmese kings. Recorded marriage alliances include the marriage of Chakpa Makhao Ngambi, the daughter of King Charairongba in 1702 to King Taninganwe of the Tongoo (Toungngoo) dynasty, the marriage between Princess Satyamala, daughter of Garib Niwaz again to King Taninganwe, and others. These marriage alliances fostered friendly peaceful relationships between Burma and Manipur, and led to stability in the eastern frontier.

The Manipuri kings also sought Burmese military assistance to ascend the throne, introducing periods of dependency or vassalage. Pemberton (1835, p. 45) mentions that the period of Marjit Singh's rule as Burmese dependency led to a period of political stability, economic prosperity and trade. He recounts that the prosperity of the inhabitants was seen in the numerous herds of buffaloes and bullocks grazing on the plains, while Marjit and the other officers from their long stay at Ava also adopted many of the luxurious habits of the Ava court such as their dressing, and even the equipments for their horse.

The relationship between Burma and the frontier states, particularly Manipur went beyond the predatory nature of warfare and raids. In this context, the English's need to counter Burmese influence through soft tactics was imperative. Thus, the period leading to the first Anglo-Burmese war saw intense propaganda and lobbying by the English of the eastern tribes. While the Burmese ordered the kings of its tributary states of Assam and Manipur to respect their vassalage, the British carrot policy of conciliation offered the eastern kings asylum, pensions, zamindari rights and English military support in return for British protection (Cederlöf, 2014, p. 67).[10] The approach towards the NEF states differed; while the Burmese followed the "stick" as usual approach towards its tributary chiefs, the British who were looking for an entry into the region initiated a "carrot" or friendly approach towards the tribes.

Manipur-Anglo Relationship and the War

Manipur occupied a strategic location on the eastern frontier. The passes leading from Manipur (and Assam) into Cachar and Jaintia served both the British and the Burma, as on either side it went up to Bengal and Burma. The Burmese, therefore, could easily attack Calcutta coming *via* Manipur through Cachar down the Brahmaputra. Though even the Supreme Council at Calcutta did not seriously consider the threat and possibility of a Burmese conquest, they were, however, aware of the devastating effects of a Burmese raid both on the prestige of the Empire and its economic resources.[11] The Burmese, therefore, presented a formidable challenge to the territorial integrity of the English's eastern frontier, and the constant fight for the throne amongst the sons of the King of Manipur, escalated the uncertainty of the frontier.

Manipur's problem was, therefore, not only its geographical vulnerability to external aggression but also "the constant raids of the Manipuris into Burma, and of Burmese into Manipur" (Mackenzie, 1884, p. 149). The relentless struggle for the throne amongst the sons of the King of Manipur, also aggravated the eastern frontier issues for the English. Politically Manipur, the small eastern princely kingdom, was notoriously barbarous for what Alexander Mackenzie describes as:

> Internal wars of the most savage and revolting type, in which sons murdered fathers and brothers murdered brothers, without a single trait of heroism to relieve the dark scene of blood and treachery (*Ibid.*).

It was this combination of Burmese threat and the contestations for the throne that initiated the beginning of an Anglo-Manipuri relationship in the year 1762. The invasion of Alaungpaya in 1758, for the first time made the Manipuri's seek external support from the English East India Company.[12] However here, the request for support did not come from the Manipuri king Bhagyachandra but from Ajit Shai. Ajit Shai had been living at Cachar being expelled from Manipur 2 years before Alaungpaya's invasion and seeking to reclaim the throne from his brother king Bhagyachandra according to Pemberton "endeavoured to interest the British government in his behalf, and by representing himself as unjustly expelled from the throne, had created a feeling of sympathy for his misfortunes" (1835, p. 40). Jai Singh on becoming aware of Ajit Shai's activities deputed Haridas Gosain to Harry Verelst, Chief of Chittagong factory requesting assistance in the event of a Burmese invasion. On 4 September, 1762, Haridas Gosain on behalf of Jai Singh and Verelst on behalf of the Company signed a treaty of alliance between the Company and Manipur. The British while seeking Manipur's alliance against "every enemy of the English as his own enemy, and the English shall consider every enemy of Jai Singh as their enemy"[13] sought the help of Manipur against Burmese threat to the English forts and factory at Pegu. Any Burmese aggression towards the English was to be considered as injury to Jai Singh. The Manipuris in their attempt to recover territories from the Burmans were to be assisted with English troops, whose maintenance and expenses were to be paid by the Manipuris. In return, the King of Manipur was to make such grants of land to the English free of rent in perpetuity for the purpose of establishing a factory and a fort and providing a distance eight thousand cubits around the factory and fort, as well as provide duty free goods transit for the English and ensure protection. This treaty protected the commercial interests of the Company.

The terms of the treaty, however, could not be implemented as heavy rains halted the Company troops at Casspore, the capital of Cachar from marching ahead to Manipur. The new king Gourshyam though affirming the treaty informed Verlest his inability to pay for the troops, though he was willing to reimburse the British for any expenditure incurred. As proof, an amount of 500 meklee gold rupees (valued at 12 silver rupees each) was offered. A list of items comprising silk, iron, kupas, dammer, wood oil, wax, elephants' teeth, sandal wood, camphor, black thread, red thread, blue thread, white thread, black cuss, meklee cloth, meklee gold rupees to be paid annually to the English was also mentioned (Pemberton, 1835, p. 42).

Between 1762 and 1823 where we have the next recorded political relations between the British and Manipur the state experienced numerous raids by Burma and the Burmese occupation in 1819. Commenting on the history of this period, Pemberton observes that:

> From this period, the history of Muneepoor presents an

> unvarying scene of disgusting treachery, between the numerous sons of Jaee Sing, who in their contests for supremacy, arrayed the unhappy people of the country in hostile warfare against each other, and inflicted miseries upon them, little if at all inferior to those they had suffered at the hand of their common enemy the Burmahs (*Ibid.*, p. 44).

Increasing Burmese interference in the affairs of Manipur also marks this period of Manipur's political instability. As mentioned earlier, this political instability extends over to Cachar. It is at this juncture of increasing Burmese dominance in Manipur, in the other states of the eastern frontier and towards Sylhet that in 1823 the English began communication with Gambhir Singh, whom Pemberton called "the most enterprising of the three brothers." The Manipur Levy was formed comprising 500 Manipuris under Gambhir Singh's command who were paid, accoutered, and given ammunition by the British government. In 1825 during the Anglo-Burmese war, the Levy was increased to 2000 men and placed under the command of Captain Grant (Mackenzie, 1884).

Manipur did not participate directly in the Anglo-Burma War, though the Manipur Levy was pivotal to the Company's victory over Burma. The unfriendly difficult terrain made it practically impossible for the 6000 Company soldiers who were sent from Dacca to expel the Burmese from Manipur to go further east than the Jiri river, and their use of camels to carry supplies did not serve any benefit. It is in this context that the Manipur Levy raised from local Manipuri soldiers came to the aid of the English. These soldiers had little problem sustaining themselves in this difficult hilly riverine terrain, had immunity to malaria and far more determined to oust the Burmese soldiers and regain control over Manipur (Cederlöf, 2014). Hence no sooner did Gambhir Singh advance into Manipur volunteers joined his force—in July 1825, about 700 men armed with spears and dhows joined--who were then armed with muskets and ammunitions by the Company (*Ibid.*, p. 71). It was this Manipur Levy who played an important role in expelling the Burmese troops from Cachar and in 1825 ousted the Burmese troops from the Manipur valley and by 1826 from the western bank of the Ningthee river.

The Treaty of Yandaboo, Transforming Manipur-Burma Relationship

The political-geo-military strategic alliance signed between Gambhir Singh and the English in 1823 was, cemented by the Treaty of Yandaboo. The treaty did not annex the state of Manipur. Rather Article 2 of the treaty states:

> With regard to Munnipoor it is stipulated, that should Ghambhir Singh desire to return to that country, he shall be recognized by the King of Ava as Rajah thereof.

The Burmese translation of Article 2 reads, "Ghambhir Singh should not be molested in the government of his principality by the King of Ava." Thus conveying the importance of the independence of Manipur and that Burma should not interfere in the internal affairs of Manipur (Cederlöf, 2014). Article 2 and the treaty of Yandaboo had much wider implications for Manipur, Burma and the English in the eastern frontier.

The stability of Manipur was important to ensuring law and order in the eastern frontier. This the English aimed to control and regulate firstly by impressing upon the King of Ava that Manipur was an independent state, Burma had no right over Manipur and that they would not interfere in the internal affairs of Manipur. Secondly, an important factor that led to lawlessness and Burmese interference in Manipur was the struggle for the throne. Thus, the English aimed to again control and regulate by deciding who will become King of Manipur and for the Burmese to recognize the same, beginning with Gambhir Singh. This political interference in the succession of Kings to the throne of Manipur, was important, as it is not only attempted to legitimize succession to the throne of Manipur and hereby reduce chances of conflict for the throne. The treaty successfully began the practice of legitimizing accession to the throne; at the death of Gambhir Singh in 1834, his son Kirtee Singh was formally recognized as King with Senapati Nar Singh as Regent. This practice of appointing the King of Manipur continued until 1947. Lastly, this secured a friendly but dominating influence of the English in the state of Manipur, *vis-à-vis* any rival claimant to the throne, who might seek Burmese assistance. The Manipur state accordingly was re-established by the British Government professedly in order that between their frontier and that of Burma, they might have a neutral and independent territory (McCulloch, 1859, p. 16).

The treaty of Yandaboo consolidated British policy in the eastern frontier and in the case of Manipur its relationship with Burma was controlled and moderated. To facilitate friendly relations between the court of the Burmese King and the English in India, Article 7 of the treaty of Yandaboo provided that "in order to cultivate and improve relations of amity and peace" between Burma and the East India Company representatives were to reside at the respective Durbars. Accordingly in January 1830, Major Burney was appointed British Resident at Ava. Similarly, William Bentinck's Minute dated 7th February, 1835 stationed a Political Agent in Manipur for "the preservation of a friendly intercourse and as a medium of communication with Manipur government and as occasion may require with the Burmese authorities on that frontier, and more specifically to prevent border feuds and disturbances which might lead to hostilities between the Manipurians and the Burmese" (Mackenzie 1884, p. 153). The first Political Agent was Lt. George Gordon.

In the Company's eastern frontier plan, which extended as far as Tibet, Sichaun, Yunnan, Upper Loas and Arakan, Manipur was the centre of the map in the Imperial vision of the Empire (Cederlöf, 2014). The period post-Yandaboo and the Company's entry into the eastern frontier saw the beginning of extensive land surveys by English officers including Lt. Pemberton (Joint Commissioner of Manipur) and Captain F.I. Grant (Commissioner of Manipur). These surveys mapped the resources and the terrain of Manipur to meet the Company's military and commercial interest. Militarily Manipur was transformed into an advanced position for the defence of the eastern frontier. Pemberton's (1835) report provides detailed information on the military preparation made in Manipur against any future Burmese advancement: six companies of infantry were cantoned at Langthabal around the villages of the King's Palace, and four others were posted along the eastern borders of the valley from where they were to be deputed in case of emergencies in the hills between Manipur and Kabow valley. Other 2 battalions were posted throughout the villages. Pemberton gives the present strength of the infantry at 3000 men, cavalry and golandauz attached to four 3-pounders at 100 men each, and in case of emergency an additional

1000 men could be included. The Manipur ponies, which had equally impressed the Burmese army, were considered for military cavalry use. Commercially, the abundant forest resources like teak, sal, cotton tree, oil tree, keo, and bamboo and the state's rich wildlife like elephants "bigger than any seen so far in the eastern frontier" oxen, deer, tigers were also recorded (Cederlöf, 2014). Trade routes that would further English trade as far away with China were also explored. Manipur's strategic location on the eastern frontier close to the Surma and Barak valley along with its luxurious trade goods such as silk, salt, wax, ivory, cotton and ponies made it an important commercial site for the merchants from Yunnan and Burma. It was this trade along these routes, which Henry Lodge, the Collector of Sylhet in the 1790s attempted to control in Manipur's western foothills, on the border of Cachar (*Ibid.*, p. 46).

It was this combined military and commercial objective of the English in the eastern frontier, which continued to impact Manipur-Burma relationship in the period post-Yandaboo, and which the English persisted to control to their interests. Though Manipur was not directly annexed into the British Empire, the English continued to politically interfere in the internal affairs of Manipur. To further their interest, the English continued to regulate the border/boundary between Manipur and Burma, particularly the Kabow valley. Post-Yandaboo Kabaw valley emerged as a point of conflict between Manipur and Burma. Neither the Kabaw valley nor the boundary between Manipur and Burma was an issue discussed in the treaty (Mackenzie, 1884).[14] However, the valley was involved in the war; it was in the hands of the Burmese at the time of the outbreak of the war, and had been taken by Manipur during the war, the valley was not retroceded to Burma in the treaty. Rather, it was accepted that all places and territory in Gambhir Singh's possession at the time of the signing of the treaty of Yandaboo would belong to Manipur.

Kabow valley, however, became a source of contention, as the Burmese though recognizing the sovereignty of Manipur and Gambhir Singh, did not agree to Manipur's possession of Kabow valley. This boundary issue became an important point of discussion, however not between Gambhir Singh and Burma, but between the Government' of India and Burma.[15] After much discussions and deliberations, the Government of India in its order dated 16th March, 1833 informed:

> That the supreme government still adheres to the opinion that the Ningthee formed the proper boundary between Ava and Munnipoor; but that in consideration for his Majesty's feelings and wishes, and in the spirit of amity and goodwill subsisting between the two countries, the supreme Government consents to the restoration of the Kubo to Ava, and to the establishment of the boundary line at the foot of the Yoomadoung hills.

By the treaty of 1833, the British Government decided Manipur's boundary line at the Jeree river and the western bend of the Barak, a compensation for the loss of Kabow valley. The 1834 treaty, which transferred Kabow valley, also awarded Manipur with a monetary compensation of Rs. 6000 per annum.

The transfer of the Kabow valley to Burma was determined not by Manipur's interest but the Company's strategic military-commercial securities in the eastern frontier, and in this context the need to appease Burma. Major Burney, the British Resident at Ava opined that:

> Keeping Gambhir Singh in possession of an unhealthy and depopulated strip of territory which is divided from Manipur by a range of hills and with which our officers even cannot communicate without being always attended by large parties of coolies to convey every necessary of life for their subsistence, is worth the risk of thoroughly disgusting the court of Ava and accelerating another war (Mackenzie, 1884, p. 181).

Even Governor-General William Bentinck argued on the need to protect the strategic interest of the English, and Manipur's incompetence, including the Manipur Levy at safeguarding the eastern frontier against Burmese aggression. The loss of the Kabow valley, however, also came with additional commercial terms, which Gambhir Singh had to concede, namely—to not obstruct the trade with Burma under the Bengali and Manipuri merchants, would not exact heavy duties, nor would assert monopoly over articles of merchandise, would not prevent the Nagas in the Kalanaga and the Noonjai ranges of hills from selling or bartering the items of ginger, cotton, pepper etc., either in the Cachar plains,

Banskandee or the Oodharbun bazaars, and the rajah of Manipur in the event of war with the Burmese or any such events affecting the eastern frontier, were to provide military assistance to the British (*Ibid.*, p. 151). The restoration of the Kabow valley to Burma would also serve the capitalist needs of the colonial state as via the Kabaw valley the English would not only re-establish trade with China but also enable safe and easy access to the seaports for the transportation of Manipur's commercial resources (Cederlöf, 2014). Kabow valley was handed over to Burma on 9th January, 1834, and Gambhir Singh died on this same day from a heart attack.

Boundary issues or Manipur-Burma conflict or even cattle-pony thefts however continued, with the British controlling the outburst. In 1848, the Burmese complained of the aggression on Burmese territory by the Loohoopa hill tribes, in 1860 the Mokoo Burmese village in Manipur was raided by the Burmese, in 1871 the inhabitants of the Nat-tseng-nga Manipur village was attacked by the Burmese, such disputes continued. However, the history of Manipur-Burma relationship underwent radical transformation following the treaty of Yandaboo, and accordingly such disputes and conflicts were regulated and controlled by the English to suit the capitalist imperialistic needs of the British Empire.

NOTES

1. The region has been variously referred to as the North Eastern frontier of Bengal by Woodthorpe in 1873, while in 1884 Alexander Mackenzie called it the North-East Frontier of Bengal. See, Woodthorpe, R.G. 1873. *The Lushai Expedition 1871-1872*, London: Hurst and Blackett Publishers. Mackenzie, Alexander. 1884. *History of the Relations of the Government with the Hill Tribes of the North-East Frontier of Bengal.* Calcutta: Printed at the Home Department Press.
2. Kamei, Gangmumei, 2019 (2015). *History of Manipur: Pre-Colonial Period.* Akansha Publishing House, New Delhi.
3. Pemberton, *op. cit.*, p. 2.
4. On 24 September, 1923, the Burmese forces attacked the Shahpur island killed 3 sepoys while driving the remaining off the island. See Kitzan, Laurence, Lord Amherst and the Declaration of War on Burma 1824, *Journal of Asian History*, Vol. 9, No. 2 (1975), pp. 101-127.
5. Chittagong and some of its adjacent territories was at one time part of Arakann hence the Burmese claimed territories north of the river Naf. See Ramachandra, G.P. 1978. The Outbreak of the First Anglo-

Burmese War. *Journal of the Malaysian Branch of the Royal Asiatic Society*, Vol. 51, No. 2 (234), pp. 69-99. Pearn, B.R. "Arakan and the First Anglo-Burmese War, 1824-25," *The Far Eastern Quarterly*, Vol. 4, No. 1 (November, 1944), pp. 27-40

6. Zou, David Vumlallian and Kumar M. Satish. 2011. "Mapping a Colonial Borderland: Objectifying the Geo-Body of India's Northeast." *The Journal of Asian Studies*. Vol. 70, No. 1 (February), pp. 141-170.
7. Pemberton, *op. cit.*
8. See Mackenzie *op. cit.*, Ramachandra, *op. cit.*
9. Kitzan, *op. cit.*
10. Cederlof, Gunnel, 2014. *Founding an Empire on India's North-Eastern Frontiers 1790-1840: Climate, Commerce, Polity*, Oxford University Press, New Delhi, p. 67.
11. Kitzan, *op. cit.*
12. Pemberton, *op. cit.*
13. Sanajaoba, Naorem 2017 (1988). Ed. *Manipur Past and Present (The Heritage and Ordeals of a Civilization) Volume I: History, Polity & Law*, Mittal Publications, New Delhi.
14. In the period before the war Kabow valley was under Burmese possession for 12 years and prior to that with Manipur. Mackenzie, *op. cit.*, p. 176. According to Kamei this was a clear sign of the ignorance of Manipur-Burma relationship, See "Kabui, Gangmumei, The Lost Territory of Manipur: Cession of Kabow Valley," In *Naorem Sanajaoba*. 2017 (1988). Ed. *Manipur Past and Present (The Heritage and Ordeals of a Civilization) Volume I, History, Polity & Law*. Mittal Publications, New Delhi.
15. As early as the 19th of April, 1926, the issue of Kabow valley was raised by the Sylhet Commissioner, and by February 1827 discussed between the Burmese ministers and Mr. Crawford, the British Envoy. In April 1828, Captain Grant and Lt. Pemberton who were appointed Commissioners to settle the boundary issues with the Burmese Commissioner, See Mackenzie *op. cit.*

THEME-IV

Political Engagement

12
Garibniwaz (Pamheiba)-The Master of Manipur and Upper Burma (West of Irrawaddy) (1709—1748)

Manglemjao Singh Sorokhaibam

Garibaniwaz, more popular locally as Pamheiba was the greatest king Manipur has ever produced in its historical existence since more than 2000 years. After knowing his prowess as a warrior king and his skill in statecraft many writers even described this great king as an 'Emperor', in Manipuri Ningthourel or Maharaja. In one sense this term might have been applied in the Manipuri world. When any Manipuri king consolidated his power and positions within the core of the nine ranges of hills, the subjects and the king believes that he is the king of kings. He earned the confidence of different Clan Chiefs in the Central Valley and the village heads (Chiefs) of the hills on all four surroundings by way of conquest and agreements; and then he descended towards the Kabaw Valley since the last part of 1717 A.D.; and more violent attacks followed in Chindwin Basins, and penetrated in the Mu-Irrawaddy valley in the heartland of Burma in following years.

There is a story which instigate Garibniwaz to invade Ava (Awa). During those days Ava was the capital of Upper Burma, and hence to Manipuris its land and people were known as Ava (Awa), and even Chinese authorities used the term 'Awa'. The same term and the same spelling were also used by the Burmese before their British connection. This term is also popular in Manipur and while reading we find Awa as synonym to Burma, perhaps this term was also used by Shans even, and the immediate eastern neighbour to Manipur was Shans living in Kabaw Valley and the people of North Western Shans of the then Burma who had been known to Manipuris as Pong). According to "Samsok Ngamba" and many sources disclosed that his father Charairongba was very much broken-hearted before his death by the news that his sister who had been married to Burmese King as Awa-Leima (one of the Queens) has been dethroned or demoted after having a son to her. Charairongba, the Manipur King vowed to take a revenge against the Awa king but his fate was different, he died before taking any revenge, and he had given the task to his son Pamheiba (Garibaniwaz). The king Charairongba was broken-hearted because there were few more points of disagreements which were agreed upon before the marriage of Chakpa Makhao Ngambi to Awa (Burma) king "Tongdoi Leimaba" (King Taninganway was known to Meiteis as Tongdoi king). While instructing to his son at his (Charairongba) dead bed to invade against Awa (now Myanmar) King, he disclosed that there were following agreements before the marriage of Chakpa Makhao Ngambi that: [1]

> Chakpa Makhao Ngambi must be made one of the Queens of Awa; the following border tributary villages of Poirei land, namely, Kamu, Chirang, Kharoi, Ting-itsha Khunthak, Ting-itsha Khunkha, Kontong Maru (Khunjao), and Tarao Khundon which had been encroached by Awa (Burmese) must be allowed to remain as earlier as the tributary villages of Manipur and those Tarao villagers who had been kidnapped by Burmese authorities be released.

Above demotion of Chakpa Makhao Ngambi from the Burmese Queenship, and the agreements of those villages had not been served by the Burmese king and the heart-broken Manipur king died after giving the task of invasion against Burmese King. Now his son Garibaniwaz determined fully to invade Burma at an opportuned time. He along with his ministers and military commanders together made an agreement with the eastern village chiefs including Tangkhul Chiefs, Maring Chiefs, and Khoibus to fight jointly when war broke out with Burma and had a grand feast.[2]

During his time the king was assisted by nine 'Kurus' or Gurus, namely[3]—1. Lourembam Cha Khongnangthaba; 2. Chigong of Samurou; 3. Ningombam Cha Akong; 4. Moirangthem Cha Lalhaba; 5. Lukhoi of Laṇgol (possibly Ashangbam Cha: Longjam Sanathoi Piba); 6. Yambem Cha Phougak; 7. Thongbam Cha Himaiba;

8. Pajior Baji of Wangoo; 9. Phadiba of Kameng; and last but not the least 10. Pandit Shantidas Goswai. But he was a very controversial figure because of his closeness with the king.

These Kurus assist the king in many ways in administration and policy making. Here it may be interesting to note that Chakpa Makhao Ngambi was not the daughter of Charairongba but she was the sister of Charairongba as both were born to Tonseng Ngamba, the brother of King Paikhomba. Both Charairongba and Chakpa Makhao Ngambi were born to Tonseng Ngamba and Ngangbam Chanu Ngaikhong Ngambi.[4] Prof. Chongtham Manihar Singh and Geneologist Naoroibam Indramani also mentioned Chakpa Makhao Ngambi as sister of Charairongba, the father of Garibaniwaz.[5] On the other hand, she was sent off to Awa as "Awa Leima", as one of the Queens in the month of Lamta, 1703.[6] Saroj Nalini on the other hand mentioned that "Lourembam Chanu (maiden) Awa Leima (a queen in wait) left for Awa on 23rd of Poinu, 1704."[7]

In this regard W.S. Desai writes[8]—"In 1704, the Raja of Manipur presented a daughter to Sane the Burmese king." Here we may see the periods of the Awa Kings (Burmese King) as—Sanay (1698-1714), Tanninganway (1714-1733), Mahadhammaraza Dipati (1733-1752).[9] Henceforth whether Chakpa Makhao Ngambi was demoted from Queenship or not is a matter of discussion now as her marriage to Burmese king was during the time of King Sanay not during King Tanninganway. We need to confirm from Burmese or any other records again.

In any way the news that she had been demoted from Queenship has seriously aroused the sentiment of the Court Authorities and the military commanders as well as the common people. Now we can otherwise presume this news as one of the very effective diplomatically motivated political propaganda of Maharaja Garibaniwaz to arouse the sentiment of his people for a successful military campaign against Burma.

In the meantime on 10th of Wakching, 1716, Wednesday, a team of Burmese emissaries along with six Samsok (Thaungthut to Myanmar, Hsawng Hsup to Shan local people) people altogether 156 people arrived with rich presents at Manipur capital to seek the hand of a Meitei (Manipuri) princess. King Garibaniwaz was more angered as this team arrived along with the treacherous Samsok people but he did not apparently shown his sentiment but received them very courteously, and sent them back saying that he will send the princess with abundant gifts next year this time at an appointed place at the confluence of Yu-Chindwin Rivers at Phongta.

Then, Maharaj Garibaniwaz discussed the matter with his ministers and commanders; and taking this as an opportune moment, decided to wage war against the Burmese when they arrived to receive the princess on Chindwin next year. During the discussion King Garibaniwaz[10]—

> "My great leaders who are always at the great Hall of the king to discuss important matters of the Kingdom, the royal order of my great father Charairongba have not been away from my memory, and also I can't forget the news about my niece Chakpa Makhao Ngambi but the king of Awa (Burma) sent his emissaries with lots of presence and letters to seek the hand of my aunty again, like his tribute articles. My courteous commanders and advisors I can't even forget the issues of border tributary villages including Tarao. Now I will fight till the 10 regiments of Burmese army are routed and the Samsoks are devastated. Till then I won't turn my face to any direction."

It is worth mentioning that Yu is the river flowing in Kabaw Valley, which rises from Eastern Hills of undivided Ukhrul District as Maklang River, and another branch is called Tuyungbi River both join at or near Sorbung and flows down to Myanmar as Yu River. Maklang River rises from the ridge slightly away from Sangshak towards the east, Tuyungbi south of Lambui and west side of Sangshak ridge. In the beginning there are two branches of Tuyungbi, the eastern branch is called "Awa Lok" as it flows down to Kabaw Valley, and the other branch by flowing south eastward joins with the main branch Awa Lok. In the early days, Manipuris penetrated from this route into Burma, now Myanmar, frequently as this route is the shortest distance to reach Samjok and other towns of Upper Myanmar. Most of the time while invading Samjok, Pamheiba perhaps used this route being the shortest distance. Not only this, Pamheiba used another route while proceeding southward. There is a climb from Tumukhong side and Nongdam Tangkhul on the left ridge of Taret River and could easily reach Myanmar. This was also another route used during the time of king Pamheiba. Another third route leading to Myanmar was a climb from Bungjang-K. Leihao-Kasom Khullen-Kasom Khunou-

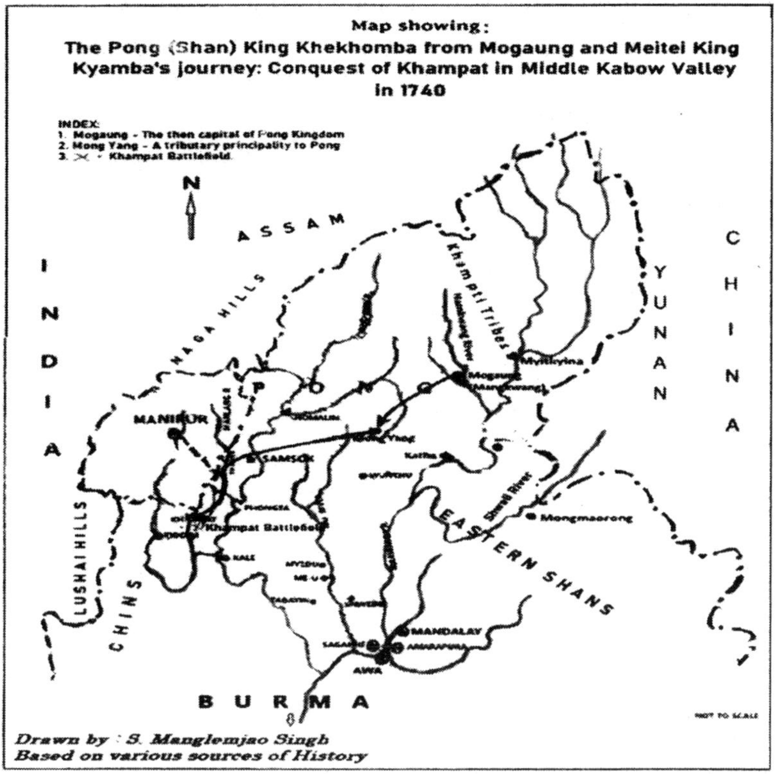

Map showing: The Pong (Shan) King Khekhomba from Mogaung and Meitei King Kyamba's journey: Conquest of Khampat in Middle Kabow Valley in 1740

Kasom K Hunthak-Nambashi, and then descending to the Kabaw Valley, Myanmar.

Samsok or Samjok is the Manipuri name of Hsawng Hsup, which the Burmese called Thaungthut. Here, in this context, we may see Grant Brown[11], *Upper Chindwin District Gazetteer, 1911*:

> "To the north of Kale, Thaungthut also claim to have had rulers since the time of Buddha, but its history is even legendary. Up to the reign of Anawrata (1010-1052) it is said to have been an independent kingdom with its capital at Gawmona, near the site marked on the map in 24 degree, 31 minutes N; 95 degree 34 minutes E, as Thap or Old Samjok, Samjok being the Manipuri form of Thaungthut. Anawrata is said to have appointed a Burmese Governor with the title of Thokyinbwa. During the reign of Tarokpyemin in

the thirteenth century, when the Burmese kingdom lost many of its outpost, it was subdued by the Manipuris, and it seem to have paid tribute to Manipuri till the conquest of that state by Alaungpaya (1753-1760)."[12]

Now Garibaniwaz Maharaja declared all his Pana Leadres as Army Commanders and ready for an all-out war against Burma. He planned it very cautiously for a fight at Phongta (Yu-Chindwin Confluence) and Samjok simultaneously. He was a skilled strategist and a matchless warrior. Even before the siege of Samjok he ordered to locate food grain storage (in Manipuri 'Kei'): Grain Houses, nearby with enough provisions and posted trusted generals.

Battle Craft of Samjok Devastation (1717-18)

Sapam Cha Kiyamba, a leader of Laipham Pana, the Pukhranba must proceed to the south, where the great Door (Gate) is located which connects Nanda village where most of the time during the wars Tangkhuls are sheltering. He must do his duty with utmost care and alertness.

Sorokhaibam Cha Apong of Laipham Pana, who is holding the mixed Department (achoibashanglen) must guard the king. He must do it with complete dedications.

Thiyam Cha Maiba Pukchao: The Commander of Khabam Pana must penetrate from the eastern side and must go to the foothills of Ango-Ching (Ango Hill range) and attack the Samjok Camp located near the Salt Spring.

Samloibam Cha Wakching of Khabam Pana: Who had been grown up with the king since childhood must guard the king with great care and there shall not be any lapses.

Tayum Loinai (Sellung Hanba): The leader of Ahallup Pana must go via the confluence of Tuyungbi and Maklang and proceed towards the side of Makal-Kamba Ching (Hill) and must control the movement of Samjok army.[13]

Ngangbam Cha Lamloi: The Wangon Keirung-hanba of Ahallup Pana, i.e. the caretaker of Ahallup Pana grain store (Granary) must guard the king with utmost care.

Sanasam Cha Honglai (The Shanglen Lakpa): The Leader of Naharup Pana must go to the south along with the Pana forces to guard the main Gate (entrance) of Samjok, so that none from

Samjok be able to do any mischief and must kept the Samjok under complete control.

Naoroibam Cha Mungyang, a leader of Naharup Pana whose works are related with boat race and boating must guard the king carefully.

After this all the four commanders swear in the name of God that they will fight the enemy till their last blood and come back to the land of Poirei (Manipur) with victory.

The Field Craft of Yu-Ningthi (Chindwin) Confluence

(Phongda War Craft: a top secret plan)

Yu River flows through Tamu in Kabaw Valley, which rises from Ukhrul District of Manipur. In Manipur the stream is known as Maklang, which has another branch called Tuyungbi or Tuyungpi. In the ancient and medieval periods, Manipuri frequently used the road for proceeding to Burma along the course of these two rivers. Major areas of Kabaw Valley is also drain by Yu River. Earlier Tamu was known as Kabaw or Kabo or Kapo and later all areas under the controlled of Kabaw (Tamu) might have been known as Kabaw Tampak (Kabaw Valley).

There were three Shan principalities in Kabaw Valley:

1. Samjok (Hsawng Hsup: to Shans, Thaungthut to Burmese) in the north;
2. Khampat at the centre; and
3. Kale in the south. Long back all these principalities were under Manipur King.

These three principalities were under Manipur king since the boundary demarcation between Pong (Shan) king Chaopha-Hkehkomba and Manipur king Kyamba after the Khampat conquest during 1470 or 1474 A.D.

Kopeng, the Wangon Keirunghanba of Naharup Pana[14] must proceed with a large army from the Naharup Pana along with Meitei Pangal sharp shooters and the skilled archer Rupak.[15] They should take the Laininthou Taibang Khaiba, the Lord Sanamahi and the following four ladies who had been treated as the consort to him—(a) Chinphuron Tangkhombi, (b) Wangam Chanu Tonu Maikhubi (Meitengu Chanu), (c) Ahongbam Chanu Chaobi

Tengbura, (d) Thounaojam Chanu Hongbi (Nungpal Luwang) to Phongta or Phongda at the confluence of Yu-Chindwin Rivers as the team of Awa Leima in disguise and fight the Burmese who came to receive the Royal Lady as decided at the most appropriate time when Manipur king along with his main army arrived there.

When reached there, Kopeng under his command must take out the royal boat "Khongchomba Tongcheng Selkoi Lokpa" which was already kept there for their use to cross the big river. They must wait for the arrival of Manipur King and his army there by satisfying the Awa (Burmese) Royal Team. Pamheiba also instructed that when he arrived there he will halt at "Tamlouren Talla Uyok-kon", a forest area nearby by constructing a camp. When seeing the smoke and hearing the sound of big gun all must acknowledge that Meidingu Pamheiba (Maharaja Garibaniwaz) arrived there and the whole team must prepare for assault against the enemy (Awa/Burmese).

Pamheiba, the Manipur king and his team arrived there after 6 days of Kopeng and his team's arrival there, and Kopeng narrated the whole arrangement to the king by sending a messenger. According to the order of Manipur king, Kopeng, the commander send an emissary to the Burmese who were waiting for the arrival of Manipur princess and reported that the princess along with all royal gifts arrived and requested to receive the princess.

Within few minutes there was a fight between Manipur army and Burmese team. Many Burmese were killed, many arrested, and the Golden Royal Barge which belongs to Awa king was completely destroyed and burnt, and its remaining parts floated down up to Awa capital along the river Chindwin (Ningthi). This scene was transliterated as—"Then the grim fight between the Meitei and Burmese forces started like thunder-clap. The bullets from the intensive fire of the Burmese stream across the sky like starled game birds winging out of the Loktak Lake. Then they also discharged piercing arrows. The Meitei force, on the other side, did not lag behind. They gave a marching reply with guns and arrows. The whole scene resembled the random flight of meteors, and the deafening sound of guns was like the roar of the approaching monsoon."[16]

Thousands of shields, swords were collected along with many war captives (captives were 90 men and 11 ladies).[17] Then with the help of Royal Boat "Khongchomba Tongcheng Selkoi Lokpa", Kopeng, the Commander with his army and all teams along with the war captives and booties collected arrived at the "Panthoibi Forest" (In Manipuri—Kabo Tamllouren Wangamlon Panthoibigi Uyok-Umang), where king Garibaniwaz was camping and reported everything all about Phongta; and the satisfied king instructed the Commander to proceed to the Poirei-Tam In archaic Meitei in Samsok Ngamba—"Lairel Meitinguna Eyu Khoiyam Lainingthou-o chingu Taibang Khaiba-o yoiheinakhoimarimabungairoinna Poirei-Tamdatangam-o, Kanglei Yoikoinungda Eyu Lairel Loiyamba chengja Nungoibidatannheba-llalluchallmlbgkhoiyammakhonloidwaithungngam-o".

Then the Manipur king further proceeded with his team to fight the Panga (Pagan related Shans) and arrived at Samsok. Meiteis called the Samjok Shans leaders as Panga because these Samjok rulers were very proud as they had been identified as descendants of Awa ruler of Pagan Dynasty during the time of Anawratha. The Manipur king says that he won't turn his face till the Panga Samjoks are devastated. The Samjok had been already cordoned off by his Commanders and Army, where he further commanded to keep Samjok under cordon further, and he is being proceed further to Chanta, from where food grains are supplying to Samjok and destroy this location first. The King said further to his all four Commanders who are responsible in cordoning the Samjoks—"Cordon the Samjoks without any deviation, thy king is proceeding first to Chanta, which is supplying food grain and other items to Samjoks along with Apong Sorokhaib, Wakching Samloibam, Lamloi Ngangbam Cha and Mungyang Naoroibam. The king arrived at Chanta and devastated the village where rich people settled on Chindwin River. Some Chanta villagers tried to escape by boat on the Chindwin River but were followed by Manipur King and his men by boat and killed all of them. The settlers of Angoching Range including Kamuching, Chirang, Kharoi, Kondong Makha, Ting-itsa Khun-kha, hill settlers Tarao Khundol were helter-skelter due to the battle at Chanta.

Then Manipur King arrived at Samjok and the four commanders who were cordoning the four sides of Samjok started to attack the Samjok with new vigour and on the other hand all the supply lines of essential commodities like salt spring on the foothills of Angoching and the supply of fire wood from the same hill; and food grain had been cut off since few days. But it was informed to the great king that there were supply of rice from the village of Chanta or

Chada on Ningthi (Chindwin to the Burmese). Garibaniwaz after instructing to his commanders for further cordoning hurriedly proceeded to Chanta to destroy the village and to cut-off the supply completely. The Chanta Chief who fled away by boat to Chindwin River was hurriedly persuaded by boat and killed, and the whole village was ravaged completely. Then the king turn hurriedly to Samjok (Hsawng Hsup in Shan), the capital of the Northern Kabaw Valley, a Shan Principality (was known to the Burmese as Thuangdut) which was underseized since quite some time.

When the king arrived there he ordered to fire a rocket inside the town, and his men did the same in no time and the same rocket falls at the court yard of a noble man of Samjok and already starved people of Samjok were frightened with great panic. They are now like fish out of water, they are so thin as they eat boiled leaves of local herb like Chongtai and even eat the flesh of horse which they never eat earlier. The starving people of Samjok were so thin that even the damsels are so thin and ugly that they became too old of their age and looked like old ladies of above 80 years and could not move even due to long days of starvation.

Here we may see the Chongtham Manihar Singh's *A History of Manipuri Literature* (p. 152):

> "since we are utterly starved, how shall we be able to subsist only on wild plants, we have now tested even horse meat which we never touched. Death is now sure to us. The pretty damsels look pale, emancipated and quite old for her age. The babies in arms are sniveling from want of the milk. How shall we let them die on stakes choked and with eyes upturned."

Then the Samjok Chief with his son Lakhamton and other noblemen together discussed and surrendered to the Manipur King Garibaniwaz and sweared that they will be the tributary country to Manipur King and they will pay tribute every year without fail; and begged to feed them as they had been starved since few days.

The noble king agreed heartily and ordered to feed the Samjok people with rice and fish from his royal stock (grain house: Kei) specially arranged for this battle. But the Samjok Chief, along with his son Lakhamton were brought to Meitei Kanglei as war captives.

It's also reported that in the Samjok War Thangjam Cha Hidang with Khagokpa and all together ten warriors were killed by gun from the Burmese Army.[18] It's also reported that all those dead bodies were brought back at Kangla and all rituals were performed in accordance with the Meitei traditions of the time.[19]

The Fongda incident has greatly angered the Burmese king Tanninganwe and feeling shame and decided to invade Manipur within no time. Before four days of return from Samjok there was a news received from Takhel of Mangsha that Burmese Army approaching towards Manipur for immediate attack. Pamheiba Maharaja immediately called his warriors and rushed towards Mangsha, and hurriedly attacked the Burmese forces and routed them at the spot in which Poliba Lamthok played the important role.

Here we may see, George Scott's *Gazetteer of Upper Burma and Shan State*s, Part 2, Vol. I—

> "In the time of Hanthawaddi Yauk Min, when Manipuris invaded the country, they attacked Thaungthut, the Sawbwa, Saw Kan Ho, brought supplies of rice from Minbu, now called Wunbu, and stored them, and having call up all his forces from western side of the river, fought the Manipuris for three years. The Burmese King however gave no help and he defeated and had to take refuge in the jungle. Then the Manipuris utterly destroyed Thaungthut, the Haw (Palace) with its triple roof, its twelve pavilions, the pyathas in front, the golden umbrella with its crystal top-setting, the throne and the white umbrellas together with all the rest of the city, and carried off the elephants, male and female."[20]

Here, we may see *Burma Gazetteer, Upper Chindwin District-1911* compiled by G.E.R. Grand Brown ICS, Rangoon about Samjok[21]—

> "To the north of Kale, Thaungthut also claim to have had rulers since the time of Buddha, but its history is even legendary. Up to the reign of Anawrata (1010-1052) it is said to have been independent Kingdom with its capital at Gawmona, near the site marked on the map in 24°31′N, 95°34′E, as 'Thap'[22] or old Samjok, Samjok being the Manipuri form of Thaungthut. Anawrata is said to have appointed a Burmese Governor with the title Thokyinbwa.

> During the reign of Tarokpyemin in the 13th century, when the Burmese Kingdom lost many of its outpost, it was subdued by the Manipuris, and it seems to have paid tribute to Manipur until the conquest of that state by Alaungpaya (1753-1760).
> Samjoks were time and again defeated by Manipuri King Pamheiba but they were very treacherous and did not obeyed the conditions agreed upon between Manipuri kings, and to teach some befitting lesson Pamheiba King attacked Samjok between (1717-1718) and (1718-1724) at least 12th times and devastated Samjok and then Samjok never ever rose again."[23]

In 1723, the Kingdom of Awa or Burma together with Tripura invaded Manipur at a time to defeat Manipur. The Burmese forces attacked Manipur from the South-east and the Takhel or Tripura forces from the south-west simultaneously. But the war specialist and the great Commander King Pamheiba @ Garibaniwaz tackled the grave situation very carefully and defeated both the enemy and win the two battles. This news has greatly enhanced his fame far and wide and the ability of Manipur's influence in the Geo-political environment of South East Asia. Prof. Gangmumei Kabui while citing *Cheitharol Kumbaba* mentioned that Pamheiba invaded Samjok seven times in the year 1717, 1718, 1720, 1722, 1737, and 1748.[24]

W.S. Desai, a former Burma Education Service and a Prof. and Head of History Department University of Rangoon, Rangoon, Burma mentioned about Garibniwaz—

> "The Manipuris entered Burma in 1724, and informed the king that they were bringing another princess for the Burmese monarch so that the princess of 1704 might have a companion. The king sent three hundred lords and ladies to receive the new princess and to escort her to the royal palace. The reception committee in good faith to the appointed place on the Yu River. They found no princess there, however. Instead, Garib Nawaz with his intrepid horsemen bore down on them, captured them all, and carried them away captive to Manipur."

Mu-Valley Campaign of Pamheiba @ Garibaniwaz the King of Manipur

Here, we may quote from *Burma Gazetteer, Shwebo District 1924,* compiled by Ma. William, Rangoon[25]—

> "Thirty years later they defeated on the Manipur frontier a Burmese army which included men from this District (Shwebo) in the Myauke-bet-myin Cavalry and the Tabayin and Myedu Regiments. In 1735 they actually attacked Myedu and carried off the 'Kalas' (Mahomedans) and Burmans living there. Two years later the King becoming aware of the activity sent out small forces to reconnoiter—one under the Pontaga Sa.ss. These were both defeated near the Chindwin, and the King immediately sent a force, stated to have consisted of 200 elephants, 700 horses, and 5000 men to occupy Kunon and Modaungh about 10 miles west of Yeu. They were attacked there by the Manipuris and partly owning to one of their generals being inebriated, were driven back. The Manipuris then destroyed all the kyaungs, tanks, and pagodas from Kunon as far south as Tabayin and retired. This was in January 1738. The following cold weather, the Generals sent out against this enemy were beaten outside the district and driven back on Tabayin, where they collected their scattered forces and spend the rains of 1739.
>
> In December 1739, the Manipuris descended in force and cleverly avoiding Tabayin and Myedu, which had in the meantime been filled with troops, where apparently content to remain passively on the defensive within the walls, marched down through Sitha, Moksobo and Halin and engaged the force hastily raised from Sagaing and the surrounding neighbourhood to defend the passage to that town between the Kaunghmudaw Pagoda and the Mingun range of hills. This time they defeated and setting fire to Sagaing, retired probably because they were to cross the great river, but in Burmese History it is stated that they had come to fulfil a prophesy of their great Brahman that if their chief bathed in the Irrawaddy at Sagaing, all evil would cease in their country. Their object was apparently plunder and not permanent conquest."

W.S. Desai, again mentioned about Garibaniwaz @ Pamheiba regarding Manipuri invasion into Mu Valley in Central Burma[26]—

> "In 1735, the Manipuris entered Myedu in Shwebo district and carried away cattle and slaves. In 1737, the king again sent an army into Manipur, but Garib Nawaz routed in a pitched battle and slew its commander. The Manipuris again entered Shwebo District, ravaged it with fire and sword, and carried away much loot. In 1738, they came again and boldly encamped near Sagaing. They burnt houses and monasteries right up to Ava, the Burmese capital, across the Irrawaddy River. The king, in order to protect the Kaunghmudaw pagoda, constructed a stockade round it. The Manipuris stormed it, however, and put the entire garrison to the sword. Garib Nawaz, while entering the pagoda, slashed at a door with his sword, and the gash may still be seen."

E.W. Dun in his *Gazetteer of Manipur* mentioned about Garib Nawaz[27]—

> "In 1725, he attacked and defeated a Burmese force at the mouth of the Maglang River; the following year repulsed an army of 30,000 men, which had penetrated into the valley, and captured three divisions. In 1735, he crossed the Ningthee River, attacked and destroyed the town of Myedu, on the bank of the Mu River, and carried off numerous captives. Two years subsequently he successively defeated two Burmese armies, amounting to 7000 foot, 700 horses, and 20 elephants, and devastated the whole country from the banks of the Khodoung Choung to Dabayen. In 1738, he again crossed the Ningthee River, attacked and dispersed a Burmese army of 15,000 foot, 3000 horses, and 30 elephants; and at the termination of the rains of the same year, at the head of 20,000 men, marched between the Burmese army, three divisions of which occupied the towns of Matsen, Dabayen, and Myedu, and to use the language of the Burmese historians, 'without stopping', attacked and carried the stockade positions around the ancient capital of Sagaing, of which he obtained possession."

During King Pamheiba @ Garibniwaz's campaign in Mu-Valley including the military town of Mydeu in 1735, 1736 and 1737 he encamped more than a month at Mydeu town and nearby areas in Shwebo District. Shwebo or Moksobo is the birthplace of the great king Alaungpaya, at that time he was a boy seeing and watching the events happening around Shwebo, Mydeu and other towns along the Mu Valley in the heartland of Burma.

In 1739 again Manipur King Garib Nawaz with a strong force of 20,000 aided by Cacharis invaded Ava (Awa), the capital of the then Burma with an aim to disperse Ava, but failing in an attack on a Burmese force, stockaded at Mydeu again.

In 1749, after spending some few years in the internal administrations appear again in the heartland of Ava by crossing Chindwin (Ningthee) River, marching along the left bank of it reach near the confluence of Irrawaddy-Chindwin rivers waiting for a favourable opportune time to cross the big river near Sagaing, to attack Ava, but his standard was blown off by the wind and he and his team thought this as a bad omen, and he was glad to negotiate rather than to fight. And later he as requested by the Ava king Mahadhammaraza Dipati Garibaniwaz sent off his niece Satyamala Devi as his daughter as Ava (Awa) Leima, a queen in wait.

In regard to Mu Valley and Central heartland of Burma campaign by Garibaniwaz, Prof. N. Joykumar Singh remarked[28] —

> "The year A.D. 1738 was the most significant period so far the military campaign of Garibaniwaz was concerned against Burma. As recorded in *Ningthourol Lambuba* king Garibaniwaz attacked and occupied several places like Metu (Mydeu), Makang, Taprang and from these places the Manipuri forces collected a large number of war booty and the entire villages were completely devastated. In this way, the repeated attacks by Manipur king Garibaniwaz from 1719 up to 1749 has weakened the Burma king considerably."

NOTES

1. Moirangthem Chandrasingh, *Samsok Ngamba,* Imphal.
2. As referred in L. Ibungohal Singh & Ningthoukhongjam Khelchandra Singh, *Cheitharol Kumbaba* (The Royal Chronicle of the Kings of

Manipur), Imphal, 1989. And also local sources from the people bordering Myanmar.

3. Longjam cha Sanathoi Piba.
4. *Sagei Salairol*, pp. 101-102, 250. Also see *Samsok Ngamba*. p. 4.
5. Chongtham Manihar, *A History of Manipuri Literature*, 1996, Sahitya Academy Edition, New Delhi, p. 149. Also see Naoroibam Indramani, *Takhel Ngamba*, N.I. Series, Imphal, 2014, p. ii.
6. Sarangthem Bormani, *Meitei Ningthourol*, 2018, p. 57.
7. Saroj Nalini Paratt, *The Royal Chronicle of the Kings of Manipur: The Cheitharol Kumbaba*. p. 114.
8. W.S. Desai, *A Pageant of Burmese History*, Orient Longmans, 1961.
9. Maung Htin Aung, *A History of Burma*, 1967, p. 339.
10. Moirangthem Chandra, *Samsok Ngangaba*, pp. 9-10.
11. Grant Brown, *Upper Chindwin District Gazetteer*, Rangoon, 1911.
12. It should be taken note that 'Thap' is pronounced as 'Tap', here we see that when Shans write 'Hs', we write 'Sh', when we write 'kh' they write 'hk', when there is 'th' most of the time 'h' is silent, e.g. when they write Kathe it is pronounced as Kate, we also write as Kate, when they write 'Hsawng Hsup' we will write as 'Shawngshup' but we called this place as 'Samsok' or 'Samjok' for pronunciation convenience. The Khoibu folk-tale still indicated that they were happily settled long back at 'Thap' or Tap means Old Samjok on the west side or right of Chindwin River. They might have been migrated to the present location in Tengnoupal Hills due to torture by the Burmese (Awa) as they (Burmese armies) were always in search of royal servants by subjugating the other ethnic border minorities in those days. This kind of slave gathering war-fare were very frequent in those days amongst the Southeast Asian kingdoms and ethnic groups).
13. Ningombam Chinglen, *Ningthourol Inot*, Imphal, 2005. In it, Ningombam Chinglen identified the leader of Ahallup Pana as Haobam Cha Akong.
14. B. Kulachandra Sharma, Meidingu Garibaniwaz, 2000, Imphal and N. Chinglen mentioned as Thangjam Cha Kopeng, but source from where they cited is not clear.
15. Ningombam Chinglen, *Ningthourol Inot*, Imphal, 2005, p. 201.
16. Ch. Manihar Singh, *A History of Manipuri Literature*, 1996, Sahitya Academy Edition, New Delhi.
17. Royal Chronicle of the Kings of Manipur, *Cheitharol Kumbaba*.
18. Ningombam Chinglen.
19. *Cheitharol Kumbaba*, Maharaja Pamheiba left Meitei Kangla for Samjok War on 7th Day of Poinu Yumsakeisha 1717, and returned to Kangla after the war on 2nd day of Wakching, Thangja 1718.
20. George Scott, *Gazetteer of Upper Burma and Shan States, 1901*, Part I & II, Rangoon.

21. G.E.R. Grant Brown, *Burma Gazetteer: Upper Chindwin*, Vol. A, Rangoon, Burma, 1960.
22. 'Thap' is pronounced as 'Taap'.
23. Samjok is the Manipuri form of Thaungthut, but in Shan locally known as Hswang Hsup.
24. Gangmumei Kabui, *History of Manipur*, Vol. One, New Delhi, 1991.
25. Ma.A.Williamson ICS, *Burma Gazetteer: Shwebo District*, Rangoon, Burma. 1924.
26. W.S. Desai, *A Pageant of Burmese History*, Orient Longmans, 1961.
27. E.W. Dun, *Gazetteer of Manipur, Calcutta, 1886*, reprinted 1992.
28. N. Joykumar Singh, *Emergence of Manipur as a Nation State*, New Delhi, 2015.

OTHER WORKS CONSULTED

1. Bryce Beemer, *The Crole City in Mainland Southeast Asia: Slave Gathering Warfare and Cultural Exchange in Burma, Thailand and Manipur, 18th and 19th Century*, The University of Hawaii, Manoa, USA, 2013.
2. Chanam Hemchandra, *Ningthourol Lampupa*, Uripok, Imphal, 2018.
3. D.G.E. Hall, *A History of South-East Asia*, Fourth Edition.
4. Emmanuel Guillon, *The Mons: A Civilization of Southeast Asia*, Bangkok, 1999.
5. Maung Htin Aung, *A History of Burma*, Columbia University Press, New York & London, 1967.
6. Konsam Manikchand Singh, *Descent of the Scion of Sorarel on the Earth*, Imphal, 2014.
7. Micheal Symes, *An Account of an Embassy to the Kingdom of Ava*, London, 1800.
8. N. Ibobi Singh, *The Manipur Administration (1709-1907)*, Imphal, 1976.
9. Ningthoukhongjam Khelchandra Singh, *Ariba Manipuri Sahityagi Itihas* (Manipuri), Imphal, 1969.
10. Oinam Bhogeshwar, *Ningthourol Lambuba*, Imphal, 1967.
11. P. Gogoi, *The Tai and Tai Kingdoms*, Gauhati, 1968.
12. R. Brown, *Statistical Account of Manipur 1873*, New Delhi, 2001 (rp.).
13. R.K. Jhalajit Singh, *A Short History of Manipur*, Imphal, 1965, rp. 1992.
14. Rajkumar Snahal Singh, *A Short History of Manipur*, Imphal, 1989.
15. Rev. H.I. Marshall, *The Karen People of Burma*, The Ohio State University, Ohio, USA, 1922.
16. Wahengbam Ibohal Singh, *The History of Manipur*, Imphal, 1986.
17. Wangjam Somorjit, *Manipur: The Forgotten Nation of Southeast Asia*, Waba Publications, Imphal, 2016.
18. U Kyi Win, *Studies in Myanma History*, Vol. I, 1999, Yangon, Myanmar.
19. Walter Hamilton, *East-India Gazetteer*, London, 1828, India, 1993 (rp.).

13
Samsok Ngamba-An Old Manuscript Showing Manipur Burmese Relation

Chirom Rajketan Singh

Manipur was an independent princely nation before it became a part of India. One could see the relation that prevailed between Manipur and its neighbour Burma (now Myanmar) during those times from various old manuscripts that are found till today. These manuscripts are written in old Meitei script and old Manipuri language. The paper used for writing was prepared manually by the *Meiteis* and was called *Meitei che* (*che* meaning paper). These old manuscripts were collectively called "Puyas" by the *Meiteis.* The hill and valley areas of Manipur were once settled by many smaller independent groups which later on came under a single rule by the end of the 17th century. The history of Manipur can be traced back long before this time. The Meitei king belonging to *Ningthouja* clan *Nongda Lairen Pakhangba* ruled from 33 A.D. at *Kangla* of *Imphal* and from this time the unification of the various groups had started. There is history of different parts of Northeast India being under the rule of different Meitei kings from time to time in the past. Not only this, along the eastern side, different parts of Burma (Myanmar) were annexed and ruled by the Meitei kings. At that time, Myanmar was not a united nation. Different groups both small and large occupied different territories and each ruled independently. The different communities mainly settled at *Kyang Lamjao* (Kabow Valley), a neighbouring land of Manipur, which was a vast fertile area with a big river flowing through it. The Old Manipuri manuscripts mention this settlement of different communities in Kabow Valley. There were also stories of inter-marriages between the *Meiteis* and the *Burmese*, their trade relations, harmonious relations as well as stories of annexation etc. The relation that existed between the *Awas* and the *Meiteis* could also be known from oral narratives. Fortunately, the Manipuri scripts were there since long time back so many stories were recorded and kept in the palace. Such records prove to be helpful in establishing the relation of Manipur and the Awas (Burmese) in the past.

A manuscript that gives a vivid account of Manipur-Awa relations in *Samsok Ngamba*. The main theme of this manuscript is that—the Awa king *Tongdoi Ningthou Chekong Leimaba* called in with two of his noblemen—*Kong* and *Tunglacha* and asked them to go to *Poireilam* (now Manipur; at that time it was not called Manipur) to seek the hand of the daughter of Meitei King *Charairongba* for the Awa king for marriage. The two messengers were sent with many gifts for the Meitei king—brass plates, iron, clothes and other valuable items. After reaching *Poireilam*, they took shelter in *Laibar Phayeng Nongphai Sang*. During that time, the king usually built and kept a separate house especially for the people coming from other lands like royal messengers, guests etc. for accommodation during their stay. It was, in fact, a guest house. This house was called *Laiber Phayeng Nongphai Sang*. *Laibar* means conversation. After taking rest for five days, the two messengers of king *Tongdoi* came to the palace of the Meitei king *Charairongba* to convey the message of the Awa king *Chekong Leimaba*. They presented the gifts to the Meitei king and requested him to sent his daughter *Tampha Wangamlon* in marriage to Khamran (Awa) land and escort her till the port of Ningthi river where the Awa king would be waiting to receive the Princess.

King Charairongba refused to accept the gifts and did not agree to the terms of the Awa king. He said that he would not easily accept their proposal as he was also a superior king. The Meitei king asked them to return to their land to give the news that he would give his consent only on one condition. He would give his daughter's hand in marriage to the Awa king only after the latter releases the *Tarao* and *Kondong* people from *Meiteis'* area who were held as captives. Only after this the Meitei king would sent his daughter *Chakpa Makhao Ngambi* to Khamran. Carrying this message the two messengers went back home and relayed it to their king. King *Chekong* again sent his two messengers with gold, silver and other costly gifts to *Poireilam*. They told the Meitei king that the Awa king had agreed to the Meitei king's demand so he should send his daughter as the Awa king would be waiting at the *Phongto Port* of *Ningthi River*. With this agreement Meitei king *Chairairongba*'s daughter *Chakpa Makhao Ngambi* was sent as Awa king's bride along with dowry. Like this the two lands strengthened their ties.

The terms of agreement for the marriage were—the daughter of Meitei king should be made the *Leimarel* (queen) and release of captives from *Tarao* and *Kondong* villages. During that time, the boundary of Meitei king extended till the western areas of the Ningthi river which runs through Kabow Valley (now a part of Myanmar). Such stories are mentioned in old Manipuri manuscripts. Pong is a powerful group of people settling in the Kabow Valley. From early times they had good relations with the Meitei king. *Khullai,* the Pong king who ruled in 80 A.D. and the Meitei king Nongda Lairen Pakhangba were relatives. Manuscripts like *Sorarel Machana Khulkumpa* and *Pongga Meiteiga Lamyen Lairek* depict the close ties between these two groups of people. When Pong king *Maganou* died his son *Sukamfa* became the king of Pong dynasty. *Sukamfa*'s brother *Samlungfa* invaded and annexed many parts of Burma. Later he intruded in Northeast India and captured the area that lies in today's upper Assam. On his way home he sent away his soldiers and he halted at the Meitei palace and stayed there for a long time. The place where he stayed is still called *Apong Engkhol*. In *Cheitharol Kumbaba,* it is recorded that this time corresponds to the time of *Meidingu Naothingkhong* (663-763 A.D.).

In 1470, Meitei king *Kyamba* and Pong king *Chaofa Khe Khomba* planned to attack *Kabo Kyang Khampat. Khampat* lies along the Indo-Myanmar Friendship Road of today and was 35 miles from Tamu. Tamu which lies close to Manipur is an important commercial centre of Myanmar. At that time the Meitei king and the Pong king divided an orchid plant (*Khonggum melei*. Sc. name *Dendrobium sp.)* into two and took one each. They promised each other to meet again when the plant blooms and then attack *Khampat*. As Pong land had a hot weather the orchid began to bloom earlier during *Lamta Tha* (March-April). Seeing the flowers Pong king came in full preparation for war to the stipulated place. There he waited for the Meitei king for one month. The Meitei king did not come. The Pong king felt cheated. He retreated from the place and on his way he met the Meitei king who only arrived then. Pong king asked the reason for his late coming. The Meitei king replied that he had come as the flower had started blooming. Now the two kings came to the conclusion that the variation in the weather conditions of their respective lands made them come in different times. Then they invaded *Khampat* and conquered it. They celebrated their victory by eating from the same gold plate and drinking wine from the same gold glass. Then they divided the lands among themselves. In this the Meitei king got *Kabow Valley*—the lands lying on the eastern side of *Ningthi River*. The two kings planted betel nut plants in this place where they rejoiced and celebrated their victory as memory. The Meitei king also allowed some Meitei households to settle in this place. Till today the place is called *Kwatha* (Kwa—betel nut plant; *tha* or *thaba*—planted).

Bayinnnaung of *Toungoo* Dynasty was one of the three greatest kings of Burma. During his time in 1560, *Kale, Mohnyin, Mogaung, Momaik, Sanda* etc. which were under the rule of the Meitei king were captured and taken back. *Samsok* was also one of the many lands in *Kabow* valley which was under the rule of the *Toungoo* king. It falls within *Sagaing* region of today's Myanmar. Among the Meitei kings, King *Charairongba* reigned from 1697-1709 A.D. In *Cheitharol Kumbaba,* it is written that in 1624 of *Saka era* (1702 A.D) in the month of *Phairen* (January-February) the Awas had come to seek the hand of the Meitei Princess. Then again on Friday 23rd of *Hiyangei* (October-November) 1704 A.D. (1626 in *Saka era*), the Meitei princess was sent off as Awa Queen.

According to *Samsok Ngamba* when the Meitei princess *Chakpa Makhao Ngambi* started for Awa from *Imphal* they stopped at *Keirao Chingtompok* for the night on the first day itself. *Makhao Ngambi* then sent her companion *Khomma* to call her father for a last meeting. As memory of this meeting she left her engraved footprint in stone at this place, it is written in the book. The King on receiving the news came to meet his daughter. He consoled her that if she was not given the place which her husband king had promised, she should immediately give the news to her father so that he would intervene and even fight a battle if necessary.

Next morning they resumed their journey. After crossing *Thoubal River* they reached *Lamding Sabal,* then after climbing *Khoiroi hill* they reached *Tenjeipokpi*. Here she wept feeling that this will be the last time she would ever see of her home. As they went they spent one night at *Senbi Tummu Lokchao*. Then they reached *Kabow Valley* and ultimately the *Ningthi River*. The *Chekong* king was waiting for her at *Phongdo Port* of *Ningthi River*. From here they sailed in *Ningthi River*, crossed *Irrawaddy River* and reached the Awa *Tongdoi* Palace. In the palace *Makhao Ngambi* was crowned the Queen by *Chekong* king.

After some years *Chakpa Makhao Ngambi* gave birth to a son *Mangdra Kengdu Ngamba*. After the birth of a son the queen title was removed from her and another woman was made queen instead. Hearing this news *King Charairongba* was very upset. The Awa king failed to keep his promise. He did not release the captives from *Tarao* and *Kondong* also. His daughter was removed from queen ship. So the Meitei king felt betrayed. He consulted his ministers and plotted to lay siege on Awa. As preparation for war started king *Charairongba* suddenly fell ill. As he became aware that he would not be able to complete the task he called his eldest son *Pamheiba* and told him to lay war on the Awa when he became king as revenge. *King Charairongba* died on Sunday 7th of *Engen* 1709 A.D. His rule lasted for only 13 years and he was only 37 when he died.

Pamheiba ascended the throne on Wednesday 23rd of *Engen* 1709 A.D. He was only 20 years old. After he became king he fought many wars and annexed many small kingdoms thereby expanding his territory. During his reign again the Awa king sent messengers asking for his daughter's hand in marriage for the Awa king. *King Pamheiba* sent back the messengers with the news of his approval for the proposal and told the Awa king to wait in the *Phongdo port*. As soon as the messengers left *Pamheiba* called all his ministers for a meeting. He told them about his father *Tubi Charairongba's* desire to take revenge on the *Awas* since the *Awas* had failed to release the captives from *Tarao* and *Kondong* and that his sister *Makhao Ngambi* had also been disgraced. He also opined that the *Awas* had taken them as subordinates who would easily give in to their demand for wives. Not only this, the *Awas* would often attack on Meitei villages and loot their properties and cattle and take the people as prisoners of war. So they all felt the need to teach the *Awas* a lesson by attacking on them, so that they would come to know the might of the *Meiteis*. So, they all vowed to take revenge. *King Pamheiba* was adamant that he was not going to change his decision of giving the *Awas* a defeat. He even stayed at the palace supervising the preparation for war.

Different military commanders were given different instructions. As for example, *Kyamba Satpamcha* was instructed to lead his soldiers and attack from the south of *Samsok*. *Pukchao Maiba* was to come with his soldiers from the eastern side after passing *Anggo Ching* and attack. *Akong Haobamcha* of *Ahallup Shang* and his soldiers were to attack from Eastern gate after passing through *Makel Kamba Hill* and *Maklang River. Honglai Sanasaba,* head of *Naharup shang* and his soldiers were to attack from the southern gate after passing *Munu Lamlaitang Pong Kansa Khullalam Saman Uyampok. Apong Sorot khaiba, Wakching Samloiba, Lamlai Ngangbamcha* and *Mungyang Naoroiba,* the four commanders were to remain beside the king. They were called *Chingkhong Puyokpa.* They were to guard the king on all sides—right, left, front and back. *Wangol Keirungba Kopeng* had to lead his soldiers along with four trained women in the guise of bride's maids. They will come in the king's boat *Khongjomba Tongcheng Selkoi Lokpa* till *Phongto port.* The king will come with his troops and set up his camp at *Lainingthou Halba Pamel Uringkol Khabi Lengnao Mombi Talla Uring Kond* in *Kabow Valley.* The different parties agreed to communicate with each other by smoke signals.

The different parties set out for Awa on an auspicious time. *Meidingu Pamheiba* performed the rituals for getting victory in the war which they were going to fight. The local priests and priestesses performed the rituals at the shrine of *Nongpok Ningthou* at *Nongmaiching Hill* for victory over the *Samsok.* They could foresee many good signs. These good signs were also seen during the time of king *Khagemba* when he defeated the *Mayangs* and *Muslims,* the priests and priestesses said. So they told the King that he will surely win this war. The King's wives also saw good signs in cooked rice and wine (traditional belief). The King started for his journey one day later on Thursday 29th of *Wakching* (December-January) on an auspicious hour. But in *Cheitharol Kumbaba,* the day was recorded as Wednesday 7th of *Poinu* (November-December) in 1639 of *Saka era* (1717 A.D). There is a one month difference. The war events were all similar. *King Pamheiba* and his troops set up his camp at *Panthoibi Umang* (forest) after crossing *Mangsa* of *Kabow Valley.*

The troop which went in disguise as bride's party reached the Phongdo Port of Ningthi River and gave the Awas a surprise attack. They fought fiercely. The Awas usually possessed good weapons and they had huge number of arms. Since they had come for receiving the queen only they got defeated easily. According to *Cheitharol Kumbaba,* 10 Meitei soldiers were killed by gun shots. It is written that 90 men and 11 women were captured as prisoners of war by the Meitei's. According to the manuscript *Samsok Ngamba*, it is written that the Awa army got destroyed, thousand swords and thousand shields were collected. The head of queen reception party *Longimuk Athouba* were captured alive. The boat of the Awa King called *Phongtohi* which was sent for the queen got destroyed and burnt. The Meitei soldiers brought their king's boat *Sengoi Lokpa* along with the prisoners of war along the Mangsa river to the Meitei King's camp. The military commander *Kopeng Keirunghanba* related the war events to the King. He asked the King to return home along with the four Meitei women and the prisoners of war and celebrate the war victory. To this King *Pamheiba* answered that he himself will fight the *Samsok*s so he refused to return.

King Pamheiba conquered other parts of *Kabow Valley* and accumulated enough food supplies. He slowly surrounded the *Samsok* palace. As planned earlier, the other Meitei troops arrived from four sides leaving no way for escape. There was a fierce battle between the *Samsoks* and *Meiteis*. The *Samsoks* locked themselves inside the palace. The nobles, soldiers, old, young and Buddhist monks remained inside the palace. They remained like this for more than one month. The food supply of the *Senbi Kabows* in the palace exhausted slowly. Ultimately, they had to survive on boiled vegetables. Even they started eating horse meat which was not eaten before.

King Pamheiba entrusted his four military commanders who led the attack from four sides *Akong Haobamcha, Honglai Sansaba, Pukchao Maiba* and *Kyamba Satpamcha* with the task of guarding the palace. While the king himself led an army of soldiers to attack on *Chantu*, a land near the *Ningthi River*. He went tirelessly day and night and after crossing *Ango Hill* reached *Chanta*. He surrounded its palace on a moonlit night. There were few soldiers as most of the soldiers of *Chanta* went to help the *Kabow* king. Next morning there was a fierce battle. The *Meiteis* made a forceful entry by destroying the fort. The *Chantas* retreated and most of them jumped into the *Ningthi River* in order to save their lives. The *Ningthi River* flowed with bloody water. Like this *Chanta* village was captured. Many other villages along *Ango Hill* were made colonies as they went. Then they reached *Samsok* and joined the other Meitei troops.

The *Samsoks* inside the palace went without food for many days. They were starving. They could hardly walk and move. Everyday the *Meiteis* would attack by shooting arrows and cannons inside the fort. They begin to fear the Meitei King's strength and valour. There was hardly anything to eat. They eat boiled herbs which were available at that time. They began to eat horse meat. The old folks could hardly walk. The young grew thinner. Young mothers could not feed their young ones. There were sufferings everywhere. The old folks went to their military commander, Buddhist Monks leaders and youngest son of the *Samsok* king to speak out their problems. They suggested that they should surrender to the *Meiteis* and remain as their colony and pay taxes in the form of gold, silver etc. (As it was done in the past since the time of King *Kyamba.*) As they did not have the strength to face the Meitei's might, they put forward the proposal of surrender. That night the youngest son of *Samsok* king, Military commander of *Samsok,* five Buddhist heads and other noblemen discussed about the proposal. They agreed to surrender before the Meitei king the next day. The next morning, the Chief of *Samsok* and youngest son of the king opened the palace gate and came out with their subjects. From far they kneeled down on their knees, called for cease fire and agreed to pay taxes. When King *Pamheiba* heard their pleas, he turned to his four commanders *Apong Sorok Khaiba, Wakching Samloiba, Lamlai Ngangbamcha* and *Mungyang Naoroiba* and told them as they were not his counterparts he could not answer them so they should go on the king's behalf and give their approval. Like this, the *Senbi Kabows* gave away gold, silver etc. as taxes. *Samsok* chief requested the Meitei king to feed his people as they went without food for many days. The Meitei king agreed and gave them food. The people ate happily and it was said that some had died because of over-eating.

Samsok chief asked the Meitei king to rebuild his village. *King Pamheiba* rebuilt it. Those in hiding came out and settled again. After resettlement King *Pamheiba* returns *to Poireiland.* While crossing the *Anggo Hill,* the king saw a beautiful flower. The King plucked the flower and asked *Aroi Laishramcha,* the head of the Pena troupe who accompanied the king, about the name of the flower. Aroi Laishramcha holds the Pena and gave the details of the flower in song form. The flower was named as "One with the leaves similar to *Kusum* flower, first identified by the king *Thongnang Mayamba,* flower that conquered Samsok, flower named by *Aroi Laishramcha,* flower found in *Senbi Anggo Ching.*" The king brought a plant along with its roots, watered it well and gifted to the queen. The Queen planted the plant in *Apong Engkhol* and nurtured it. Then the king arrived in Kangla and performed the ritual "Nunggoibida Lallu Chanba, Huiyen Lansing Thaba". After telling the tale of the war he will take rest. There was a tradition where the king after a war will go to a shrine in the palace called *Nunggoibi.* Here a ritual is performed where the names of those killed in the war especially the nobles were taken one by one. By doing this, the person and the land were considered to be under the Meitei king, it was believed. Not only this, it was believed that the person will become free from the sin of killing a person. This was called *Nunggoibida Lallu Chanba Huiyen Lansing Thaba.* After this ritual the war accounts will be narrated and the people will leave for their homes.

After three days of their return one of the Meitei King's man called *Takhel Lousingba* brought the news that the *Awas* had come for war. King Tongdoi of Awa called the Meitei king a liar because he pretended to give his daughter in marriage but instead declared war on them and captured *Phongdo* port. They also burnt the royal boat called *Phongdo Khongnet Hi.* The Meitei king came by his boat *Sengoi Lokpa,* crossed the *Ningthi River* and defeated *Samsok* taking away many captives. They also looted them. For all these reasons, the Awa King had sent two of his men *Lanjingba Chaothap* and *Tarung Tekwa* with troops of soldiers to attack the *Meiteis.* This was the news brought by *Takhel Lousingba.*

On receiving the news, the Meitei King called all his noblemen and soldiers. That night itself they had set out for war and waited for the *Awas* at *Tuhang* (Tuhang is a place in Kabow Valley). The Meitei warriors and the king vowed to fight till the last hour. Next morning the *Awas* and the *Meiteis* fought fiercely in *Khukeep laopal Thong.* The *Awas* fought relentlessly owing to large number and skilled warriors. At this moment *King Pamheiba* himself led the attack. He charged forward shouting encouraging war cry. Hearing the cry, the Meitei soldiers as well as the commanders became stronger and fought more fiercely. *Cheksa Tante Thangsaba* and Awa leader *Chaothap* had a fierce fight. The *Meiteis* fought so bravely that the Awas retreated. Awa leader *Chaothap* was killed. The Awa army got disorganized. *Tarung Tekwa* was captured alive. Many brave Awa soldiers died while others were captured as prisoners of war. The Meiteis collected 10 elephants and 1000 rifles from the *Awas.*

With this victory king *Pamheiba* decorated his commanders and chiefs with different titles as reward for their contributions. *Karamba Satpamcha* was given the title *Kraksu Phaba* (one who captured

Kraksu). *Apong Sorok Khaiba* with the title *Senbi Chaikha Mirongkhan Phaba, Wakching Samloiba* with the title *Lasak Kadeng Thangsaba Phaba, Akong Haobamcha* with the title *Senbi Pongnong Phaba, Ngangbamcha Wangol Keirungba* with the title *Lasong Lanthouyang Phaba, Hongai Sanasam* with the title *Luthak sara Phaba, Mungyang Naoroiba* with the title *Lakeng Lanthouyang Phaba* and *Kopeng Wangol Kairuhanba* with the title *Tarung Thangsuba Phaba. King Pamheiba* was given the title:

> "Lairel Meidingu Nongpok Wairang Pamheiba Awa Thonglen Lanthaba Senbicha Chota Ngamba Samsok Changna Khomba Taret Senbung Lokpa, Mapari Lakhamton Mathok Lakpa Awa Chaothap Lalchingbabu Kaina hunba Langoi Sagol cha Tara Khomba Khouyeng Maru Panda Telsingba Chakpa Anggo Chingda Thellen Marai Langna Tanfangba."
> (Lairel Meidingu Nongpok Wairang Pamheiba = Original Name of king Pamheiba; Awa Thonglen Lanthaba = one who invaded Awa; Senbicha Chota Ngamba = one who conquered Chota of Kabow; Samsok Changna Khomba = one who captured Samsoks alive; Taret Senbung Lokpa, = one who collected many wealth; Mapari Lakhamton Mathok Lakpa Awa Chaothap Lalchingbabu Kaina hunba = one who killed the Chaothap—youngest son of Awa king; Langoi Sagol cha Tara Khomba = one who collected 1000 horses; Khouyeng Maru Panda Telsingba = one who danced with arrow at Khouyeng Maru Pan; Chakpa Anggo Chingda Thellen Marai Langna Tanfangba = one who returned from Chakpa Anggo Hill with victory).

Meidingu Pamheiba after ordering his general *Kopeng Keirunghanba* to come along with the royal boat *Sengoi Lokpa*, returned to the palace, performed *Nungoibida Lallu Chanba*, related the war events and moved to his chamber.

After the war, the King ordered *Aroi Laishramcha* and *Atibar Yumnamcha*, to write the book called *Samsok Ngamba*. They wrote the book in song form which they sung it. *Aroi Laishramcha* was a *Pena* singer who accompanied the king in the *Samsok* war.

It was a rule for all the Meitei manuscripts to start with an obeisance to creator God, god that was worshipped and the king who ruled at the time of writing the manuscript. It will conclude with *Mikol Thakonba* (Mikol Thakolba—at the end of any religious ceremony an act called Mikol Thakolba is usually performed which is aimed at embracing the hearts and minds of the people which might have gone haywire during the ceremony). The Book *Samsok Ngamba* starts with a verse "Haya he Liklaio Ebudhou Nongthourel Pumaba-o" (meaning greatest God who is high up in the sky). It was some sort of prayer said by the writer or writers so as to complete their works without any interruption. Most stories were sung in *Pena* so they were composed in *Pena* tunes (hepli). It was a tradition to start with obeisance to God, teachers and the elderly listeners and asked for forgiveness if there be any mistake. This tradition was also maintained in written books. At the end also there will be a prayer asking for forgiveness and for the removal of any bad incident and to free the minds of the listeners which is called Mikol Thakolba. This book concludes with *"Hayicha Haya Hari-o"* (last ward of Mikol Thagonba).

Meidingu Pamheiba was called *Thongnang Mayamba. Lairel Meitengu Thongnang Mayamba* written in the beginning of the book *Samsok Ngamba* was usually referring to king *Pamheiba*. It was during the reign of king *Pamheiba* in the beginning of 18th century when Hindu religion first made its entry in *Poirei land*. This land also came to be known as Manipur during his time. Along with Hindu religion came Hindu names, words, language, festivals etc. The king was called Maharaja, Queen (*Leimarenbi*) was called Maharani, *Wangol Ningthou* (crown prince) came to be known as *Yuvaraj* etc. King *Pamheiba* changed his name to *Garebniwaz* after he got baptized into Hindu religion. As king *Pamheiba* was the first to follow Hindu religion he was called *Thongnang Mayamba.* He ascended the throne on Wednesday 20th of *Thawan* (July-August) 1709 A.D. He vowed that he would attack Awa as his father *Charairongba* had said before his death. In 1717, when the *Awas* asked again for his daughter's hand he took it as an opportunity to attack upon them. With this intention he agreed to send his daughter and attacked them. In *Samsok Ngamba,* the description of the war is written in such a way that it look like the war took place only one or two months before. But from the concluding part of the book we can know that king *Pamheiba* conquered and ruled certain areas in Awa for about seven years. The time corresponds to that given in *Cheitharol Kumbaba. Pamheiba* first attacked *Samsok* in 1717 A.D. He attacked *Chanta* in the month of *Poinu* (November-December) 1722 A.D. *Samsok,* which was conquered by king *Pamheiba,* lies in *Sagaing* Division of today. It is said that *Kaunghmudaw* Pagoda that lies in this division was marked on its door with 7 sword marks by king Pamheiba to show that it was under his control. This Pagoda is called *Koumodo* Pagoda by the Meiteis. It is of oval shaped in design. Most of the Burmese Pagodas are of pyramid shaped. This *Koumodo* Pagoda is quite different from other Pagodas. It looks like Buddhist *Stupa* and is one of the biggest temples of Theravada Buddhism. This pagoda was built during the time of King *Thalun* of *Toungoo* dynasty who ruled from 1629-1648. The work was started from 25th April, 1636 and completed on 12th May, 1648. It took 12 years to build the pagoda. Its height is 46 metres and circumference is 274 metres. It is of an umbrella shaped Pagoda. There is a 24 ft. tall Buddha statue made of white marble inside the Pagoda. This Pagoda is one of the many well known Pagodas of Burma. *Sagaing* was developed as the capital of *Sagaing* Kingdom (1314-1364). Different dynasties of Burma had its capital here. This was mainly settled by Bamar which means Burmese Ethnic group. At present, *Sagaing* is the capital of *Sagaing* Region. It is famous for its Buddhist monasteries and Pagodas. If one stands in any part of *Sagaing* he could see the tips of Pagodas on all sides.

When *Charairongba* and *Pamheiba* married off their daughters, Burma was ruled by *Toungoo* Dynasty. The war also occurred during the rule of this dynasty. At this time, the *Toungoo* Dynasty was in its downfall. King *Sanany* (1698-1714) ruled Burma during the time of King *Charairongba*. King *Taningnway* ruled from 1714-1733. King *Maha Dhanmayaza* was the last king of this dynasty. He ruled from 1733 till 1752. The war fought by king *Pamheiba* was during the King *Taningnway*'s time, i.e. from 1714 to 1733. During this time, *Inwa* or *Awa* was the Capital. Presently, *Inwa* is in Mandalay Region. The *Irrawaddy* River runs between *Sagaing* and *Inwa*.

The *Meiteis* called the *Toungoos* as *Tongdoi*. The golden period of *Toungoo* dynasty was from 1510 till 1752. In Burmese history this period was called *Toungoo* Period. They were the descendants of Shan. The first king of this dynasty was *Mingyi Nyo*. Around 1485 they first established their dynasty at *Taungoo*. Their religion was Theravada Buddhism and they speak Burmese language. *Toungoo* lies near Sittaung River on the south of *Inwa*. *Inwa* was conquered by the *Shans* in 1527. Most of the *Barmar* settling in *Inwa* migrated to *Taungoo*. As a result *Taungoo* became a new centre. *Taungoo* is now a district level city in *Bago* Region of Myanmar. It lies on the north-east of Yangon at a distance of 220 km. It was the famous capital of Burma during 1510-1539 and 1551-1552. *Taungoo* was a newly established dynasty hence called *Taumgoo* or *Toungoo* Dynasty. Among the well known kings of this dynasty mention may be made of *Tabinshwehti* and *Bayinnaung*. After establishing *Toungoo* dynasty at *Taungoo Mingyi Nyo* died in 1530. His son *Tabinshwehti* became the king in 1530 at the age of 14. He annexed many parts of Burma including the areas in the *Irrawaddy* Delta. *Tabinshwehti* was recognized as the Emperor of Burma in 1544. During this time, the European traders being to enter Burma. Portuguese Empire entered from the south and captured Malacca. The capital was shifted from *Taungoo* to *Bago* to enhance trade and commerce. Lower Burma was also under his rule. Lower Burma included *Irrawaddy Delta* (comprising *Ayeyurwady, Bago* and *Yangon* Regions) and coastal regions like *Rakhini,* Mon states and *Tanintharyi* Regions. The people living in Lower Burma were called *auk-tha* (men) and *auk-thu* (women) in Burmese language. People of upper Burma were called *a-nya-tha* (men) and *a-nya-thu* (women) in Burmese. Upper Burma includes *Mandalay, Sagaing, Magway* Regions, *Shan States* and *Kachin states*. After Second Anglo-Burmese War of 1852, Lower Burma came under the rule of British Empire. Upper Burma remained independently under Burmese Empire.

Tabinshwehti was known as the Founder of *Toungoo* Empire. He died in 1550 at the age of 34. Actually, he was assassinated on his 34th birthday on the advice of his closest adviser *Simim Sawhtut.*

After *Tabinshwehti Bayinnaung Kyawhtin Nawrahta* (*Burengnong Kayodin Norotha*) became the King from 1550-1581. His father *Mingyi Swe* was the elder brother of *Tabinshwehti*'s father *Mingyi Nyo. Bayinnaung* was born on 16th January, 1516 while *Tabinshwehti* was born on 16th April, 1516. The *Toungoo* Empire flourished under these two brothers. When *Tabinshwehti* was the king *Bayinnaung* had led many battles. It took two years to overthrow *Smin Sawhtut* and established *Toungoo* Empire again. During his 31 years rule *Toungoo* Empire became the greatest empire in South-East Asia. This 31 years tenure is considered "greatest explosion of human energy ever seen in Burma." He conquered many parts of today's Burma. Above this he expanded his empire till Chinese Shan States, Lan Na, Lan Yang, Manipur and Siam. Kings who succeeded him called him Cakkavathi (Universal Ruler). In Siam (Thailand), he was called Phra Chao Chana Sip Thit meaning "Victor of the Ten Directions." The three greatest Kings of Burma were *Bayinnaung, Anawarhta* and *Aloungpaya*.

In the history of Burma, *Bayinnaung* conquered Manipur in 1560. At that time Manipur was ruled by *Meidingu Chalamba* (1542-1562 A.D.). In the history of Manipur such records are not found in the chronicles like *Cheitharol Kumbaba, Ningthourol Lambuba* etc. *Poirei land* was also not called Manipur then. The Manipur in their history would mean the lands in the *Kabow Valley*. On 2nd December, 1559, Manipur was invaded. A warrior named *Binnya Dale* from *Chiang Mai* led the invasion. He came with 10,000 soldiers, 300 horsemen and 30 elephants. It was recorded that the annexation was completed on February 1560. The main aim of the invasion on Manipur was expansion of *Bayinnaung*'s empire. Manipur was accused for wrong infiltration into Kale Territory. They annexed *Kale, Mohnyin, Mogaung, Momeik, Sanda* and forced the people to work as soldiers. *Bayinnaung* died on 10th October, 1581 because of his illness. His son Nanda ruled from 1581-1599. The dynasty had a downfall during his time. *King Nyangyan* ruled from 1599-1605. During his time, the capital was shifted from *Bago* to *Inwa*. The Dynasty flourished again. *King Anaukpetlun* ruled from 1605-1628. During his time, *Bago* was again made the capital. His son *Minve Deibba* ruled for one year only. Then *King Thalun* ruled from 1629-1648. The capital shifted to *Inwa* again. He was considered a strong ruler. *King Pindale* (1648-1661), *King Pye* (1661-1672), *King Narewa* (1672-1673), King Minye Kyawhtin (1673-1698), *King Sanay* (1698-1714), *King Taninganway* (1714-1733) and *King Maha Dhamma Yaza* (1733-1752) were some of the kings of this dynasty who ruled later on. After king *Thalun,* the Dynasty faced downfall. During *King Taninganway Min*'s reign (1714-1733), the land faced attacks from different sides. Even his uncle who was the Governor of Pagan also attacked him. In 1724, the *Manipuris* attacked North-west parts of Burma and conquered them. In retaliation, the Burmese attacked Manipur in November 1724 but got defeated—it is written in Burmese history. According to *Cheitharol Kumbaba* of Manipur, *Pamheiba* attacked *Chanta* in November 1722 while the Awas attacked Manipur in retaliation in the month of *Kalen* (April-May) 1723. It is written that on Wednesday 8th of Kalen 1645 of Saka era (1723 A.D.) King Pamheiba returned home with the victory over

Samsoks. There is difference of about one year in the two records. But still all the stories are similar.

As the *Toungoo Dynasty* disintegrated the *Meitei Cavalry* often attacked them and collected tribute from them. This record is found in the history of both sides. The Burmese were afraid of the Meitei cavalry and at the same time hold them in high esteem. This was because of the Meitei soldiers' skill in warfare. For this reason, the Burmese captured the Meitei soldiers and let them settled in their land to help the Burmese set up a Cavalry of their own. Then they used this cavalry while attacking Lower Burma and Siam. When *Alaungpaya* invaded Manipur, he captured the Cavalry men, took them and organized them as his strong Cavalry in *Kongbaung* Army. The people of *Myintut* village in present Mandalay Division are the descendants of Meitei Cavalry who were captured in the war. In Burmese language, *Myin* means *horse* and *Tut* means *soldiers*. During the time of *Toungoo Dynasty*, the *Meiteis* invaded the *Awas* and annexed them. Then again during the reign of *Kongbaung Dynasty*, the *Awas* attacked Manipur again and again. The *Awas* ruled Manipur for seven years. This period is called "Seven Years Devastation" in the history of Manipur.

Inwa, the capital of *Toungoo Dynasty* is also known as Ava. It is in Mandalay Region. It was the capital of Burma from 14th to 19th century. This city was completely devastated by series of major earthquakes in March 1839. The literal meaning of *Inwa* is *Mouth of the Lake*. It is derived from *Innawa* meaning *nine lakes*. Lake is called 'In'. There are nine important lakes in *Inwa*. The Ava kingdom flourished from 14th-16th century in *Inwa*. This was the capital of *Toungoo* and *Kongbaung* Period from 16th-19th century. During the time of King *Bodawpaya, Amarapura* was the Capital (1783-1821). It was again the capital during King *Bagyidaw*'s time in 1821. Ava came to be known as Awa after the western people arrived. *Irrawaddy River* basin was settled by South East Asian ethnic groups called *Baman*. Out of the total basin area of *Irrawaddy* 91 per cent are in Burma, 5 per cent in China and 4 per cent in India. The language spoken by *Baman* is called Burmese. In *Inwa*, the *Burmarised Shan* groups settled in small groups and created their own kingdoms. These small kingdoms were merged together to form Ava Kingdom in *Inwa* by *Thado Minbya* in 1364. He then annexed *Sagaing* and *Pinya* kingdom. In January 1555, the Awa kingdom got defeated and perished in the hands of *King Bayinnaung* of *Taungoo Dynasty*.

After two centuries, the Awa Dynasty returned again as *Kongbaung Dynasty*. This dynasty was also known as *Alompra Dynasty* or *Alaungpaya Dynasty*. This dynasty ruled between 1572 and 1885 and was considered the Second largest empire in Burmese history. After *Toungoo* dynasty *Alaungpaya* built this dynasty in 1752. He was born in 1714 at *Shwebo*. He became king in 1752 at the age of 38 and he made Shwebo his capital. The downfall of Toungoo coincided with his rise in power. His father *Min Nyo San* was the hereditary chief of *Moksobo*—a village which consisted of 100 households. They were under the *Toungoo* rule. As the *Toungoo* became weaker, they could no longer give protection to the lands under them. For this reason, the *Manipuris* had started annexing many parts of upper Burma. Not only this, the *Manipuris* invaded often and collected wealth from them. In 1724, the Manipuris had occupied major parts of Mu Valley. *King Pamheiba* invaded the western parts of *Kabow Valley* after crossing Chindwin River and Mu River. He then annexed *Myeda*. He also annexed *Sagaing* which lies on the other side of *Irrawaddy*. Awa and *Sagaing* lies on other side of *Irrawaddy*.

Mu Valley consisted of areas along the *Mu River*. This river runs through Upper Central Myanmar and is a tributary of *Irrawaddy River*. It runs through the dry zone of *Kabow Valley*. *Ayeyerwady (Irrawaddy)* lies to the east and Chindwin to the west. It runs from north to south through *Sagaing* and is 275 km long.

Moksobo, the birth place of Alaungpaya is a village in Mu Valley. It lies at 60 miles to the north-west of the Awa Capital. The lord/chief of *Mu Valley* whose name was *Kyawswa Htin* was his uncle. *Alaungpaya* was married to *Yun San* in 1730. *Yun San* was the daughter of the chief of the neighbouring village *Siboktara*. In 1736, he was made the deputy chief of Mu valley by the *Toungoo* King and he served under his uncle. He consolidated 46 villages of *Mu valley* with his power. During that time, the Mu valley was a source of tax for the *Awas* and least protected. For about 30 years, the *Awas* did not give protection to this land from invasions. This condition made the consolidation work of *Alaungpaya* much easier. In 1740, the Mons build *Hanthawaddy* kingdom and ruled at Bago. This kingdom was carved out from *Toungoo*'s parts of Lower Burma. Till 1751, the *Hanthawaddy* and *Toungoo* (Bago and Awa) were at constant wars. This gave *Alaungpaya* the opportunity to build *Konbaung Dynasty* while still under *Toungoo*. In the early part of 1752, the *Hanthawaddys* and the French East India Company occupied Ava. This ended the rule of *Toungoo* king *Maha Dhamma Yaza*. The parts that got separated from the *Toungoo* joined with *Alaungpaya* to form a strong nation. In 1752, *Alaungpaya* completely defeated *Hanthawaddys* and conquered *Bago*. In 1754, Ava was conquered. The whole of Upper Burma came under his rule. In 1755, he occupied *Irrawaddy* Delta. He renamed Dagon as Yangon and started its development. In 1756, he occupied the cities in *Thenlyin* Port which were in the hands of the French. In 1756, he invaded Manipur. It was during the reign of *Meidingu Maramba* (*Gaurashyam*). The Meiteis got defeated. In 1758, again he himself led another attack on Manipur. A battle was fought in *Pallel* and *Kakching*. Manipur was disintegrated and Imphal—capital of Manipur, was captured. This is the record according to Burmese history. There is some difference in the time period with that of Manipur history. In 1759, *Alaungpaya* annexed Northern Shan and Tai states. In 1759, he invaded Siamese. This war is called Burmese-Siamese War (1759-60). Amidst the war in April 1760, he got ill in *Ayutthaya* (also spelled "Ayudhya" or "Ayodhya" was a Siamese kingdom that existed from 1350 to 1767 centred on the city of Ayutthaya. The Kingdom of Ayutthaya is considered to be the precursor of modern Thailand and its developments become the main part of History of Thailand. He could not win the war. But he won back *Tenasserin Coast*. He died on Sunday 11 May, 1760. He ruled for eight years only and he died at the age of 46. Within these eight years he could build a united Burmese nation.

The kings after him invaded Manipur quite often and showed their might. They took Manipur as a land dependent on them. The Meitei princes were not united and always fighting for the throne. This gave an advantage to the *Awas*. The Meitei princes took the help of the *Awas* for getting the throne and this resulted in Seven Years Devastation in the hands of *Awas during the reign of King Bagyidaw (1819-1837). 1819-1825 is the darkest period in the* history of Manipur. Manipur was ruled from time to time by kings chosen by the Awas. The *Manipuris* fled to *Cacchar,* Tripura and *Bangladesh* and settled there. During *Bagyidaw*'s reign some parts of Assam were also annexed. *Meidingu Gambhir Singh* succeeded in driving out the *Awas* from Manipur in 1825 and again annexed the areas in *Kabow Valley*. The last king of *Konbaung* Dynasty was its eleventh king *Thibaw* (1878-1885). He had his Capital at *Mandalay.* He is considered the last king of Burma. He was defeated in the Third Anglo Burmese War. The British sent him to exile in India.

While discussing the relation between Manipur and Burma one need to have an insight into the history of both the lands. Since the Burmese and the *Meiteis* have different accents there is vast difference in the names of people, place etc. The names of place, river, persons which the Meiteis had known were known by different names in Burma. What the *Meiteis* called *Ningthi Turel* (*Ningthi* river) was known by the name Chindwin by the Burmese. There is no 'R' sound in Burmese. So when the Burmese say 'Myanmar' they would say 'Myanma'. The places in Kabow Valley in *Samsok Ngamba* were places all known to the *Meiteis*. Similar names were also there. *Samsok Ngamba* is a historical piece of Literature written in song form which can be sung. It is a record of the Meitei's courage and bravery. It does not give any historical day, date, month or year. *Cheitharol Kumbaba* was written by the *Maichous* (learned pandits) in the royal palace. Here they recorded everyday significant events of the Meitei kings. This record started from *Nongda Lairen Pakhangba* when he ascended the throne in 33 A.D. till the *Shradha* ceremony of *King Budhachandra*. (*King Budhachandra* died on 26th *Hiyangei* 1955, The *shradha* falls on Wednesday 7th of Poinu, 1955). It is the royal chronicle. There is also another manuscript called *Ningthourol Lambuba*. This mainly recorded the war stories of the Meitei kings.

Meidingu Pamheiba is a very important King in the history of Manipur. His good and bad qualities as a king can be discussed in detail. While trying to bring in Hindu religion to Manipur, he burnt many valuable old manuscripts of Manipur called *Puya*. He abolished many traditions. He created new traditions based on Hinduism. At some important Manipuri sacred sites he allowed worshipping of Hindu Gods together with Meitei Gods. A great change came in the religion of the people. On the other hand, he spread the message of the Meitei's valour by fighting wars. He annexed many parts of Burma. He had defeated Tripura (*Takhel*) also. The *Awas* and the *Takhel*s had plotted against Manipur and they invaded simultaneously from different sides. When the *Awas* invaded from eastern side, the *Takhels* attacked from Western side of Manipur. After fighting the Awa war he went to fight the *Takhels*. He won both wars. For the second victory, a book called "Takhel Ngamba" was written. From these books one could know that Manipur was a well known nation state in the South East Asia before it finally merged with India.

REFERENCES

Amubi Singh Irom (ed.). *Awa Ngamba*, Imphal, 1979.

Ashokumar, L. *Ariba Manipuri Sahityagi Paring*, Yumnam Ibopishak, Imphal, 1992.

Ashokumar, L. *Ariba Manipuri Sahityagi Paring (18 amasung 19 gi Manipuri Sahitya)*, Jenifar, Jenita, Shibadata, Imphal, 2000.

Bhogeshwor Oinam (ed.), *Ningthourol Lambuba (Ahanba Saruk)*, Imphal, 1967.

Bhogeshwor Oinam (ed.), *Sanamahi Laikan*, Tamara Publication, Imphal, 2nd Edition, 1995.

Bhogeshwor Oinam (ed.), *Takhel Ngamba*, Imphal, 1986.

Bormani Sarangthem. *Meitei Ningthourol*, Barsa Publication, Imphal, sixth edition, 2014.

Chandra Singh Moirangthem (ed.). *Samsok Ngamba*, Manipur Naharol Sahitya Sava, Imphal, 1980.

Hemchandra Chanam (ed.). *Ningthourol Lambuba*, Imphal, 2018.

<*https://en.wikipedia.org/wiki/Myanmar*>, accessed on 23 August, 2020, at 03:46 (UTC).

Ibungohal, L. and Khelchandra, N. (ed.). *Cheitharol Kumbaba*, Manipur Sahitya Parishad, Imphal, 1967.

Khelchandra Singh, N. *Ariba Manipuri Sahityagi Itihas*, Chirom Yaimabi Devi, Imphal, 1972.

Manikchand Singh Konsam, (Tran. & Ed.). *Sorarel Machana Khulkumpa*, Konsam Imo Singh, Imphal, 2014.

Pemberton R.B., *The Eastern Frontier of India*, Mittal Publications, New Delhi (India), 2015.

14
Awa Ngamba-The Last War of Manipur and Burma

Chirom Rajketan Singh

Awa Ngamba is a literary work of Medieval Manipuri Literature. It is a work which portrayed the courageous feat of *Meidingu Gambhir Singh*. This book was written during the time of *Meidingu Chandrakirti* in Meitei script. In *Cheitharol Kumbaba*, it is mentioned that this book was written on Thursday 7th of *Kalen* in 1793 of *Saka era* (1871 A.D.), the year of Laishram Purna Singh's *Cheithaba* on the royal order of King Chandrakirti by four scholars, namely *Khumujamcha Pandit, Chingakhamcha Chaobaton, Sarangthemcha Surpananda* and *Thoudamcha Chaobaton*. These four writers were all renowned scholars (*Maichous*) during the time of King Chandrakriti. At that time *Khumujamcha Pandit* was the head *Pandit* in the palace. He was also called Khumujamcha Purnachandra Singh. There were other books written by these four scholars together. "*Chandrakirti Jilla Changba*" was written by a team of scholars headed by Khumujamba Pandit, The team comprised Sarangthem Surpananda, Thoudam Chaobaton, Khundrakpam Jagat Singh, Yumlembam Pena Khongba, Yambem Angangton, Erungba Pabung, Khundrakpam Nungnang and Khomdram Leisang. Chingakham Chaobaton Pandit was also among the writers of *Khahi Ngamba, Chada Laihui* and *Ningthourol*. During that time seeking permission of the king and joint writing was the tradition that was followed for writing a book. Skilled writers, the one with knowledge of stories and Pena singers usually sat together and wrote the books. There was a tradition of singing all the stories by Pena singers.

In the book *Awa Ngamba* which was transcribed in *Bengali*

script in 1979 by *Shri Irom Amubi Singh, Pandit* of Royal Palace, there is no mention of the four writers. But in *Cheitharol Kumbaba,* it is mentioned that this book was written by four writers. At the end of the book it is written that one *Chandrashyam Naoremcha* also took part in the writing of the book *Awa Ngamba.*

Awa Ngamba is a book which portrayed *Meidingu Gambhir Singh Chinglen Nongdrenkhomba* as a brave king, a skilled warrior and a staunch follower of *Vaishnavism*. The storyline of the book goes as—In 1819 Manipur got defeated in the hands of the Awas and Meitei king Marjit fled to *Cacchar*. The Awas occupied Manipur and ruled over it through kings chosen by them. Among the Meitei princes who took refuge in *Cacchar,* Gambhir Singh was one who had organized an army of soldiers in *Cacchar* with the sole aim of attacking the Awas and taking back Manipur. At that time, the Awas had reached *Cacchar,* Assam and other British occupied lands. Gambhir Singh helped the British in the War against Awas in *Cacchar* thereby defeating them. Later with the help of the British, Gambhir Singh defeated the Awas and he became the king of Manipur. He again annexed the places in the *Kabow Valley* expanding his territory till the *Ningthi River*. As the story was based on the journey of conquest, the book was titled *Awa Ngamba* (Conqueror of Awas).

In order to understand the story of the book better a small part of the history of Manipur could be highlighted. *Meidingu Pamheiba* (*Garibniwaz*) conquered and ruled over many parts of Burma by defeating the Awas. After him his sons started fighting each other for the throne leading to instability of the kingdom. In 1748 A.D., *Pamheiba* crowned his son Chitsai the King. At that time Pamheiba was only 58 years old. (Pamheiba was born on Saturday 22nd of *Poinu* 1690 A.D). King Pamheiba had many queens who bore him sons. Instead of giving the throne to *Shyamjai Khurailakpa,* the son of his first wife, king Pamheiba gave the throne to his son Chitsai from his another wife *Wayenbam Chanu Gomati*. The people were not satisfied with this action of the king as it was out of tradition. After entrusting the throne with Chitsai King Pamheiba left the palace and lived at Ramsala. King Chitsai had five brothers (Queen Gomati gave birth to six sons—Chitsai, Nandasai, Angasai, Saibyasachi, Bharatsai and Satrughanasai). Chitsai was the third son of Pamheiba Maharaj. The names of twelve wives and sixteen sons of Pamheiba are mentioned in *Cheitharol Kumbaba*. After

Chitsai ascended the throne, Pamheiba was thrown out from the palace. Pamheiba's eldest son Shyamjai was an ardent follower of *Ramandi* religion—the religion that was introduced in Manipur by his father king Pamheiba. *Ramandi* religion was the religion of Ram worshippers. In order to keep his father's promise Lord Rama had went to exile for 12 years. So Shyamjai believed that serving his father was itself a religious commitment and as such he always accompanied his father. After his son Chitsai drove him out, King Pamheiba took shelter in different places. In 1750 in the month of *Hiyangei* Pamheiba fled to Burma. After staying there for more than one year he returned to Manipur in the month of *Hiyangei* 1751 A.D. Hearing the news of his father's return King, Chitsai sent his men to kill his father on the way. On Wednesday 26th of *Poinu* king Pamheiba, his son Shyamjai and Kishoresai, Moirang Lalhanba Pandit, Bamon Wari Liba and his son, Monk Lokdas, Selungba Angom Chandramani, Naoroiba Selungba and other companions of Pamheiba were killed on their way home.

In the month of *Sajibu* 1752 A.D., king Chitsai was also deported by his own brother Bharatsai (fourth brother) and Chitsai fled to Cacchar. Bharatsai became the king and after one year and eight months rule he was thrown out of the kingdom by his noblemen with support of the people. Bharatsai fled to Burma. On the 20th of *Hiyangei* 1753 A.D., Maramba (Gourashyam) became the king. Gourashyam (Maramba), Bheigyachandra (Chingthangkomba) and Krishnachandra were the sons of Shyamjai Khurailakpa and Wayenbam Chanu Chakha Maring Loikhombi. The noblemen in the palace asked Gourashyam and Bheigyachandra to rule for five years alternately. During the time of Gourashyam, the war with Awas had started. In 1758, crown prince Bheigyachandra along with army commander Anantasai proceeded towards Tamu to face the Awas. The Awas retaliated with strong power so the Meiteis had to retreat up to Kakching. The Meiteis had set up their camp at Kakching and fought the Awas. But the Awas were too powerful. Bheigyachandra failed to stop the Awas with his army at Leisangkhong. The Meiteis were badly defeated in this war. The Awas captured the palace, ruled for nine days and left. The Meiteis returned and continued with their rule.

As per agreement Bheigyachandra became king again on Thursday 7th of *Sajibu* 1759. During his rule also there were constant fightings with the Awas. In 1761, Bheigyachandra forsook the throne and gave it to his elder brother Gourashyam. The main reason for this was that one of his men killed a Brahmin in *Tangkham* (a village in Imphal East). King Bheigyachandra felt that he was unfit for the throne as even a Brahmin was not spared during his rule. King Gourashyam died on Tuesday 29th of *Thawan* 1763 because of his illness. Bheigyachandra became king again. In 1764, the Meiteis and Awas fought a war at Tamu. Haricharan, son of Pamheiba was the commander of the Meitei soldiers. The Meiteis were defeated in this War. Two Meitei warriors namely Naharup Hajari and Kshetri Cheiteinya got killed in this war. The Meiteis set up their camp at *Kakching*. The Awas were aggressive and advanced rapidly. In this war, the *Meiteis* set up *Unapal. Unapal* were barriers made of leaves, trees etc. (*Una*—leaves; *pal*—barrier). *Maha* River, *Tusarok* River and *Sekmai River* were dammed by constructing *Unapal* so as to block the pathways of the Awas. The Meiteis were defeated in this war and the Awas captured the Meitei palace. King Bheigyachandra fled to Cacchar and then reached Tekhao. He took shelter in Tekhao king Swargadev Rudeshwar's place. *Shija Fongdolokpi* who was the daughter of Gourashyam, Bheigyachandra's brother was married to the *Tekhao* king. (She later became the queen of *Tekhao* and known by the name *Kuranganayani*). With the help of Tekhao king Bheigyachandra tried to overthrow the Awas.

In the war that was fought between the Meiteis and the Awas at Kakching, Moirang King *Khelemba* took the side of the Awas. This was a main factor that led to the Meitei's defeat in the war. *Wayenbamcha Khelamba* was the maternal uncle of King Bheigyachandra. When Gourashyam was king he was made the king of Moirang in 1757. When Khelemba asked for land to the Meitei king for the expansion of Moirang kingdom, the latter refused to give. He also had a desire to become the king of Meitei kingdom. So he took the side of the Awa king. At that time, the Awa king was *Hsinbyushin,* the third king of *Konbaung* dynasty. This period was the golden period for the Awas. *King Alaungpaya* had founded *Konbaung* dynasty. He was a powerful ruler who put Burma under his rule. He even annexed major parts of Kabow Valley which was previously a part of Manipur. In 1756 and 1758, he invaded Manipur and captured Meitei Cavalry and other skilled craftsmen. With these Meitei Cavalry, he established Cavalry Corps which was called *Cassey Horse* in Burmese Army. This strengthened the Burmese Army. After him his son *Naungdawgyi* also attacked

Manipur in his time. Gourashyam was the King of Manipur during this time. The Burmese stayed at Imphal for 9 days. *Hsinbyushin* was the second son of *Alaungpaya*. He was king from 1763 till 1776. In 1764 he himself led an attack on Manipur. This war took place in December 1764 according to Burmese history. In this war Imphal Capital was easily captured. Many *Manipuris* were captured and taken as prisoners of war. It is recorded that King Hsinbyushin returned to Awa kingdom with his Army in April 1765 A.D. While in *Cheitharol Kumbaba,* it is mentioned that defeated Bheigyachndra fled to Tekhao while most of the people fled to Moirang. After the Awas had left Khelemba ruled Meitei Kingdom. He killed four noblemen namely Dhulavsai (son of King Pamheiba), Loukrakpam Hajari, Chingakham Hinaohanba and Shanglen Shriram. Khelemba married his daughter Shija Samjumani to the Awa King. The terms of agreement between him and the Awa king are clearly written in the old manuscript *Shija Samjumani.* He also killed his own brother Chandramani. By destroying his enemies he tried to rule as a king in Meitei Kingdom under the Awas. News of Bheigyachandra coming with an army of soldiers from Tekhao reached Manipur in 1767. On Thursday 6th of *Lamda* Bheigyachandra reached the Palace of *Sangaithel.* People who fled to Moirang returned and started settling at Imphal. In 1768, Moirang king Khelemba was killed by Meitei soldiers on the way while he was coming back from Awa to Manipur. In 1769, the Awas invaded again and Bheigyachandra fled to Cacchar. The Awas seized the palace for 20 days. A man of their choice called Keibiram was made to rule the kingdom. In 1770, Nandasai killed Keibiram and made his brother Kukilananda the ruler of the kingdom while he himself proceeded to Awa. Nandasai was the son of Mansai and he was the Senapati (Army Commander) and Mansai was again the son of Mungyamba Khwairakpa (chief of Khwai Pana) the youngest brother of Garibniwaz). The Awas came back again to fetch Meitei captives by waging war. But they were stopped by the Meitei soldiers led by Nandasai near the banks of Ningthi River and there a fierce fighting ensued. In this war about 700 Awas were killed. In 1772, the news of Bheigyachandra's arrival reached him and he tried to prevent Bheigyachandra from entering Manipur. Bheigyachandra's soldiers defeated them and they reached Sangaithel. Sangaithel is a village located at the foothills of *Ngaprum Chingjin* Road (New Cacchar road) and is 17 kms to the west of Imphal. A palace was made here. If a war in Imphal got severe the king would come to this place. In case of defeat they would easily proceed towards Cacchar from here. This palace was specially made for this purpose. After two days Bheigyachandra moved to the palace at Imphal. In the month of *Phairen* of the same year the Awas invaded again. Bheigyachandra was defeated again and he left for Cacchar. The Awas seized Imphal for 5 months. On the 11th of *Hiyangei*, Sunday 1773 Bheigyachandra reached Imphal. He drove away the Awas and resumed his rule. Like this till 1776, there was never a stable rule in Manipur. Many of the Meitei princes who were ambitious of becoming the king of Manipur seek refuge in Awa. This resulted to the frequent invasions on Manipur by the Awas. For this reason, Bheigyachandra was not able to establish a stable rule in the Meitei kingdom. On the 8th of *Sajibu*, Friday 1776, Bheigyachandra made his palace at Lamangdong and he ruled from there. He started making the statue of *Shree Shree Gobindajee* from 12th of *Hiyangei* (Friday). This was called *Nirpon of Shree Shree Gobindajee*. King Bheigyachandra maintained good relations with the *Mayang, Takhel* and *Tekhao* and started establishing a harmonious rule. He shifted his capital from Lamangdong to Canchipur on Tuesday, 3rd of *Kalen* 1779 A.D. On 11th of *Hiyangei*, Friday, in the *Raas Mandal* pond of Canchipur Palace *Shree Shree Gobindajee* was worshipped for the first time. This day fall on the day of *Hari Uthan* and *Raas Leela* was held for the next five days. The *Raas Leela* concluded on the day of *Mera Wa-fukpa*. This is the record found in *Cheitharol Kumbaba*. This was the first *Raas Leela* that was played in Manipur dedicated to *Shree Shree Gobindagee* and it was patronized by King Bheigyachandra. The Ramandi religion that was brought in Manipur by Garibniwaz was soon replaced by *Gouriya Vaishnava* religion by King Bheigyachandra. The Manipuri *Raas Leela* that had its roots in this religion has become so developed and unique that it has now become a well known dance form throughout the world. Manipuri *Raas Leela* was considered a Classical dance form of India before Manipur merged with India. Manipuri culture flourished during the time of King Bheigyachandra. Many new art forms were developed by blending Meitei and Hindu culture. King Bheigyachandra had developed three forms *of Raas Leela—Maha Raas, Kunja Raas* and *Basanta Raas*. Bheigyachandra died on Friday 3rd of *Mera* 1798 A.D. Manipur had witnessed a stable rule from 1776 till 1798. The Awas did not attack during this time also. The hill and valley people could be integrated. The people turned towards religion instead of fighting wars. Dance and music were more preferred. This period was called Golden age of Manipuri Culture.

According to *Cheitharol Kumbaba,* King Bheigyachandra had nine wives and 13 sons. Of these 13 sons 5 sons became Kings. The conflict amongst these sons for the throne gave the Awas undue advantage and they ruled Manipur for nearly seven years. This period is called Seven Years Devastation in the History of Manipur. After Bheigyachandra his son Labnachandra ruled from 1798-1800. After him Modhuchandra ruled from 1800-1803. Then Chourajit ruled from 1803-1813. Then came Marjit from 1813 till 1819. Labnyachandra was king for only three years and he died at the age of 46. After Modhuchandra had ruled for 3 years, his brothers had waged war upon him so he fled to Cacchar. When Chourjit became king Modhuchandra attacked Manipur with an army from Cacchar in 1804. On 14th of *Kalen* Wednesday Chourajit and Modhuchandra fought a battle at Keinou. Modhuchandra died in this battle. On Monday 28th of *Hiyangei* 1806 crown prince Marjit started a rebellion against Chourjit. But he was unsuccessful. So along with 273 men he went to Burma and set up his camp at Tamu. King Chourjit sent his men to appease his brother. Marjit refused and came for war instead in the month of Wakching. In spite of Chourjit's resistance Marjit marched till Yaiskul. But he could not enter the palace. Chourjit was ready to give his brother half the kingdom or the full kingdom whichever he like as he was ready to go to Cacchar. But Marjit was unrelenting. So Chourjit shunned him and they fought over the kingdom. Marjit was defeated and he fled to Burma. This war lasted for seven days and the kingdom was in chaos. Even the market was deserted. Then in 1808 Marjit came for war again. He was again defeated. Like this Marjit came again and again for war over the throne. Then at last on Sunday 11th of *Langban* 1812 A.D. Marjit seek refuge in the Awa King and asked for his help. The Awa king Bodowpaya advised Marjit not to fight with his brother but Marjit was adamant so the Awas had to help him. They reached Kakching on Sunday 6th of *Sajibu* 1813 A.D. Chourajit and Marjit fought the war for 11 days. Chourajit got defeated and he fled to Cacchar. On Wednesday 17th of *Sajibu* Marjit became the King of Manipur.

King Marjit ruled from 1813 till Tuesday 12th of *Wakching* 1819. He was king of Manipur for 6 years and 8 months. He invaded

Cacchar and defeated them. For this reason he was also called *Mayang Ngamba*. He had forgotten that the Awas had helped him in getting the throne so he broke off all ties with the Awas. The Awas on the other hand were thinking that the Meitei king was sub-ordinate to them. The Awa king Bodawpaya died on June 5, 1819 and his grandson Bagyidaw became the 7th king of *Konbaung* Dynasty. The coronation Ceremony was held on June 9, 1819. The funeral ceremony as well as Coronation ceremony were attended by many kings which were under the Awa king. King Marjit failed to attend the ceremony. Many of the vassal kings came with gifts, tributes etc. except for the Meitei king. This made Bagyidaw furious. When his grandfather Bodawpaya was king he had helped Marjit in the war of 1813 which made Marjit the king of Manipur. During this time, Bagyidaw was the Prince of Sagaing and was a well known leader but when his father the crown Prince Thado Minsaw died on April 9, 1808 his grandfather made him the Crown Prince. In the Burmese history, it is written that the war in which the Awa king had helped Marjit took place in February 1814—(During his stay as crown prince, his grandfather Bodawpaya renewed his expansionism in the west. In February 1814, a Burmese expanditionary force invaded Manipur, placing Marjit Singh, who grew up in Ava, as vassal King).

The first war that Bagyidaw fought as a king was the one which was fought with Marjit. In October 1819, General Maha Bandula led an army comprising of 25,000 infantryman and 3,000 cavalries and invaded Manipur. Maha Bandula conquered Manipur but king Marjit had already fled to Cacchar so he could not be captured.

According to *Cheitharol Kumbaba* when king Marjit heard of the invasion of the Awas he went to face them. The war started from Tuesday 5th of *Wakching*. There were fierce fightings for 8 days. By Tuesday the 12th of the same month, the Awas had intruded forcefully and they occupied Imphal. The people ran for their lives. It is written that Marjit also ran to Cacchar.

Manipur became deserted as most of the people left Imphal and went into hiding in the hills. The Awas took thousands of Meitei war captives. Majority of the Meiteis fled to Cacchar, Tripura and Bangladesh out of fear for the Awas. The Meitei prince Jaising was called out from his hiding place in the hills by Meiteis who were allies of the Awas in order to make him king. Instead of making him the king, the Awas took him to Awa. The Awa nobleman Kane-un stayed behind with 2000 soldiers and he ruled the Meitei Kingdom.

Starting from this time till Sunday 26th of *Inga* 1825 A.D., Manipur remained under the Awa's rule. This period is called the *Seven Years Devastation* in the history of Manipur.

During the Seven Years Devastation, the Awas did not actually sit and rule. They chose Meitei princes from time to time and made them rule. Herachandra, son of King Labnyachandra came down from the hills and started killing Awa soldiers through Guerrilla warfare. In the history of Manipur, he was called the *Taku Ningthu* (Dacoit King). On Tuesday 9th of Kalen 1820, he led on attack on the Awa Camp with 500 soldiers at Moirangkhom. 200 Awa soldiers were killed while others escaped. During this time King Modhuchandra's son Yumjaotaba returned from Cacchar and together with Herachandra, planned to attack the Awas. Herachandra only had 800 soldiers, 50 horses and 20 rifles. His mode of attack was guerrilla warfare type. He could not openly challenge the Awas as the latter were larger in number. About 200 to 300 Awa soldiers usually came out to collect their food. Such soldiers were ambushed by Herachandra and his men. He would hide in the trees and then attack with arrows, *Arambai* etc. Logs of wood were placed in the path of the Awa soldiers blocking them and he would attack from behind. The Awas could not resist such sudden attacks. It was said that the Awas stumbled and fall whenever they come out of their camps as their fear for Herachandra made them look upwards among the trees while walking. "Awa Mityeng" (Mityeng = gaze) is the Meitei proverb that is used till today. It means a person who constantly looks upwards while walking making him stumble and fall. Because of this the Awas were reluctant to come out of their camps. During this time Yumjaotaba and Herachandra had plotted another scheme. Yumjaotaba along with four men went to the camp of the Awas. He met Awa leader Kane-un and offered to help the Awas. He introduced himself as the son of King Modhuchandra who was an ally of the Awas and who was slained by his uncle King Chourajit. This convinced the Awas. He took about 100 Awas to Sekmai and collected food materials to feed the Awas. This action of Yumjaotaba won the confidence of the Awas. On the pretext of confronting Herachandra, he took 200 Awa soldiers, 40 cavalries and 20 rifles to Heiyen village. There he met Herachandra and together they kill all Awas and took their horses and rifles. Like this, the two brothers fougth the Awas for about eight months thereby helping the people in times of trouble. In the month of Hiyangei,

1820 Pakha-un led an army of 10,000 Awa soldiers and reached up to Kakching. A fierce battle was fought between the Awas and the brothers at Thoubal. The Awa army outnumbered the Meiteis so the two brothers were defeated and they fled to Cacchar. The Awas took with them many common people of Manipur. Kane-un and Pakha-un returned home with their soldiers. *Laipham Lakpa* (Chief of *Laipham Pana*) Huidromcha Subon was made to look after the kingdom.

Herachandra returned from Cacchar and fought with Subon. But they came to an agreement and soon stopped fighting and ruled the kingdom together. On Friday 14th of *Phairen,* Yumjaotaba came back from Cacchar and reached Maklang. Herachandra and Subon went to receive him and crowned him the king on 16th of *Phairen,* Sunday. On Thursday 26th of *Sajibu* 1821 A.D., Gambhir Singh returned to Manipur. Yumjaotaba gave him the throne and went to Cacchar. On Tuesday 21st of *Mera,* the Awas proclaimed Jai Singh as the king of Manipur and they marched to Manipur reaching up to Thoubal. Jai Singh set up a palace at Thoubal and stayed with the Awa soldiers. Ghambhir Singh could not face Jai Singh so he went to Cacchar. On Monday 13th of *Hiyangei,* Jai Singh shifted to the palace at Canchipur and ruled from there. King Jai Singh was the grandson of Pamheiba's son Anantasai. Anantasai was married to Naoroibam Chanu and gave birth to Kokilananda. Kokilananda was then married to Aheibam Chanu and gave birth to Jai Singh. Jai Singh was king till Wednesday 18th of *Langban* 1822. He went to Awa as he was called in by the Awas. On Friday 2nd of *Hiyangei,* the Awas appointed Jadu Singh Nongpok Chinglen Khomba as the King of Manipur. King Jadu Singh was the son of Bhadra Singh Nongchup Lamgai Ngamba and Thangjam Chanu Haripriya. Bhadra Singh was the son of Ngoubramsai who in turn was the son of King Garibniwaj.

King Jadu Singh died on Sunday, the new moon day of *Mera* in 1823. Ibungo Raghav Singh was proclaimed King the next day, i.e. 1st of *Hiyangei.* The Awas attacked Cacchar by using the Meitei king. In this war more than 300 Awa soldiers died. In 1824, the Awa army commander Atongbun led an attack on Cacchar. Many Awas died in the war also. Raghav Singh proceeded to Awa while his father Bhadra Singh Nongchup Lamgai Ngamba was proclaimed king on Monday 24th of *Sajibu.* There were two months of *Inga* for the year 1825. In the first *Inga* month, on Friday the 24th, Gambhir

Singh reached Maklang along with British army. They fought with the Awas on Saturday the 25th. The Awas were defeated and they fled. Bhadra Singh and Gambhir Singh stood on the same side. Gambhir Singh became King of Manipur on Sunday the 26th and Nara Singh became the Senapati (army commander). Nara Singh was the son of King Bhadra Singh and he played an important role in organizing Meitei army in Cacchar together with Gambhir Singh in order to overthrow the Awas in Manipur. On Friday 20th of *Hiyangei,* Nara Singh went for Awa invasion. He halted and set up his camp at Tamu. On Friday 5th of *Poinu,* Gambhir Singh joined him at Tamu. On Monday the 14th, the Meiteis surrounded the Awa army at Tamu and they kept them like that for five days. The Awas escaped at midnight. The Meiteis kept the Samsok King and Kale King as captives, and collected rifles, swords, gold, money etc. from them. Samsok capital was destroyed. The lands extending up to Ningthi River were again occupied and they become parts of Manipur. The Meiteis who were captured by the Awas were bought back again. Gambhir Singh and Nara Singh the two brothers reached the palace on the full moon day of *Wakching*. During that time Bishnupur was the capital. The capital shifted to Langthabal on Sunday 10th of *Mera* 1827. On Monday 22nd of *Kalen* 1829, King Gambhir Singh went to *Sylhot* in order to help the British in the war against the Khasis on the request of David Scott (the agent to the British Governor General for the Northern Territory). Sylhot was also called *Srihatta.* It is the Sylhet of present day Bangladesh. David Scott himself welcomed the King. The British army and the Meitei army attacked separately from different sides. The Meitei army faced the Khasis first. King Gambhir Singh captured Khasi King Tirot Singh and handed him to the British. The manuscript called *Khahi Ngamba* was written and kept and it described this war between the Meiteis and the Khasis. In Sylhet a dispute erupted between the Muslims and the Meitei Hindus as a Muslim religious festival and the *Rath Jatra* of Meitei Hindus fall on the same day. In order to settle the dispute, the British had asked the Muslims to celebrate their festival first. The Meiteis were unhappy at the British decision. As per the wishes of the people, the King of Manipur himself led the *Rath Jatra* festival in spite of the Muslims hindrance, on the same day, The King had defeated the Muslims who had come to interrupt the *Rath Jatra* festival. Instead of using swords and arrows, the Meitei soldiers easily defeated the Muslims by using sticks. The *Rath Jatra* continued without shedding any blood. After this the Muslims did not give any hindrance to the *Rath Jatra* festival. On Sunday 23rd of *Langban,* King Gambhir Singh returned from Sylhet and reached at Royal Palace. On Tuesday 13th of Hiyangei 1832 A.D., his son Chandrakirti was born. Gambhir Singh died on the new moon day of the month *Poinu* 1833 A.D. He was king for nine years only and he was only 47 when he died. Chandrakirti was made king when he was only one year and 3 months old. The actual rule was carried out by Nara Singh, the army commander.

Awa Ngamba tells the tale of how Manipur was saved from the hands of the Awas after the defeat of the Meiteis in their hands and the devastation of seven years that followed thereafter. On the other hand, *Cheitharol Kumbaba* is the record of how Manipur was ruled during these seven years. The events and wars that occurred in Cacchar are not recorded in *Cheitharol Kumbaba.* In *Awa Ngamba* it is clearly written how Gambhir Singh tried to conquer back Manipur from the Awas after he fled to Cacchar. It is also written how Gambhir Singh had helped the British in defeating the Khasis and the celebration of *Rath Jatra* in Sylhet after the conquest of Manipur. The manuscript may be written in the form of a literary piece of work but it contains many important historical facts which prove to be helpful in establishing the history of Manipur. *Awa Ngamba* is an indispensable part while establishing the history of how Kabow valley was annexed again from the Awas. After Chourajit's defeat in the hands of Marjit, Chourajit fled to Cacchar taking his brother Gambhir Singh along with him. Both the brothers took refuge in the kingdom of Cacchar during the time of King Gobinchandra. The king of Cacchar gave the two brothers separate lands where they were allowed to rule. Meanwhile, Marjit too got defeated in the hands of the Awas and he also reached Cacchar. He took shelter in his brother Chourajit's place. Chourajit forgave his brother. The brothers then overthrow Cacchar King Gobinchandra and they divided the lands of Cacchar amongst themselves and ruled. Chourajit and Marjit did not have the thought of invading the Awas again. On the other hand, Gambhir Singh started organizing Meitei army for Awa invasion in order to claim Manipur. Gambhir Singh along with Nara Singh developed an army of 500 men which was then called *Manipur levy.* The Awas were a powerful group of the people during that time. In 1822, the Awa King Bagyidaw made his general Maha Bandula to lead an attack on Assam with an army of 20000 men. The Ahom King was defeated and Assam was conquered by the Awas. The conquest of Assam hit a massive blow to British India. The Awa leader Maha Uzana then led attacks on Cacchar and Jaintia successively, The British asked for help to Gambhir Singh in the war of Cacchar. Gambhir Singh had also helped in this war. This record is found in *Awa Ngamba.* Gambhir Singh took his army and started witnessing the battle between the Awas and the British. The British did not have any idea of the war tactics of the Awas. They started attacking by firing arms and using bombs. The Awas were hiding secretly in pits and they did not retaliate. This made the British to advance rapidly towards the Awa camp when suddenly the Awas surrounded and attacked them from all sides. Many British soldiers were killed and others trapped. The Awas tried to capture British leader *Iska Saheb* (David Scott). At this time Gambhir Singh along with his army rode through the Awa soldiers and brought out *Iska Saheb* thus saving him. Many Awa soldiers died while others flee the place. Gambhir Singh had saved the British and he faced the Awas and by midnight he captured the Awa Frontier at Tilain Hills. The Awa soldiers retreated and they searched Manipur. Gambhir Singh after chasing the Awas till Barak River could catch only three Awas alive. He brought them and handed them over to *Iska Saheb. Iska Saheb* was very impressed by Gambhir Singh's courage and after appreciating them, he returned to Sylhet with his army. David Scott (called *Iska Saheb* by the Meiteis) invited Chourajit and the Gambhir Singh to Sylhet. After introducing them to the British at Sylhet Scott informed them that the Queen had agreed to extend help in the overthrowing of Awas from Manipur. They were told to return to Cacchar and organize their army and the British had agreed to provide all the expenditure, rifles and other weapons. Chourajit and Gambhir Singh gladly agreed.

King Chourajit told his brother Gambhir Singh that he had already ruled for twelve years as king of Manipur so it was time for him to retire. As Gambhir Singh showed immense courage in Cacchar while defeating the Awas and saving the British, he would be able to face the awas in Manipur also with the help of the British, Chourajit said. He also told Gambhir Singh to go and rule the kingdom while he decided to go to *Nabadwip* on pilgrimage. Like this he handed over the King's *hee-yai* (certain things which were entitled only to the king) to his brother Gambhir Singh. Gambhir

Singh then started organizing his army in Cacchar in preparation for war with the Awas. He started for Manipur but could not proceed further because of the rain as it was rainy season so he turned back and set up his camp at Badarpur. During that time Gambhir Singh heard the news of the Awas reaching Lakhimpur so he went to the British camp at Badarpur to confront the Awas. Seeing the Awas and the Meiteis coming together towards Badarpur, the British took it as a combined attack so they left Badarpur and returned to Sylhet. Gambhir singh stayed at Badarpur check post which was formerly the camp of the Birtish. The British soldiers returned after knowing the situation. At that time, the Awas had set up their camp at Tilain Hills. Soon war started between the British army and Awa Army. When the British had their camp at Jainagar, the Awas attacked them on all sides by coming along the Barak River. The British asked Gambhir Singh to help them which he obliged. Gambhir Singh again saved the British from the Awas. The weapons collected by the Awas and the prisoners of war from the British side were again saved and brought back. Gambhir Singh set up a British camp at Jatrapur and he returned to Badarpur.

Additional British forces arrived and they positioned themselves on the top of Kukmbra hills where they placed cannons in preparation for attack on the Awas. After full preparation they called Gambhir Singh to help them. The attack of the cannons dispersed the Awa army but there were no casualty on the side as they hid in pits which were dug out already. The war went on for some days. As it was rainy season, the British soldiers fell sick with fever. They could no longer face the Awas so they moved to Jatrapur camp. As the number of sick soldiers increased, the British had to go to Sylhet leaving the war to Gambhir Singh. The Awas also left the battlefield. Hearing this, Gambhir Singh ran after the Awas and completely evicted them out of Cacchar. After getting the news, the jubilant British invited Gambhir Singh to Sylhet. In the Darbar of Sylhet, Gambhir Singh Was felicitated. He was offered the post of *Captain Maha Fadrut Janera* for the North-east by the Queen of Englend. For this post customary uniform, Sword, Sword belt, Scabbard etc. shall be provided. Gambhir Singh and his men will be allowed free movement in every British Camp even if they possess arms and weapons. This post was being offered to Gambhir Singh. To this Gambhir Singh replied that he was not helping them for his personal gain but he was doing so in return for the help they extended during the difficult times of struggle to drive away the Awas from his motherland Manipur. The British officers took Gambhir Singh as no ordinary man. The court was scheduled for the next day and they returned. Gambhir Singh and his men deliberated on whether to accept or not to accept the post. If he accept the post the British would claim Manipur as their land even if they succeed in driving away the Awas. If they do not accept the post then they will not be able to defeat the Awas alone. Then at last they decided to surrender to their fates and take the help of that greater power for the sake of their motherland. In the next darbar (court), Gambhir Singh accepted the post offered by the British. Like this, Gambhir Singh and the British became allies. Gambhir Singh gathered around 4000 soldiers in Cacchar and get prepared to enter Manipur. During that time King Chourajit was staying at Narasingh Tilla in Sylhet. He sent message to his brother Gambhir Singh in Cacchar to come and meet him. Gambhir Singh went to meet his brother. King Chourajit told his brother that if he became the king of Manipur, the British would levy tax upon them. If the British asked to repay the help they extended weapons, soldiers and food then they will not be able to do it and so they were likely to become slaves. If Gambhir Singh became the king, the British would not impose tax on the people because he had helped the British in several ways many times. They would surely treat him like a friend. So Chourajit Singh told Gambhir Singh to take the throne and rule. He blessed him to be able to succeed in defeating the Awas. As for Chourajit Singh he chose to go to Nabadwip. The two brothers wept and that was their last meeting. Chourajit set off for Nabadwip on an auspicious day. Gambhir Singh returned to Cacchar, took the soldiers and started for Manipur. As it was rainy season they could not proceed beyond Jiri. *Iska Saheb* advised Gambhir Singh not to proceed further as the condition of roads worsened because of the rain. Above that the food supplies were being wasted. So Gambhir Singh returned to Cacchar. He felt frustrated when *Iska Sahed* told him not to enter Manipur as it would be an impossible task and it would be much better if he stayed as the king of Cacchar and ruled there. Gambhir Singh looked for an auspicious hour and set off for Manipur. After four days of journey he reached Manipur valley. A fierce battle took place with the Burmese. He made the British officers to return from Thoubal so as to take the news to Calcutta by giving three Awa prisoners-of-war. Gambhir Singh had arranged relay teams to facilitate the movement of the British officers from Thoubal to Leishangkhong, Leishangkhong to Lamangdong, Lamangdong to Chandrapur and Chandrapur to Calcutta. When the news of the defeat of Awas and their subsequent expulsion from Manipur reached Calcutta there were jubilant celebrations with fireworks. The Queen of England engraved words of appreciation for Gambhir Singh's courage on Copper plates and presented one to Gambhir Singh and kept another one at Calcutta.

After Gambhir Singh became the king of Manipur by defeating the Awas, his Queen Langmaithembi who stayed behind at Sylhet reached Manipur. She brought the news that the Muslims had shut down all the Hindu temples, prohibited the ringing of bells in the temple and *Rath Jatra* etc. On hearing these news, King Gambhir Singh left the responsibility of looking after the kingdom to Nara Singh, his army commander and left for Sylhet with his soldiers. After reaching Sylhet, King Gambhir Singh then allowed the opening of Hindu temples in every villages and normal prayer services were resumed with the use of bells and drums as usual. He instructed his soldiers to look for sticks (*lathis*) and beat up any miscreant. So 200 soldiers were put on duty with poles and sticks. On the day of *Rath, Jatra* the Muslims blocked the path of the Hindus resulting into a riot. In this conflict the Meitei soldiers used sticks and poles instead of rifles, swords, arrows etc. to fight the Muslims. The Muslims were badly beaten up and they ran helter skelter. They went into hiding in fear of the Meitei soldiers. Like this, the *Rath Jatra* was celebrated in a proper way. When the Muslims complained to the British, the British replied that they should not interfere in other's religion. Instead they should follow only their religion. As the king of Manipur was a religious man he did not take their lives. So they should be grateful to him. Like this, the British gave their judgments. The Muslims did not interfere in the religious matters again. For this reason King Gambhir Singh was praised by the people. After returning to Manipur, King Gambhir Singh invaded Awa. He pushed out the Awa soldiers who had set up their camp at Tamu and occupied up to Samsok. While he was in Tamu three British officers namely *Premtol, Giral* and *Ajiton* came with gifts from the Queen of England. They were astonished when they opened the box. The gift was actually a sword which meant a great honour. The three officers presented the aword to the King. (*Premtol*—Robert Boilean Pemberton; *Giral*—Major Grant; *Ajiton Saheb*—Captain George Gordon).

Later Gambhir Singh again defeated the Awas and annexed the lands extending up to Ningthi River. By destroying the forts at Loi-jiri, Gambhir Singh had saved several Meiteis who were captured as prisoners of war by the Awas. These Meiteis were sent back again to Manipur with money, food and cattle. The lands along the Ningthi River were under the control of the Awas. These Awas were also driven away by the Meiteis and annexed by Gambhir Singh. The Awas had run away so far that they had reached the Capital of Awa kingdom. After knowing that the Awas had reached the capital King Gambhir Singh knew that there will be no use chasing the Awas. So he cleaned his sword in the Ningthi River and returned to Manipur. This was called *Ningthi Turelda Thang Chamba* (*Turel*—River; *Thang*—Sword; *Chamba*—cleaned). There is a story behind the cleaning of sword in the Ningthi River. King Gambhir Singh had once swore that he will invade the Awa Kingdom, defeat it and ruled over it. His sword which would be stained with the blood of Awa soldiers will then be washed in the Ningthi River and that would serve as an offering (Tarpon Katpa) to the lost souls of the Meiteis. The fleeing of the Awas was a sign of their defeat. So King Gambhir Singh annexed their lands and they became a part of Manipur. To fulfil his vow he cleaned his blood stained sword in the Ningthi River before returning to Manipur.

During King Gambhir Singh's rule in Manipur the Khahis had killed two British officers. So Scott Saheb seek help from Gambhir Singh in the war with the Khahis. King Gambhir Singh went to help the British. The Khahi war details were recorded in a written form called *Khahi Ngamba*. But the time of this war as recorded in *Cheitharol Kumbaba* and *Awa Ngamba* showed a great difference. In *Cheitharol Kumbaba* it is written that the *Rath Jatra* conflict at Sylhet happened after the Khahi war. Whereas in *Awa Ngamba,* the Khahi war occurred after the *Rath Jatra* conflict. Nevertheless, these two episodes were all historical facts. *Cheitharol Kumbaba* recorded the day, date and year of historical events but *Awa Ngamba* did not give any such time records. Instead beautiful literary words, proverbs etc. were used in presenting the story for good reading purpose. In *Awa Ngamba* it is written that it took four months to capture Khahi king Chabar Singh. Gambhir Singh caught Chabar Singh along with his two ministers Uma Mantri and Thibal Mantri and handed them over to Scott Saheb. It is written that the two ministers were hanged while Chabar Singh was not put to death. In *Cheitharol Kumbaba* and British records, the name of the Khahi / Khasi king is written as Tirot Singh. In appreciation of the Manipur king's bravery by the British, it was agreed that Cacchar would be considered a part of Manipur. But on the request of the Cacchar King half the kingdom was retained by him, the British record mentioned.

The later part of *Awa Ngamba* is mainly about the British and Manipur. The Awa Manipur episode is not written anymore. This part mainly reflected Gambhir Singh's childhood reminiscences of his father King Bheigyachandra's stories about Hindu religion and the principles of administration taught by him. Many stories of Hindu *Puranas* are written in this book in parts. As Gambhir Singh was a devout Hindu there are also many instances that try to show that the Meiteis are the descendants of the *Mahabharata* hero Arjuna. After a thorough research on the various Puyas relating to creation Myth and various religious belief systems, the British opined that the Meiteis were not the descendants of Brabubahan. Gambhir Singh tried to prove that the Meiteis were the descendants of Hindu ancestors by consulting many priests and learned scholars and other related books also. His quests for the answer form the story line of the book *Awa Ngamba*. Remembering the religious stories of the Hindus told by his father Bheigyachandra when he was a child and the administrative principles taught by his father and their relevant application during his rule formed the main part of the book.

Awa Ngamba is a manuscript written in Meitei script. It begins with a prayer on Lord Ganesh—the protector from all evils according to Hindu belief which read as "Om Ganeshai Namah". Next the writing starts with a prayer of *Shri Hari* which said "Shri Hari Haya hey Khoimom Lainingthou". This prayer is actually a combination of Meitei and Hindu religion. 'Haya hey' is a word which is used while offering prayer to the Meitei creator God. The Meitei God and Shri Hari are taken as one and worship. It is a mixed form of culture of the Meiteis after the coming of Hinduism. The book concludes with "Mikol Thagonba". (Mikol Thakolba—at the end of any religious ceremony an act called Mikol Thakolba is usually performed which is aimed at embracing the hearts and minds of the people which might have gone haywire during the ceremony. This tradition was also maintained in written books. At the end of the book there will be a prayer asking for forgiveness and for the removal of any bad incidents and to free the minds of the listeners which is called Mikol Thagolba).

REFERENCES

Amubi Singh Irom. (ed.). *Awa Ngamba*, Imphal, 1979.

Ashokumar, L. *Ariba Manipuri Sahityagi Paring* (*18 amasung 19 gi Manipuri Sahitya*), Jenifar, Jenita, Shibadata, Imphal, 2000.

Ashokumar, L. *Ariba Manipuri Sahityagi Paring*, Yumnam Ibopishak, Imphal, 1992.

Bhogeshwor Oinam. (ed.), *Ningthourol Lambuba* (*Ahanba Saruk*), Imphal, 1967.

Bormani Sarangthem. *Meitei Ningthourol*, Barsa Publication, Imphal six edition, 2014.

Chandra Singh Moirangthem.(ed.). *Gambhir Singh Nongaba*, Poknapham Publication, Imphal, 1967.

Chandra Singh Moirangthem.(ed.). *Samsok Ngamba*, Manipur Naharol Sahitya Sava, Imphal, 1980.

Chandra Singh Moirangthem.(ed.). *Shija Samjumani (Samjureima)*, Kh. Surendra Singh, Imphal, 1966.

Chandra Singh Moirangthem.(ed.).*Khahi Ngamba*, Manipuri Sahitya Parishad, Imphal, 1967.

Hemchandra Chanam.(ed.). *Ningthourol Lambuba*, Imphal, 2018.

https://en.wikipedia.org/wiki/Myanmar, 23 August 2020, at 03:46 (UTC).

Ibungohal L. & Khelchandra N. *Cheithrol Kumbaba*,(ed.), Manipur Sahitya Parishad, Imphal, 1967.

Ibungohal Singh Lairenmayum. *Narasing* (*Awa Ngamba*), Poknapham Publication, 4th Edition, Imphal, 1986.

Khelchandra Singh N. *Ariba Manipuri Sahityagi Itihas*, Chirom Yaimabi Devi, Imphal, 1972.

Manikchand Singh Konsam, (Tran. & Ed.). *Sorarel Machana Khulkumpa*, Konsam Imo Singh, Imphal, 2014.

Pemberton R.B., *The Eastern Frontier of India*, Mittal Publications, New Delhi (India), 2015.

Sorojini Kh. (ed.). *Tiline Landa Narasing*, Imphal, 1981.

15
The Problem of the Kabaw Valley

Leisangthem Chandramani Singh

The Kabaw Valley is a narrow strip of level land between the mountains which form the eastern boundary of the Manipur Valley and the Ninghthee River. "The term Kubo (Kabaw)" Pemberton writes, "is employed by the people of Muneepoor (Manipur) to designate not only the Shans, but the extensive race Itself together with the tract on the opposite bank of the Ningthee River, extending to the Naojeeree Hills, was called by then Meithei Kubo and by the Burmese Kathe Shan, while that portion of Shan comprised between the eastern foot of the Naojeeree Hills and the right bank of the Irawathi (Irawadi) River was Ava Kubo or Mrelap Shan."[1] The Valley was divided into the Sumjok, the Khambat and the Kule divisions respectively. Apart from its economic importance arising from rich teak woods, the Rajas of Manipur and Burma thought the possession of the valley indispensable for the border security of their respective countries and naturally they endeavoured to extend their sovereignty over that valley. No wonder, therefore, successive border disputes arose in that valley during the years following the First Anglo-Burmese War (1824-26). The necessity for demarcation of a well defined boundary was, therefore, keenly felt by both the parties and the Government of Bengal came forward as the arbitrator over the intricate problem. In fact, no mention, whatever, was made of the valley in the Treaty of Yandaboo and nothing was discussed at that time about the boundary between Manipur and Burma. The Government of Bengal felt it to be just and proper that all the places and territories in the ancient country of Manipur, which were in possession of Raja Gambhir Singh should belong to that Raja as the authorities in Calcutta, hitherto, calculated the importance of keeping Manipur as a buffer State between British

India and Burma. The Sumjok and Khambat Divisions of the valley as far east of the Ningthee or Kyendwin were accordingly given to Manipur[2] on April 1826 and the Ningthee formed the boundary between the countries.[3]

Soon after the conclusion of the treaty of Yandaboo some Burmese troops crossed the Ningthee River and entered the Valley. Instead of renewing hostilities, Gambhir Singh thought it wise to leave the matter to the decision of the British. The Supreme Government, therefore, took great pains to demarcate a proper boundary between Burma and Manipur. The Burmese, on the other hand, made no friendly offers. Several attempts had been made subsequently saw no sign of amicable settlement. In early 1828, the Government of Bengal appointed Captains Grant and Pemberton, the two British officers in Manipur, as the Commissioners to settle the dispute. In that same year, the latter met the Burmese Commissioners on the bank of the Ningthee River, but the season was far advanced and the two parties decided to postpone the meeting till the following year.

In the meantime, the Burmese interpreted that the Ningthee was not the Kyendwin (Chindwin).[4] They falsely represented that it was a river flowing to the west of the Kabaw Valley and tried to back their claims by sending a map to Calcutta showing the Ningthee and the Chindwin as two different rivers. The authorities in Calcutta returned the map to the British Commissioners in Manipur to enquire into the report whether any such river shown as the Ningthee in the map existed. Grant and Pemberton proved the deception of the Burmese and their report was forwarded to the Resident at AW.[5]

The date for the next meeting was fixed in early 1829; but no Burmese Commissioner appeared. The Supreme Government desired the settlement in favour of Gambhir Singh and directed Grant and Pemberton to proceed to the Ningthee. The Burmese were, however, invited to meet the British Commissioners, in January 1830, pointing out to them that if they failed to come on the appointed date, the boundary would be fixed in their absence permanently.

As scheduled, the meeting with the Burmese Commissioners, accompanied by Major Burney, British Resident in Burma was held in January 1830 on the bank of the Ningthee River. The Burmese strongly denied the conquest of the Kabaw Valley by Gambhir

Singh during the late war and rejected the boundary demarcated by Grant and Pemberton.[6] They asserted that the Manipuris had come secretly into the valley and taken possession of the country while the boundary question was under discussion with Sir A. Campbell, the Commander of the Oversea Expedition, in the First Burmese War. But Grant and Pemberton did not agree with their argument and recommended the valley in favour of Gambhir Singh pointing out that the valley was in possession of Manipur occasionally in earlier periods as well as for twelve years during the reign of Raja Chourjit Singh (1800-1813), the then Raja of Manipur. The Burmese on the other hand claimed the valley as their own and cited that the Khambat and the Sumjok divisions of the valley, 1,300 years ago were under them. They denied the possession of the Kabaw Valley to Manipur occasionally in the ancient times as well as for a period of twelve years during the reign of Raja Chourjit Singh. They also rejected the claims of possession of the Sumjok, the Khambat etc. by Manipur before the conclusion of the Treaty of Yandaboo. The strongest argument in support of their dales was that the Kabaw Valley was separated from the authority of the Chief of Manipur and annexed to the Burmese Empire under the Burmese Governor for a period of eleven or twelve years before the First Anglo-Burmese War.[7] In support of their contention they produced an old inscription on a stone in the Pagoda of Koungnhoohan to show that Sumjok was subject to Ava in the Burmese year 1012 or 1650 A.D. and denied that any grant of the territory eastward of the Kyendwin was ever made to Manipur by the great grandfather of the then Raja of Pong, an important and powerful Shan kingdom of Upper Burma. They challenged documents and other proofs produced by Manipur as to date and manner in which she originally came into possession of the town of Tamu, Khambat etc.[8]

The British Commissioners denied the Burmese claims and maintained that the valley belonged to Manipur and produced records from the chronicles of that State and proved that Kyamba (1467-1508), the then Raja of Manipur, with Khikhomba, the contemporary Raja of Pong, both agreed to fix a boundary between their countries and Kabaw was ceded to the former in 1485 A.D.[9] They laid before the Burmese Commissioners a book which proved that: (1) the Pong Raja was not a tributary of Ava 400 years ago, (2) that the Khambat and the Sumjok were tributary of Pong ,and (3) that the Pong Raja then ceded to Raja Kyamba all the country comprised between the Naojeeree and the Muyalong Hills on the eastern side of the Ningthee River.[10]

The Commissioners, no doubt, agreed that the Burmese had been for twelve years, in possession of the Kabaw Valley before the last war. This transaction took place in consequence of a successful attempt through the aid of the Burmese made by Raja Marjit Singh to deprive his elder brother Raja Chourjit Singh of the Chiefship of Manipur. Kabaw, which for the preceding 15 years had belonged to Manipur, was then annexed to Ava—it was a reward for the good service rendered by the latter.[11] They, therefore, reminded the Burmese Commissioners that the reconquest and the former possession were the only two points for the consideration and that the Ningthee River must be the boundary between Burma and Manipur.[12] Grant and Pemberton further told them that the conquest of the Kabaw Valley by Raja Gambhir Singh before the treaty of Yandaboo was correct, because, they were present at the time of the capture of Tamu. In support of their argument they also produced printed narratives of the Burmese war—one, dated 23 January, 1826, written from Tamu and the other dated 3 February, 1826 from Monfu, on the western bank of the Ningthee River as proofs of their statements.[13]

The Burmese Commissioners paid little heed to the argument put forward by the British Commissioners. In these circumstances, Major Burney, the British Resident at Ava, therefore, invited Pemberton to have a further discussion with the Burmese ministers. On his arrival at Ava, the latter found it impossible to convince the Burmese of the rightfulness of the claims of Gambhir Singh to the Valley.[14] Major Burney brought home to the Burmese Ministers that the deputation of Captain Pemberton to Ava was itself a proof of the desire of the British Government that the question regarding the boundary of Manipur should be settled in the most amicable manner. He added that Pemberton's earlier actions had recalled entire approval from the Governor-General and that the officer was not empowered to renew or enter into any further discussion of the subject.[15] The King and ministers of Burma firmly believed that if they could secure, in the same manner as Gambhir Singh had done, the aid and services of the British officers to represent their case before the Governor-General, His Lordship would not decide the question against Ava. The Burmese ministers further enquired of Major Burney if the Governor-General could remove Raja Gambhir

Singh and place Marjit Singh on the throne of Manipur, for under such an arrangement they hoped to maintain friendly relations between Manipur and Burma.

Major Burney informed that the decision made by the Government in favour of Raja Gambhir Singh had already been reported to the authorities at England and as such the discussion could not be reopened. To conciliate the Ministers, he pointed out that the Government might sacrifice a part of the indemnity (under the terms of the Peace treaty of 1826). If there was no objection on their part to the Inclusion of the Kabaw Valley in Manipur. The Ministers considered, the proposal favourably, but dared not to communicate their feelings to the King, who, they knew, would burst out into a violent rage, the consequences which sight be a serious one.[16] The Burmese King, till then, bore an implacable hatred against the British and was determined on retrieving the losses which the last war had inflicted upon him. He was keen on the subject of the Kabaw; he expressed his vexation that the British not only supported the Manipuris but also desired to give them a portion of his own territory. Major Burney felt that if the matter was pressed further, it would bring another war. He remarked: "Had our determination regarding the Kabaw Valley been communicated to the Court in 1827 at the time when it sought so much to obtain some delay in the payment of the Third instalment and at the time when the king's weak mind had not taken up this subject, I think, there would then have arisen little or no difficulty. But now, there are grounds of probability that the determination of the Governor General-in-Council in favour of Munneepore may ultimately produce a collision between the British and the Burmese States."[17]

In the meantime, a Burmese deputation went to Calcutta and waited upon the Governor-General to make an appeal against the British decision in the Kabaw Valley. Major Burney was, therefore, called upon by the Supreme Government to reach Calcutta so that he could join in the discussions. A perusal of the official records of Ava convinced Burney that the claims put forward by the Burmese could not be so lightly set aside. Apart from this, the political insignificance of Manipur as a buffer state, had led him to support the Burmese case notwithstanding vehement opposition from Grant and Pemberton. Though convinced of the right of Manipur to the Kabaw Valley, the Supreme Government concurred in the views of the Resident on the problem. It was felt that Burma being more important than Manipur it would not be expedient to uphold the right of the latter, and subsequently it was decided to accede to the request of the King of Ava that the valley should be restored to him and the eastern foot of the Maring Hills should be considered the boundary between Manipur and the Burmese territories.[18] Lord William Bentinck, in his Minute, 26 February, 1833, remarked: "........... to the humiliation to their pride and to their reduced if not extinguished power I think it will be both generous and expedient to grant them this gratification .... and Gambhir Singh be awarded a compensation for the loss."[19] Major Burney was, therefore, directed to announce to the King that "the Supreme Government still adheres to the opinion that the Ningthee forms the proper boundary between Ava and Munneepore but that in consideration for His Majesty's (i.e. of the King of Burma) feelings and wishes and in the spirit of amity and goodwill subsisting between the two countries the Supreme Government consents to the restoration of the Kobo Valley to Ava and to the establishment of the boundary at the foot of Yoomadoung Hills."[20]

Grant and Pemberton persuaded Gambhir Singh to accept the new arrangements. They appealed to him in the name of friendship and assured him that the new arrangement would be found highly beneficial both to him and as well as to his country.[21] They communicated to the Raja the final approval of the Government to the sum of Sicca Rs. 500 P.M. to be paid by half yearly instalments as compensation for the loss of the valley and if circumstances arose by which the territory in question ever again reverted to Manipur, the compensation granted would cease from the date of such restoration.[22] Grant and Pemberton thus handed over the valley to Burma on 9 January, 1834, and a treaty was concluded on the same day between Manipur and Burma.[23] Gambhir Singh expired on 9 January, 1834, the very day on which the valley was transferred to Burma. The arrangement for carrying out this agreement into execution was entered into by his successor.

It will be evident, from the above that the transfer of the valley had been decided without any reference to the Raja of Manipur. The surrender of the valley as apprehended by Sir E. Barnes, the then Commander-in-Chief, would do but little good in appeasing the wounded pride and the angry feelings of the Court of Ava and did a great deal of harm to Manipur. He felt it to be an unwise attempt to conciliate an enemy and a very probable means of converting a friend into an enemy. Sir E. Barnes, therefore, strongly desired that the Government should revise the decision.[24] But the latter paid little attention to what the Commander-In-Chief entreated. The relations with Burma continued to be unfriendly for the Burmese Kings could neither forget nor forgive the lessons they received in the hands of the English only a few years before and determined to undo the Treaty of Yandaboo. The Burmese monarch Tharrawaddy (1837-1845) expressed: "The British beat my brother, not me. The Treaty of Yandaboo is not binding on me, for I do not make it."[25]

Actually, within 18 years of the transfer of the valley, the Second Anglo-Burmese War broke out in the time of King Pagan (1845-1852). Sir James Johnstone observed: "We had an agent Colonel Burney at Ava, and the Burmese who were not disposed to be at all friendly, constantly tried to impress on him the fact that all difficulties and disputes would be at an end if we ceded the Kabaw Valley to them—that territory belonging to our ally Gambhir Singh of Manipur. Of course, the proposal should have been rejected with scorn and a severe snub given to the Burmese officials .... it was not realised that a display of self-confidence and strength is the best diplomacy with people like the Burmese and with a view to winning their goodwill we basely consented to deprive our gallant and loyal ally on part of his tributaries."[26]

NOTES

1. R. Boileu Pemberton (1835, rp. 1966), *Report on the Eastern Frontier of British India*. Gauhati: DHAS, p. 116.
2. Iboogohal Singh, Lairenmayum, *Introduction to Manipur*, (Imphal: 1963), p. 137.
3. Meckenzee, Alexander, *North East Frontier of Bengal*, p. 176.
4. Meckenzie, *Op. cit.*, p. 177.
5. Jhaljit, Rajkumar, *A Short History of Manipur*, p. 215.
6. National Archives of India, New Delhi. *(A) Foreign Department, Secret Consultations (SC)*, 30 April, 1830, Nos. 3-4.
7. National Archives of India, New Delhi. *(A) Foreign Department, SC*, 19 November, 1830, Nos. 4-11.
8. National Archives of India, New Delhi. *(A) Foreign Department, SC*, 30 April, 1830, Nos. 3-4.
9. *Ibid.*
10. *Ibid.*
11. National Archives of India, New Delhi. *(A) Foreign Department, Secret Proceedings Volume (SPV)*, 19 March, 1833, No. 1.

12. National Archives of India, New Delhi. *(A) Foreign Department, SC,* 30 April, 1830, Nos. 3-4.
13. *Ibid.*
14. *Ibid.*
15. National Archives of India, New Delhi. *(A) Foreign Department, SC,* 19 November, 1830, Vols. 4-11.
16. National Archives of India, New Delhi. *(A) Foreign Department, SC,* 21 January, 1831, Nos. 6-8.
17. National Archives of India, New Delhi. *(A) Foreign Department, SC,* 19 November, 1830, Nos. 4-11.
18. National Archives of India, New Delhi. *(A) Foreign Department, Secret Proceedings Volume (SPV),* 16 April, 1833, No. 77.
19. National Archives of India, New Delhi. *(A) Foreign Department, Secret Proceedings Volume (SPV),* 19 March, 1833, No. 1.
20. *Ibid.,* No. 2.
21. National Archives of India, New Delhi. *(A) Foreign Department, SC,* 11 July, 1833, Nos. 14-15.
22. National Archives of India, New Delhi. *(A) Foreign Department, SC,* 10 January, 1834, Nos. 4-5.
23. *Aitchison, Treaties etc.,* Vol. I, pp. 220-221. See Appendix D & E.
24. National Archives of India, New Delhi. *(A) Foreign Department, SC,* 19 March, 1833, No. 11.
25. Dodwell, *The Cambridge History of India,* Vol. V, p. 560.
26. Johnstone, Sir James, *op. cit.,* p. 86.

16
How Manipur Lost Kabaw Valley to Burma During Negotiation[1]

Th. Suresh Singh

What is Kabaw valley? It is a bone of contention between Manipur and Pong/Burma (present Myanmar). At present, it is under Burmese control. Up to mid-18th century, before Pong kingdom (Shans are the inhabitants) was overrun by Burmese king Alampara, it was under the Shans. In the majority of period it was under Manipuri king and in the minority of period, it was under Pong or Burma.

Boundary

The Pong kingdom with Mogaung (Burmese name/ Mongmaorang-Shan name) as capital was inhabited by the Shans. The Kingdom is known as Pong Kingdom to the Manipuris and the people are generally called "Kubo" or "Awa". However, the two terms, Kubo and Awa, are often used in a general sense and often give confusion to the readers. These terms often refer either to the place or to the people as the situation demands. One has to interpret it according to the context. The river Ningthee (Manipui name, Chinsuin-Shan name and Chindween-Burmese name) prominently occupies an important and unavoidable part in its turbulent history.

The Burmese called the eastern side of the river as Mrelap Shan and the western side as Kasi Shan as per the different names given to the Meiteis by the Burmese. The Burmese called the Meiteis as Kasis/Kathees/Cassayers. The Manipuris called the eastern side as Awa Kabo and the western side as Meitei Kabo. In northern and central portion of the Kabo Valley, the Manipur and Burmese languages were very often generally spoken of though later subdued by the rising power of the Burmese. The Maglung valley, which lies between Maglung river course and Angoching hills, is 2 miles broad and is occupied by the Shans or by the Manipuris who manufactured salt there.

According to Pemberton[2], the Pong Kingdom is divided into 3 valleys: (i) the Kabo Valley, (ii) a 2nd Valley, and (iii) a 3rd longitudinal one. Three rivers flow through it—the Ningthee (Chindween), the Moo and the Irrawaddy. These 3 are the most known and extensively used for communication. Other smaller rivers are the Ooroo which flows to Ningthee and Mezashwelee and Namyan Khoyoung which flows to Irrawaddy on the western bank.

(i) Kabaw Valley proper i.e. the Valley

Pemberton[3] described it as lying between the present north-east Manipur boundary which starts at the foot of Yoomadoung hills and Ningthee River. It starts from the foothills in 24° 30° Lat. North and 22° 30° Lat. South where Manipur (Kathekhyoung) river falls into the Ningthee. This is the southern Unit of Kule Raja's territory. However, the actual southern limit is Mutootgaundee, a short distance beyond the confluence of the two rivers and on the left bank (eastern) of Ningthee.

According to the Chieftain during Pemberton's survey, the former Kule principality extended up to the junction of the Ningthee and Irrawaddy Rivers. Though not a single book mentioned the length of this valley, Pemberton described its breath between two to eight miles in circumference and when viewed from a height, presents a vast expanse of dark Primeval Saul forest, in the very heart of which cleared spaces are discerned.

Famous and valuable trees are available here—Varnish tree (Khewoo to Manipuris), world famous Teak tree and the finest specimen of Saul (Khangra to Manipuris).

The whole valley is watered by Ningthee and very fertile. An inferior and broken range of subordinate hills run parallel to and close upon the left bank of Ningthee as far as Maukandan Myoo, then gradually disappears. The superior range of Noajeeree (beyond Ningthee) terminates a little beyond it on the east.

The valley has three principalities or subdivisions— 'Samjok' (Thangdent), 'Khumbat' (Kendat) and Kule (present Kale). Pemberton had stated that '*the boundary of these subdivisions of the ancient Pong Kingdom have fluctuated with the success or failure of the Burmese arms.'*

There are two routes for reaching Kabaw Valley or Samjok. The first one is the southerly route known as Moreh/ Imole road, an easier and most frequented by traders and the second one is the Yanjonpokpi route and is the northerly one. The second one lies east from Imphal and is the direct route to Kabaw Valley and Samjok. According to Regional Integration[4], a new Kuki village named Phaikot had settled besides border Post 102 (new) across the stream Wamaya where Manipuri 'Kongal Thana' outpost used to be. The 'Tangkhuls' know this place as 'Huimi' and is the north-easternmost corner of present Manipur. 'From here, Angoching and Somra Tract begins'.

This valley is important from Manipur's perspective in that many battles were fought in various places situated in this valley.

Controversy about its Boundary

Pemberton's double standard and deceptive description of above definition of Ningthee river as the eastern boundary of Kabaw Valley is unfortunately followed by all Manipuri historians/writers and also by all foreign historians/writers without scanning the true historical perspective. Let us scan as below:

The same Pemberton[5] at page 122 described Noajeeree or Dzeebyootoung range as the eastern boundary of Kabaw Valley. At page 125, he described Noajeeree as the eastern limit of Khumbat woon. At page 128, he again mentioned Noajeeree as the western boundary of 2nd valley described above. Pemberton's (p. 20) often quoted and famous line *'The territories of Manipur have fluctuated at various times with the fortunes of their princes, frequently extending for three or four days' journey east beyond the Ningthee or Khyendwen river, and west to the plains of Cachar...'* is itself a true reflection of Manipur frontier. I find him sincere here.

I also found Dr. Brown[6] (page 60) mentioning the state's boundary during Garibniwaj's time as : West—up to Cachar, South—as far as water-shed flowing sea wards (means up to Irrawaddy basin on Bay of Bengal) and North—about 9 days journey from capital (means Manipur capital). He is the only foreigner giving a true perspective.

Hence, Pemberton was the originator of this deceit boundary definition of Kabaw Valley. No doubt, the British were trying to find a true natural boundary of Kabaw Valley in order to solve the troubled Manipur-Burma frontier. Here they find 'Ningthee River' as the same and Raja Gambhir Singh agreed to it (though no historical documents available) thinking that the valley up to Ningthee will be handed over to him permanently.

Intermingled it with the fact that various Manipuri kings crossed the Ningthee during their conquest of the valley, every Manipuri historian/writer/intellectual now should be clear that Noajeeree Range, and not Ningthee, is the Eastern Frontier of Kabaw Valley.

An Outline of Ningthee River

This is most often quoted, most often misunderstood but most beautiful river in the region. Ningthee is a Manipuri term meaning beautiful. Hence, Ningthee River means beautiful river. How the river is known as Ningthee is beautifully described in '*Ningthourel Lambuba*'.[7]

Kabo Senbi people knew the pillow as 'Yeng'. One day, Pangka (a principality in Kabaw Valley) King's pillow was taken away by one wild cock and thrown away to the mid-stream of the river there. The pillow was recovered by one of his noblemen Yangsanam Yaurou Shafa Ngamba. From that day, the river was known as 'Yingthee River'. The present 'Ningthee' is the corrupt version of 'Yingthee'. The Shans knew it as Nupurong and Burmese as Kyondwen/Chindween/Thanlawattee. This river is the water communication line for the whole Kabaw valley and beyond.

Fascinating History of the Three Kingdoms: Manipur-Pong-Burma history will be incomplete without the fascinating account of Kabaw Valley. Brief outlines are as below:

Period of uncertainty: It covers from 33 to 1467 A.D. and known as 'before King Kyamba Period'. Starting 33 A.D., 37 Kings reigned in Manipur during this period according to *Cheitharol Kumbaba*.[8]

However, the first contact with the Pong must have started at least centuries ago. This is a period where the valley is either under Manipur or under Pong by virtue of their respective military might and subsequent dominance.

The period of settled boundary where Kabaw Valley was a part of Manipur: This period covers from 1467-1709 A.D., where 12 Manipuri Kings reigned, i.e. from Kyamba to Charairongba. Hence, it is referred to as 'Kyamba to Charairongba period'. That the Manipur boundary extended far beyond Ningthee River and subsequently Kabo Valley at that time means up to Noajeeree hills is being proved by the following events:

Combined forces of Manipur king Kyamba (1467-1508 A.D.): The king along with Pong King Soohappha (known as Chaupha Khekhomba by the Manipuris) destroyed Khumbat thus extending Manipuri boundary up to the famous celebrated mango tree near Mongkhong Mawai which lies between Ningthee and Noajeeree range to the north. Noajeeree range of hills which lies between the Ningthee and the Moo River was the eastern boundary of Manipur by virtue of this conquest and division of geographical area between the two kings.

Kabomba (1525-42 A.D.): The King invaded and defeated the Kabos at Pallu Village on eastern border hence the name of Kabomba (i.e. the one who conquered Kabo).

Mungyamba (1562-97 A.D.): The king invaded Samjok and other parts of Kabo valley 7 times, i.e. in 1571, 1572, 1573, 1582, 1588, 1591 and 1592 A.D. respectively. By virtue of the king's conquest of Kabo Mungsha, he was called Mungyamba, i.e. the conqueror of Mangsha after this battle as per *Ningthourol Lambuba* (pp. 265-277).[9]

Khagemba (1597-1652 A.D.): The king ruled 55 years. and invaded Kabo valley eight times and won. Awa invaded Manipur twice, but were defeated by the King (*Cheitharol Kumbaba*, 2nd ed.).[10] *Ningthourol Lambuba* (pp. 280, 297 & 301)[11] also mentioned four invasions by the King and 2 invasions by his queen Taipombi to the valley. In one invasion of a big Chinese village, the king defeated its Chief Choupha Hongdai and many noblemen, hence, the name Khagemba, i.e. Conqueror of China. Though this Chronicle did not indicate the specific year, T.C. Hudson suggests it to be 1630 A.D. and R.K. Jhalajit thinks it to be 1631 A.D. as quoted by *Gangmumei* (p. 212).[12] This battle must have definitely taken place around the Chinese border of present Yunnan province. The Manipur King captured the Chinese chief by jumping about 25 feet up and 120 feet length. That shows his ability and courage. After this important battle, the king was known as 'Khagemba' (conquerer of China) and had never changed his name afterwards. An important event during his reign was the visit of prince Khwairakpa to China in 1631. This also shows that Manipur had some relationship with the Chinese, diplomatic as well as trade since centuries.

Khunjaoba (1652-1666 A.D.): In 1657 A.D., the King destroyed Kabo Mungsha and conquered Khuntlaisung, Tonsensung and

Mahousung. In 1659 A.D., the king again invaded Samjok and stayed there for three months (i.e. November-February).

Paikhomba (1666-1697 A.D.): This king invaded Samjok 4 times as per *Cheitharol Kumbaba* (2nd ed., pp. 52, 56 & 57).[13] For the 4th invasion, the king left on 2nd November, 1694 and returned on 18th February next year, that means he stayed there for 3½ months. *Ningthourol Lambuba* (p. 314) also mentioned his invasion of a Chinese main village in the east where many glasses and silk cloths were produced. Hence, if we take it by its face value, the above war was fought at the present Burmese-Yunnan frontier and probably during the Manipuri King's stay of three and half months at Samjok as stated above. Or, it may be in a large Chinese village situated somewhere at the present Kachin state of Burma bordering China. If one corelates this period with that of Pong kingdom, one can find that during 1662-1672 A.D., the Pong kingdom was ruled by one of the Ava king and then reverted to the lineal descendants of the ancient race of kings. Hence, this was a period of uncertainty and instability in the Pong Kingdom. If one again looks back to the Burmese Empire based at Ava, it was a period of consolidation as well as decline of the second Toungoo Empire. Paikhomba's reign tallies with the religious fanatic Aurangzeb's rule in Delhi.

Charairongba (1697-1709 A.D.): An important event was the marriage of his daughter Chakpa Makhao Ngambi to the Burmese king Awa King Tanin-Gane-we (Manipuris call him Awa Tongdoi King Chephong Leiaba) of Toongoo dynasty at Ava. Manipuri writers and historians refer to the ill-treatment of the Manipuri princess by the Ava king in the later part of the marriage. This became a sour point in the relationship between two countries. Charairongba wanted to invade Awa to take revenge for the same but could not due to old age. He communicated this as one of his last wishes to his son, future king Garibniwaz, who executed it perfectly.

The period of expansion beyond Kabaw Valley: 'This period belonged to Maharaja Garibniwaz—the most adventurous, the most fearless and the ablest general Manipur ever had'. 'During his reign, the famous king made a web of Tsunami attacks on both the Pong Kingdom and the Ava Burmese Kingdom from all directions uninterrupted, unpararalled and whenever he wanted. From one principality to another, from one prince to another, the Shans and the Burmese succumbed to the might of the Manipuri king. There was a total of 8 invasions by him personally, another 17 invasions either by his sons or by his Guru or by his noble warriors. The Burmese invaded Manipur four times during this period all of which were defeated by him.... That means he fought a total of 29 battles on the Burmese front during his reign, according to Dr. Suresh (pp. 108-09).[14]

In two of his campaigns, his conquest reached Sagaing situated on the western side of Irrawaddy and opposite to Ava, the Burmese capital. Dr. Suresh further added (p. 110)[15] '...*Awa men and women described the Manipuri King as God's incarnation and not a simple human...*' In one of these, he destroyed the whole city, surrounded the Kyangamdo Payodo temple and opened it by placing one mark each on its 4 walls by his famous sword as a mark of his conquest. Thus during his period, the Manipur empire extended not only up to Kabaw Valley but up to western side of Irrawaddy river.

These accounts are corroborated by Pemberton, Dun and many western writers; and also by many Burmese chronicles.

'Shrinking of boundary to Kabaw Valley again' (refer to map 1, 2 and 3): After Garibniwaz's death, Manipur boundary shrank to Kabaw Valley again. The same continued till the beautiful valley was handed over to Burma in exchange for his Manipuri throne in 1813 by incompetent king Marjit. Kabaw Valley was, however, regained by Maharaj Gambhir Singh in December 1825 with British help. Thus, the Valley was under Burma for a brief period of 12 years only.

Gambhir Singh's hard earned victory and re-conquest of Kabaw Valley was made negative by the British and by our own failure at the negotiations will be clear from the following presented historical facts:

Starting of dispute: The dispute started around April 1826. With the rising tension on the Manipur-Burma frontier throughout the subsequent years, the British were trying to find an honourable solution to the Kabaw Valley dispute.

Now, let me repeat here again that Naojaree range of hills, and not Ningthee, were the eastern boundary of Kabaw Valley.

How Manipur Lost Kabaw Valley due to Bad Negotiation Strategy?

The Governor General, after hearing various evidences, believed that the Ningthee was the true and natural boundary

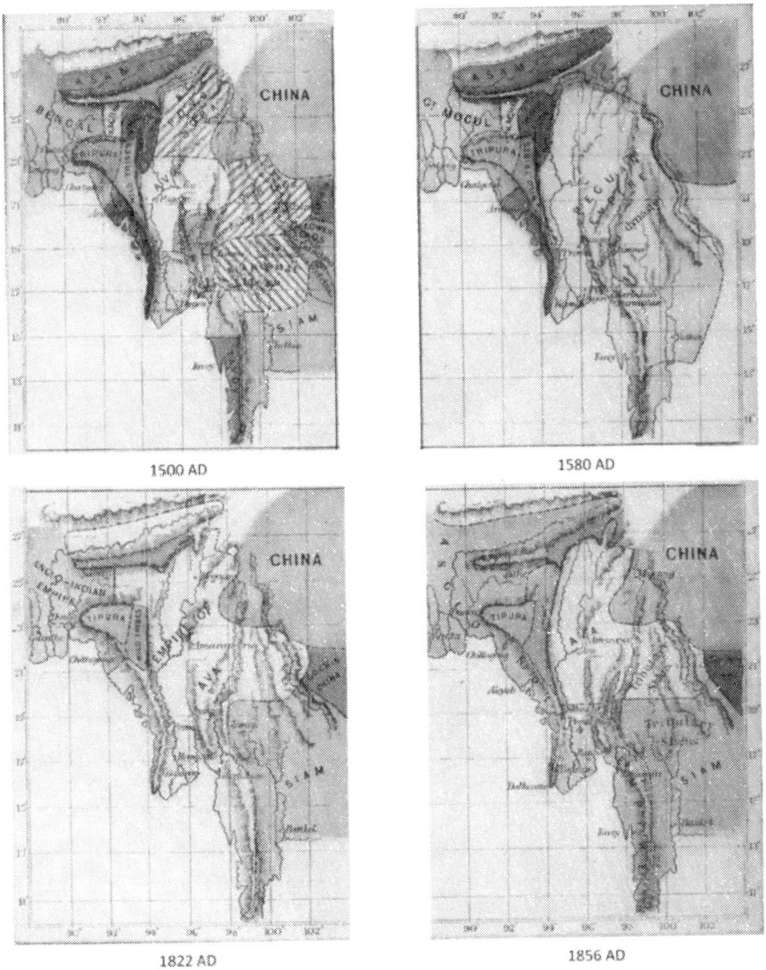

Map 1: Map in A Narrative of the Mission sent by the Governor General of India to the Court of Ava in 1855 by Captain Henry Yule, London[16]: Smith, Elder, and Co. 65 Cuornhill, 1858. Authors note: 1500—King Lamkyimba period, 1580—King Mongyamba period, 1822—Seven year devastation period where Kabaw Valley was a part of Burma; hence Manipur was included in Burma boundary, 1856—Chandrakrity period, i.e. after handing over Kabaw Valley to Burma by the British in 1834.

of the two countries. Major General Campbell and the Viceroy at Rangoon decided that officers should be deputed by each state at the Ningthee River and settle the dispute. Accordingly, British appointed Major Grant and Captain Pemberton as Manipur Commissioners while Lt. Montorency of the 3 Regiment, Madras Cavalry, was deputed to Ava to accompany the commissioners to be appointed by the court of Ava.

Map 2: Rennell's Map, Dominion of Meckley, 1769.
Source: Mutua Bahadur, Manipur Arts ki Wari Shngbul, 16.05.1973.

On 15th June, 1826, His Excellency in the Council's clear instruction to Major General Sir A. Campbell was to maintain Gambhir Singh's right to Samjok and Kendat bounded on the east by Ningthee. In case of Kule, Nurinjurah River was to be the southern boundary. However, Kule's annexation to Manipur had to be a subject of negotiation.

Various Negotiation Meetings

The 1st negotiation was between February and April, 1828.

Pemberton and Grant reached the banks of Ningthee in early February. As the Burmese Commissioners had not yet arrived, they left the place for a healthy place keeping their agents with instructions to inform them of the Burmese arrival. After two months, at the end

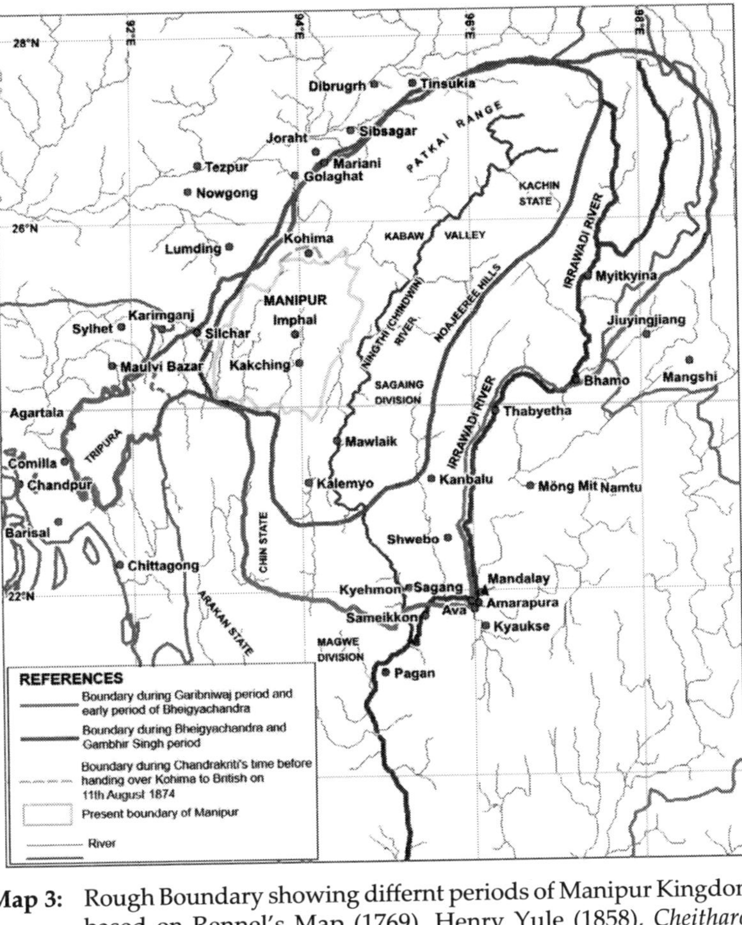

Map 3: Rough Boundary showing differnt periods of Manipur Kingdom based on Rennel's Map (1769), Henry Yule (1858), *Cheitharol Kumpaba, Ningthourol Lambuba.*

of March, Lt. Montmorency and Burmese Commissioner arrived, i.e. after 2 months. The Burmese Commissioner tried to convince Lt. Montmorency that the Ningthee was not the Chindween River, but a separate river to the westward of Kabow valley by producing a map. Because of setting of monsoon and unfortunately for Manipur, Montmorency left the Burmese Commissioner to manage for himself and returned without waiting for the arrival of Grant and Pemberton. Actual meeting took at in 1st week of April where Pemberton exposed the inaccuracy of the above Burmese map.

The second negotiation took place in January 1830. Prior to this, Pemberton and Grant were authorised to fix Manipur thanas (police stations) on certain places indicated on the sketch of the boundary without further reference to the Burmese authorities in case they don't come to the meeting.

In the meeting, the Burmese admitted their incorrectness of the river presented in the 1st meeting. Accordingly, Ningthee was fixed as the boundary between Manipur and Burma, and planted flags accordingly. However, Burmese Chief Commissioner, Woondouk Moung Khanye, objected to this without producing any proof or refusing to hear any witnesses.

Manipur's two commissioners sent in their report to the Supreme Government before the arrival of Major Burney to Ava. It is important to remember who Burney is as he was instrumental for the Supreme Government favouring Kabaw Valley to Burma in the last part of the negotiation.

Burney was a Major of the 25th Regiment of Bengal Native Infantry and was appointed as 1st British Resident at Burma on 31 December, 1829, as per the 7th Article of the Treaty of Yandaboo, which stipulated permanent residence of a British officer at Ava Court. Mackenzie (p. 180) mentioned presence of Burney in the second meeting which was wrong perception. The meeting took place before Burney joined at Ava as given in *Historical Review* compiled by G.T. Bayfield (pp. i-v) and revised by Burney. It is given as supplement to Pemberton book.

Thus in the second negotiation, Kabaw Valley was accordingly settled to the satisfaction of Gambhir Singh as his territory.

The third negotiation took place in August 1830 at Ava. On 3rd June, after Burney joined as Resident of Burma, he had a meeting with the Burmese Minister regarding the letter sent by Gambhir Singh in English dt. 15th May, "declaring that, after 40 days, all persons found to the westward of *Ningthee, would be considered and treated as subject of Gambhir Singh*". Seeing the hostility of the Burmese Minister, Burney persuaded them to allow him to invite Pemberton to join him at Ava and explain the grounds of Gambhir's claim to Kabaw Valley.

At the same time, on 5th June, 1830, Burney sent a letter to Grant and Pemberton requesting to wait till the result of his previous reference to the Supreme Government where he reported his proceedings at Ava stating the inconvenience of further inquiries and discussions and the advantage of communicating at once its determination that the Ningthee should be the boundary.

Ignoring Burney's well-intended advice, Pemberton along with Manipuri followers, arrived at Ava on 12th August, 1830. The 1st discussion was held on 16th where Pemberton exposed Burmese fabrication of Ningthee River in their map and Woondouk Moung Khanye's false statement of Manipuri Commissions giving him only one interview instead of four. The second discussion took place on 18th. Here, based to very ancient dates on their ancient records, historical works and original writings, the Burmese Ministers strengthened Ava's claim to Kabaw Valley. The Burmese allowed Burney to verify these records which show their possession of the disputed valley 30 years before 1075 and further possession after 1475 A.D. Pemberton based his defence on a Shan Chronicle made available to him by Burney where it was stated the cession of a portion of the valley to Manipur by a Pong King in 1475 A.D. (meaning destruction of Khambat by combined forces of Pong and Manipur King Kyamba).

The third discussion took place on 25th where the Burmese hardened their stand shown a complete change in negotiation strategy. They shown "offence as the best form of defence". They demanded not only dethroning of Gambhir Singh and enthroning of Marjit Singh, but also getting back of Tenasserim provinces and rising of Salween boundary question. This visit, Pemberton's last, strengthened Burmese argument of Kabaw Valley in their favour.

Final Order: Based on Burney's letter dt. 5 July, 1832, favouring Burma giving details of research, history, testimony etc., British gave a final order dated 16th March, 1833, restoring Kabaw Valley to Burma. This order was handed over to Burney only in November 1833 where he carried it to Ava. With this, the British ended their blowing hot and cold alternately with Burma and Manipur.

In an unending controversy and ragging till today, the signing of this "Agreement Regarding the Kubo Valley, 1834" was signed on 9th January, 1834 at 'Sunnyachil Ghat', opposite to 'Gendu' on the right bank of Ningthee (Annexure 1). It was signed by Grant and Pemberton without Raja Gambhir Singh's signature. The Raja heard it from reliable sources on 7th and had a heart attack, next day he had another attack and the condition worsened around 10 pm and died around 3 am next morning, i.e. 9th. *Cheitharol Kumbaba* (2nd ed., p. 244)[17] gave this date as Thursday, 30th December, 1755 Sakabda. If we convert it into English Calendar, it is probably 9th January, 1934 A.D.

The second agreement referred to as "Agreement Regarding Compensation for the Kubo Valley, 1834" was also signed by Grant and Pemberton as Commissioners on 25th January, 1834 A.D. but at Langthabal, the Manipur capital (Annexure 2). No Manipuri representative stamp was seen in it and it is significant. By this time, nothing can be done except the Manipuris sucking their thumbs with sorrow and disappointment.

The Missed Opportunities

Had Pemberton and Grant waited for Lt. Montmorency in the first meeting held in February 1828, the matter would have been finalized once for all in favour of Manipur as he was very unhappy at the treatment meted out to him by the Burmese at Ava. Silently, he would have favoured Manipur. Unfortunately, the two Manipuri commissioners withdrew back two miles from the meeting place and stayed to a healthy and comfortable place. Lt. Montmorency didn't wait for them as rain was approaching and went back to Ava leaving the Burmese representative to deal with himself.

The second one was Pemberton and Grant's refusal to heed to Burney's advice as contained in his letter to them dated 5th January, 1830 where he asked them to wait for the Supreme Government's decision on the proceedings sent by him to the Supreme Government. If waited, the British Government would have given a final order to Manipur's favour and would have ended again permanently in Manipur's favour. In the said proceedings sent by Burney, he pleaded Ningthee to fix as the natural boundary.

The third one was Pemberton's failure to stand firmly on his ground, thus giving upper hand to the Burmese during the three meetings held at Ava in August 1830. The man, who knew every corner of Manipur too well, depended too much on the *Pong Chronicle* supplied to him at Ava. He was too confident, thought the Burmese could not counter his well-documented argument based on Shan Chronology. The man, who read history well and also surveyed the entire North East region of present India and neighbouring Burma, was thoroughly ignorant of our history which was exclusively available at *Cheitharol Kumbaba.*

Manipur authorities were also to be blamed to a certain extent for not briefing him thoroughly. Had Pemberton represented Manipur's true historical perspective as given in the preceding paras, i.e.:

- First, during 663-1467 A.D., a part of Kabaw Valley was under Manipur even though repeated war broke out;
- Second, from Kyamba to Charairongba period (1467-1709), the whole Kabaw Valley belonged to Manipur;
- Third, it was expanded to the whole Pong Kingdom and middle Burma up to Irrawaddy basin during Garibniwaz's period (1709-48 A.D.);
- Fourth, from Chitsai till Gambhir Singh's last conquest (1748-1825 A.D.), the whole Kabaw Valley belonged to Manipur except on 5 occasions, *viz.*, Alampra's 9 days' conquest in November 1758, 3 years' Burmese invasion during 1764-66, another 20 days' invasion in 1769, yet again another invasion and 5 months occupation starting February 1773, and finally, the famous seven years' devastation period of 1819-1825 where King Marjit took flight to Cachar; and
- Fifth, that the Manipur boundary extended up to the origin of Ningthi River is proved by the agreement signed between the British and Raja Goursam Singh on 11 September, 1763 (Annexure 3).

Possibility of Bribery

Circumstantial evidences strongly suggest that Burney and Pemberton were heavily bribed during the last negotiation. Burney, who sent a letter to Supreme Government on 5th June, 1830, recommending to declare Ningthee as natural boundary of the two neigbours, had a sudden change of heart and did a U-turn during the third negotiation. It is because of his final recommendation that the Supreme Government gave the final order favouring Kabaw Valley to Burma.

The same applies to Pemberton. The man, who was given so much name and fame by the Manipuris from his insignificant post of Assistant Surveyor of erstwhile North-East India, did not defend Manipur cause to the core during the final stage of third negotiation. Not only that, he cheated Gambhir Singh as he did not come back to Manipur boycotting the meeting and reporting the inner minutes to the king. The Raja and Manipur Darbar depended too much on the man who came to Manipur at his own will along with Gambhir Singh Levy in May 1825. This became Manipur's downfall. Manipuris should never forget and forgive him.

During those periods, gift-taking/giving both for the host and visiting dignitaries was the order of the day. When Pemberton arrived at Alva on 12 August, 1830, the Burmese treated him with hostility. But when he left on 13 September, the Burmese treated him fairly because of their upper hand in the negotiation. What it implies? Though the writer does not have concrete evidence, there are strong circumstantial evidences that both Burney and Pemberton were heavily bribed in the Burmese court by the Burmese ministers during the third and final negotiation.

Manipur's bad strategy and bad negotiation is seen everywhere—in this Kabaw valley negotiation, in Bodh Chandra Maharaj's 1949 Merger negotiation at Shillong—an unfortunate one indeed.

Manipuris failed to cross the bridge when needed.

Last Hurrah by Nehru

Meanwhile, India's First Prime Minister was barking under the sunshine of non-alignment. Burma Prime Minister U Nu was extending a helping hand to strengthen Nehru's non-aligned movement. India and Burma also signed a "Treaty of Friendship" in 1951. However, during that volatile period of Manipur, he was planning to hand over our Kabaw Valley to Burma without considering Manipur's sentiments.

Amidst such atmosphere, he visited Manipur twice in succession. He came to Manipur 1st on 23 and 24 October, 1952, then 5 months later again on 28-31 March, 1953. Nehru praised Manipur and its people as very beautiful, Manipur women very hard working and Manipuri dance world famous etc.

Manipur was already suspicious of his intentions. In the 2nd visit, Burmese Prime Minister U Nu also came down to Imphal. The two Prime Ministers together went to Kohima on 30th and there Nehru handed over our precious Kabaw Valley to Burma on a platter even without the compensation clause. It was without the consent of the Manipur people and without the approval of India's Parliament. India's First Prime Minister added insult to injury. This has created an apple of discord between Manipur, Burma and India. Manipur has lost Kabaw Valley, we have lost Kabaw Valley for ever.

Before this Nehru's handing over of Kabaw Valley to Burma as elicited above, Kabaw Valley was leased to Burma as testified by the second Treaty of *"Agreement Regarding Compensation for The Kubo Valley, 1834"*. The matter was taken up in the Lok Sabha question hour session on 25th November, 1952 by two MPs, namely L. Jogeshwar and A.G. Guha according to Professor Jonh Parrat of the University of Birmingham as quoted by Madhumangol. Home Minister Dr. Katju, in his reply stated that the Burmese Government was paying 500 Sicca Rupees (i.e. more than Indian Rs. 6,270 at that time) per month. That means Manipur was getting the same rent since 25 January, 1834 till Nehru's second visit to Manipur.

The British at least kept a scope to revert the beautiful Valley back to Manipur (Compensation Agreement). At least they have a partial favour to the Manipuris.

But, India's First Prime Minister finally handed over Manipur's precious Valley permanently to Burma illegally without the State's approval and/or without Parliament's approval. This is the last straw. State's approval and Parliament approval is required as per the provision of Article 371(c) the Constitution of India.

Wish list

1. Manipur has the habit of presenting incomplete facts or wrong facts in respect of various important historical perspectives. This is the failure of the Manipuri historians/ writers/intellectuals because of their incomplete research/ study. The writer sincerely hopes that this gap will be fulfilled by the present lot new generation researchers so that future generations have a clean glimpses of the true Manipur historical perspective.
2. Also wish that present lot politicians—State Assembly, MPs take up Kabaw Valley in appropriate forum—Assembly, Parliament, other forums etc. in order to regain the beautiful Valley back as we have a strong historical and legal background favouring us.

ANNEXURE 1
Agreement Regarding the Kubo Valley-1834

First: The British Commissioners Major Grant and Captain Pemberton, under instruction, from the Right Honourable, the Governor-General in Council, agree to make over to the Woandauk Maha Mingyan Rajah and Tsarudangicks Mvookyautheo, Commissioner appointed by the King of Ava, the Towns of Tummao, Khumba, Surjail, and all other villages in the Kubo Valley, the Ungoching Hills and the strip of valley running between the eastern foot and the western bank of the Nintha river and Khyendan river.

Second: The British Commissioners will withdraw the Munnipore Thannas now stationed within this tract of the country and make over immediate possession of it to the Burmese Commissioner on certain conditions.

Third: The conditions are, that they will agree to the boundaries which may be pointed out to them by the British Commissioners, and will respect and refrain from any interference, direct or indirect, with the people residing on the Munnipooree side of those boundaries.

Fourth: The boundaries are as follows:

1. The eastern foot of the chain of mountains which are immediately from the western side of the plain of the Kubo valley. Within this line is included Morehand all the country to the westward of it.
2. On the south a line extending from the eastern foot of the same hills at the point where the river, called by the Burmahs Nansawing and by the Munnipoorees Namsaulung, enters the plain, up to its sources and across the hills due west down to the Kethe-Khyaung (Munnipooree River).
3. On the north the line of boundary will begin at the foot of the same hills at the northern extremity of the Kubo valley, and pass due north up to the first range of hills, cast of that upon which stand the villages of Choatao, Naonghe, Noanghur of the tribe called by the Munnipoorees Loohooppa, and by the Burmah Lagumsauny, now tributary to Munnipoore.

Fifth: The Burmese Commissioners hereby promise that they will give orders to the Burmese officers, who will remain in the charge of the territory now made over to them not in any way to interfere with the Khyens or other inhabitants living on the Munnipor side of the lines of boundary above described and the British Commissioners also promise that the Munipoorees shall be ordered not in any way to interfere with the Khyens or other inhabitants of any description living on the Burmah side of the boundaries now fixed.

(Seal) Sd/- F.J. Grant, Major } Commissioners
(Seal) Sd/- AR.B. Pemberton
Sunnyachil Ghat, Ningthee. 9th January, 1834

- Aitchison's Treaties, Engagements, etc., p. 360.

ANNEXURE 2
Agreement Regarding Compensation for The Kubo Valley, 1834

Major Grant and Captain Pemberton, under instructions from the Right Honourable the Governor-General-in-Council, having made over the Kubo Valley to the Burmese Commissioners deputed from Ava, are authorized to state:

1. That it is the intention of the Supreme Government to grant a monthly stipend of five hundred Sicca Rupees to the Rajah of Munnipore, to commence from the ninth day of January One Thousand Eight Hundred and Thirty-four, the date at which the transfer of Kubo took place, as shown in the Agreement mutually signed by the British and Burmese Commissioners.
2. It is to be distinctly understood that should any circumstances hereafter arise by which the portion of territory lately made over to Ava again reverts to Munnipore, the allowance now granted by the British Government will cease from the date of such reversion.

(Sd/-)
FJ. Grant, Major } Commissioners
(Sd/-)
R. Boileu Pemberton,
Captain

Langhthabal Munnipore,
January 25, 1834

ANNEXURE 3
Proposals of the Treaty Mentioned in Appendix XIX

Proposals made by Anund San, Podullo Singh and Chitton Singh Hazarry in the name and behalf of Goursah Singh, Raja of Meckley for an explanation of a former treaty of alliance bearing pate the 14th September 1762 made by Hurry Dass Gussein in behalf of Jai Singh and Harry Verelst etc. Gentlemen of Chittagong (Home Department, Public Proceedings, Volume 1763, pages 1330-1331).

I, Goursah Singh, Raja of Meckley do confirm a treaty of alliance dated the 14th September 1762 made between Harry Verelst, Randolf Marriot and Thomas Rumbold in behalf of the Honourable East India Company, on one part, and by Hurry Dass Gussein in the name and behalf of my brother Joy Singh, on the other part, approving and ratifying all and every article of the said treaty of alliance.

The second article of the said treaty stipulates all and every expense and contingent expenses of the said English troops employed in the service of my brother Joy Singh to be paid by him at the immediate expiration of every month.

To this I am to observe that since the Burmese have overrun and destroyed a great part of .the Dominions of Meckley, it is not in my pcwer to make such payments in actual species either of gold or silver.

But I agree to pay all such expenses as have already accrued in the English late march towards Meckley and all such expenses as hereafter may accrue in their future march to Meckley to be paid from time to time in such goods and merchandise as are procurable in my country and which I agree to deliver to the English at Raung Roong at their annexed rates and conditions, but such quantities as are specified in· the annexed lists shall be delivered as the first payment immediately on the English troops getting up to Meckley. And I am now willing to pay in ready money towards this agreement, hundred Meckley gold Rupees to be valued at twelve-silver rupees each.

So soon as the English shall enable me to work the gold mine on the banks of the River Barrampooter in the Dominions of Meckley, as

Products of Meckley that Goursah Singh, Rajah agrees to pay annually towards the defrayment of the expenses of the English troops employed on his account, viz.,

Silk	10 mds.	Rs. at 5 per seer	Rs. 2,000
Iron	1,000 mds.	at Rs. 4 per md	Rs. 4,000
Copal	1,000 mds.	at Rs. 1 & ½ per md	Rs. 1,500
Dammar	1,000 mds.	at Rs. 1 & ½ per md	Rs. 1,500
Wood oil	1,000 mds.	at Rs 1 &1/2 per md	Rs. 1,500
Wax	500 mds.	at Rs. 20 per md	Rs. 10,000
Elephant teeth	100 mds.	at Rs. 20 per md.	Rs. 2,000
Agar	100 mds.	at Rs. 4 per seer	Rs. 16,000
Camphor	10 mds.	at Rs. 80 per md	Rs. 800
Black thread	100 mds.	at Rs. 20 per md.	Rs. 2,000
Red thread	100 mds.	at Rs. 20 per md.	Rs. 2,000
Blue thread	100 mds.	at Rs. 20 per md.	Rs. 2,000
White thread	200 mds.,	at Rs. 20 per md.	Rs. 4,000
Black coss	10 mds.	at Rs. 2 per seer	Rs. 800
Meckley cloth from 2 &1/2 to 3 cubits broad and a cubit long	500 pes.	at Rs. 1&1/2 per piece	Rs. 750
Meckley gold rupee	500	12 silver rupees each	Rs 6,000
		Total...	Rs. 56,850

Out of the above, Goursah Singh can now give within the period of one month after the arrival of the troops at Raung Roong.

Silk	5 mds.
Iron	500 mds.
Copal	500 mds.
Dammar	500 mds.
Wax	250 mds.
Elephant teeth	50 mds.
Agar	20 mds.
Black thread	50 mds.
Red thread	50 mds.
Blue thread	50 mds.
White thread	100 mds.
Meckley clothes	500 pieces
Meckley gold rupees	150

NOTES

1. In this chapter, the author at the very start gives the pointer that:
   a. Names given in the ancient books are retained as far as practicable;
   b. The name Burma is retained instead of Myanmar as Manipuris called the eastern neighbour as Burma.
2. Pemberton, R.B. *The Eastern Frontier of India*, Mittal Publications, New Delhi, Photograph reproduction, 2008.
3. *Ibid.*
4. "Molcham Revisited: 23 to 26 December, 1933" in *Regional Integration* (A quarterly Journal), Vol. IX, issue No. 1, July 1984, pp. 19 & 20.
5. *Op. cit.*, Pemberton, R.B.
6. Brown, R. Doctor. *Statistical Account of Manipur*, Calcutta, Reprint 1975, p. 60.
7. Bhogeshwore, O. *Ningthourol Lambuba, A detailed history of the kings in Manipur*, 1st part, self-published, J.M. Printing Works, Imphal, 1967.
8. Ibungohal, L. and Khelchandra, N. *Cheitharol Kumbaba*, Manipur Shahitya Parisad, 1st edition, 1967, 2nd edition, 1989, 3rd edition, 2005 and 4th edition, 2012.
9. *Op. cit.*, Bhogeshwore, O.
10. *Op. cit.*, Ibungohal, L. and Khelchandra, N.
11. *Op. cit.*, Bhogeshwore, O.
12. Gangmumei Kabui. *History of Manipur*, Vol. I, Pre-Colonial Period, National Publishing House, New Delhi, 3rd edition, 2011.
13. *Op. cit.*, Ibungohal, L. and Khelchandra, N.
14. Suresh Singh, Th, Dr. *The Endless Kabaw Valley* (British Created Vicious Cycle of Manipur, Burma and India), a Quills Ink Publication, 2014, pp. 108-110.
15. *Ibid.*
16. Source: A narrative of the mission sent by the Governor General of India to The Court of Ava in 1855 by Captain Henry Yule, London: Smith, Elder, and Co. 65 Cornhill, 1858.

    Authors note: 1500: King Lamkyimba period, 1580: King Mongyamba period, 1822: Seven Year Devastation period where Kabaw Valley was a part of Burma; hence Manipur was included in Burma boundary, 1856: Chandrakinty period, i.e., after handing over Kabaw Valley to Burma by the British in 1834.
17. *Op.cit*, Ibungohal, L. and Khelchandra, N.

THEME-V

Socio-Cultural Relations

17
Matrimonial and Social Relationship between Manipur and Myanmar

Before the Reign of Nongda Lairen Pakhangba (33 A.D.–158 A.D.)

Mangangcha Thoudam Achou

The relation between Myanmar and Manipur was in different subjects from the pre-historic period out of those relationships, the matrimonial and social relationship is worth to mention.

Myanmar use to call Manipuri as Kathe or Kase. Whereas, Myanmar was known as Awa by Meiteis. In the earlier period, the different places of the present Myanmar was known by different names. Shan people who were settled near the bank of Chindwin river was known as Pong, the place where Kabow-Shan people settled at the bank of Chindwin river in the northern portion of present Kabow Valley was known as Samjok, Shan people who were settled of the river bank of Chindwin river was known respectively as Kabow.

In the earlier period, there were transport and communication between Myanmar and Manipur. The transport and communication was done through the hills passes of Manipur valley. The Heirok hill pass, Aimol hill pass, Ngarachingjel hill route and Maring hill pass were used as a main communication routes between Manipur and Myanmar in the ancient period. The said hill routes used to connect Manipur with Kabow, Awa, Khagi and Southeastern Asian countries (Nandalal, *Meitrabak*, pp. 28-29).

If the people from India and Western countries would like to travel at the eastern and southeastern countries like Awa, Khagi (China) etc. then they have to pass Manipur. Trade and commerce, immigration and settlement were done by the help of those hill routes (Khelchandra, *Ariba Manipuri Sahityagi Itihas*, pp. 3-4).

The present name of Manipur was entitled during the reign of Maharaj Garibniwaz (1709 A.D.-1748 A.D.) before this name, there were different names in different eras (Chak/Juk). According to old manuscript 'Sakok Lamlen Ahanba' the names of this land were written as Tilli Koktong during Hayichak, Mira Pongthoklam in Khunungchak, Tillikok Leikoiren in Langbackak and Muwapalli in Konnachak. Before this four chaks (eras), the four Hangko (Hangko indicates the meaning of Chak), i.e. Kohangko, Thoihangko, Tayohangko and Poihangko, which were again divided into eight chaks from the creation of Universe till now. It was written in old manuscripts like Leithak Leikharol, Thirel Layat, Sakok Lamlel, Malem Leisemlon, Malem Leisemlon Ariba, Ningthou Kangparol Ponglen Puya Meihoupa etc. About the reign of kings during the above mentioned chaks, were also given in those old manuscripts, i.e., Purel Sidaba in Kohangkochak, Nongthou Kurusidaba in Thoihangkochak, Sana Phuhing Sidaba in Tayohangkochak and Koubaren in Poihangkochak (Nityai, *Ningthou Kangparol Ponglel Puya Meihoupa*, pp. 1-2). Not only this, the names of Kings, those who reigned during these four hangkochak were given in "Kanglei Langba Pakhangba". The said four hangkochaks were related with the creation of Universe.

About the reign of kings after this four hangkochaks were also found in these old manuscripts. They were king Kangba during Hayichak period, Mariya Phambalcha in Hayachak (Khunungchak), King Koksuba in Langbachak (Khunungchak) under Nongda Lairen Pakhangba in Konnachak respectively.

According to old manuscripts of 'Malem Leisemlon' and 'Leisemlon Ariba' more appropriate writing about the reign of Kings during those four chaks (eras) were found out.

According to these books, King Kangba, King Tari, King Sakappa, King Wankappa, King Kaksuba, King Tolongba, King Pitingkoi, King Lambicha, King Sapaiba, were in the period of Hayichak and in the beginning of Konnachak (era), Chronology of kings after Nongda Lairen Pakhangba had continued one after another. The above mentioned chak or Hangkochak was in vague about the fixing of years in a particular chak (era).

So, we can analyse the matrimonial and social relationship between Manipur and Myanmar in two contexts, one from the reign of Nongda Lairen Pakhangba, 33 A.D. to 158 A.D. in the beginning of Konnachak (era) and another before the reign of King Nongda Lairen Pakhangba.

Before the Reign of Nongda Lairen Pakhangba

The analytical view of matrimonial and social relationship between Manipur and Myanmar before the reign of Nongda Lairen Pakhangba during four Hangko and three chaks (i.e. Hayichak, Hayachak, Langbachak) needs to look after the Meitei's cosmology, belief, religious traditions etc. which were found in the related old manuscripts.

Social relationship: According to the contents in the old manuscripts, the social relationship between Myanmar and Manipur can be divided into two ways—i.e. view from creation of Universe and another view from religious matter.

Analysis of creation of Universe and religious matter: According to old manuscripts, Pong (*Pong : The Shan kingdom of Pong was formerly bounded on the north by the range of hills dividing Burma from Assam; South it extended to Khampat, west to Yoma range; east to the Yunan. The capital was Mogoung. After vaying fortunes, it was annexed to Burma in 1752: Gazetteer of Manipur* by Captain E.W. Dun, Culcutta, 1886, p. 188) and Khamaral (*Awas are known as Khamaral*) group of People were originated, born and associated with the history of Manipur. The old manuscript of Meitei like 'Leihou Naophamlon' had indicated that the birth place and burial place of placenta for their aboriginal forefathers were— "Koipung was the burial place of placenta for Pong, ... Lokloupung was the burial place of placenta for Senpi Khamaral (*Ponggee Naopham Phumfamdi Khoipungne......Senpee Khamaralgee Naopham Phumfamdi Loklou Pungne*, p. 13)". Thus, it indicated that Pong and Senpi Khamaral were the aboriginal people of this land.

Not only this, about the birth place of the aboriginal forefathers of this land in their stones found at Kangla were in the writing of old manuscript like 'Nunglon' for example— "There was one stone known as Yai, just like a human statue. White colour, face directed eastward. Pong was born [*Yai Koupa Nung Ama Leiyae. Masakti Migee Masakne. Machu Ngouae. Mamai Nongpok Pangae. Mamimg Pong Kouae. Pong pokae*" (p. 32)]. Thus, it indicated that Pong people were originated from this land.

On the other side, according to old manuscript like 'Leithak Leikharol' and 'Pudin', Pong was born by Kongkoi, the eldest son out of nine sons of King Kangba and his consort Leima Tarinu during Hayichak period. Thus, it indicated that the forefathers of Pong people were the grandson of King Kangba.

The above analysis indicates that the present Pong Khamaran (Awa) people of Myanmar were originated from this land. Thus, it expresses the relationship between the two countries from the early period.

Relationship in relation to migration and settlement: There were written record in the ancient manuscript about the migration and settlement at ancient period from the neighbouring countries into this place. Out of those manuscripts, one manuscript known as Khununglon wrote about the pre-historic migration and settlement in Manipur from different places. In the said book migration and settlement in Manipur from different directions wrote about migration and settlement of Senbi-Tekhao and Awa from their land, i.e. "Your forefather, who migrated from the land of Phatlou Laimakon used to settle and speak Tekhao language,....... Your forefather who migrated from the direction of Thanghi-Ngangoi (Moirang direction) use to settle and speak Kabow language,...... your forefather, who migrated from the direction of Nayum Meiram used to settle and speak Awa language (*Nabudhou Fatlou Awang Laimakongi Lamdagi Khunthorapa Laidi Senbi Tekhao Marol Londuna Khunthorakae ... ... Thanghi Ngangngoi Haram Pangbadagi Khunthorakkhiba Nabudhoudi Kabow Marol Londuna Khunthorakae..... Nayum Meiram Pangbadagi Khunthorakkhiba Nabudhoudi Awa Marol Londuna Khunthorakae.*)." From the source of these stories, clearly reveals the pre-historic migration and settlement of people from the neighbouring country of present Myanmar into Manipur.

As shown in the above manuscripts, the people of Myanmar and Manipur used to migrate and settle in the pre-historic period, according to their convenience.

So, it shows the relationship of migration and settlement of these two neighbouring countries from the pre-historic period.

Matrimonial relationship: The matrimonial relationship of two groups of people, who settled in Manipur and Myanmar from pre-historic period was found in old manuscripts, out of those manuscripts, Malem Leisemlon and Leisemlon Ariba give the account of matrimonial relationship between Meitei and Pong.

Pong was a Tai group of people, who settled at Yunnan province in southern part of China. Burmese used to call them Shan, when these group of people came down to Shan province in the area of upper Burma. Thus, Meitei used to call them as Pong, when these Pong settled at Kabow Valley, they were known as Kabow.

There was an account that the said Pong group of people during Langbachak period, the King Lambicha (Lambicha: Lambicha was the son of King Pitingkoi and Leima Koirembi during Langbachak, Sapaiba was the son of Lambicha and Lairichanu, Sapaiba was King during Langbachak. 'Panthoibi Khongul' gives account of the reign of this King as a King of Kanglei) married with Leirinu and Leiyainu, the daughter of Pong King Kakma.

This reveals the matrimonial relationship between Myanmar and Manipur in the early Pre-historic period from Hayachak to Langbachak.

Reign of Nongda Lairen Pakhangba

Konnachak was started from the first King under the name of Nongda Lairen Pakhangba, who ruled during 33 A.D. in the history of Manipur. Nongda Lairen Pakhangba was the son of Lollang Pakhangba and his consort Leinung Yabirok. He was the last incarnation of Pakhangba. He was known as Konjin Tingthokps during the creation of Universe. Lainingthou Konjin Tingthokpa continued his incarnations one after another as a Loinai Pakhangba.

The incarnations of Pakhangba during four chaks were Loinai Pakhangba in Hayichak; Leinung Lonja Pakhangba (Tangja Lilla Pakhangba) in Hayachak; Lollang Pakhangba in Langbachak; Nongda Lairen Pakhangba in the beginning of Konnachak and he became the King of Kanglei.

In the pre-historic period different groups of people like Mangang, Nungban Luwang, Khuman, Khaba, Nganba, Haorok, Konthou, Chakpa, Heirem Khunjal, Kege Moirang, Urok Usai, Thagga Kambong, Selloi Langmai, Chenglei, Nongban Angom, Fantek, Lokkha Haokha, Khunfam Ngangcheng, Lera Khongnang, Lokkhu Lokhan etc. with the present hill men like Maram, Koireng, Mahaou, Kabui, Maring, Tangkhul, Tarao, Chothe, Anals, Kharam etc. were settled in different places in this land. Under these groups of people, there were many small groups of people. A common Meitei community was started to organise from the reign of Nongda Lairen Pakhangba.

The views regarding the formation of Meitei community were the unification of powerful Khaba clan into Meitei community was brought by Nongda Lairen Pakhangba during his period after defeating Khaba Nongjengba, a leader of Khaba. Haokha Lokha was brought under Meitei community after defeating them by Meidingu Taothingmang (264 A.D. to 364 A.D.) with his elder brother Yoimongba. King Mangang Konkhucha Atengba with a group of Mangang people, those who were settled at Loijing Saronya was defeated by Meidingu Naotkingkhong (663 A.D. to 763 A.D.) after achieving the title of "Mangang Ngamba" and brought them under Meitei community. There was no King of Luwang clan after the death of Luwang Ningthou Punshiba during the period of Meidinggu Chenglei Ipan Lanthaba (949 A.D. to 969 A.D.) and thus Luwang clan also united with Meitei community. Thawanthaba (1195 A.D. to 1231 A.D.) had conquered Heirem Khunjal group of people, those who were settled at Kereching of Kakching and kept them under the fold of Meitei community. The unification of Kuman group of people into Meitei community was during the reign of Meidingu Kongyamba (1324 A.D. to 1335 A.D.). The unification of Moirang into Meitei society was during the period of Meidingu Ningthoukhomba (1432 A.D. to 1467 A.D.) after defeating Sanahongba, King of Moirang. In this way, the present day Meitei community was build up by assimilating different groups of people. The above mentioned groups of people were settled during the reign of Nongda Lairen Pakhangba.

During the reign of Nongda Lairen Pakhangba from 33 A.D. to 154 A.D. about 120 years as a King, the relationship with Myanmar was recorded in the old manuscript like Thanglon Thagchat, Poireiton Khunthok etc., out of those relationship, the social relationship is given below:

Social relationship: The social relationship between Manipur and Myanmar in the early period was maintained during the reign of Nongda Lairen Pakhangba. In the old manuscript like 'Thaglon Thangchat' Pong people were recorded as the descendant of Pakhangba. The said book recorded that—Pakhangba and his two consorts Leisuk Leisoi Yambi with Lilanbi gave birth two sons, i.e. Pong and Paikhu. They were sent to protect the eastern side by handing over Tarung sword with stick sword to Pong and Kairemba Sword to Paikhu respectively. With this, Pong had established Pong group of people and Pong become the first King.

According to 'Ariba Manipuri Sahityagi Itihas' (Khelchabdra, p. 6), it has opined that the foremost King Khullai of Pong was the same Pong, which was the son of Nongda Lairen Pakhangba and his consort Leisu Leisoiyambi.

Later on, during the reign of Meidingu Naothingkhong (663 A.D. to 763 A.D.), in the year 698 A.D. Samlung (Samlung/Samlong: ......Samlong, the second brother, was dispatched by Sookampha at the head of powerful force, to subdue first the countries to the eastward, including probably the principality of Bhmo, which extended from the left bank of the Irrawattee river to the frontier of Yunnan. This expedition was successful; the Samlongpha again leaving Maongmarong is described as having in the western country of the Basa king, which probably means Banga (Capt. Pemberton, *Report on the Eastern Frontier of British India,* 1966, p. 113), the younger brother of King Sukanfa (Sookampha) of Pong conquered up to Pasa (Basa) and in the return journey, he used to stay 10 years in Meitei Leipak (Manipur). After that the army of Samlung travelled towards the source of Iril River (*Cheitharol Kumbaba,* p. 6), still home yard of Pong is there and their return journey is known Pong roadway.

It clearly reveals that Pong was the descendant of Pakhangba because Samlung accompanied and use sword Kairemba when he invaded western side (Manikchand, edit, *Thanglon Thangchat,* p. 44) which was given away by Pakhangba to his eldest son Pong with Paoikhu to protect eastern side. Samlung used to stay in Manipur for a longer period due to close relationship with Meitei people. This matter is clearer from the history of Meidingu Kyamba (1467 A.D. to 1508 A.D.) when he conquered Kabow Kyampat with the help of King Chopha Khe Khomba of Pong and distributed the land of Khampat among Meitei and Pong (*Cheitharol Kumbaba,* pp. 19-20). Captain Pemberton also stated that during those days Kabow Valley was occupied by Manipur. (A tract of country was then made over to the Rajah of Muneepoor by the king of Pong, extending east to the Noajeeree, a range of hill running between the Moo and Kyendwen river, which was then established as the boundary between the two countries, South, the limit extended to the Muyatoung or Muyu hills, and north, to a very celebrated mango tree near Moongkhum, between the Noajeere hills and Kyendwen river (R.B. Pemberton, *Report on the Eastern Frontier of British India,* p. 118).

After invasion and occupation of Khampat by King Kyamba

(1467 A.D. to 1508 A.D.) of Meitei and King Khekhomba of Pong as a grandson and grandfather used to ask about their agedness was recorded in 'Cheitherol Kumbaba' along with 'Sorarel Machana Khungumba' indicated the close relationship and reveals the descendant of Pong and Paikhu, the sons of Pakhangba, who were sent to protect the eastern boundary.

That is why, king of Pong used to call the King of Meitei as grandson (Khelchandra, *Ibid.*, pp. 10-12). This shows the close relationship between Meitei and Pong.

In the old manuscript like 'Poireiton Khunthok' shows the main relationship during the reign of Nongda Lairen Pakhangba with Kabows. It gives account about the migration of Poireiton with his companion from a place known as "Khamnung". Meitei believed that Khamnung was situated in the southern side. Not only this, it was taken as the land of Khambat, which was situated inside Kabow Valley.

According to the manuscripts 'Malem Leisemlon' Poireiton was migrated from Kiyang region. Kabow Valley is stretching from north to south having narrow breadth with long length and it is divided into three portions, i.e. Samjok in the north, Kiyang Khambat in the middle and Kale in the south. Therefore, the place of Khamnung is nothing but it is Kiyang Khambat, which is situated in the middle portion of Kabow valley (Indramani, *Ibid.*, pp. 211-212).

"Poireiton Khunthok" recorded about the migration and settlement of Poireiton with his companion in Manipur. The another name of Poireiton was Tangkhongtek (Khagemba Yumbi). The book also recorded about the assimilation of Poireiton and his companions to the Tangkhul, Kabui, Kharam, Chakpa, Kege-Moirang, Meitei group of people.

There were many major changes in tradition, religion, customs etc. after the migration of poireiton. This was mentioned in the book— *"Khaningpa Hongnate. Mikonpa Hongnate. Khaning Mikon Ama Teipati, Yeyuwa Chingkhong Poieiton Makhuwonpu Konpane"* (p. 1).

The forefathers of Luwang and Khuman were the descendants from the sons and grandsons of Poireiton after his migration and settlement in Manipur. Thus the chronology of these two Salais is continued. Poireiton with Leinaotabi along with his companions migrated from Kyang Khampat of Kabow valley and settled at Lamdeng. His son Singdabung was born there and Singdabung born Arong and Pamingnaba. Arong become Khuman and

Pamingnaba born Luwang Khunthiba, when he became Luwang. Thus, the progeny of Luwang Salai had continued one after another. Arong and his wife Chinphurol Laitonglen Chinkhubiborn Tumahaba. Tumahaba had no son. So, he adopted Lungba, the son of Luwang Ningthou Punshiba and his fifth wife Nganurol Thongaiba Chanu. Afterward his adopted son was handed over to Khuman. Thus, the progeny of Lungba spread Kuman Salai (Indramani, *Meitei Yek Salai*, p. 232).

Even in the later period many people from the surrounding and neighbouring areas were migrated and settled in Manipur. Out of those group of people, who migrated from eastern side of Manipur especially from Kabow Valley, Awa etc. are known as easterners (Nongpok Haram). Thus, 'Nongpok Haram Khunthok' recorded that the place of migration of different people in the reign of different Kings and in which place of Manipur where they were allowed to settle and what type of Meitei's clan and surname was given to them by the then King.

According to the writings of this book, Kase Shan Hokham, who came from Mirlap of Kabow Valley married one girl of Nongthombam family and settled at Chingmeirong as Ngaseppam family during the reign of Meidingu Kabomba (1524 A.D. to 1542 A.D.). He was given Kousik Gotra, during the reign of Meidingu Chalamba (1545 A.D. to 1562 A.D.). One Kase Shan Tailongpha married a girl of Louriyam family and settled at Phoijing as Nandeibam family. He was given Bhardwaj Gotra etc. etc.

An account for the migration of Easterners from reign of Meidingu Kyamba (1467 A.D. to 1508 A.D.) up to reign of Meidingu Mungyamba (1562 A.D. to 1597 A.D.) was also recorded in the said book.

Thus, the firm relation of migration and settlement pattern between present Myanmar and Manipur was indicated by some manuscript like 'Poireiton Khunthok', 'Khagemba Yumbi', 'Nongpok Haram Khunthok' etc.

Inter-marriage relationship: The ancient inter-marriage phenomenon between Myanmar and Manipur was continued up to the reign of Nongda Lairen Pakhangba in the same manner. In this kind of relationship, the marriage of Nongda Lairen Pakhangba and Kanglei's queen Laisans, the younger sister of Chingkhong Poireiton, who was migrated during the reign of Nongda Lairen Pakhangba is worth mentioning. Thus, old manuscripts recorded about the marriage of Nongda Lairen Pahkangba and Laisana as a queen (Leima), who was accompanied during the migration of Poireiton as his younger sister.

About the writing in *'Cheitharol Kumbaba'*, "Meidingu Pakhangba became the King in 3135 Kali kumsing. When Laisana was married, he existed for a longer period as a god in day time and turned into human being during night time and one night Leisna said, ... I would like to become a god, but Pakhangba said that you are not allowed to become a god but you are allowed to be a human being because you are accompanied in Poireiton's migration" (*Ibid.*, p. 1).

As a Meitei King predecessors of Nongda Lairen Pakhangba and his consort Laisana, were Meidingu Khuiyoi Tompok (154 A.D. to 264 A.D.); Meidingu Taothingmang (264 A.D. to 364 A.D.); Meidingu Ningomba (364 A.D. to 379 A.D.); Meidingu Pengsiba (379 A.D. to 394 A.D.) etc. Ningthouja clan become from these Kings. Thus, Ningthouja clan was progeny of Nongda Lairen Pakhangba and Laisana. So, it indicates that there was an intermarriage relationship with Myanmar during the period of Nongda Lairen Pakhangba.

In short, the above analysis proves that there was a matrimonial and social relationship between Myanmar and Manipur from pre-historic period up to the reign of Meidingu Nongda Lairen Pakhangba.

REFERENCES

D.G.E. Hall, *A History of South East Asia*, 1968.

E.W. Dun. *Gazetteer of Manipur*, 1992.

Gangumei Kabui, *History of Manipur*, Volume-1, Pre-Colonial Period, 1991.

Hemchandra Chanam (Ed.), *Pakhangba Laihui*, 1997.

Irom Amubi (Ed.), *Leihou Naofamlon*, 1981.

I. Amubi, N. Khelchandra, O. Bhogeshwor and O. Ibochouba (Ed.), *Sagei Salairol (Meiteigi Yek Salaigi Yumfam Puya)*, 1994.

Khulem Chandrasekhar (Ed.), *Sakok Lamlen Ahanba*, 1992.

Kokngang (Ed.), *Kangleilangba Pakhangba*, 1955.

Konsam Manikchand (Ed.), *Thanglon Thangchat*, 2006.

—, *Poirei Nattki Wareng*, 2015.

— (Ed.), *Malem Leisemlon*, 2017.

— (Ed.), *Pudin*, 2015.

— (Ed.), *Sorarel Machana Khungumba*, 2014.
L. Ibungohal and N. Khelchandra (Ed.), *Cheitharol Kumbaba*, 2012.
Laishram Nityai (Ed.), *Ningthou Kangparol Ponglen Puya Meihoupa*, 1982.
Laishram Udoi (Ed.), *Nonglon Sakok Puya*, 1996.
— (Ed.), *Ningthourol Singkak*, 1995.
Lila Gogoi, *The Tai Kamtis*, 1971.
Moirangthem Chandra (Ed.), *Poireiton Khunthok*, 1995.
Nameirakpam Ibochouba (Ed.), *Thirel Layat*, 1981.
Nandalal Sharma, *Meitrabak*, 1960.
Naoroibam Indramani, *Meitei Yek Salai*, 2019.
—, *The Socio-Culture and Historical Account of Manipur*, 2019.
Ningthouja Manisana (Ed.), *Nunglon*.
Ningthoukhongjam Khelchandra, *Ariba Manipuri Shahityagi Itihas*, 1969.
Pebam Ibomcha (Ed.), *Thirel Meiram Liba Khngngoi Yangoi Sekning*, 1992.
R.K. Kokngang (Ed.), *Kanglei Langba Pakhangba*, 1987.
Thingbaijam Tuteshwor (Ed.), *Malem Leisemlon Ariba*, 1994.
Y. Bheigy (Ed.), *Leithak Leikharol*, 1988.
—, *Leimarel Nunglon*, 2003.

18
Satyamala Devi-The Most Fortunate Manipuri Princess in the 18th Century Southeast Asian History

Manglemjao Singh Sorokhaibam

Satyamala Devi was the daughter of Maharaja Garibaniwaz @ Pamheiba's brother Khamlang Pamsaba, the Wangkheirakpa who had been brought up by Garibaniwaz as his own daughter. Manipur during the time of Garibaniwaz (1709-1748) was at its peak in its military expeditions in the neighbouring kingdoms. His tactics in war complete and always successful. None could revenge against him during his time that made him the greatest conqueror as well as a great fighter. There were repeated invasion and devastation in the northern Upper Burma west of the Irrawaddy River by the Manipuri Cavalry under the command of Maharaja Garibaniwaz and the Kingdom of Upper Burma at Awa (Ava) was very much weakened by this invasion from Manipur. Here we may quote from—*The Mons: A Civilisation of Southeast Asia* by E. Guillon[1]—"The last episode in Mon history, at last in terms of power, had its origin partly in the events which left on their mark on Burma and Thailand around 1724. It was at that time that horsemen from Manipur (where the Burmese had lost the influence they once possessed) began their raids on Upper Burma, specially Sagaing. During these raids which went on for almost twenty-five years, they made off with peasants and herds and massacred the Burmese soldiers. At their head was Garibniwaz, a mercurial warrior whom they had made a national hero. Some of these horsemen who had newly been converted to Hinduism became convinced that if they bathed in the Irrawaddy at Sagaing they would become invincible. These disturbances, which the Burmese court had not been able to quell, considerably weakened the kingdom of Ava."

During this time Burmese king Mahadhammaraja Dipati send Burmese emissaries repeatedly to the court of Manipuri king to seek the hand of a Manipuri princess.[2] Ultimately, Maharaja Garibaniwaz send princess Satyamala Devi as Awa Leima in 1749 and she became one of the queen of Mahadhammaraja Dipati, the last king of Toungoo Dynasty and titled as "Maha Devi". Her son Khura Letpa was titled—Minye Sithu.[3]

The later periods were the bloodiest time in the history of Manipur also. The ex-king Garibaniwaz on his returned journey from Awa he was attacked slightly north of Myedu by tribal forces and bandits in the north Upper Burma and on return to Manipur, again he was expelled by his son Chit Sai in 1750 and he went back to Ava but no help received from Ava king as the Burmese kingdom was under attack from Mons and with great disappointment he returned to Manipur again but was mercilessly killed by forces of Tollen Tomba (Satrughan Sai), the youngest son of Garibaniwaz who were sent by Chit Sai near Tonphang on Ningthi River.[4] In the meantime, Mons in the south became very strong and the Pegu Court chose Binnya Dala, an ethnic Shan who hails from Chiangmai as the king of Pegu, and sacked and destroyed Ava in 1752 and hundreds of royal families including the king were deported to Pegu including Princess Popa and Maha Devi and there were massacred. But fortunately "Maha Devi" was not killed but made the queen of Pegu by king Binnya Dala and conferred her the title "Thirizeya Mingala Devi".

This historical period in South East Asia was one of the most bloody and there were great wars of leadership in Burma and Manipur. Alaungpaya the leader from Moksobo was firm to occupy Ava and he after consolidating his position at his village with 46 village leaders he came down to Ava to fight the invading Peguers under the leadership of Binnya Dala.

Satyamala Devi, who had been queen to Burmese King Mahadhammaraja Dipati (1749 to 22nd March, 1752) and Mon king Binnya Dala (1752 to 1756) who had been so fortunately survived the mass slaughter had been again submitted to Alaungpaya on 29th December, 1756 as Pegu was devastated by the forces of Alaungpaya. Actually, she was escaped from Pegu along with Mon General Dalaban (Talaban) and she was submitted to Alaungpaya and later became a concubine of Alaungpaya.[5] According to Bryce Beemer[6], slave gathering warfare and cultural exchange in Burma, Thailand and Manipur, 18th-19th Century narrated this incidents—"A few years later in 1757, Alaungphaya forces attacked Pegu where it was reported that dead bodies were piled so high at the city gates that residence

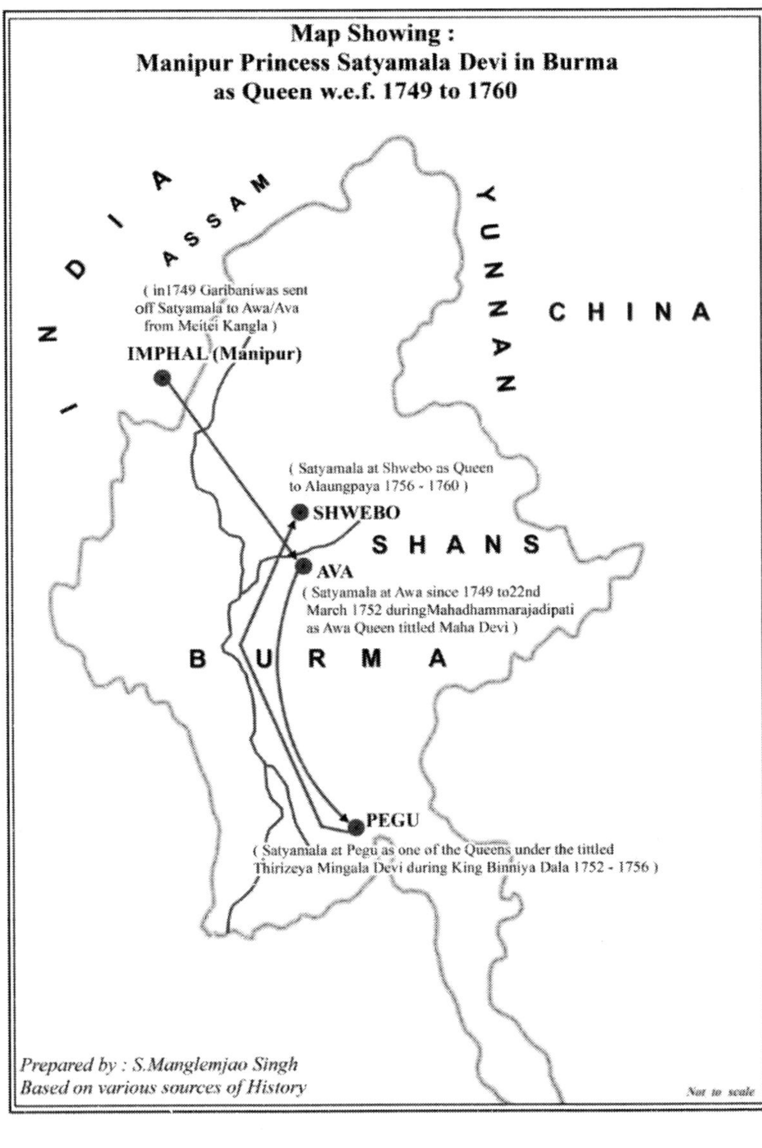

Map Showing : Manipur Princess Satyamala Devi in Burma as Queen w.e.f. 1749 to 1760

become trapped inside the wall. Maha Devi was captured yet again and made the wife of the Aluangphaya. Meanwhile, the assassination of Gharib Nawaz had destabilised the monarchy in Manipur."

Thus, Satyamala Devi, the daughter of Khamlang Pamsaba, one of the brother of Maharaja Garibaniwaz, who was Wangkheirakpa became the queen of two kings in successive events of Burma and lastly became a wife of the great king Alaungpaya in 1756 can be described as one of the most fortunate Manipuri princess in the history of Southeast Asia and South Asia.

Alaungpaya after consolidating his positions in Burma, he turns his attention towards Manipur and invaded it in 1758. He started the Manipur campaign on 12th November, 1758 and took the town on 2nd January, 1759.[7]

"In 'Konbaung-zet Mahayazawin', Alaungpaya is reported explaining that he decided to invade Manipur out of an obligation to his wife, Maha Devi. The Manipuri queen is 'under my golden foot,' the king explained, meaning he is responsible for her protection and by extension the peace of her homeland. Therefore, I will capture Manipur and put on the throne a righteous successor."[8]

We may see a Proclamation of King Alaungpaya as described in Royal Order of Burma, Part-III on his conquest of Manipur: King Alaungpaya's Proclamation on Manipur on 12th January, 1759: Alaungpaya, the Most Excellent King, Defender of the Buddha's Religion, Possessor of Arindama, Lance Master of White, Red, and Spotted Elephants, Lord of the Golden Palace, Liege of Various Kingdoms in Jambudipa, proclaimed that all lands known as Manipur is annexed to his empire from this day of 12th January, 1759 and make to it a lasting record for all generations to come, this proclamation is inscribed on stone. Any ruler over this land of Manipur shall send either his sister or his daughter as bride to his liege lord in Burma once in every three years.

The yearly tribute is as:

- 10 viss of gold,
- 100 horses,
- 500 bows,
- 5000 arrows with poisoned iron tips, and
- 1000 viss of tree gun.

In the time of war he has to join the imperial army with a force of 2000 men (1000 Horsemen, and 1000 Archers). He shall be allowed to rule Manipur so long as he accepts Burma's suzerainty. But in case he becomes disloyal, the Burmese king, may he suffer all the great miseries enumerated below:

- The curse of all guardian spirits of the Buddha's Religion
- The curse of all guardian spirits of the Burmese King
- The curse of all Hindu Gods
- The horrible death of being eaten alive by leopard, lions, tigers
- Ogres on land or crocodiles and sharks
- The horrible death of being struck by a thunderbolt
- The horrible death of being burnt alive
- The affliction of all the ninety six kinds of illness
- The affliction of the loathsome disease of leprosy
- The inexplicable failures in all trade ventures
- The loss of property like water in an ebb tide
- The horror of war, epidemic, famine and plunder
- The disintegration like salt in a sunken boat.

On the other hand, if he remains loyal, may he be healthy and prosperous in this life and in all lives to come and ultimately may he be obtained the bliss of *nirvana*. This record was inscribed on stone by Thet Shay Nawyatha and the inscription stone was erected right in front of the Manipur palace on 19th January, 1759.[9] In the month of Sajibu (April-May), 1759, Meiteis destroyed one memorial build by Burmese forces to commemorate their victory over Meiteis.[10]

NOTES

1. Emmanuel Gillon, *Mons: A Civilisation of Southeast Asia*, Bangkok, 1999.
2. *Cheitharol Kumbaba* (Royal Chronicle of Manipur).
3. New Ni Hlaing, "The Meitei (Kathe): Crown Service Group in Myanmar from the earliest times to the end of Monarchial Rule" in *Journal of the Myanmar Academy of Arts and Science*, Vol. XIII, No. 9, June 2015.
4. Sarangthem Bormani, *Meitei Ningthourol*, Edit-2018, p. 73.
5. *Konbaung*, Vol. I.

6. Bryce Beemer, *The Creole City in Mainland Southeast Asia : Slave Gathering Warfare and Cultural Exchange in Burma, Thailand and Manipur 18th-19th Centuries*, University of Hawaii, Manoa, 2013.
7. Than Tun (tr.), *Royal Order of Burma*, Part III, p. 55.
8. Bryce Beemer (2013), University of Hawaii at Manoa.
9. *Royal Order of Burma*, Part III, pp. 54-55.
10. L. Ibungohal Singh and N. Khelchandra Singh, *Cheitharol Khumbaba*, Imphal, 1989.

OTHER WORKS CONSULTED

1. George Scott, *Gazetteer of Upper Burma and Shan States*, 1900.
2. Maumg Htin Aung, *A History of Burma*, Columbia University Press, New York and London, 1967.
3. W.S. Desai, *A Pageant of Burmese History*, Orient Longman, 1961.

19
Cross-Border Ethnic and Historical Connect
Manipur and Myanmar

Konsam Himalay Singh

Introduction

The geographical and the historical setting of the sub-Himalayan region which is bounded by the mighty Irrawaddy river to the East, the river Brahmaputra to the West, Himalayan range to the North and the Bay of Bengal to the South is marked by mountainous and hilly landscape interspersed by the beautiful valleys and riverine terrain. The region is abound with thick vegetations, jungles, hills, and are remote, underdeveloped, and ravaged by the fury of the nature through the centuries. The area is very sparsely populated except in the valleys of Brahmaputra, Surma and Imphal. The region is also home to over 300 ethnicities, many of whom have amalgamated with the larger groups or are in the process of doing so over the years. Scholars opine that large scale migrations of Austeric stock speaking Sino-Tibetan languages to the region took place around 5 B.C. Bodos are believed to be the earliest settlers in the Brahmaputra valley. Another wave of migrations came to the region from the present day South West China and settled themselves in the hilly region between the present day sub-Himalayan regions of Patkai Bum ranges and the Irrawaddy river basin. The migrations of Tai-Ahoms from the South East Asian region during the 13th century further pushed the Bodos further to the west and southwards. More migrations of Bengalis, Nepalese and others from mainland Indian civilisation throughout the 7th century onwards added to the diverse mosaic of the ethnicities of the region.

Ethnicity and Kingdoms

Among the most powerful and historically documented kingdoms that existed in the areas which lie to the West of the Patkai Bum range, which include present day East Arunachal areas of Tirap, Nagaland, Manipur and Mizoram region were the Tripuri, Chutia, Koch, Kachari and Dimasas (All of them affiliated to the Bodo origin). The kingdoms of Kamrup, Kamtapur, the Ahoms, the Jaintias are recorded to have been in existence in the region around 9th century A.D. in the river valleys and highlands which were considered suitable for human habitation and economic activities. On the other hand, the kingdoms of Shans and the Burmans were established in the valleys and highlands which existed to the East of the present day Naga Hills but West of the Irrawaddy river in early 10th century. The Pagan empire during the 9th century was the first kingdom in the Irrawaddy basin which was formed after bringing the many ethnic groups in the area under one kingdom in present day Myanmar. There are vast tracts of the region inhabited by the various Naga, Chin speaking peoples, the Arakanese, Kachins, mostly unadministered in the true sense due to the terrain where the political boundaries of the various kingdoms fluctuated according to the priorities of the rulers. The Burmans were mostly concentrated in the Irrawaddy river basin and other highlands/ valleys.

Kingdom of Manipur

In the middle of this vast geographical region, existed the kingdom of present day Manipur, established around the 1st century A.D. There are many theories of the origin of the inhabitants of the people of Manipur including Indo-Aryan origin. T.C. Hodson rejects these theories and asserts the people are indigenous to the valley, he notes that "the Meitheis were as the hill people now are. The successive waves of foreign invasion, Shan, Burmese, and Hindu, have each left permanent marks on the civilization of the people so that they have passed finally away from the stage of relatively primitive culture into one of comparative civilization, but their ultimate homogeneity with the Nagas and Kukis of the hills is undoubted, and in my opinion needs no further insistence." It is also pertinent to note here that certain ethnic nationalities, for instance many of the Chins and the Naga affiliated groups, inhabit in both Myanmar and Manipur borders. At least a lac of Tangkhuls are believed to be in the Somra Tract area of Myanmar in addition to the many tribes of Nagaland who have spill over populations on both sides of the border. Anals and Moyons inhabit some areas in Tamu and around.There are approximately 60 tribes affiliated to the Naga/ Kuki tribes in Indo-Myanmar border region. Many Kuki-Chin tribes also are residing in the Chin Hills in Myanmar with approximate population of a million. Together, the Chin speaking and Naga groups comprise about two to three per cent of the population of Myanmar today. These ethnicities were generally accepted to be within the lost administrative boundaries of the various kingdoms from time to time.

Manipur and Ava (Myanmar)

The fluctuating geographical boundaries of the kingdom of Manipur included the south bank of Brahmaputra to the South, Surma Valley to the East and the Kabaw valley to the West from time to time during 18th century. The geo-political location of the Kingdom enabled commercial and cultural exchanges far and wide to the East and to the West in particular and also to the north (beyond Kohima) and south (present day Mizoram and Chin Hills) in a limited manner due to the geographical realities. It was also inevitable that competitive expansion of their influence resulted in frequent wars between the Kingdom of Manipur and the ruling powers in Burma (Ava) since the beginning of 15th century even though limited social and cultural exchanges grew between the powers during the period. *Cheitharol Kumbaba* records that the first invasion of the Kabaws on the Khumans in Manipur after which some kind of demarcation of the boundary between the Kabaws and Meiteis was carried out which was roughly aligned to the present day Kabaw valley during 1475 A.D. Attacks and counter-attacks continued between the two kingdoms of Ava and Manipur during the next three centuries. The teak rich Kabaw valley was a territory of Manipur till the Burmese took control of it in 1560 when the Toungoo dynasty conquered Manipur and made it a tributary state. The valley was re-occupied by Manipur in the 18th century.

The precise, surveyed and accurate modern day boundaries between Myanmar and Manipur as we see today, took shape only in the 19th century with the coming of the British and its administration. In the pre-British era, the borders and boundaries of the states and kingdoms the world over were more fluid in nature. Exacting tributes and conquest of one state over the other was considered to be reason enough for these territories to be included in the territory of the powerful state. The Burmese considered present day Assam and Manipur to be included in their boundary after exacting tributes from these principalities in early 19th century. To the Meiteis, for example, there was no such country as Burma. There was only the Ava kingdom with whom frequent fighting was the norm.

Wars and Forced Migrations

At different junctures in history, interactions happened between the Meiteis and the Shan kingdom as well as the Avas. G.E. Harvey wrote in 1824 that: "The Manipuris were living in an obscure valley, knowing nothing of the outside world, they thought themselves to be heroes able to take on Burma as they willed. They didn't realise that Burma was by this time far bigger power and they were laying up for a frightful vengeance (from the Burmese)." Harvey's account is attested by Thant Myint-U (*The River of Lost Footsteps*, 2007), who writes: "For decades fierce Manipuri horsemen had been raiding up and down the valley of the nearby Mu River, torching villages all around, ransacking pagodas, and stealing away captives. Led by their rajas Jai Singh and Gharib Newaz and riding the stylish little ponies for which they would later be renowned, the Manipuris defeated again and again the soldiers despatched to stop them. The first raids into Burma had taken place in the middle and late seventeenth century, but they were now increasing in frequency and destructiveness. The Burmese Court seemed powerless against the rising menace, and its frailty lost its support at home and even the nominal allegiance of its eastern tributaries. In the summer of 1739, Gharib Newaz's cavalry reached the Irrawaddy itself, burning the monastic libraries on the north shore and halting, the Burmese believe, to bathe in the holy waters of the river."

> **1743:** The famed Manipuri teacher Maha Tharapu arrived in person at Ava, intending to instruct the Burmese king in the ways of Hindu faith. The dynasty founded two

hundred years before by Bayinnaung was on its last legs.
1764: Ava invaded Manipur and took some Manipuris to Ava (it was the capital city between 1364-1555 and 1629-1752) as captives and settled them around the outskirts of the city. King Alaungpaya developed a cavalry battalion out of Manipuri settlers. Then, king Alaungpaya invaded Siam (Thailand) with the help of 500 Manipuri cavalries.
1769: A Sino-Myanmar War took place during the time of king Myeidumin. A combined force of Kate horsemen, numbering around 500 and Myanmarese army, launched an attack against the Chinese.
1820-21: King Bagyidaw of Myanmar invaded Manipur and the Seven Years Devastation took place in Manipur during 1819-1826. During the Seven Years Devastation, king Bagyidaw brought thousands of Manipuris to Myanmar by promising job opportunities. Under two instances, each numbering 30,000 of Manipuris were taken to Myanmar in the year 1820 and 1821.

Contribution of the Kathes (Manipuris) in the Making of Burmese Empire

Alaungpaya had already ravaged the kingdom of Manipur in 1758, and this brutal invasion was followed up by another in 1764. Thousands of people were deported, and the valley was left nearly empty for years. Many of the captives were smiths, weavers, craftsmen of all sorts. They were formed into hereditary groups owing special service to the crown, and for generations they and their descendants laboured as servants and agricultural workers for the Burmese nobility. They also formed the new Cassey Horse, an elite cavalry regiments that supplied some of Ava's best polo players. Two more invasions followed together, and a Burmese-educated puppet prince was installed. The people of Manipur were famous for their skill in handicraft, and the Burmese valued them highly, settling them in the capital, in the riverine villages of Sagaing district, and at Amarapura. They served as boatmen and silversmiths; as silk workers they introduced the acheik patterns; they gave the Burmese army its best cavalry (the Cassey Horse), and they supplied the bulk of the court astrologers intoning benedictions, as the king took his seat on the throne.

Trade and Commerce

Manipur had trade relations with countries like Burma, China, and British India. India's trade with China and South East Asia went through Manipur and *vice versa*. The earliest mention of trade links between Manipur and the Yunnan province of China is recorded in the chronicle of Manipur in 1630 A.D. According to historian Gangumei Kamei, trade continued till 1813 A.D. The khamenchatpa cloth which is worn by royalty and during religious ceremonies in Manipur was, "...first made in the country by Chinese, who are said to have visited Manipur in the reign of Khagenba" (circa 1630 A.D., Hodson, 17). The Chinese merchants are also attributed to imparting the art of manufacturing gun powder to the Manipuris (Hodson, 21). Trade was one of the most important aspects of these exchanges. British colonial reports and writings talk about trade exchanges and the popularity of Manipuri craftsmen, horsemen and silk in Burma—The Burmese traders who frequent Munnipore, buy up greedily all the silk they can get.

Ethnic and Cultural Connect

It can safely be assumed that, the broad culture and traditions among the hundreds of ethnic groups in the region had broad common ancestry and could not be separated from each other. There are many similarities among the languages of Chin-Kuki groups and the Naga groups. Similarities between the Manipuri language, Burmese and Tibetan language exist. The Bodo language itself had its origin from Indo-Tibetan backgrounds. The Bodos are closely related to the Tripuris, Garos, Cacharis, Dimasas and so on. The Burmese language itself is classified in the Tibeto-Burmese group of language in the family of Tibeto-Chinese languages. The Manipuri language is also grouped in the Kuki-Chin group in the Tibeto-Burmese family by the scholars.

The two 'nations' also experienced cultural exchanges with one another. Manipur was especially close to the Shans of Myanmar (Hodson, 31). Hodson's account clearly states that the horsemen, boatmen and good craftsmen and goldsmiths in the Ava kingdom were primarily Cassayers. The Meitei Brahmins who practised astrology were also highly regarded and patronized by kings and high officials. They were brought to the Ava kingdom as prisoners of war. The places where the Cassayers or Meiteis, settled are mostly in Mandalay and Amarapura. The Meitei villages 'or Poana-Gok' still exists to this very day in Mandalay as well as Yangon. 'Poana' in Burmese refers to Brahmins and Gok means a village or locality.

The Royal Historical Link

It was during the Bagan period in the Eleventh Century that the Manipuris started settling in Myanmar, the wife of king Kyan Sit Thar happened to be a Manipuri princess. The present-day polo or 'goolie game' which has its origin in Manipur was played during the time of king Bayiunaung (1551-1581) who belonged to the Taungoo period (Manipuris called it as Tongdoy). Many Kate horsemen served under this king. It is recorded in history that King of Pong (Shan) gifted image of Lord Vishnu to king Kiyamba during 14th century well before the Hinduisation of the Manipuris in late 16th century. It can be assumed that the influence of Vishnu cult could have been introduced from Siam (Thailand) through the Shans who were already in practice of some form of Buddhism at that time.

Some of the important recorded historical and ethnic connect between Manipur and Myanmar through the ages are as under:

- **1558 A.D.:** Many members of the Manipuri royalty settled in Taungoo.
- **1702 A.D.:** King Charairongba of Manipur gave his daughter, Chakpa Makhaongambi, to the then Awa king.
- **1732 A.D.:** King, Jayashree Garibaniwaj offered his daughter, Hmin Long Khang, to king Sa-ne.
- **1749 A.D.:** Manipuri princess Maha Devi was installed as a queen by the Mon king and the title, Thirizeya Mingala Devi was conferred on her, after defeating the Ava king of that time to whom the princess was married.
- **1757 A.D.:** King Alaungpaya took some Manipuris as captives and along with some others settled them at Sagaing and various parts of Amarapura district. He established a Kate cavalry with the number ranging around 2000.

Places Settled by Manipuris in Myanmar (Extract from the Speech by Mutuabahadur, published in *The Sangai Express*)

The Manipuris who were taken to Myanmar were settled at different places according to their vocation. Those settlers were—skilled weavers, carpenters, painters, goldsmiths, rowers, soldiers, cavalry, indigenous physicians, priests and astrologers etc.

Manipuris were scattered in different parts of Myanmar, such as—Kachin state, Yangong division, Sagaing division, Shan state, Ayeyarwaddy division etc. Some of the old villages have vanished. Even the names of the settled areas are not known to the new generations of the Manipuris settled there. Some of the existing Manipuri villages have been absorbed into Myanmarese society.

Those Manipuris settled at Myintut are believed to be the descendants of Manipuri cavalries that settled in this locality. The word '*Myin*' is for horse and '*Tut*' is for army in the Myanmarese language. Around 15 km from Myintut is the village of Aheneitaw. The word '*Aheneitaw*' stands for a village inhabited by very skilled medical practitioners. These people are the descendants of those Manipuris who were forcibly taken to Myanmar to serve as medicine men. Just to the south-western side of the past capital arc villages—Kha-Kshetri, Awang Kshetri, Bamon Khunjao (Paonasu), Kshetri Khul, (those inhabitants were serving Myanmarese kings as purohits), Lairikyengbam Leikai and Myint Mo Geve etc.

There is Dal Dale and Latthamar villages (the latter is known as Konjengbam Leikai) just near Amarapura (it was the capital of Myanmar from 1783 to 1823) of Mandalay division. A little distance away from Amarapura is Shrigram or Senga Manipuri village and also Gaave (Myanmarese know it as Yekyipauk) village. Before reaching Sagaing, there is a Manipur village known as Shwekyet by the Mandalay road.

A Manipuri village called 'Hypi-kathe' (supplementary residents) in Mogok which is situated to the northern side of Mandalay. In 1780, king Bodawpaya settled Manipuris at Mogok to use them for ruby mining.

And again in 1812, the king added another 45 families, and had to settle them there. There are more of Kate (Manipuri) villages near Kyatpayen due to an increase in their population.

In 1916, one written silver scroll was found near an old pagoda in Kathe (Manipuri town). In that scroll, it was written that in 1785, the right of ruby mining was in the hands of Thungyi of Kathe, Mogok. The Kathe town is adjacent to Kyatpyen.

In 1783, during Bodawpaya's time, Manipuri captives were used in the ruby mine. The place was known as Myaukywar by villagers during those days. They have identified themselves and the villages as Kathe for a long historical period. Lots of beautiful folk tales and man-made stories for those Kathes and Kyatpyen, settled around Mogok, were written in the parabaiks of Myanmar from an early time.

Present Status and the Reality of the Historical and Ethnic Connect

Shared in ethnicity, linguistic affinity, social and cultural beliefs, folklore, food habits, traditions, rituals and traditional attire have much in common with the eastern neighbour. Geographical proximity and historical connect did have significant impact even in post-colonial periods.Today insurgents from Manipur, both hill and valley-based, are believed to have taken sanctuary in Myanmar since the beginning of the insurgency movements in the region. There are also reports that many who have left the insurgency movements have taken to Myanmarese society particularly in the Sagaing Division among the Shan community. There are reports today of entire villages populated by Kathe-shans, meaning thereby that the population in these villages are of mixed stock between the Kathes (Meiteis) and the Shans located in the Chindwin river valleys in Sagaing Division of Myanmar.

Today, Myanmarese Manipuris are known to have two ways of dressing. Men wear Longyi when they are out of their homes and they wear Pheijom on customary and religious occasions. The traditional Kang Chingba (Rath Yatra), Ramayan Leela, Sankirtanas, Holi and Lai Haraoba festivals are observed with gaiety even today. Brick temples of Lainingthou Pakhangba and Lairembis are also known to be found among the Manipuri households in Myanmar till date. With the gradual disappearance of some of the cultures, language and customs of the Meitei community in Myanmar, many Manipuris settled in Myanmar today have little choice but to adopt Myanmarese names to ensure their livelihood and the future of their kith and kin. Casteism and clan hierarchy in the local society in Myanmar is known to have been one of the factors in their losing identities to a great extent. Most Myanmarese Manipuris today do not identify themselves with Manipuris except those living in the vicinity of Mandalay and Ningthi River (Chindwin River) such as villages of Mangsa, Tanan, Tekshigong, Homalin etc. Even if 50 per cent of the population of Manipuris, mostly men folks, who were transported to Myanmar during 1820-21 (Approximately 60,000), the present population of Manipuris or with Manipuri descent in Myanmar should be close to a million. The census of Myanmar do not find details of Kathes/Meiteis in their records. However, considering the fact that there were about 7,000 Manipuri speaking people in 1931 in Myanmar excluding those who have converted themselves to Myanmarese identity, it could be extrapolated that there would be approximately 40-50 thousand or more Manipuri speaking people now.

But, some time in the future, the generations of the Manipuris or of Manipuri descent living in Myanmar would trace their roots once again and look westwards towards their paternal home. Similarly, with the democratisation of Myanmar, many who have ethnic linkages on this side of the border are bound to do the same thing. It must also be noted here that, owing to the various ethnic nationalities that inhabit the two regions there were no such thing as one sacrosanct Manipuri culture or Myanmar culture prior to the advent of Hinduism and Christianity in the kingdom of Manipur. Geography prevented the various tribes of the yore to have social intercourse and understanding among the tribes. In the modern world today, such social gaps are drastically reduced even though localised ethnic political unrest among the various groups continue unabated due to many other factors.

India's Act East policy is expected to create the requisite ecosystem in the long term, for greater understanding and interactions between the Manipur and Myanmar in terms of cultural and traditional exchanges too besides strategic and other commercial activities. It is hoped that more and more socio-cultural and economic linkages in the region will improve the quality of life in both sides of the International boundary and add force to the strategic outreach by India to the South East Asian countries. The ethnic and cultural linkages should have no political overtones or even cause any threat to either country. On the contrary, the linkages should be exploited for better understanding between the two neighbouring countries, just as Free Movement Regime

(FMR) agreed between the two countries attempted to achieve in post-independent era.

To conclude, it is hoped that the much talked about ancient wisdom in the old Manipuri Puyas that "Nongpok Thong Hangba" (Opening of the Eastern Gate) of Manipur would bring greater peace and progress in the Manipur-Myanmar relationship within the larger framework of Indo-Myanmar Friendship in the future.

20
Cross-Border Migration and Cultural Dynamics of Ethnic Groups Between Myanmar and Manipur

Sanasam Amal Singh

Introduction

We know that interrelationship of human being and land is rather intrinsic and both exist under a systemic environment. The systemic environment is sometimes forced to change when political and economic factors disturbed the social balance. Under such conditions people's migration took place from one place to other. It is evident that migration of people has taken place to different areas in different directions in groups as well as individuals. Many of these migrations are recorded in the context of Manipur. Racial groups of people, like Mongoloid, Austroloid, Proto-Mongoloid, Proto-Austroloid have entered in this area. The influx of people brought about a mix of cultural aspects and also racial characteristics. Moreover, we are aware of the fact that people from China, Burma, Cambodia, Vietnam, Tibet, etc. came and settled down in the valley and adjoining areas. The ancient manuscripts of Manipur such as *The Nongchup Haram, Nongpok Haram, Chakpa Khunda Khunthok, Poireton Khunthok, Chinggurembi Khonglup, Bamon Khunthoklon* etc., reveals that people, by and large, migrated into the region and settled down. The accounts of the detailed information of the migrated Pangals (Muslims) also recorded properly. Thus in this background, the chapter highlights the early Shan migration in Manipur and the Meitei settlement in Myanmar. The Meities in Myanmar are commonly known as Kate, *Kathe, Kasse, Kathe Ponna* or *Cassay*. Almost everyone in Myanmar country knows

Kathe Ponna. The Myanmarese are also known to the Manipuris as Awa a derivation of the name Ava, one of the ancient capitals of Myanmar. The ethnic Shans are known to Manipuris as *Pong* and the Shans inhabiting Kabo valley as *Kabo* and so on.[1] The chapter also briefly looks into the cultural influence brought by the ethnic migrant groups in both the regions, i.e. Myanmar and Manipur.

Routes of Migration

There are a number of routes which connected Manipur and various parts of the adjoining countries. The most important old routes are Imphal to Burma, Imphal to Silchar and Imphal to Kohima. The former one connected six important routes to Imphal via Chasad to Bhamo and subsequently to the Southeast.[2] It is the offshoots of the Himalayas—separating Manipur from Burma. By these routes the Shans and other people of Burma could easily come to Manipur.[3] This reveals that Manipur had a good relation with South East Asia and also towards the west. Through the mainland these routes were interconnected and the subsequent migration and immigration of people can be traced. Even long distance and short distance trades were carried through these routes. When a foreign missionary of South East Asia had to visit the Indian mainland or *vice versa*, they had to go through Manipur. That is why Manipur was regarded as gateway to South East Asian people.[4] Still farther north, there was a route connecting to China through Upper Burma and Yunnan.[5] There is clear evidence that this route was used from the beginning of the second century B.C.[6] Thus, it can be speculated that by this route there was Indian influence, after affecting Upper Burma and reached Nanchao. Through these routes migration and immigration had evolved. Consequently, people from the eastern and western sides settled in this early state, and also at the same time several Manipuris had also migrated into neighbouring countries as well.

Shan Migration in Manipur

The Shans are in the category of Tai or Tai Loung race and speak Tai dialects.[7] The inhabitants on the west bank of the Cambodia river, the Siamese, the Laos, and Shans of the Salween river, the Chinese Shans of Yunnan, the Shans of Northern Burma of the Kyendwen river, and in the Kabaw valley; besides which the Ahoms of Assam are of the Shan race. The similarity in feature, language and religion between these people prove that they belong to the Shan origin.[8] Chinese Shans are the Shans of the Shan states in Yunnan, the most important of which lie in the area south of Tengueh and west of the Salween. Many of the Shans now resident in Burma in the Bhamo and Myithyina district are recent immigrants from the Yunnan and are classed by the Burmese as Chinese Shans. Hkamti Shans are looked upon as a sub-type of Burmese Shan.[9] This widespread distribution of Tai speakers in Southeast Asia has been pictured as the end of a mass exodus out of China in response to Han Chinese pressure.[10] Historically, as today, these people appear as valley-dwelling wet-rice growers, a fact that gives to the cultures of most Tai-speaking populations, a certain uniformity. The Shans established a power base in upper Burma (Myanmar), with their capital at Inwa outside of modern Mandalay.[11] Following the Mongol sack of Bagan in 1287 A.D., the Shan kingdom was formally bounded to the North by the range of hills dividing Burma from Assam. In the South it extended to Khampat, in the west to the Yoma range, east to the Yunnan, the capital was Mogoung.[12]

It is believed that the Shans came to Manipur in the 15th and 16th centuries, when the Chinese and Burmese attacked on their land in Upper Burma. The Chinese attacked from the north and the Burmese from the south.[13] Many Shans who fled to Manipur had settled here and merged with the local population. In Manipur, the word Kabo and Pong are synonymous with Shans.

According to R.B. Pemberton, the term Kabo is employed by the Meiteis to designate not only the country of the Shans, but that extensive race itself. Likewise in Assam, the Shans are known as Ahoms. T.C. Hodson rejected the Meitei connection with the Tai origin on the basis of the Meitei being a Tibeto-Burman language and the Tai being of the Siamese-Chinese linguistic family.[14] Though not of the Tai origin, there was a relationship between the Shans and the Meiteis, because of historical connection.

The people coming from the east into Manipur during the reign of different kings were known as *Nongpok Haram*. The literal meaning of 'Nongpok' means 'East' and 'Haram' means 'Direction' i.e., people coming from the eastern side. The history of their migration into Manipur were properly arranged and recorded in the form of literature by the *Pandit Loishang* (Royal Scholars' Office) under the patronage of the kings. These groups of people came from places like Kabo, Senbi, (Shan) and Khagi (China). They were settled mostly at *Kabo Leikai* (DM College Campus) and to some other places in the valley areas like *Khurai, Angom Leikai, Phumlou*[15], etc. In the year 1891 just after the establishment of British colonial administration, the people of *Kabo Leikai* were evacuated outside the 'British Reserved Areas'.

The literature of *Nongpok Haram* mentions that these people came into Manipur during the period of Meitei king Naothingkhong (663-763) A.D. and Moramba (1709-1753) A.D. and they were assimilated into the social and cultural fabrics of indigenous people. They were given *yumnaks* (sub-clan). Most of them came without wives, and so they married local girls. They strictly maintained the patriarchal system. The names of their wives (local girls) are properly recorded in the *Nongpok Haram* manuscript. With the help of this manuscript one can make an easy access to a person who belongs to *Nongpok Haram*. This shows that in Meitei society every migrated group was recorded in Meitei genealogies. Thus, their diasporas spread in the valley.

The following are the list of the *Sageis* (sub-clan) of Nongpok Haram: *Senjam, Ngaseppam, Konsam, Chingsubam, Khongbantabam, Nandeibam, Chaphamayum, Hikham, Usham, Huritsabam, Irungbam, Samjetsabam, Lakwanmayum* etc. But, these pouring groups were not allowed to occupy or hold high ranking post like the head of department of offices. Again they were not allowed to serve the traditional deities like *Sanamahi, Nongsaba*, etc. (see Table 20.1) However, they were allowed to worship these deities. During the period of Khagemba (1592-1652 A.D.), the Khagis (Chinese) with their brave leader Chaopha Hongdei led an expedition to Manipur. Khagemba defeated the Khagis and killed Chaopha Hongdei who belongs to the clan of Waisi Thomangba.[16] A number Khagis became war captives and made their settlement at a particular place called *Suisa Kameng* in the Imphal East District. From the Khagis, the Meitei learnt the art of brick making and the art of silk reeling. These new technologies rendered a lot of contribution in the developmental process of the Meitei society. It also extended a great help in the economic development of Manipur.

Cultural Elements of Shan in Manipur

(i) *Kiyang Liphang*: It is an ornament used by the Manipuri women. It is from Kiyang which is an ancient Shan state in Upper Burma.

(ii) *Kaboloo*: A typical fishing trap widely used in Manipur.

(iii) *Taijeploo*: A rectangular fishing trap made of piece of bamboo and cane.

(iv) *Kabak Thang*: A typical sword of the Shans used by the Manipuris.

Naming of places by prefixing the word Kabo is also used in Manipur since the early period. It is in use even today. For example:

(i) *Kabo Leikai*: A place or locality which indicates the settlement of the Shans. Presently, this locality is identified with DM college compound. It is believed that after Anglo Manipur war in 1891, the people of this locality were evacuated to other places by the British Govt. because they apprehended some land of revolt in the area.

(ii) *Kabo lou*: It is a rice field used by the Shans. It is presently located near Sekta village which is on the Northern side of Imphal.

(iii) *Kabo Wakching*: It is a place to the western side of Imphal.

(iv) *Kabo Pali*: A Place in Thoubal district near the DC office.

In addition to this, materials like *Kabo Kang* (Water herbs), *Kabo rang* (colour), *Pong Hawai* (bean), *Pongdon* (Guava) etc. are attributed to the Pongs and the Kabos. There also took place a great innovation in the Meitei society regarding cotton thread processing pots and tools like *Lashing Pollang* (a cone shaped pot made of piece of bamboo and cane), *Huitree* (bow like tools made of piece of bamboo and cane), *Kaptreng* (a tool made of wood which is used to take out cotton seeds), *Tawot* (a tool made of wood is used to roll thread). Besides, there were found cultural similarities between the *Pongs* and the Meiteis. In Shan society, traditionally after sunset, sweeping in the household was debarred. *Likon shanaba* (playing of cowrie) was performed in Shan society. These aforesaid customs are prevalent in Meitei society. Like the Meiteis, the Shans or Pongs were not allowed to cut nail and hair on his or her birth day. It is customary amongst the Shans or Pongs that when a girl's or boy's teeth is broken then it is to be thrown up on the roof of the house. Such a practice shows a belief that the tooth will grow fast in the years to come. The same tradition is still in practice in the Meitei society. The Shans also keep high respect to their father. So, they do not allow anyone to sit to their father's seat.[17]

These Shan elements were a factor influencing the knowledge of the Meities. An intermingling of such culture caused social movements in the Meitei society. The close relationship and the communication that took place between the two regions is a kind of social interaction from which a social change emanated. The socio-cultural contacts during the historical period also produced Tai influence on the language and culture of the Meiteis. Later, a process of amalgamation of individual groups occurred. This in turn led to develop sub-clans and clans in Manipur's society thus evolving a social structure.

Kathe (Meitei) Migration in Myanmar

Throughout history Kathe-Myanmar relations took the form of both hostile and friendly relations. The frequent outbreak of war prevailed between Myanmar and Manipur from Taungoo to the first half of Konbaung dynasties. King Bayinnaung (1551-1581) of Taungoo Dynasty, King Thalun (1628-1648), King Minye J Kyawhtin (1673-1698), King Taninganwe (1714-1733), King Maha Dhammar-rajadipati (1733-1752) of Nyaung-yan Dynasty, King Alaungmintaya (1752-60), Myeidu Min (1763-1776), Badon Min (1782-1819) and Sagaing Min (1819-1826) of Konbaung Dynasty waged the war against Manipur. As the Myanmar kings launched expeditions and occupied Manipur, Kathe rajas occasionally over-ran Myanmar territories. Some Manipuri rajahs also established friendly relations with the kingdom of Myanmar through the matrimonial alliance, i.e they submitted their daughters to the kings of Myanmar to establish amicable relations. Thus, according to the origin and history of migration, the Kathe communities had emerged in Myanmar through the conscription of war captives by the successive kings. Kathe people and their descendants were organized into miscellaneous crown service groups and were allotted lands for residence and subsistence. The Kathes were skilled weavers, carpenters, painters, goldsmiths, rowers, soldiers, cavalry, indigenous physicians, priests and astrologers etc.[18] Notably one of the most valuable contributions of Manipuris to the Myanmar society is the Myanmarese cavalry known as the *The Cassay Horse* which is almost exclusively composed of Kathe Manipuris. In the battles against the British at Arracan, Pegu and other places during the Second Anglo-Burmese War, the *The Cassay Horse* had played very significant roles.[19] Thus, a process of cultural assimilation started in Myanmar society with the advent of the Kathes.

The Kathes in Mayanmar have two identities. They have come to be referred to as *Ponna* or *Kathe* community, even though it is officially not recognized. The Meities in Myanmar are commonly known as *Kathe-Ponna*. Almost everyone in Myanmar country knows *Kathe-Ponna*. Though the Myanmarese recognize them as *Kathe-Ponna* but the Meitie community itself comprises of the *Kathe* and the *Ponna* which are two separate groups. The *Kathe* are the group of Meities belonging to non-Brahmin/Bahmon whereas the *Ponnas* are the Meities that belong to the Brahmin class or higher section of Hindu society.[20] The tradition of Hinduism created a wide gap of difference between these two sections in matters of identity. These two groups lead separate lives and do not intermingle with each other. Thus, the same groups of people from the same original place live as separate entities in a foreign land.

The reason behind Manipuri Brahmins being called *Ponna* was that they served as '*Purohit*' (Priest) under the king of Myanmar.[21] The Manipuri Brahmins served as the priests and counsellors at the royal court and also practiced the art of astrology. The *Ponna* Meities are larger in number than the other group. They took along with them their Brahmanical rites and beliefs and continued the same in the host country. The superstitious native of the Burmese society provided a good opportunity for advancement to the *Ponnas* with their traditional professions of Palmistry, Medicine, Astrology, etc. Later, they began to play a crucial role even in the court circles.

The role of Ponna in the Burmese court included presiding over the naming ceremony of child, consecration and coronation of the King, ritual performances so as to achieve success in war etc. During King Alaungpaya's reign, Hanthawarry, king of Burma, sent en envoy on 20th Dec., 1753, to make a proposal of marriage of his daughter to Alaungpaya. The Ponnas Adapti Brahma, Mulla Brahma and the Agga Brahma formed part of the envoy's party. In the field of literary works, the Ponnas were found engaged in translating the script and text of several works from Bengali and Sanskrit into Burmese. In the year 1829, King Bagyidaw appointed

Table No 20.1: Shan Migrants in Manipur

Sl. No.	*Name of the kings & periods*	*Original place of the Outsider*	*Person who came with wife*		*Person who came without wife*		*Absorption of Subclan*	*Absorption of clan*	*Remarks*
			Names	*Wife's name*	*Names*	*Wife's name*			
1	2	3	4	5	6	7	8	9	10
1.	Naothingkhong (663-763AD)	Kabo (Shans)			Haoningkhaikham	Heirom Chanu	Yuiham, Senjam	Khuman	
2.	Khumomba (1263-1278AD)	-do-			Tampathok	Yunam Chanu	Usham	Angom	
3.	Ningthoukhomba (1432-1467AD)	-do-			1. Chaokhunpung 2. Khambin 3. Taokhapyum 4. Chaoshem	Laishram Chanu	Khumbongmayum Sendangmayum Akhangbam Louriyam Shankhubam	Angom Angom Angom Ningthouja	
4.	Kiyamba (1467-1508AD)	-do-			1. Taothoklang 2. Rashoi 3. Taokhapyum 4. Taokrucha 5. Loutaneng 6. Chahasena 7. Toudaruja 8. Taongakhong 9. Nangtharej	Leichonbam Chanu Lokwanmayum Chanu Laishram Chanu Lourembam Chanu Sorokhaibam	Khongbantabam Khongbantabam Nandeibam Chaphamayum Konsham Haikam (Heikham) Huijam Nandeibam	Luwang Angom Angom Khuman Khuman Luwang Khuman Angom Ningthouja	

1	2	3	4	5	6	7	8	9	10
					10. Larong 11. Tairongpha 12. Taojarung 13. Taokhun 14. Taokhunlik 15. Hemdaucheng	Chanu Khoibam Chanu Mubi Lourembam Chanu Laishram Chanu Samom Chanu Thangjam Chanu Nameirak-pam Chanu Oinam Chanu Meihaubam Chanu Huirom Chanu Mairungbam Chanu	Charai Mayum Akanbam Usham Phuritsabam Tangjam Konsam Sarungbam	Angom Moirang Ariba Salai Angom Khuman Khuman Moirang Aiba Salai	
5.	Koirem-ba(1508-1512 AD)	Kabo	Chaosoikham	Mangsaba Chanu Nin-gee			Konsham		
6.	Kabomba (1524-1542 AD)	Kabo			Hokham	Nongthon-bam Chanu	Senjam Ngas-epam	Angom	
7.	Chalamba (1545-1562 AD)	Kabo	2. Ikham Singh 12. Lalhan-gamba 13. Lacha	Nongsai Likhom Hanbi	1. Chaosoinok 3. Langoo 4. Taudanga 5. Chaurei	Huyam Chanu Khongbanta-bam Chanu Sansenbam	Konsham Usham Nandeibam Nandeibam Senjam	Khuman Moirang Ariba Salai Khamba	

					6. Lilanda 7. Lamloi 8. Tairongpha 9. Lokon 10. Inkham 11. Taokham Amu	Chanu Chaphama-yum Chanu Usham Chanu Louriyam Chanu	Monphang Ma-yum Hikhambam Nandeibam Nandeibam Chapha Mayum Heibi Thabam Nandeibam Khongbantabam	Ningth-ouja Luwang Angom Angom Khaba Moirang Ariba Salai Ningth-ouja Ningth-ouja Angom Luwang	
8.	Mungyamba	Kabo	3. Chothi 5. Chourai 6. Laku 7. Kakiyang	Aung Nangden Langshen	1. Chaumingk-hang 2. Taokhut Hei 4. Loutong 8. Nungjai 9. Chaokha-mseng 10. Loutong 11. Shingun 12. Choukh-anpung 13. Khulakna	Huirongbam Chanu Chapha Ma-yum Chanu Lourembam Chanu Sanjenbam Chanu Loushigam Chanu Lourembam Chanu	Chingsubam Usham Senjam Phuritsabam Heitham Heikham Phuritsabam Konsam Louriyam Phuritsabam, Shungkhubam Nandeibam	Angom Angom Luwang Ningth-ouja Luwang Luwang Ningth-ouja Angom Angom	

						Yumnam Chanu Yumnam Chanu Akham Chanu	Khumbongma-yum Chingangbam	Ningth-ouja Angom Angom Angom Angom	
9.	Maramba (1761-1763 AD)				1. Kabeng	Chaphan Ma-yum Chanu	Senjam	Angom	

Source: M.S. *Nongpok Haram*

a committee of scholars to write a chronicle of the Myanmar Kings. The committee consisted of 'learned monks', learned Brahmins, learned ministers, who came together and compiled a chronicle which they translated and prepared in accordance with all credible records in the books. Various texts were translated with the help of Ponnas from Bengali to Myanmarese.

When the Second Anglo-Myanmar War broke out in the reign of King Bagan (1846-1853) two sagacious Ponnas, two planet worshipping Ponnas and two astrologer Ponnas were made to go along with the expedition column, not because of their military skill nor for engagement in the battle but to make arrangements for the winning of the war.[22] Through their performance and participation in royal occasions and ceremonies, the Ponnas obtained a high status in the Myanmar society especially during the time of the Burmese empire.

Thus, the advent of Kathes in Myanamr society prevailed since the Taungoo period. They served Myanmar kings in various capacities. They arrived into Myanmar not only as the captives but many of them moved into Myanmar since the time immemorial. Variety of Kathe strata including royalty, servicemen, commoners, Kathe Ponnas, and slaves came to Myanmar through ages. Successive Myanamr kings employed them in accordance with their expertise and offered titles and insignia of ranks to the Kathe servicemen and officials. As also mentioned above, ordinary servicemen were granted lands for their subsistence and residence. Over time, Kathe Cavalry commandant, Kathe scholars and royal advisers prevailed in Myanmar officialdom. Kathe scholars served the kings with their mental prowess and Kathe horsemen, elephanteers, boatmen faith-fully served the king with their skilfulness in respective service groups including armed groups and small groups of craftsmen. Finally, we can say that the advent of Kathe in Myanmar society brought about the changes in Myanmar culture and way of life to certain extent.

NOTES

1. Hareshwar Goshwami, "Relationship of the Erstwhile Kingdom of Myanmar and Manipur: A Historical Perspective", in *Souvenir Indo-Myanmar Fraternal Alliance*, Imphal, Manipur, Sept. 2005, p. 9.

2. Amal Sanasam, *Social Dynamics of Chiefs and their Cheifdoms in the State Formation in Early Manipur (From the Earliest times to the 16th Century A.D.)*, unpublished thesis submitted to Dept. of History, Manipur University, 2003 p. 90.
3. R.K. Jhalajit Singh, *History of Medieval Manipur*. Seminar Paper.
4. E.W. Dun, *Gazetteer of Manipur*, 1975 pp. 245-282. Also see. N. Khelchandra, *Ariba Manipuri Sahitya Itihas*. 1969 pp. 3-4.
5. Gordon H. Luce, *JBRS. XXIX*, 1939, p. 264.
6. Krishna Murari, "Burma-Manipur Corridor", in Sanajaoba N. (ed.) *Manipur Past and Present*. Vol. 4, 2005, New Delhi, p. 51.
7. Gogi. L. *The Tai Hkamtis of North East India*. 1971, New Delhi, p. 49.
8. *Ibid.*
9. *Ibid.*, p. 84.
10. Frank M. Lebar, Gerald C. Heckley, John K. Musgrave, *Ethnic Groups of Mainland Southeast Asia*, 1964, p. 187.
11. *World Infoṗaedia, Myanmar*. Pragun Publication. New Delhi, 2007, p. 107.
12. N. Tarunkumar Singh, "The Pan-Manipuri", in Sanajaoba, N. (ed.), *Manipur Past and Present*. Vol. 4, 2005, p. 11.
13. *Ibid.*
14. Gangmumei Kabui, *History of Manipur*, Vol. 1. 1991, p. 16.
15. M.S. *Nongpok Haram*, in possession of Dr. N. Debendra Singh of Uripok Archaival Library, Uripok Ningthaukhonjam Leikai, Imphal-795001.
16. O. Bhogeshwor Singh, *Ningthourol Lambuba*, Imphal, 1967, p. 280.
17. A.R. Colquhan, *Ethnic History of Shans*, New Delhi, 1985, pp. 97, 100.
18. Dr. Nwe Ni Hlaing, The Meitei (Kathe) Crown Service groups in Myanmar from the earliest times to the end of Monarchical Rule, *Journal of the Myanmar Academy of Arts and Science, Vol. XIII, 9, June 2015, History, International Relations, Anthropology and Archaeology*, p. 65.
19. Hareshwar Goshwami, *Ibid.*, p. 9.
20. Interview with Mutua Bahadur, a Cultural activist, Freelance Archivist and Museologist, 17th September, 2018.
21. *Ibid.*
22. New Ni Hliang, *History of Myanmar Ponna*, M.A. Dissertation, Mandalay University, Unpublished, 1999, p. 36.

21
Manipur and Kabaw Mangsa (Min Thar)
Revisiting the Linkages

Ngangom Jayshree Devi

Introduction

Kabaw[1] Valley, now an integral part of the Sagaing Division of Myanmar occupies an important place in the discourse of Manipur-Myanmar relationship. It is the 'narrow strip, of level country [2] lying between the mountains forming the eastern boundary[3] of Manipur and the Chindwin River in Myanmar known as the *Ningthee Turen* to the Manipuris. Traditionally, this valley housed many Shan principalities such as—Samsok/Samjok, Khumbat, Kule, Khamran, Tamu, along with smaller ones some even equivalent to villages which have Chiefs or '*Lakpa,*' of which Mangsa[4] or Minthar is an example. Except for a few principalities like Samjok and Tamu[5], knowledge of their relationship with Manipur throughout the course of history has fallen into oblivion. This chapter is an initial endeavor to fill up the void starting with a small place named Mangsa[6] known as Minthar in Myanmar, located at the western border of Kabaw valley almost next to the mountain circling the Manipur mainland and its linkages with Manipur from a historical perspective.

This chapter is developed on the basis of few primary as well as secondary sources mainly Manipuri and Colonial ones but faced the lacuna of Shan and Burmese sources. As for exploring the people to people contact in recent time, interview of few related persons have been incorporated.

Background of Manipur and Mangsa Relationship

The foundation of relationship between Manipur and Mangsa can be assessed from the very name Mangsa itself which is believed to be given by Poireiton.[7] In Myanmar, the place is known as Min Thar, presently identified as a village under Myothit Sub-Township in Tamu District of Sagaing Region.[8] *Poireiton Khunthok* or 'Migration of Poireiton' an old Meitei manuscript, gives account of how the protagonist Poireiton while having fallen asleep at a place in Kabaw saw his brother in the dream and named that place as Mangsa, in Meitei language '*Mang*' means dream.[9] Though we can take this account as mere imagination of the writer it does clearly indicates that Mangsa was well known to the Manipuries since an early time.

The Maring community of Manipur also has a strong connection with Mangsa. According to Gimson, they migrated to Manipur from Mangsa, the first Maring village whereas Maring tradition cites Kulbi—song near Mangsa as the first one. Nowadays-no Maring is found in Mangsa though Maring villages in Manipur near the border conduct irregular trade with its Shan villagers.[10]

Pre-Colonial Period

It is an accepted fact that territories of the kingdom of Manipur expand or contract with the might and fortune of its ruler. During certain period its eastward expansion was even beyond the Chindwin River which naturally implies subjugation of the Kabaw valley. The Royal Chronicle of Manipur, *Cheitharol Kumbaba* recorded the first skirmish with the Kabaws in 1263 A.D. during the reign of Meetingu Khumompa.[11] But it was Kyamba who brought it under Meitei rule, when he in collaboration with the Pong king Khekhomba annexed and divided the Valley between themselves in 1470.[12]

Historically one comes across Mangsa in the context of Manipur in the 16th century A.D. during the reign of king Mungyamba (1562-1597 A.D.). The *Ningthourel Lambuba* [13] describes his conquest of Mangsa whereby he defeated and captured the *Ningthou* (king) called Kancham along with its famous warrior named Khenchong as war captives. From that time Mungyamba's name came to be known as Meidingnu Mungyamba Mangsa Ngamba or 'Conqueror of Mungyam, Mangsa.[14] This type of slave raiding warfare a common aspect of pre-modern Southeast Asia[15] was frequently practiced by Manipur on many principalities in Kabaw valley as well among themselves too. Though the *Cheitharol Kumbaba* is silent on the conquest of Mangsha, it is recorded that in 1570 A.D., Kancham the king of Mangsha was involved in a fight in Mangsamkei resulting in his death. The place Mangsamgkei now known as Mongsangei is a place in Imphal West, where one of the royal granary was built. This place with all probability was named after *Mangsha, Mangsa + Kei = Mansgamkei*. Kancham was possibly appointed as the first caretaker of the *Kei*.

Many of the Shan principalities which came under Meitei king's rule due to lack of direct administration as well as large physical distance from core mainland were found to challenge Manipur's authority from time to time which were dealt with an iron hand. Likewise, Mangsha also seems to need strong handling from time to time. It is said that during the time of King Khunjaoba (1652-66 A.D.), he raided Mangsa in 1657 A.D. and devastated the land.[16]

The Samjok Factor

The importance of Mangsa is apparent from another angle which is its proximity to Samjok. Kabaw valley is a fertile region with high level of rice production and among the principalities Samjok occupies a special position. It is said that "Samjok was a great source of revenue because of the tribute in form of paddy. For any eventual conflict with Ava, Manipur's hold over Kabaw valley especially the principality of Samsok was absolutely necessary."[17] It seems to be the main source of rice to feed the Manipuri officials and soldiers who were present in the Kabaw valley. In 1694 A.D., king Paikhomba himself led a raid to collect paddy and war captives.

"Hyankei 2, Wednesday, Ningthem and others left for Samsok to thresh paddy. They captured nine people in battle. Also captured two horses. Many people fled. Friday they returned."[18]

Samjok continued to be a source of rice as well as war captives for Manipur administrators till the time of Garibniwaz. The royal chronicle recorded that during his reign even dredging of irrigation canals in Samjok was carried out in 1737.

The importance of Mangsa in this context lies in the fact that the granary to store the rice was built not at Samjok but at

Mangsa. Samjok now popularly known as Thaungdut is about approximately 27 kms from Mangsa by proper road.

Consolidation of Manipur's Rule

All along after the initial phase of subjugation, Manipur and Mangsa seems to have a cordial relationship. The construction of Royal granary at Mangsa can be taken as an indicator of the consolidation of Manipur's administration over Kabaw Mangsha. Another incident which further highlighted the deeper affiliation of Mangsa to the Meitei administration is, in 1693 A.D. when a Wangkam man tried to flee to Samsok (from mainland) he was captured by Mangsa and got killed in the resultant affray.[19] The consolidation may be because of its proximity to the Manipur as well as other policies adopted by the Manipuri kings such as matrimonial relationship.

Matrimonial Alliance

Matrimonial alliance was an important part of Meitei statecraft which the Manipuri kings adopted with almost all of his neighboring kingdoms and principalities. *Cheitharol Kumbaba* recorded the first Manipur-Mangsa marriage alliance in 1688 A.D. during the reign of Paikhomba (1666-1697 A.D.).

> "Thoipi, the Ningthoucham maiden was given to the Mangsha Rakpa of Kapo (for marriage)."
> Again during the reign of Meetingu Mayampa (Garibniwaz) 1709-1748) in 1720 A.D.,
> "the year of Keisham Womma, Lamta (Februray/March) 4 sunay, Tummurakpa and Mangsarakpa, these two chiefs presented their daughters (to the king). Palanquins were made and they were carried in them."[20]

These events indicate the consolidation of Manipur-Mangsa ties and also exhibit the importance of Mangsa.

Political Significance of Mangsa and the Ava Factor

The conquest of Kabaw valley by Kyamba brought Manipur to

close proximity with Ava or Burma now known as Myanmar. Burmese chronicles claimed Manipur as a vassal state as early as the first Taguang kingdom[21], a semi-legendary state which the Burmese chronicle *Glass Palace Chronicle (Hmanna Yazawin)* links Burma's foundation with.[22] Manipuri records on the other hand show its active involvement in the valley affairs from the time of Mungyamba (1562-97 A.D.). The Ava interference reached a turning point by the time of Garibniwaz. Thereafter, Kabaw valley became an area of great contention between the two powers. The controlling measures adopted by Meitei administrators over the Kabaw principalities were officials from Manipur were constantly posted there and also Meitei villages were established in strategic positions in Kabaw Valley and the routes connecting the Valleys.[23]

Mangsa due to its strategic location provided the crucial base through which Manipur could monitor as well as protect its interest in the valley by stopping Ava's influence. For instance Garibniwaz seeking revenge over the Avas for the ill treatment of his sister who was the queen of Ava and the associated reassertion of Manipur's authority over Samjok are well known events in the history of Manipur. These events have another aspect, the tussle for authority over Kabaw valley between Ava and Manipur which reached a serious stage during his time. At that juncture, Samjok began to lean towards Ava making King Garibiwaz to look out for an opportunity to curb it. Another chronicles *Samjok Ngamba* or 'Conqueror of Samjok'[24] describes how Mangsa offered the perfect excuse for invading Samjok but without any dates. This event must have taken place in 1723 as *Cheitharol Kumbaba* describes how he totally vanquished Samjok that year.

Mangsa was also where the Manipuri warriors stood as vanguard against invaders to stop them from entering the mainland or core of the Manipur kingdom. In 1724, Poinu, 11 Sunday, as it was reported that Awa was marching to attack, Haopam Cha the Pukhranpa and the people of Naicha and others left for Mangsaram.[25]

Meitei Settlement at Mangsa

Till date one does not come across records giving specific information of Meitei settlement at Mangsa in the pre-colonial time, nevertheless, its existence is indicated by different factors. The construction of the royal granary of the Manipuri king, presence of Manipuri officials, and marital relationship[26] all point towards Mangsa having a Meitei settlement. The Meitei sub-lineage called the Mangsatabam or the one who settled at Mangsa seems to be an indicator of it. At the same time, its existence seems to be tied with the fortune of the Manipuri kings.

After king Garibniwaz, the political situation of Manipur nose dived which only worsened post king Bhagyachandra as war of throne amongst the princess reduced the kingdom to such a condition that by early part of 19th century, it collapsed before the Ava power. The situation reached to the point where the Avas ravaged it for years pushing Manipur to a dark phase still remembered as the *Chahi Taret Khuntakpa,* 1819-1825 A.D. or 'Seven Years Devastation of Manipur.' With the new developments, the Meitei settlement at Mangsa must have lost its significance as in the early 19th century A.D., the colonial officials assigned in Manipur failed to mention the presence of any Meitei settlement there, or another possibility is that they failed to make out the Manipuris from the Kabaw Shans.

Colonial Period

Manipur entered a new phase when king Gambheer Singh with the assistance of British colonial power finally freed Manipur from Ava's clutches which was marked by the Treaty of Yandaboo 1827. Manipur paid a huge price for taking British assistance by being coerced to give away Kabaw Valley to the Ava. Post Anglo-Manipuri War of 1891, the kingdom was reduced to a princely state. The new colonial administrator had already made Ava a part of British India by 1886. Under that context Tamu proved more convenient for taking different routes towards proper mainland of Ava and henceforth the relevance of Mangsa declined though not totally neglected. Capt. Dun one of the colonial officers posted in Manipur who compiled the *Gazetteer of Manipur* when writing about Kambang Thana in the Maring route, regarded as one of the second line of defense of Manipur, situated 20 miles from Yangoupokpi, suggested that a signal-station be formed there so as to communicate with Mangsa. He also wrote about two roads leading to Mangsa while travelling from Yangoupokpi to Moreh Thanna.[27] The place significance as a route to Manipur for the

Shans, Avas and other from Southeast as well as East Asia was still recognized.

Meitei Settlement in Mangsa after Ava was brought under British India

Burma was a part of British India from 1886 till 1937 A.D. This must have brought Manipur and Ava especially the Kabaw valley more closure. The Nikhil Hindu Maha Sabha under the leadersip of Hijam Irawat even managed to organize its Third Session in Mandalay from 28 February to 2 March, 1937. Manipur's interaction with Mangsa must also have increased, especially the people to people contact. Oral accounts as well as references found in different events mentioned the Meitei settlement of Mangsa. It is said that at one point of time, the Meitei population of Mangsa was of a significant number that even a Rath Yatra festival was organized by them.[28] This is significant as the festival is organized at a community level with mass participation under the direction of a Brahmin or *Bamon* who is responsible for the ritual aspect.

Second World War and Mangsa

During the Second World War, better known as '*Japan Laan*' in Manipur, the Meitei village of Mangsa came into light. It is narrated that in 1944 May, a team made up of members of Manipuri Paona Independence Party, INA and Japanese army which entered Manipur from the southern path of Chandel around Libung village had to retreat from Bongli in Chandel district when the tides of war turned against them. Majority of them choose the Yangoupokpi-Mangsa road to retreat. As it was rainy season, the road was found immersed in water at many parts even up to waist at some points. When they reached the Meitei village at Mangsa, it was almost midnight. Most of the houses were found burnt with bullet marks on almost everything. The retreating troop spend the night there and the next morning, the Meitei villagers helped them to carry their luggage up to Tamu.[29]

Post-Independence and Merger with India

Hijam Irawat and Mangsa

After the British left the kingdom on 14th August, 1947, the first elected government was formed in 1948, which ended abruptly after Manipur merged to India on 21 September, 1949. The new political developments led to the emergence of new breed of Manipuris who dreamt of a new Manipur. Their thoughts were shaped by the modern education introduced by the colonial administrators and interaction with mainland India. One such person was Hijam Irawat, regarded as one of the most important history makers of modern Manipur. His life also had a Mangsa connection.

Post Pungdombam incident he was declared a fugitive and forced to go underground. For furthering his dream of a new modern and better Manipur he escaped to Burma in September, 1950. He went there to seek cooperation from the numerous groups revolting against the national government of Burma. Many of them warmly welcomed him. His entry to Burma was through Mangsa from there he shifted to Ango hills where he expired at a village called Taungbo due to ill health on 26, September, 1951. In the beginning of that very month he came back to Mangsa and attempted to launch his political movement in Manipur with Mangsa as his base camp but Burmese army's movement compelled him to went back to Taungbo.[30] The reason for his choosing Mangsa is easily understandable as it could be easily reached after crossing the Heirok hills through the Maring route which is interspersed with many paths leading to Mangsa. The Meitei settlers there are closely associated with people of places around western foothill of Heriok hill. In fact Irawat reached Mangsa under the guidance and protection of Red Army members mainly belonging to Heirok and Salungpham villages which are around Heirok hills.

People to People Contact

Most of the Meiteis settled at Mangsa are said to have their origin in villages of Thoubal district which lie near the Heirok hill. Post harvesting season there was the tradition of '*Kabaw Chatpa*' or '*Going to Kabaw* ' among the villagers. They travelled on foot and if one starts at dawn Mangsa was reached by dusk. [31] Many of them were involved in trans border petty trade too. The popularity of the route is evidenced by the development of a transit trading place at Yangoupokpi which was mainly run by Meiteis with active participation from Kabaw Shans from Burmese side particularly those from Mangsa as well as tribal inhabitants of the border area.[32] By late 1960s, the place lost its significance and fades out. The main factor being, Meities in Mangsa were forced to leave due to new political development in Myanmar and on the Manipur side it was tribal politics. Those who choose to stay back adopted Burmese identity. Many from Mangsa who facilitated trade at Yangoupokki shifted to Moreh to start afresh. Some of them emerged as leading traders at Moreh, many credit their Burmese linkages as key to their success.

Look East Policy/Act East Policy

A new chapter in the Indo-Myanmar relationship is opened with India's 'Act East Policy' launched in 1992, the development took for a better turn with the transformation of the Policy to 'Act East Policy' in 2014. The new Indian policy provides reopening of the Manipur-Myanmar relationship in a wider manner. This Act provides provisions for interface between Manipur and Myanmar with opportunities to develop and strengthen connectivity through trade, culture, people-to-people contacts and physical infrastructure. The new policy has consequently removed the political wedges blocking the connection between Manipur and Myanmar thereby offering the right time and opportunity to revive the past linkages. Though the focus is mainly on Tamu township as the main centre in the Sagaing region this can be taken as opportunity to reach out to Mangsa or Min Thar. The distance between the two places is calculated to be about 29 kms by proper road. Minthar which lies north to Tamu is connected by a road which bifurcates from the Asian Highway 1. If situation permits, the old route to Mangsa via Yangoupokpi can be revived which may result in speedy development of the newly formed border district of Tengnoupal.

Conclusion

Manipur and Kabaw Valley now divided by a political boundary, much shaped by the British colonial power, irrefutably shared a close relationship. Much lamentation is still observed of the division while the shared linkages which no boundary can do away are pushed to forgetfulness. The reason may be that the valley was not easily accessible to the common Manipuris for a long time. India's 'Look East Policy' now 'Act East Policy' provides an interface between Manipur Myanmar by developing connectivity through trade, culture, people-to-people contacts etc. thereby offering Manipur an opportunity to reconnect and rebuild the linkages for mutual growth and development without losing affiliation to their respective countries. A delve into the past proves that the relationship had its ups and down, bitter and sweet phases; history provides positive explanation for that on the basis of time and space. From these perspectives, the study of Manipur's relation with Kabaw calls for minute study by dividing the valley into different units as found in the past. This chapter which explores linkages and relationship between Manipur and Mangsa from historical perspective can be considered as a preliminary attempt which still requires further investigation.

NOTES

1. Kabaw is also as spelt as Kabo, Kapo or even Kapu.
2. Pemberton, R.B. *The Eastern Frontier of India*. Mittal Publications, Delhi, 2015, First Published 1835, p. 116.
3. The mountain ranges runs across four border districts of Manipur—Chandel, Tengnoupal, Kamjong and Ukhrul.
4. Sometimes the chief of Mangsa is referred as *Ningthou* or king.
5. Samjok is also known as Thaungdut.
6. Mangsa ia also spelt as Mungsa by some.
7. Poireiton who is believed to have come from a place called Khamnung, identified by some scholars as a place somewhere in eastern Tibet is taken to be a contemporary of Pakhangba the first historical king of Manipur who ascended the throne in 33 CE.
8. *The 2014 Myanmar Population and Housing Census Sagaing Region, Tamu District Myothit Sub-Township Report,* Department of Population Ministry of Labour, Immigration and Population Office, No. 48, Nay Pyi Taw, p. 8.
9. Moirangthem Chandra Singh (ed.), 1995, *Poireiton Khunthok,* Poknapham Publications, Imphal, Manipur, p. 29.
10. Das, Rajat Kanti Das. *Tribal Social Structure : A Study of the Maring*

Society of Manipur. Inter-India Publications, New Delhi, 1988, p. 34.

11. Parratt, Saroj N. (ed & trans.). *The Court Chronicle of The Kings of Manipur: The Cheitharo Kumbaba, Vol. 1*, Routledge, London, 2005, pp. 33-34.
12. Singh, K. Manikchand. (ed & trans.), *Soraren Machana Khunkumba: Descent of the Scion of Sorarel on the Earth (A Shan Chronicle in Meitei).* K. Imo Singh, Imphal, 2014.
13. Another royal chronicle of Manipur.
14. Singh, O. Bhogeswar (ed.), *Ningthourel Lambuba, vol. 1*. Author, Imphal, 1967, p. 270.
15. Beemer, Bryce. "Southeast Asian Slavery and Slave Gathering Warfare as a vector for Cultural Transmission : The Case of Burma and Thailand." *The Historian*, Vol. 71, No. 3, 2009, pp. 481-506.
16. Parratt, Saroj N. *op. cit.* p. 84.
17. Kabui, Gangmumei. *History of Manipur Pre Colonial Period*, 3rd ed. National Publishing House, New Delhi, 2003, p. 243.
18. Parratt, S. *op. cit.* pp. 102-10.
19. *Ibid*., p. 102.
20. *Ibid*., pp. 99, 128.
21. U. Tin, *Myanmar Min Ok-chok-pon sa-dan hnit Bodaw Paya-gyi ei Ya-za-that Khawthaw A-meint-daw tan-gyi* (Royal Edicts by King Bodawpaya), V volume, Yangon, Seik ku-Cho Cho Press, 2012, p. 196 (Henceforth: Tin, 2012). quoted in 'The Meitei (Kathe) "Crown Service groups in Myanmar from the earliest times to the end of Monarchical Rule" by Nwe Ni Hlaing, *Journal of the Myanmar Academy of Arts and Science*, Vol. XIII, No. 9, 2015, pp. 65-86.
22. D.G.E. Hall. *A History of South-East Asia*. 4th ed., Macmillan Press Ltd. 1994, pp. 151, 153.
23. G. Kabui, *op. cit*., p. 211.
24. Singh, Moirangthem Chandra Singh. *Samsok Ngamba*. Manipur Naharol Sahitya Parishad Sabha, Imphal, 2010,
25. Saroj N. Parratt, *op. cit*., p. 132.
26. The tradition of Manipuri maidens who officially married rulers of other places were being accompanied by a huge entourage leading to the establishment of a small settlements there, examples, Tekhao, Ava etc.
27. E.W.Dun. *Gazetteer of Manipur*. Akansha Publishing House, New Delhi, 2013, (first published in 1886 by Suprintendent, Government Printing, Calcutt under the ordrs of Quarter-Master General in India), pp. 112, 260.
28. Informal talk with Mutua Bahadur in November, 2015, at his home.
29. Singh, Wairokpam Mangol. *Prithivigi Anisuba Lanjao Amadi Manipur Party 1939-1945 (The Second World War and The Manipur Party)*. Author, Imphal, 1984, pp. 86, 112.

30. Thounaojam, Chanu Ibemhal. *Taungbo: Irawatki Aroiba Yahipha,* Meino & Khomdon Foundation, Imphal, 2015, pp. 150-192.
31. Now there is a motorable road reaching Yangoupokpi village.
32. Interview with residents of Wangjing who took part in the trans-border trade with Mangsa via Yanoupokpi. Naorem Mangijao Singh, Wangjing Hodamba age, 83, 19th December, 2015.

THEME-VI

Strategic Opportunities

22

Comparative Studies on Manipur and Myanmar (Burma) within the South East Asian Paradigm

An Overview

Nongthombam Jiten

Manipur in North East India and Myanmar are immediate neighbours in terms of physical and human geography, as well as culture, and interlocked historical development. In the academic discourse of international community which essentialised formations of 'area studies' in three broad geographical regions as South Asia, South East Asia and East Asia (Van Schendel, 2002), the studies of the peoples and culture of the Northeast Indian states including Manipur are ushered into the backward recesses of academic minds. Because of this reason, this region had remained a blank spot in the cultural understanding of its people within the South East Asian paradigm. Scholars of South East Asia also begin their investigations on the history and culture of those regions from the immediate geographical reality of Myanmar as a starting point. In this regard, Peter Bellwood (1992) viewed that "[Though] the very perception of South East Asia seems to be a post-war construct, that the term is a modern and external perception, the South East Asians themselves, though were aware of local, ethnic and cultural identities, they did not, until very recently, perceive a South East Asian identity"(p. 1). In fact, in locating South East Asia, historians normally writes that "In a purely geographical sense, South East Asia falls conveniently into two parts, mainland comprising China—south of the Yangtze, Burma (Myanmar), Thailand, Indonesia, peninsular Malaysia and island, comprising Indonesia, East Malaysia, Brunei, the Philippines, and Taiwan" (Peter Bellwood, 1992: 56). Scholars often follow official discourses of boundary formations of established political communities, without discreet hindsight of silenced lifeworlds that connect spaces, peoples and cultures which overlap recognised administrative and territorialized formations of governments and nations. Northeast India, including Manipur had remained as an 'obscure' spot in the minds of the scholars on South East Asia.

Again, the term "North East India" was initially conceptualised by the British to identify a geographical area and even considered as an extended frontier of Bengal, inhabited by tribal peoples in the states of Assam and Arunachal Pradesh. Further, the area was transformed into a frontier zone of the British Empire by imposing their colonial legislations such as Inner Line Permit, Protected Area Permit and Restricted Area Permit in order to expedite their colonial rule, which is also familiarised by the post-colonial India in identifying the geography of this region. It was the contemporary Dutch scholar Willem Van Schendel (2002) who made the statement that Northeast India is not only the North Eastern borderland of South Asia, but it can also be described as the North-Western borderland of South East Asia (p. 647). He also commented that scholarly research on these borderlands is an essential prerequisite to a proper understanding of its peoples and the far-reaching social and religious transformations they are engaged into. The rationale is that the region had been a part of South East Asia but was interrupted during the British colonialism and its subsequent merger to the post-colonial India. This is how "we" and "they" have perceived the region in the line with the discourse of "geography of knowing" and "geography of ignorance".

The other more important issue is the nature of the complications in international diplomacies within the geo-political contexts of Indo-Myanmar ties. Due to the presence of borderland 'disturbances' from ethnic political dissidence within the nation-state of India and the very complex political realities within Myanmar, the maintenance of international boundaries and heightened perceptions of internal security had inconvenienced the free-flow of information, person to person contact and institutional collaborations amidst the academic establishments of these two nation states. In spite of the official opening of trade and commercial relations through the international transit town of

Moreh-Tamu sector since 1994-95, the diplomatic activities within the cherished Asean, and the declared intentions within the "Look/ Act East Policy" of the Government of India since the late nineties, the region has been defined as "sensitive" with a suspicious eye from the security perspective. There has not been convenient free movement and travel of researchers, scholars or teachers in the universities/institutions for well informed exchange of knowledge for studies of past cultures and roots of historical development of the two immediate neighbours from the regional perspectives. Hence, academic information about the very ancient structures of polities, the social and cultural developments through time, their adaptations to the environments, their response to external stimuli as well as relationships in war and peace, and the organization of authority relations between their own rulers and the ruled etc. have not been comparatively studied by contemporary scholars.

The challenges before modern scholars interested in comparative studies of the two pre-colonial polities are enormous. Though substantial work had been done by many Western Scholars (namely: G.H. Harvey; Snodgrass; William J. Koening; Arthur P. Phayre; V.C. Scott O'Connor; Robert H. Taylor; Victor B. Lieberman; Henry Yule; Michael Symes; J.S. Furnivall; Michael W. Charney etc.), and Myanmarese Scholars like (Than Tun; Maung Htin Aung; Thant Myint-U; Michael Aung-Thwin etc.) on Myanmar Proper, yet a Manipur-Myanmar comparison in terms of polity construction, organisation and impact on social and political histories are still to be undertaken by the native scholars. The tracing of their own historical development, in their own worldview, in their own contexts within the global environment of the times, their own relationships within their histories as independent nations would be a proper framing of the studies. There is a need for an autonomous treatment on the studies of Manipur and Myanmar of pre-colonial times till the present.

South East Asian histories are never narratives of peaceful friendly development of regional powers within cultures, but a dynamic of intense rivalries, hostilities and mutually destructive wars. Survivors of their past confrontations had as a result inherited cultures and traditions of deep phlegmatic philosophical import with an ability to contain violence within the womb of society, and subsequently to transcend them in the serene atmosphere in the precincts of the Buddhist pagodas, with meditation and freeing of the minds from complexities of internal turmoil. The experiences of historical violences had also bequethed to the following generation's intense cultural expressions in terms of lively dances, theatre and music reflecting the unique energy and vitality of these ancient races.

For the Manipuris, the Myanmarese occupy an indelible space in their collective memory. Tales and narratives of mutual hostilities and confrontations, destructive wars, fights for survival from extinction as a race, periods of bondage and vassalage, liberation struggles for the people of Manipur twice in their remembered history in the eighteenth and early nineteenth centuries in the heyday of the Konbaung Dynasties, the heroic achievements of the kings and the subjects who brought freedom to Manipur, notably Maharaja Garibaniwaz, Maharaja Bhagyachandra and Maharaja Gambhir Singh, their courage, bravery and noble deeds remain as markers to the national identity formation of the Manipuris. The devastations of the region from the onslaughts from powerful Burmese conquerors like Alaung-Paya (Aung-Zeyya) in the eighteenth century and the devastation by the Burmese General Maha Bandula in the second decade of the nineteenth century form the historical memory of the sufferings, humiliation and subjugation of Manipur. Naorem Joykumar, a Manipuri historian commented the situation as *"the degree of their [Burmese] tortures was so severe that it reached even to the verge of extinction of this group of people [Manipuri]. Therefore, still the people remember this particular period of time as Chahi Taret Khuntakpa"* (p. 3). These devastations within the two hundred years remain as "chosen traumas" in the collective psyche of the people, which sustain narratives of the peoples' struggle against oppression.

On the other side of the spectrum, the Myanmarese intellectuals do remember the impact of the people of Manipur on their national psyche. Thant Myint-U (2007), writes *"For decades fierce Manipuri horsemen had been raiding up and down the valley of the nearby Mu River, torching villages all around, ransacking pagodas, and stealing away captives led by their Jai Singh and Garib Newaz and riding the stylist little ponies for which they would later be renowned, the Manipuri defeated again and again the soldiers despatched to stop them. The Burmese court seemed powerless against the rising menace, and its frailty lost its support at home and even the nominal allegiance of its eastern tributaries. In the Summer of 1739, Garib Newaz's cavalry reached the Irrawaddy itself, burning the monastic libraries on the north shore and halting, the Burmese believe, to bathe in the holy waters of the river."* (p. 88).

Mutually differing impacts by the same events on contending nations form qualitatively received impressions which help provide distinct narratives on the aspects of nation formation and nation continuation in the historical experiencers of their peoples and cultures of South East Asia. However, these impressions drawn from the experiences of an early remembered history retain amorphous contours in the memory of new generations experiencing different historical events of greater force and impact on new societies. The profile of past events lay disfigured, but its universal impressions on the psyche of individuals and groups are re-structured and super-imposed on the new traumas which the new societies experience in different events at different time spans. Such inter-plays on the historical consciousness of neighbouring nations on the verge of early continual war and hostility act upon one another which sometimes transform those memories and impressions themselves.

The wars and devastations between the two peoples of Manipur and Myanmar are now completely transformed; both had different trajectories of development, where the past lay dead and buried. Now three hundred years after those cataclysmic events, in the new environment of the times, there is a discovered tinge of new humanism amongst the grassroots citizens who are interacting with one another in daily experience of trade and work in the international networks of economic transactions between these communities in the borders. There is a spirit of comraderie amongst these peoples which seem to reflect an invisible sense of unity and bonding, perhaps compelled by the impact of global forces and complexities of the market upon marginal players. This intrinsic sense of unity and comraderie which are not mutually advantageous manoeuvres within the impersonal imperatives of the market economy, but which are probably borne and nourished by mutually shared civilized traditions whose values lingered unhindered by forces of antagonism, war, crisis and change. This basic ingredient of grace and civilizing behaviour even in the context of war and confrontation could have been inherited either through long process of socialization by harmonising cultures, or through sheer unconscious experiencing of common historical roots and traditions between these two neighbouring nations, the subject which need to be investigated by students of culture and polity.

The processes of formation of the respective polities of Manipur and Myanmar may not be similar due to diverse historical circumstances of their evolution. But certain common strands in the principles of territorial organization of the states and of similar geographic and economic impacts on the respective formations seem to operate within the two polities. Though Myanmar was a much more powerful empire and Manipur was a thorn in her western expansionist ambitions, both of them seemed to possess certain common characteristics of polity formation and organization of territorial administration within their countries.

Though war was unavoidable, marriage relationship amongst kings and nobility were necessary concomitants to the maintenance of the polity, strengthening of powers of the state and avoidance of disloyalty, disaffection and rebellion. Besides, the Meiteis (Kathes) were brought to Myanmar as war captives and retinues, they also brought in different forms, the core socio-cultural characteristics of their community, such as religion, language, art, values, habits, crafts, clothing (costumes), and cuisine. Than Tun (2010) has rightly pointed out that 'Myanmar got some Manipuri culture' that Manipuri were skilled in many crafts and introduced the *Acheik* (a kind of sarong especially made for the royals) pattern in Myanmar, their horsemanship who could serve as "Cassay Cavalry" under the Myanma kings and their contribution as Court Astrologers (p. 33). With time, some of these characteristics have disappeared and some have survived, while others have undergone a synthesis and, yet, others have been assimilated. Besides, the cultural history of the Burmese population who were captured during the war expeditions to Burma (Myanmar) by the Manipur Kings and their transformation of identity as Manipuri need to be focus in the academic discourse.

British colonial conquests in three phases of 19th century Burma and of Manipur at one stroke in 1891 and thereby created conditions for more or less similar transformation of the two pre-colonial cultures and polities in the geographic north-western borderlands of South East Asia and Northeast India. Robert H. Taylor (2009) wrote that the social structure of the pre-colonial state (of Myanmar) with its clear correlation of power with status and wealth, was replaced in the twentieth century with the creation of the rise to the centre of indigenous political life of a new class which became the main force behind the development of modern political nationalism (p. 10). This phenomenon was also true in Manipur, though the character, actions and attitudes of this class towards the hegemonic empire had variables through their own contexts and environments. The old pre-colonial aristocratic orders of the feudal monarchies were subsumed into the new middle class ushered in by colonial education and economic transactions based on property. The conflictual penetration by the capitalist economy into the cultural mores of traditional ethnic societies, leading to ruptures and destruction, relentless pursuit of profit and gain by racial others in the exploitative networks of commerce and trade and attitudes of social superiority by imperial agents over the native population led to the rise of ethnic nationalism and self-determination movements in the colonial domains. Armed strife was soon to follow, which transformed the modern historical landscape of Myanmar and Manipur.

Of late, many new native scholars of Myanmar are now seriously working on the historical relationship between Myanmar and Manipur from different perspectives. Many Ph.D. thesis and research articles focusing on the *War captives in Myanmar, Crown service groups in Myanmar, Myanmar Cavalry, Cultural History of Kathe, Kathe Settlement, Slavery in Myanmar, Role of Astrology in Myanmar,* Cassay *(Manipuri)-Myanmar Relations, Myanmar Polity,* and many more are found in the University libraries of Myanmar. New array of areas which were not highlighted in the earlier works of the Pre-colonial times of Myanmar and Manipur relations are discovered from these works. The classification of Kathe into three categories: Kathe Ponna, Kathe Servicemen and Kathe Commoners and their assigned duties according to their skills and the role shared by the Kathe communities for the Burmese Kingdom were minutely written in these works. How a Manipuri Princess "Maha Devi" was made a Queen of Mon and again how she was captured and made the wife of Alaungphaya, could also be confirmed from these works. This story goes beyond the narratives of Crown servicemen, cavalry and commoners. It highlighted how the Manipuri women took part in the process of diplomatic relationship between the two Kingdoms and their role in shaping the Burmese polity. Moreover, one Western Scholar, Dr. Bryce Beemer, a Fulbright scholar at the University of Hawaii, in his Ph.D. thesis *"The Creole City in Mainland South East Asia: Slave Gathering Warfare and Cultural Exchange in Burma, Thailand and Manipur, 18th–19th C"* (2013), also critically analyzed the reason of warfare in the pre-colonial Kingdoms in South East Asia with relation to slave gathering and the cultural influences from the captive communities within the society ultimately transformed into a hybrid culture. A few scholars of Manipur are as well taking keen interest on this area of studies. The only skeptic question to these scholarly works is whether the intention of the studies are giving more attention towards emotion or to cognitive. This could be a new challenge for the contemporary scholars.

Comparative Studies on Area Studies is a part of International Studies. It is also an indispensable technique of analytic research. Research works on the comparative studies particularly on Manipur and Myanmar within the South East Asian paradigm will be a holistic approach for understanding Myanmar in particular, and South East Asia in general. This could be an asset for the policy makers and planners too.

REFERENCES

J.D. Legge, "The Writing of Southeast Asian History", in Nicholas Tarling (ed.), *The Cambridge History of Southeast Asia*, Vol. 1, Cambridge University Press, 1992.

Naorem Joykumar Singh, *Colonialism to Democracy: A History of Manipur: 1819-1972*, Spectrum Publications, Delhi, 2002.

Peter Bellwood, *"Southeast Asia before History"*, in Nicholas Tarling (ed.) *The Cambridge History of Southeast Asia*, Vol. 1, Cambridge University Press, 1992.

Robert H. Taylor, *The State in Myanmar*, HURST Publishers Ltd., London, 2009.

Thant Myint-U, *The River of Lost Footsteps*, Faber and Faber, New York, 2007.

Tun, Than, *A Modern History of Myanmar*, Loka Ahlinn Publishing House, Yangon, 2010.

Van Schendel, "Geographies of Knowing, Geographies of Ignorance: Jumping Scale in South East Asia", in *Environment and Planning: Society and State*, Vol. 20, 2002.

23
India-Myanmar Connectivity
Prospects for a Land-Linked Manipur under the 'Act East' Policy

Puyam Rakesh Singh

Introduction

Unlike other South East Asian countries, India and Myanmar share long land and maritime borders making Myanmar the focus country under the 'Act East' policy. Naturally, Myanmar is the gateway to South East Asia for India with NER as the land bridge connecting the two countries. This is also underscored by the speech delivered by Prime Minister Narendra Modi during the 12th India-ASEAN Summit held in Myanmar on 12 November, 2014.[1] In the early 1990s, India's policy towards Myanmar took a new turn following the announcement of 'Look East' policy under the leadership of the then Prime Minister Narasimha Rao which led to the opening border trade posts in Moreh (Manipur) and Zokhawthar (Mizoram). The period under the military junta in Myanmar saw gradual improvement in ties with India in many sectors.

However, there has been a qualitative change in the bilateral engagement between the two neighbouring countries since democratic elections were held in Myanmar in November 2010 under the new 2008 Constitution of Myanmar. The bilateral ties have further deepened following the landmark victory of National League for Democracy (NLD) in the November 2015 general elections. This was acknowledged by the joint statement issued at the first meeting of the India-Myanmar Joint Consultative Commission held in July 2015 stating that the bilateral relations have entered a "new phase" following political and economic reforms in Myanmar.[2]

Over the last few years, high-level exchanges between the two sides have increased thus enhancing political mutual trust, cooperation in various economic sectors, strengthening security and defence cooperation and coordination in the United Nations and other regional and sub-regional groupings. The political transition and economic reforms in Myanmar have provided immense opportunities for India to strengthen partnership with Naypyitaw including cooperation in the sectors of security, defence and connectivity.

Though the opening of the Indo-Myanmar Friendship Road in 2001 was a landmark development towards establishing road connectivity, signing of the framework agreement for the Kaladan Multi-Modal Transport Project in April 2008 marked the major shift towards cooperation in the connectivity sector. In addition to the Rih-Tedim Road Project, the two countries have widened cooperation for connectivity project following the signing of deals for the Trilateral Highway Project connecting India, Myanmar and Thailand.

With gradual improvement in security situation along the Indo-Myanmar border, the geographical advantage provided by NER in general and Manipur in particular have gained recognition in the regional discourses on connectivity. This has been underscored by the several trans-national events holding car rally that passes through Manipur and the NER at large.

Negotiations for motor vehicles agreement, signing of the land border crossing agreement, proposal for opening two border haats along Manipur section (398 km) of the Indo-Myanmar border and the proposed bus service between Imphal and Mandalay are important developments towards better connectivity between India and Myanmar. Following the signing of the Land Border Crossing Agreement between India and Myanmar on May 11, 2018, Moreh and Zokhawthar border gates were opened for immigration on August 8, 2018.[3] Along with this agreement, the signing of the MoU between Shwe Mandalar Express, Yangon and Seven Sisters Holiday, Imphal on February 14, 2020 to start the Imphal-Mandalay bus service from April 7, 2020[4], are the biggest achievements towards enhancing India-Myanmar connectivity.

India-Myanmar Connectivity

Geographical contiguity provides opportunities for both India and Myanmar to develop connectivity both maritime and overland. Myanmar is India's gateway to ASEAN and Myanmar is ASEAN's gateway to South Asia. It, therefore, calls for greater cooperation and coordination between India and Myanmar on the subject of connectivity. Recent developments regarding opening of border land crossing and the planned launching of bus service between Imphal and Mandalay are indications of serious efforts on both sides to enhance people-to-people exchanges.

In terms of greater opening up of the Indo-Myanmar land border stretching a distance of 1,643 kilometres, construction of the Indo-Myanmar Friendship Road (16 km) connecting Tamu to Kalewa *via* Kelemyo with financial assistance from India was the first major step to develop road connectivity between the two countries. The road constructed by Border Road Organisation (BRO) was opened by the then External Affairs Minister Jaswant Singh in February 2001.

However, the most significant move towards opening India's NER under 'Look East' policy began in May 2012 when the then Prime Minister Manmohan Singh visited Myanmar. During the visit, the two sides signed a total of 11 deals including three deals for development of border markets (*haats*) along India-Myanmar border and construction of the India-Myanmar-Thailand Trilateral Highway Project.[5]

Under this, the Indo-Myanmar Friendship Road connecting Tamu to Kalewa will be extended further with the construction of a two-lane highway in the Kalewa-Yargyi section of the proposed Trilateral Highway. The National Highway Authority of India (NHAI) has issued the letter of award to Punj Lloyd and Varaha Infra joint venture in January 2018 for construction of the project. This project puts Manipur in the centre of regional connectivity thus acknowledging the geographical advantage of the state towards building a land-linked state.

Another major connectivity project undertaken by India is the Kaladan Multi-Modal Transport Project. A framework agreement for building the Kaladan Project was signed in April 2008. In its last stage of completion, the project financed by the Government of India is on its last leg with the beginning of the construction of

Paletwa-Zorinpui road which will connect the Kaladan river port at Paletwa to Zorinpui on Mizoram border. The Kaladan Project, built at a cost of US$484 million, will provide transit facility through Myanmar's Sittwe sea port located on the coast of Rakhine State in Myanmar. It connects Kolkata seaport to Sittwe port and then to Paletwa *via* the Kaladan river.

Logistically speaking, goods coming from Kolkata port to Sittwe port will be carried by boats to Paletwa Inland river port from where the Paletwa-Zorinpui road will take it to Mizoram. India has handed over vessels for service on the Kaladan River as part of this project. Despite the logistical issues involving unloading and re-loading of goods at Sittwe port and Paletwa, this transport project is the only transit route for the landlocked Northeast India to get access to the sea.

In April 2017, India handed over the Sittwe Port and the Inland Water Terminal at Paletwa to Myanmar. On February 1, 2020, a Port operator to operate and maintain Sittwe port and Paletwa Inland Water Transport Terminal and associated facilities was finalised marking major progress towards completion of the connectivity project. The final leg of the project is the Paletwa-Zorinpui road which will provide overland access to Paletwa river port on the Kaladan River. The progress of the Kaladan Project has been hampered by the conflict in Rakhine State where the Myanmar forces are fighting against the Arakan Army (AA). Kidnapping of Indian officials engaged in the Kaladan Project was also reported causing death of an official.

Another important road project is the Rih-Tedim road that will connect the Trilateral Highway through Zokhawthar border gate in Mizoram. The NHAI is undertaking the works for construction of this vital link in the Chin State of Myanmar to develop more connectivity with Myanmar through Mizoram. As discussed in the section below, development of border trading post at Behiang in Churachandpur district (Manipur) immensely contribute to transport infrastructure along the Manipur-Mizoram section of the Indo-Myanmar border.

Similarly, the border *haat* at Pangsau Pass in Arunachal Pradesh on Indo-Myanmar border will revive a section of the Stillwell road constructed during the WWII connecting Assam and Kachin State (Myanmar) *via* Arunachal Pradesh. Also the Land Customs Station (LCS) at Avangkhu in Nagaland located opposite Somara (known as Somra in Manipuri) will facilitate trade and economic exchanges between the two sides. The proposed bridge across the Chindwin River at Htamanthi will provide better connectivity for the two peoples along the Indo-Myanmar border. Already, Myanmar has completed construction of Homalin bridge thus improving transport network in the region.

Broadly speaking, the potential for connectivity with the eastern neighbours of India through NER has been explored during the BCIM car rally from Kolkata (India) to Kunming (China) in 2013. Similarly, India-ASEAN car rally of 2012 also underscores the possibility of regional connectivity. Also, the Bhutan-Thailand Friendship car rally held in 2019 envisages more such overland connectivity in the future. It is interesting to note that all the rallies passed through Manipur.

If these trans-national events passing through Northeast India have any significance, the message is that there can be seamless connectivity between South Asia and South East Asia. Under the 'Act East policy', the Government of India can engage these neighbouring countries for bringing the possibilities into realities. Towards realising this, the Trilateral Highway project has been extended to connect India with Cambodia, Lao PDR and Vietnam following the Delhi Dialogue VII in March 2015. To fructify the connectivity between India and ASEAN nations, roads and railway projects connecting Assam, Nagaland, and Manipur need to be on priority basis. This will advance eastward movement of India's economic, cultural and strategic interests.

Towards a Land-linked Manipur

Manipur is a small landlocked Northeastern state of India with ranges of hills encircling the central valley of Imphal. Geography has tremendously shaped the evolution of its culture, history, economy and socio-political life. Despite such topographical difficulties, Manipur shares international border with Myanmar and its proximity to Bangladesh and Bhutan make the small state a strategic real estate in the larger Asian geo-political chessboard. The Asian Highway (AH 1) enters into Manipur through Moreh-Tamu international border gate. Again, the Trilateral Highway connecting India and Thailand *via* Myanmar is another major transport connectivity project.

Several multilateral and sub-regional mechanisms such as BIMS-TEC, Mekong-Ganga Cooperation, India-ASEAN strategic partnership, Bangladesh-China-India-Myanmar (BCIM) economic corridor will push regional/sub-regional integration with various connectivity projects as pillars of socio-economic and political transformation. As a matter of fact, connectivity projects will enhance trade, economic cooperation, power grid connectivity, integration of energy resources, tourism, health tourism, educational exchanges and cultural and people-to-people exchanges.

Strategic location of Manipur is underscored by the Battle of Imphal which is commemorated as the most important battlefield during the WW-II along with the battle of Kohima. Before this, the British Empire noted the strategic importance of the then kingdom of Manipur to control the frontiers and check the Burmese onslaughts towards the British India. Time has brought changes to the size and shape of Manipur. However, its strategic importance again re-surfaced with the 'Look East' policy which has been re-christened into 'Act East' policy in 2014 by Prime Minister Narendra Modi. Both 'Act East' policy and 'Neighbourhood First' policy of India for engagement with the eastern neighbours could be prioritised with three major transport routes that connect Manipur with Myanmar and beyond. Tusom in Ukhrul, Moreh in Tengnoupal and Behiang in Churachandpur district are important locations in Manipur through which international trade and connectivity with Myanmar and other ASEAN nations can be undertaken. In addition, construction of the Thoubal-Kasom Khullen road with funding from Asian Development Bank (ADB) has created another alternative route to open the India-Myanmar border.

While poor infrastructure for transport connectivity remains true till date security situation along the border has restricted the flow of goods and people. Nevertheless, smuggling is flourishing across the border with the Moreh Integrated Check Post (ICP) unable to rope in the informal trade sector. In fact, security dominates the discourse on connectivity. Growing security and defence cooperation between India and Myanmar in last few years points in the direction of faster pace of negotiations for opening the Indo-Myanmar border for trade, economic cooperation and people-to-people exchanges.

Recent developments that could contribute to transformation of Manipur from landlocked to land-linked state include the proposed

Imphal-Mandalay bus service. An MoU between private operators to launch a coordinated bus service between Imphal and Mandalay by 7 April, 2020 was signed. However, the Covid-19 pandemic has delayed realisation of such an eventful thing in the history of Manipur. During the state visit of Myanmar President Win Myint from February 26 to 29, 2020, the two sides deliberated on the issues concerning demarcation of boundary, centrality of connectivity, opening of two international border gates and development of integrated check post in Tamu, Myanmar.

The joint statement of February 2020 also emphasised border areas development as agreed in the MoU of 2012. As per the document, the two sides are looking forward to set up border markets (*haats*) after finalising the mutually agreed Mode of Operation. India-Myanmar Border Area Development Programme undertaken in Naga Self-administered Zone and Chin State with grant assistance from India also contributes to centrality of Manipur in opening the India-Myanmar border.

Construction of Sittwe Port and the Kaladan Multi-Modal Transit Transport Project will contribute to socio-economic development in southern part of Manipur bordering with Mizoram (India) and Chin state (Myanmar). The completion of the project will provide opportunities for trade with improvement of road connectivity between Churachandpur district in Manipur and Mizoram.

Behiang, located near the international border, is another potential border crossing gate in Manipur and the same has been reportedly inspected by the concerned authorities. Located about 122 km. from Imphal, it has been proposed as second trade corridor to Southeast Asia. Behiang village with a population of just about 1000 individuals could grow into a thriving border town provided necessary infrastructure development is undertaken along with development linkages with Myanmar in Chin State.

Another long-term project to reap the trade and economic benefits is the proposed ring road with an estimated cost of Rs. 100 crore for construction of a ring road along the Indo-Myanmar connecting the last village in Manipur bordering Mizoram to the last village bordering Nagaland. While the proposed ring road can bring socio-economic changes in the life of the villagers in the border areas, the road is no doubt closely associated with security aspects. Border fencing along the Indo-Myanmar border is a difficult and costly project with difficult terrain, heavy monsoon and other environmental concerns.

Besides, the unresolved issues associated with demarcation of border have created problems between the two sides during construction of a short stretch of border in the recent past. Moreover, some section of the demarcated border remains hotly debated in Manipur especially by the villagers who have alleged encroachments from the Myanmar side. The issue is reflected in the joint statements issued during high-level visits to respect the demarcated sections of the border.

Behiang's close proximity to Zokhawthar border gate along Mizoram-Myanmar section of the border provides it immense potential for development of border trade. Moreover, Behiang-Kalay road *via* Teddim passing through Chin State of Myanmar will integrate Behiang with air connectivity in Myanmar as the Government of India is working towards redevelopment of Kalay airport. As Myanmar develops roads, bridges and air connectivity in Chin State, Behiang-Churachandpur corridor could provide an alternative trade route connecting Manipur with Myanmar.

In addition to Moreh and Behiang, Tusom in Ukhrul district of Manipur also has the potential to develop into a viable border trading post along the Indo-Myanmar border. As part of Myanmar Sustainable Development Plan (2018-2030), Myanmar government is constructing several bridges across the Chindwin River in Sagaing Region. Five major bridges have been completed so far, namely Hkamti, Homalin, Kalewa, Monywa, and Sinphyushin. Moreover, Myanmar is planning to construct four new bridges across the Chindwin River to facilitate movement of goods and people across the river.

In fact, the Tusom-Somra-Htamanthi route could provide another trade route along with the development of Avangkhu LCS in Nagaland. Border area development programme in Naga Self-Administered Zone in Sagaing Region would eventually connect Avangkhu to Leshi (Lay Shi) and Htamanthi on the Chindwin River. This route has ample opportunities to tap the rich natural resources in Kachin State of Myanmar.

Development of new roads and bridges in Chin State and Sagaing Region of Myanmar will also facilitate development of border *haats* along the border. Signing of the MoU on India-Myanmar Border Area Cooperation has led to infrastructure development and other projects including upgradation of roads, construction of schools, health centres, bridges, agriculture and related training activities mainly in Chin State and Sagaing Region.

As of now, the most important overland transport link connecting Manipur with the outside world will be provided by the Trilateral Highway. Construction of the Kalewa-Yargyi road section by the Indian authorities and upgradation of 69 bridges along the road has been put on priority basis. Delays in the construction of this road section has again raised question regarding the target of completing this road section by 2021. Although Bangladesh-China-India-Myanmar (BCIM) economic corridor is still discussed along the four participant countries, the fate of BCIM economic corridor remains uncertain. However, various connectivity projects completed and undertaken in India, Bangladesh and Myanmar will eventually bring greater integration of South Asia, China and South East Asia.

Another important dimension of connectivity which could raise the profile of Manipur is the development of rail infrastructure. At present, the early phases of Imphal-Jiribam railway have made progress. In 2019, survey works for a rail line from Moreh (Manipur) to Kalay *via* Tamu has been conducted by the Rail India Technical and Economic Service (RITES). In the past, survey of the line from Imphal to Moreh (about 12 km) has been done.

In this regard, completion of the railway line connecting Imphal to Kalay (Myanmar) will strengthen the land-linked strategy of Manipur under India's 'Act East' policy. The rail line will constitute an important missing link of the 81,000 kilometres long Trans-Asian Railway Network. In this connection, Railway Minister Piyush Goyal has tweeted 'Act East' and 'Act Fast' referring to fact that lack of rail connectivity is causing a major hindrance to India's 'Act East' policy.[6]

Similarly, Myanmar has proposed a rail line connecting Monywa to Tamu as part of establishing rail connectivity with India. Myanmar's expanding cooperation in the sector of railways with India, Japan, China and South Korea will contribute to establishment of new rail lines connecting major border cities/ towns in Sagaing Region. Despite such interest, Naypyitaw will give priority to establish rail line connecting Sittwe Port in Rakhine coast with the rest of the country.

Another driving force towards rail connectivity between India and Myanmar is the proposed Myanmar-China railway line. At the moment the main rail line serving western part of Myanmar is the Myitkyina-Mandalay line. Westward extension of rail line from Sagaing city to Tamu in the course of time will subsequently bridge the missing link connecting India and Myanmar.

Energy and power are two other sectors with potential for further cooperation. The two sides have agreed to explore the benefits of integration in energy sector and export of oil and gas from Myanmar to India from the output where Indian oil and gas public sector undertakings (PSUs) have made investments. It could revive the history of Burma Oil Company (BOC) in its new *avatar* with energy products from Myanmar reaching markets in NER. Cooperation in the sector of energy could facilitate development of oil and gas pipeline connecting NER and Myanmar. Exploring the potential for developing an oil refinery and retailing of petroleum products remains a viable energy project in Manipur for further cooperation in energy sector between India and Myanmar.

India and Myanmar have agreed to continue negotiations on various pending treaties such as a Mutual Legal Assistance Treaty on Civil and Commercial Matters and the Extradition Treaty. Moreover, the two sides agreed to enhance bilateral cooperation in sharing information and intelligence. Progress towards legal and security cooperation between the two countries would definitely facilitate easy movement of passenger and cargo across the border. Hence, finalisation of the pending Motor Vehicles Agreement and expeditious development of infrastructure are part of the comprehensive strategy to open the Indo-Myanmar border under 'Act East' policy while ensuring security along the long stretch of land and maritime borders.

Why is Connectivity the Key?

Connectivity in NER and connectivity through NER are two interconnected aspects of India's engagement with its neighbours. In fact, partition of India in 1947 has created problems for India's Northeast with a narrow strip of land connecting the region with the rest of India. Thus, transport bottleneck in NER has been a major factor hampering trade and economic development of the landlocked region. The search for alternative routes to provide the region access to the rest of the country through Myanmar and

Bangladesh is a valid ground for some of the connectivity projects discussed in the chapter.

While some of the projects undertaken in NER are aimed at addressing this problem, other projects are vital links to enhance India's engagement with the neighbouring countries to deal with various security, strategic and economic issues as India aspires to become an important player in the regional and global affairs. The chapter, therefore, acknowledges the strategic aspects of India's 'Act East' policy with connectivity as the backbone for strengthening cooperation and partnership between India and its Eastern neighbours.

Development of Northeast Region

A major underlying problem in enhancing engagement between India and its Eastern neighbours is the underdevelopment of NER and poor transport infrastructure in the region. It has also hampered growth and development in the region. North East Region Vision 2020 document prioritizes infrastructure development and connectivity as a major thrust area. It accounts for the increasing investments on rail, air and road connectivity in Northeast India. Development of transport infrastructure in NER will further boost India's connectivity with the neighbouring countries.

China Factor

Myanmar shares a 2,204 kilometre long land border with China. In the last few years, China has been expanding its strategic footprints in Myanmar through hydropower projects, oil and gas exploration, energy pipelines, the proposed Kyaukpyu deep sea port and SEZ, China-Myanmar railway and various other projects under the framework of China-Myanmar Economic Corridor (CMEC). Following the suspension of the Myitsone Dam worth US$ 3.6 billion on September 30, 2011 by Myanmar, a series of protests targeting Chinese funded projects have hit hard the investment confidence of the Chinese companies in Myanmar.

Amidst the ongoing political transition in Myanmar, China's changing external environment has caused concerns in Beijing. The protests against Chinese-funded projects underscored the rising anti-Chinese sentiments in Myanmar and need for enhancing people-to-people contacts for shaping the public opinion in favour of closer China-Myanmar ties.[7] Under Xi Jinping's leadership, the topic of connectivity has been on the agenda of bilateral and multilateral engagements between China and Myanmar.

Towards this, Myanmar Vice President Henry Van Thio, who is also the chairman of the Myanmar SEZs Central Committee called for speeding up the implementation of Dawei and Kyaukpyu SEZs at the first meeting of the Central Committee held in August 2018 in Nay Pyi Taw. He further reported about completion of the bid for construction of the Kyaukpyu SEZ and progress of the work for signing a framework agreement on the Kyaukpyu deep sea port.[8]

Taking into account strategic importance of Myanmar, China has been supporting Myanmar on the Rohingya issue despite strong international condemnation. Also, Beijing continues to mediate between the Myanmar government and the ethnic armed groups operating in northern Myanmar. Such actions could be instrumental for gaining Myanmar's cooperation to build CMEC under Belt and Road Initiative (BRI).

During Xi Jinping's state visit to Myanmar on January 17-18, 2020, both sides exchanged views on deepening connectivity and start substantive construction of the BRI projects in Myanmar. To strengthen the partnership and *Pauk-phaw** ties with Myanmar, Xi Jinping emphasized the importance of public support and called for China-Myanmar community with a shared future. Further enhancing China's focus on Myanmar, Chinese President Xi Jinping referred to the bilateral ties as "a bond as close as between lips"[9] underscoring the importance of strengthening the comprehensive strategic cooperative partnership. Thus, China's push towards Myanmar remains a potent force influencing the foreign policy of many other regional powers towards Myanmar. Similarly, India cannot take China's increasing influence over Myanmar and the proposed construction of CMEC lightly in order to safeguard and promote its interests in Myanmar and the Bay of Bengal.

Maritime Security in Bay of Bengal

During the visit of then Myanmar President Htin Kyaw's visit to

---

* Phauk-phaw is a Myanmar word meaning cousins. It is used only to refer to Myanmar-China close fraternal ties.

India in August 2016, both sides agreed that Maritime Security Cooperation in the Bay of Bengal is vital for both countries. In 2019, the two countries have reached agreement on sharing information regarding White Shipping in the Bay of Bengal. Construction of the Kaladan Project not only serve the transit facility but also provides immense scope for maritime and coastal security and surveillance to check piracy, illegal immigration, drugs and small arms trafficking along the western coast of Myanmar.

In addition, Chinese footprint in the Bay of Bengal with the establishment of crude petroleum pipeline and the proposal to construct Kyaukphyu deep sea port and special economic zone (SEZ) necessitates further strengthening of naval and maritime cooperation with Myanmar.

India-ASEAN Connectivity

India's connectivity with ASEAN nations is also an important factor driving connectivity in the NER. With its long history of deep cultural and civilisational linkages with South East Asia, India's 'Act East' policy aims at strengthening partnership with the countries of South East Asia. Under this, overland connectivity is another important component to facilitate exchanges of people, ideas and goods as part of India-ASEAN partnership.

Besides, ASEAN is located in the strategic region stretching from Bay of Bengal to the South China Sea and will play an important role in shaping the Indo-Pacific region. The document entitled "ASEAN Outlook on the Indo-Pacific" underscores the "geopolitical and geostrategic shifts" taking place in the Asia-Pacific and Indian Ocean regions or the Indo-Pacific. The document also recommends ASEAN to continue playing the role of "an honest broker" to deal with competition among major powers. The document envisages the principle of ASEAN centrality and promotes dialogue and cooperation instead of rivalry.

The emerging geostrategic environment and India's vision for Indo-Pacific underlines the important position of ASEAN. It is, therefore, important for New Delhi to engage ASEAN in view of the changing global order amidst tension with China along the Line of Actual Control (LAC). Under the 'Act East' policy, India's strategic reach to its eastern neighbours will be limited without commensurate works towards greater connectivity between India and ASEAN.

Challenges and Problems of Connectivity

Besides difficult topography and geological challenges, financing major connectivity projects remains a crucial issue in improving connectivity within NER and without. In some cases, financial availability does not lead to implementation of the projects smoothly. In fact, financial cost and implementation of works across Indo-Myanmar border are not free from lack of enthusiasm, coordination failure and differences over modalities of financing and execution of the projects. Another major problem affecting connectivity project is armed conflict, particularly in the case of the Kaladan Multi-Modal Transport Project.

Various projects to enhance transport connectivity within Manipur and beyond require apt handling of the domestic issues as well as concerns of Myanmar. Construction of Thoubal to Kasom Khullen road with financial assistance from Asian Development Bank (ADB) has shown that many key arterial roads can be developed along the Indo-Myanmar border which can bring long-term transformation of the people living in the borderlands. The cost incurred by the inhabitants of such road projects, however, need to be studied carefully to minimise major health and social impacts.

As an impact of such projects, demographic composition along the border towns and villages will see fast changes with the establishment of such road connectivity. Such sensitivities and cultural barriers continue to dampen the pace of various projects. Land acquisition and environmental clearance are part of the larger discourse affecting approval and implementation of works.

An important dimension of constructing such a road leading to the border is the flow of goods and people for various purposes. Smuggling is one such aspect of borderland life. Ethnic affiliations across the border can also cause wider problems of security. Drug trafficking and human trafficking are some good examples. Establishing physical connectivity will increase people-to-people connectivity across border. This will naturally enhance the flow of ideas, goods and technology. The trend is as old as human civilisation.

The Westphalian model of modern states emphasise on regulating the flow of ideas, people, goods and pathogens. Sealing of the borders in the wake of the spread of corona virus is a vivid example. Not only pathogens causing diseases states are engaged in various activities to control the flow of people, goods and ideas. One can recall how Singapore is actively working towards restriction of import of chewing-gums. The Indian authorities are deploying several agencies to monitor and check illegal border crossings, smuggling and trafficking of people, drugs and other contraband items. Most importantly, cross-border insurgents and small arms trafficking are put on high priority in its engagement with Myanmar. This security paradigm of protecting the citizens and its realm from unwanted influence and goods remains the greatest hurdle in establishing greater connectivity between NER and Myanmar. Manipur is frequently in the news for such activities.

On the other hand, the general perception of the people in Manipur (also NER) towards connectivity projects is another important factor towards realisation of connectivity. Penetration of capital in the erstwhile regions located far from centres of economic modernisation with capital formation as the main objective of economic activities is being debated. Trans-national transport networks are the best channels through which large capital investments flow across the globe changing the face of the earth and the socio-cultural life of the inhabitants. These networks of road, rail and waterway also expose the people to various modes of exploitation. Many such issues are bracketed within the discussion halls where corporate social responsibility, social and environmental impacts are topics of exchanging views in the larger interest of the people affected by such large-scale projects.

In the recent past, India and Myanmar have enhanced cooperation and coordination on institutional connectivity. Here also, the topic of security is the central theme. The two sides have expanded the platform for limited cultural, educational and sporting exchanges. With the opening of the Moreh-Tamu international border gate of immigration, curiosity and eagerness to see the other side of the border is increasing. Packaged tour services have become a reality for people in Manipur (and others) to visit Myanmar. At the moment, the authorities on both sides are working towards modalities and mode of operation for launching coordinated bus service. Air services cooperation between the two countries has been on the agenda with plan to launch air connectivity between Manipur and Myanmar. Major aspects of connectivity such as physical and people-to-people connectivity are dependent on institutional connectivity to operationalise on the ground.

A land-linked strategy of Manipur (or the NER as a whole) will revive the debate over the beneficial impacts of maritime and overland connectivity between India and South East Asia. No doubt, the maritime dimension of India-Myanmar connectivity will continue to be the main pillar of trade and economic engagement between the two countries. However, the overland transport connectivity will provide immense benefits to revive and remember the close historical, cultural and civilisational ties between the two peoples. Compared to air transport, rail and road transport connecting India and Myanmar will boost tourism and other aspects of people-to-people exchanges. Cheaper modes of transportation can also bring peoples from many countries to explore the historical sites and places associated with the British Imperial rule and the World War-II. Thus, the chapter argues in favour of a balanced approach to overland and maritime dimensions to enhance transport connectivity with Myanmar. Centrality of NER in the 'Act East' policy will be revealed through execution of land transport projects while the overall designs for regional integration and engagement with South East Asia under 'Act East' policy demand demand-based emphasis on both maritime and land-based transport networks. Nonetheless, access to sea ports in Myanmar and Bangladesh are important for Northeast India to connect with the larger global supply chain. Clarity on this subject will enhance enthusiasm and visionary aspects of deeper engagements with the Southeast Asian countries through closer contacts among the peoples.

Conclusion

Manipur is located in a dynamic region in Asia lying between two major Asian rivers, namely the Brahmaputra and Ayeyawady Rivers. India's 'Act East' policy component targeting socio-economic development in NER must be undertaken with close coordination with development projects taken up by Myanmar in western Sagaing bordering India (and also Bangladesh). This vibrant region has close historical, socio-economic, cultural and civilisational linkages, ethnic and linguistic affiliations with the Southeast Asian countries.

While Mekong-Ganga cooperation mechanism adheres to broader engagement of India in the South East Asia, a coordinated development strategy between India and Myanmar to develop the peripheral regions lying between the Brahmaputra and Ayeyawady under the framework of 'Act East' policy could cater to socio-economic and developmental discourses of the people inhabiting the geographical space. Therefore, the policy makers should explore the possibility of the Brahmaputra-Ayeyawady Growth Corridor with quick impact projects to fasten the economic growth and social progress of the NER.

Although the Kaladan Multi-Modal Transport Project and the Trilateral Highway are the two main connectivity projects, a futuristic proposition of a land-linked Manipur under 'Act East' policy is unthinkable without rail connectivity between India and Myanmar. Besides, discussion on connectivity through NER is bound to bring backlashes from the various interest groups in the region without bringing on board the people of NER. This calls for quick impact development projects in NER in coordination with development projects undertaken in Myanmar's Chin State, Kachin State and Sagaing Region including the Naga Self-Administered Zone.

As far as the nature and composition of trade is concerned, Myanmar mainly exports farm, marine, forest, mining and CMP (cut-make-pack) products to the outside world while importing capital goods, pharmaceutical products, industrial raw materials, personal goods and CMP raw materials. Rice, fish, fruits, vegetables, pulses and energy resources from Myanmar can find markets in NER without much difficulty. In fact, lack of industrial outputs in NER remains a major drawback of economic cooperation between India and Myanmar.

The underdeveloped NER requires good transport connectivity and energy supply to become a hub of global supply and logistics chains. Transforming the economic activities in NER cannot happen without some serious planning and research on the part of the state governments and the Central authorities. It also requires closer cooperation with Myanmar, Thailand, Laos and China.

Moreover, any serious deliberation on NER and Myanmar is incomplete without the China factor. China's increasing footprints in India's neighbourhood is reality today. The question is how the policy makers will engage China to address the major issues for mutual benefit and cooperation. Writing a success story of India's 'Act East' policy depends on achievements of the development programmes being undertaken in NER to build the region into a vibrant economic and technological hub to engage India's eastern neighbourhood. This study concludes with the statement that India's connectivity with Southeast Asian countries through NER is bound to happen sooner or later and Manipur will get the opportunity to transform itself from a landlocked state into a land-linked state under the 'Act East' policy. The land-linked strategy of Lao People's Democratic Republic (in short Laos) is a model worth studying towards turning Manipur into a hub of logistics and financial centre with greater engagements between India and ASEAN coming in the near future.

NOTES

1. Remarks by the Prime Minister at 12th India-ASEAN Summit, Nay Pyi Taw, Myanmar, November 12, 2014, <https://mea.gov.in>
2. Joint statement by India and Myanmar on First Meeting of the India-Myanmar Joint Consultative Commission, July 16, 2015.
3. India Myanmar land border crossing pact comes into force, *The Hindu*, August 9, 2018.
4. Signing of MoU Ceremony for Coordinated Bus Service between Mandalay and Imphal by M/s Shwe Mandalar, Yangon and M/s Seven Sisters Holidays, Imphal in the Consulate, February 17, 2020.
5. Joint statement by India and Myanmar on the State visit of Prime Minister of India to Myanmar, May 28, 2012, <https://www.mea.gov.in>
6. How poor rail connectivity is acting as a hindrance to India's Act East policy, *The Economic Times*, October 20, 2019.
7. Yang Jie, "China-Myanmar exchange in SW China", *The China Daily*, May 2013, <http://www.chinadaily.com> accessed on July 22, 2020.
8. "Dawei, Kyaukpyu SEZs to be speeded up", *Global New Light of Myanmar*, August 3, 2018, p. 3.
9. Xi, Myanmar leaders celebrate 70th anniversary of diplomatic ties, *The China Daily*, January 18, 2020.

24
Indo-Myanmar Region
A Geo-Strategic Study

Rajkumar Ranjan Singh

A geo-strategic study of the Indo-Myanmar region needs a detailed analysis of the tactical relations in between the tri-nations, namely India-China-Myanmar. The main objective of this chapter is to study the vibrant geopolitical pulses throbbing along Myanmar's border. Myanmar shares common borders with five countries: Bangladesh 193 km., China 2,185 km., Laos 235 km., Thailand 1,800 km. and India 1,463 km. India dominates Myanmar's western side just as China dominates its northern borders. Thailand borders the entire east of Myanmar except for a narrow strip that borders Laos. The location of Myanmar is one of the strategic and bridges of India, linking South and South East Asia. But at the same time, the geostrategic location of Myanmar at the tri-junction of East Asia, South East Asia and South Asia is of critical significance to India. Obviously, China's security interest in Myanmar is to gain promising land access to Indian Ocean and the Andaman Sea. In terms of energy security, this has become increasingly important with China's growing dependence on imported oil.

Secondly, as a littoral of the Indian Ocean, Myanmar's strategic value further increases. Its 1,930 km. long coastline dominates the eastern arch of the Bay of Bengal, leaning Asia just as it provides convenient external land and sea communication option to India's landlocked north-eastern states. The oceanic boundaries of Myanmar are extremely concerned with maritime security of India, in particular the surrounding areas of the Coco Islands which is barely 30 km. away from the Andaman Islands. The setting up of a modern maritime reconnaissance and electronic intelligence system on the Great Coco Island by the Chinese is really a matter of serious concern for the Indian Ocean. This in conjunction with electronic surveillance facilities at the Alexandra Channel in the Andaman Sea, Indian military activities in Andaman Nicobar islands and the missile testing activities at Chandipore in Orissa can be monitored effectively by China.

Thirdly, both sides of the regions bordering Myanmar are mostly populated by ethnic communities with their own distinct ethnic, religious and linguistic identities from the rest of the country. However, the majority of Burmese populations, who are Buddhists, live in the fertile and more developed southern Myanmar with easier access from China. Thus, the northern ethnic regions have been neglected and remain underdeveloped. This caused the ethnic wars happening all along the Naga, Kachin and Chin areas bordering India. Similarly, the northeast India is a home of varied ethnic communities with different dialects and languages, indigenous belief and values of its own and ruled by different independent kingdoms before the establishment of the Union of India. Subsequently, many of the tribes in India's northeastern region are ethnically linked to the tribes on the Myanmar side of the border. Thus, different kinds of ethnic militancy and war of independence have always affected the region.

Topographically, the mountain ranges and rivers of Myanmar were running north-south direction. Therefore, construction of road communication and movement from India's north-east with the same terrain feature to Myanmar are facing more hardship. At the same time, it facilitates easier movement from Chinese border and provides for natural flow of communication. The Chinese have more favourable terrain configuration to build road from the Chinese border to Mandalay Division and up to the Ayeyarwaddy Delta. Further, Union of Myanmar provides the shortest access from Yunnan Province of China towards India's eastern borders and these developments have special strategic significance while India's northeastern states bordering Myanmar are not as well developed as Yunnan province of China bordering Myanmar in the northeast. Thus, trade relation with China is faster than with India's northeastern region. Over the last two decades the Chinese have built very close economic, political, military and developmental relation with Myanmar. Further, the Chinese have used the geophysical advantage they enjoy to gain access to Myanmar's mineral and natural gas resources.

Following a policy of non-interference in the affairs of the country, China has become the main supplier of arms to Myanmar. Since 1980, China has been exclusively involved in Myanmar strategically and economically. Naturally, it worried the Government of India over the growing strategic links in between Sino-Myanmar. Currently, China has more leverage than India in seeking influence in Myanmar. There are more Chinese than Indian immigrants in the northern town of Myanmar, engaging in different kinds of trade and business. An estimation of the Chinese Embassy in Yangon revealed that there were more than two million Chinese in Myanmar in 2005, including half a million ethnic Chinese. In the cities of northern Myanmar, such as Mandalay, the influence of new Chinese migrants in almost all economic sectors is on the rise. These new Chinese immigrants have also become an important influence in Myanmar society. Over and above, China produces cheaper goods to sell in comparison with India.

Considering all the viewpoints cited above, the issues of Indo-Myanmar relationship shall have to be more pragmatic strategic approach while framing the national policies on external affairs. Further, it is also necessary to look into the matters related with the population of about 3-4 lakh of Indians who have settled there and the issues of territorial boundaries with the States like Manipur. The relationship between India and Myanmar was close during the first years after independence and during the formation of Non-Aligned Movement. Both countries signed a Treaty of Friendship, which was to remain in force "for ever thereafter". Because of this Friendship Treaty, the Kabow Valley was formally transferred to Myanmar which is against the interest of the people of Manipur. However, after the 1962 coup, relationship came to a standstill. India ignored its eastern neighbour due to the undemocratic regime that had taken over the assets of Indians living in Myanmar. After three decades, i.e. from the early part of 1990 India's relationship with Myanmar began to restore and recuperate. The restoration of relationship may be related with the growing concern and changing attitude of Myanmar from their traditional "strategic neutrality" policy to more tilting towards China. However, India's policy may try to remove Myanmar from China's orbit or sphere of influence.

India's strategic thinking may have greater cooperation with

Myanmar on cross-border counter-insurgency efforts, building of pipeline for importing hydro-carbon resources from Myanmar through its northeastern region. The northeastern region is basically one of the most underdeveloped regions in the country and it may be the most effective way to neutralize the secessionist movements in the region.

Gas Pipe Line

But more importantly, the geopolitical position of Myanmar in South East Asia is the key stepping stone in India's 'Look East Policy' which seeks to develop and expand political, economic and security ties with ASEAN. Thus, the Northeast India, the most remote part of the country may become the centre of development in the country. In the long scenario, India may wish Myanmar becomes an independent market as well as the transit country and the link between South and South East Asia. Given the geopolitical significance of Myanmar to both India and China, and the potential for rivalry between the two growing powers, i.e. India and China, India's relation with Myanmar needs to be examined taking into consideration the complex relation along the three dimensions, *viz. Security, Energy and Economics.*

For the strategic Economic reasons, Myanmar's military junta has since the early 1990s pursued an "open-door" economic policy, embarking upon an ambitious programme of building roads, bridges, dams, hydroelectric scheme and import-substituting state-owned industries. Since 1988, China enjoys considerable share of benefit from Myanmar. Statistics showed that by 2005, China's total aid to Myanmar reached about US$ 100 million. After four years, in January 1994, India signed Border Trade Agreement with Myanmar and implemented it in April 1995, with the opening of a cross-border point between Moreh (Manipur) and Tamu in Saigang Division of Myanmar. However, economically, India started to engage Myanmar through sub-regional organisations like Bangladesh-India-Myanmar-Sri Lanka-Thailand Economic Cooperation (BIMSTEC) and the Mekong-Ganga Cooperation (MGC) which was founded in the later part of 2000. These projects under cooperation in tourism, culture, education and language training emphasize links between Indian traditional culture and Southeast Asian culture.

By involving in ASEAN infrastructure project India will cooperate for extension of railway from New Delhi to Hanoi, passing through Myanmar, Thailand, Laos and Cambodia and opening of new trade corridor in the Mekong sub-region. In order to make the involvement fruitful, India recently initiated a major project to link its isolated states of the northeastern region to Bay of Bengal *via* the Kaladan River and is investing in a new port in Sittwe. Further to improve connectivity with Myanmar, India has taken up a number of road and port construction projects. India has constructed the 160 km Tamu-Kalewa-Kalemyo road in Myanmar from Manipur border town Moreh. It is also assisting in the proposed Trans-Asian Highway project to connect Moreh in Manipur to Mae Sot in Thailand *via* Bagan in Myanmar. A proposal to construct a rail link from Jiribam in Manipur to Hanoi in Vietnam through Myanmar is also on the cards. Over and above, India is taking steps for extension of airlines with cooperation in areas like agriculture, telecommunications etc.

Security Sector

From the perspective of security, China and Myanmar have enhanced their military cooperation and exchange since 1988. The most significant move in this aspect was the 1990 deal involving weapons and military equipment worth an estimated US$ 1.2 billion; another agreement to supply weapons and equipment worth US$ 400 million in 1994. In 2003, China assisted Myanmar in building an 85-metre jetty to naval facilities on Great Coco Islands, which lies 18 km from Nicobar Island of India. Further, China has built a deep-sea port in Kyaukpyu in Rakhine state. Kyaukpyu is located on the route connecting southwestern China's Kunming city with Myanmar's Sittwe. It is also interesting to note that China has been a net oil importer since 1993 and ranked second position among oil consumers after the US and accounted for 40 per cent of the world's crude oil demand growth since 2000. Even then China is facing sporadic power shortages while growing car ownership and air travel across China and growing industries, agriculture, construction etc. make more pressure on energy resource. As a result, energy security has become an area of vital importance to China's stability and security. Therefore, China is stepping up to control over the Indian Ocean maritime operation by investing in construction of ports at Gwadar in Pakistan, Arabian Sea coast, Chittagong port of Bangladesh and Colombo port etc. Considering the prevailing circumstances in and around the Indian Ocean and the insurgency in the North Eastern States of India, smuggling of arms, drug trafficking and narco-terrorism is the main security concern along the Indo-Myanmar border. The imbroglio of ethnic secessionism, religious and political insurgencies, large-scale smuggling and above all transnational links across border supports, have long undermined the relations between New Delhi and Yangon. Furthermore, courting the junta would also enable India to open up the North-East and in the long term crack down on all the smuggling in the region, particularly small and light arms proliferation, since Myanmar had become a well-known trafficking corridor.

Energy Sector

Expecting an exponential growth in its energy demands due to expanding economy India has been trying hard in recent times to secure energy supplies. But unfortunately, India's oil diplomacy has not been sufficiently geared up to meet this challenge. As a result, its oil companies have been outsmarted or rather outbidded by Chinese firms in several deals. Most embarrassingly, India has also lost a deal in Myanmar where no such bidding was held. This deal was lost purely because we could not respond properly to the prevailing situation in the subcontinent. India is planning to import gas from Iran, Myanmar and Turkmenistan *via* transnational gas pipelines to meet the growing energy needs, as domestic production is unable to meet its requirement. But the Union of Myanmar declined the gas supply to the Myanmar-Bangladesh-India pipeline. Instead Yangon signed an agreement with Hong Kong-listed Petro China, under which Myanmar's Ministry of Energy agreed to sell 6.5 TCF from Rakhine coastline reserve through an overland pipeline to Kunming (China) for 30 years. India has been eyeing huge hydrocarbon resources of Mynamar with Chinese firm Petro China. It is definitely a setback to India's Oil diplomacy and its energy security. Considering the facts and circumstances of the prevailing geopolitics in the region, India will also have to integrate its Oil diplomacy with its foreign policy.

Since China is one of the most important players in Myanmar's domestic economy and foreign relations, India's relationship with Myanmar must be established with a vision of close and practicable long-term relationship. As South East Asia begins with Myanmar, the Indian diplomacy has to include Myanmar in its eastern diplomacy and could no longer isolate it as in the past. The Mekong Ganga Cooperation (MGC) may strengthen the relationship among the countries having common civilizational background like Myanmar, Thailand, Cambodia, Vietnam and Laos for the riparian states of the Mekong River, and India for the Ganges River to counterbalance the Kunming Initiative of Mekong Basin Project. In this strategy, the Asian Development Bank (ADB) sponsored Greater Mekong Sub-Region (GMS) project to integrate the economies of the countries like Thailand, China's Yunnan Province and Myanmar. In this context, more efforts be made for the development of historic Indo-Burma roads to transform them into economic, diplomatic and business corridors linking India and the South East Asia. Lastly, to have a better understanding and peaceful coexistence with Myanmar, India needs to resolve its border disputes with China and also to improve its relationship with neighbouring countries like Bangladesh, Sri Lanka and Pakistan. Resolving territorial disputes and reducing the ongoing uprising movements in the Northeastern region will become important for India if it is to fully exploit proximity to a region on its eastern border.

Conclusion

After decades of isolation, India's eastern neighbour—Myanmar is now perceived as a link to new capacity building of trade and commerce. The transformation of 'Look East Policy' into the much coveted 'Act East Policy' has also added to the significance of Myanmar in India's considerations of foreign policy. Over the years, India's policy towards Myanmar has been largely shaped by security and stability at the borders, diffusing cross-border insurgent groups, and economic development of its North-eastern states. Accordingly, Myanmar has extended all support for curbing insurgency and militancy on its borders.

According to Indian Prime Minister Narendra Modi, "the extent and depth of the India-Myanmar relationship is visible in the robust development cooperation partnership, which has a strong "people first" philosophy ".....India stands ready to enhance our development partnership with Myanmar......And, do so as per the priorities of the Myanmar Government." Along with the shared cultural and historical lineage, India has a great deal to offer. Religion, spiritualism and film industry in the form of 'Buddhism, Yoga and Bollywood' have been the strength of India's 'soft power diplomacy' and it has been a connecting ground with Myanmar for centuries. Therefore, it may be said that India is a neighbour which Myanmar cannot afford to ignore.

Reciprocity on the Indian side is visible in supporting Myanmar to promote democratic values and re-build its institutions along with socio-economic reforms. So far as India's interest in Myanmar is concerned, it is stepping up its development cooperation in the light of Myanmar's continuing reform process. It is also rejuvenating its historical and cultural ties. Though shared historical-cultural linkages between India and Myanmar abound our mythologies and literature, the influence that India has on this captivating land cannot be underestimated. The range of areas covered by Indian projects includes roads, railways, telecom, power, energy, hydrocarbons, remote sensing, agriculture, industry, IT, health-related services and education. Several Indian companies are already making inroads such as ONGC Videsh Limited, Jubilant Oil and Gas, Escorts, Tata Motors, Essar Energy, RITES, Apollo, CIPLA, Ranbaxy, Cadila Healthcare Ltd. etc. Nevertheless, its engagement with India in recent times in the economic field and trade statistics has not been satisfactory.

The two countries have also signed several bilateral investment promotion agreements facilitating their venture in each other's country. As of April 2019, India's investment in Myanmar reached $763 million, ranking 11th in the line-up of foreign investors with 30 permitted enterprises. India has also promised a $550 million as line of credit to Myanmar for the development of railways, transport, power transmission lines and oil refineries. The Kaladan Multi-Modal Transit Project once completed is expected to transform trade and commerce in the Rakhine and Chin states as well as the north-eastern states of India. The 3,200 km Trilateral Highway Project connecting Moreh in Manipur to Mae Sot in Thailand *via* Myanmar is expected to be completed soon. The building of rail-road connectivity through Myanmar to other South East Asian countries and reviving old rail-road links from Assam to Vietnam calls for much attention. Investment in agriculture, industry, banking sector, education, health, transport and communication is urgently required by India, besides its existing share in pearls and pulses, timber, oil and natural gas projects. Last but not the least, engagement with the Tatmadaw, NLD and the ethnic parties and Track II diplomacy at the level of civil society, cultural and academic exchanges may go a long way in strengthening ties between the two countries. There is also demand that Indian Government should introduce International bus service linking Moreh with Mandalay. The bus service linking Moreh with Mandalay would not only just help the traders, but also bring in tourists from Myanmar to India.

Both India and Myanmar have agreed to start a Cultural Exchange Programme (CEP) with wide range of activities including dance, music, yoga, Thang-Ta, Martial Arts etc. to deepen the close bonds between the peoples of India and Myanmar. To foster and strengthen cultural relations and mutual understanding between India and other countries, Indian Council for Cultural Relations (ICCR) was established in 1950-51 and many cultural exchange programmes have been organised between India and Myanmar for the last many decades and keeping efforts to leverage on 'soft' power diplomacy and fostering deeper economic and business links. Education is a crucial area where India exercises competitive advantage in Myanmar for building a sustainable academic partnership between the two countries. Myanmar attaches high priority to education and is calling for increased investment in this sector. Enhancing strong academic links between institutions of India and Myanmar and replicating best learning practices will help in human resource development and contribute to social and economic transformation of the country.

For boosting its engagement with Myanmar, India has kept its focus on 'Development Assistance', supported through grants-in-aid, lines of credit, training programmes, and provisions for expert knowledge and capacity building initiatives. The 'High Impact Community Development Projects' and the 'Border Areas Development Projects' have been crucial in reaching out to States in the border regions of Myanmar and boosting people to people contacts. While India-Myanmar shares trade relations in many areas but post-COVID-19, it can expand trade relations in areas such as Pharmacy, Healthcare, Transport, Food Processing, Steel, Renewable Energy, Communication, Education and others which can help both the countries to revive. The region is yet to prepare for the opportunity and there is a need to strengthen the region's infrastructure and rejuvenate the cultural connection. Here, we may emphasize on 3Cs such as Culture, Commerce and Connectivity.

Regime transformation and political developments in Myanmar since the last few years have opened a new chapter in India-Myanmar relation. Given the political transformation taking place in Myanmar, the country offers immense opportunities for re-engagement which India may use to its strategic advantage. The traditional relation of friendship and cooperation between the two countries could be deepened and intensified further to each other's mutual benefit.

REFERENCES

Poon Kim Shee, "The Political Economy of China-Myanmar Relations: Strategic and Economic Dimensions", *Ritsumeikan Annual Review of International Studies*, Vol. 1. (2002), pp. 33-53, The International Studies Association of Ritsumeikan University, Japan.

S.P. Kim, "The South China Sea in China's Strategic Thinking", *The Journal of East Asian Affairs*, Vol. 22, No. 1 (Spring/Summer 2008), pp. 175-194, Institute for National Security Strategy. Retrieved from *JSTOR*.

Thin Thin Aung and Soe Myint, *India-Burma Relations*, retrieved from <http://www.idea.in>

Tarique Niazi, "Asia between China and India", *Japan Focus*, May 31, 2006.

Erica Downs, *Energy Security Series: China*, The Brookings Foreign Policy Studies, December 2006. Available at: <http: www.brookings.edu>

Index